Visions of the End

Apocalyptic Traditions
in the Middle Ages

Number XCVI of the
Records of Civilization: Sources and Studies

Visions of the End

Apocalyptic Traditions
in the Middle Ages

BERNARD MCGINN

Columbia University Press
New York ••• 1979

BT
876
.V58

Library of Congress Cataloging in Publication Data
Main entry under title:

Visions of the end.

  (Records of civilization, sources and studies; no. 96)
  Bibliography: p.
  Includes index.
  1. End of the world—History of doctrines.
2. Millennialism—History of doctrines.
3. Apocalyptic literature.   4. Church history—
Middle Ages, 500–1500.   I. McGinn, Bernard, 1937–
II. Series.
BT876.V58   236   79-4303
ISBN 0-231-04594-8

79497

Columbia University Press
New York   Guildford, Surrey

To Daniel and John

Contents

Preface   xiii

Introduction   1
   Classical Apocalypticism   2
   Patristic Apocalypticism   14
   Messianism, Millenarianism, and Apocalypticism   28

Part One A.D. 400–1200   37

   Introduction   39

   1. The Tiburtine Sibyl   43
      The Oracle of Baalbek   45
      The Latin Tiburtine Sibyl   49

   2. Antichrist in the Fifth Century   51
      Sulpicius Severus, *Dialogues* 1:41   52
      The Progress of Time   52
      The Book of the Promises and Predictions of God   53
      The Revelation of the Holy Theologian John   54

   3. The Legend of Alexander   56
      The Discourse of Jacob of Serugh   57

   4. Pseudo-Ephraem   60
      Sermon on the End of the World   61

   5. Gregory the Great   62
      Homily on Ezekiel 2:6   62
      Two Letters   64

   6. Byzantine Apocalyptic   66
      Procopius, *Secret History*   67
      Vision of the Prophet Daniel   68

7. Pseudo-Methodius 70
   The Alexander Legend 73
   The Moslem Crisis 74
   The Last World Emperor 75

8. Beatus of Liébana 77
   Commentary, Book IV 77
   Commentary, Book XI 78

9. *Muspilli* 80
   Lines 37–59 80

10. Adso's *Letter on the Antichrist* 82
   The Origin of the Antichrist 84
   The Last Emperor 85
   The Destruction of the Antichrist 87

11. Apocalyptic and Non-Apocalyptic Themes
   of the Eleventh Century 88
   The Year 1000 89
      Abbo of Fleury; Ralph Glaber
   Apocalypse and the Origin of the Crusade 90
      Benzo of Alba; Guibert of Nogent; Ekkehard of Aura

12. Apocalypticism and the Great Reform 94
   "The Calamities of the Church of Liége" 97
   Otto of Freising, *The Two Cities* 98
   Gerhoh of Reichersberg, *The Investigation of the*
     Antichrist 99
   Hildegard of Bingen, *Scivias* 100

13. Gerhoh of Reichersberg 103
   The Fourth Watch of the Night 104

14. The Ages of the Church 108
   Rupert of Deutz, *The Holy Trinity,* Prologue 110
   Hugh of St. Victor, *The Mystical Ark of Noah* 111
   Bernard of Clairvaux, *On the Song of Songs* 112
   The Letter of Gerard to Evermord 113
   Anselm of Havelberg, *Dialogues* 114

15. Imperial Apocalyptic 117

Otto of Freising, *The Deeds of Frederick Barbarossa*   118
The Play of Antichrist   119

16. The Erythraean Sibyl   122
    Selections from Parts I and III   123

17. Joachim of Fiore   126
    Joachim's Vision of the Meaning of Revelation   130
    Commentary on an Unknown Prophecy   130
    The Three *Status*   133
    The Papacy and the Spiritual Men   134
    The Antichrist   137
    The New People of God   138
    Joachim's Testament   140

Part Two A.D. 1200–1500   143

Introduction   145

18. Moslems, Mongols, and the Last Days   149
    The Toledo Letter   152
    The Prophecy of the Son of Agap   153
    William of Tripoli, *Treatise on the Condition of the
        Saracens*   154
    Roger Bacon, *The Longer Work*   155

19. The Joachite Movement before 1260   158
    The Letter Explaining the Figures   161
    The Commentary on Jeremiah   161
    The Joint Encyclical of 1255   164
    The Protocol of Anagni   165
    Salimbene of Parma, *Chronicle*   166

20. Frederick II vs. the Papacy   168
    Nicholas of Bari, Sermon   172
    Gregory IX, Letter, "Ascendit de mari bestia"   173
    Frederick II, Letter, "In exordio nascentis mundi"   174
    Innocent IV as Antichrist   175
    Frederick and his Seed in the Joachite Tradition   176
    A Curial Version of the Last Emperor   179

21. Merlin, the British Seer   180
       Geoffrey of Monmouth, *History of the Kings of Britain*   182
       Merlin in Italy   183

22. The Angelic Pope   186
       The Commentary on Jeremiah   189
       Roger Bacon on the Coming Holy Pope   190
       Salimbene on Gregory X   191
       The Angelic Oracle of Cyril and Pseudo-Joachim's
          Commentary   192
       Robert of Uzès on the Papal Crisis   193
       The Papal Prophecies. First Set   194

23. Bonaventure's Apocalyptic Theology of History   196
       Bonaventure's Joachite Exegesis   197
       The Ages of the Church   198
       St. Francis and the Contemplative Orders   200

24. The Franciscan Spirituals   203
       Peter Olivi, *Commentary on Revelation*   208
       Ubertino of Casale, *The Tree of the Crucified Life*   212
       Angelo of Clareno, *History of Seven Tribulations*   215
       Jacopone da Todi, Lauda 50: *The Great Battle of the
          Antichrist*   217
       Bernard Gui, *The Inquisitor's Manual*   218

25. Arnald of Villanova   222
       The Time of the Coming of the Antichrist   223
       The Sword That Swallows the Thomatists   224

26. Fra Dolcino and the Apostolic Brethren   226
       Bernard Gui, *The Sect of the Apostolic Brethren*   227

27. John of Rupescissa   230
       The Companion in Tribulation   231

28. The Fraticelli   234
       The Papal Prophecies. Second Set   235
       Letter to the Citizens of Narni   237

29. Rome and Avignon during the Captivity   239
       Cola di Rienzo   241

Petrarch, Sonnet 137   244
Bridget of Sweden, *Revelations*   244

30. Political Prophecies: French versus German Imperial
    Legends   246
      Telesphorus of Cosenza   249
      The Second Charlemagne Prophecy   250
      John of Winterthur   251
      The Prophecy of Gamaleon   251

31. Apocalypticism, the Great Schism, and the Conciliar
    Movement   253
      "In That Day the Eagle Will Come"   255
      St. Vincent Ferrer   256

32. The Hussite Movement   259
      John Hus   263
      The Beginnings of Tabor: Jakoubek of Stříbro; Bzí Hora;
        Lawrence of Březová; John of Příbram   263
      Taborite Views   266

33. Germany on the Eve of the Reformation   270
      John Lichtenberger, *Pronosticatio*   272
      Wolfgang Aytinger, *Commentary on Methodius*   274

34. Savonarola and Late Medieval Italian Apocalypticism   277
      Renovation Sermon   279
      Compendium of Revelations   280
      Marsilio Ficino on Savonarola as Antichrist   282

35. Christopher Columbus   284
      Account of the Fourth Voyage   285

Notes   287

Bibliography   347

Name Index   365

Subject Index   370

Preface

In the course of teaching the history of medieval apocalypticism over the past seven years, the absence of any comprehensive introduction to the subject in English came to prove such a limitation that four years ago I decided to attempt to fill the gap. The result is the present book.[1]

My intention from the outset was to write what I have come to call a textual history, one in which an anthology of translations from the wealth of apocalyptic writings would play a central role.[2] The reason for this was obvious. Unlike the apocalyptic texts of the Old and the New Testaments, and those of the intertestamental period in general, later Christian apocalyptic materials are not only little known, but with the exception of the patristic texts up to about A.D. 400 also rarely available in English.[3] The purpose of my history, then, was to make available a selection of these significant works together with an appropriate interpretive structure that would enable the interested student to follow the main lines of Christian apocalypticism and to grasp the significance that it had during the medieval period. Many of the original versions of these texts are to be found only in manuscript form or in rare early printed editions; most are here translated into English for the first time.

A word about the chronological limits observed. My original plan included sections devoted to the canonical and non-canonical apocalyptic materials of the period c.200 B.C. to A.D. c.100, as well as early Christian apocalypticism up to A.D. 400. The texts of the initial period of "classical" apocalypticism are of great moment, not only for our very notion of apocalypticism, but also for the influence they continued to exert on the later tradition. This is especially true of the canonical texts—the Book of Daniel, the Epistles to the Thessalonians, the "Little Apocalypse" of the Synoptic Gospels, and the Great Apocalypse, or Revelation of John; but non-canonical texts, such as First Enoch, Fourth Esdras, and the Jewish Sibylline Oracles, remained important for centuries. There are, however, a number of translations and selections from these materials, and any inclusion here would have swollen this book to excessive length.[4] My omission in no way reflects upon the indispensability of some knowledge of classical apocalypticism for a full understanding of the later history.

Similarly, knowledge of the main lines of apocalypticism in Christian circles from the early second century to the early fifth, especially the attitudes taken by the most influential of the Fathers, is indispensable for an understanding of many later Christian texts, both Eastern and Western. But here, too, the inclusion of selections from the patristic period, especially since much of this material is available in English translation, would have made this book unduly long. Therefore, I have chosen to discuss important elements of the relation between the earlier periods and the succeeding medieval centuries in the Introduction that follows.

The other chronological limit has been set at roughly A.D. 1500. The outset of the sixteenth century does not mark an important change in the form or content of the apocalyptic tradition itself—most, if not all, of the themes used by the Reformers and their Catholic opponents, including the identification of the papacy and the Roman Church with the Antichrist, had their origin in the late Middle Ages. The apocalyptic cataclysms of the Peasants' Revolt and Münster had predecessors in the left wing of the Hussite movement a century before, and the use of apocalyptic as imperial propaganda did not end in 1500, as the career of Charles V shows. Although there is remarkable continuity, nevertheless apocalypticism is a mirror held up to the age, an attempt by each era to understand itself in relation to an all-embracing teleological scheme of history. When the age changes, a new visage begins to become visible in the mirror, and with the beginnings of the Reformation and the opening up of the New World certain major currents had been set in motion whose later developments were to produce a different world. There are then some reasons for closing this story at 1500, but I do so with a full recognition of the intimate connection between these texts and their successors in later Western history.

This book has received the cooperation of many hands, not all of whom can be thanked in individual fashion. Students in my seminars have given me the opportunity to try out ideas, and have provided both stimulus and critique. Colleagues, both at the University of Chicago and elsewhere, have offered suggestions, criticism, and a variety of assistance. Among those who must be singled out for individual thanks are John and Adela Collins for many insights into the apocalypticism of what I have called the classical period, and for advice on patristic use of apocalyptic. E. Randolph Daniel,

Jeffrey Burton Russell, Robert Lerner, Charles Davis, and David Burr were more than generous in sharing their knowledge of medieval materials. My friends and colleagues Paolo Cherchi, Peter Dembowski, and Kenneth Northcott have provided help with vernacular materials, as noted below; and James Tabor allowed me to make use of an unpublished translation from the Greek. Howard Kaminsky and the late Paul J. Alexander showed great generosity in giving permission for the use of previously published translations without which this survey would have been much poorer. Several translations from earlier works in the Columbia Records of Civilization Series have also been included here, as well as a few translations from older works now in the public domain. Finally, Michael Hollerich gave valuable assistance in checking most of the translations, and Kimberly LoPrete prepared the bibliography.

The translations themselves aim at the most literal rendering compatible with reasonably correct English. Very few of these texts are important for literary worth alone. Many make no pretense to stylistic polish of any kind; others are highly contrived, but in a rhetorical vein that is difficult to appreciate in English dress. Quite a few aim at a deliberate prophetic obscurity which the original authors would be pleased to see is even more evident in translation than it was in the language of composition. With full awareness of these many difficulties, so imperfectly surmounted, I believe that there is still value in offering this collection to those who may wish to learn more of how our predecessors perceived the meaning of history and its coming End.

Bernard McGinn   University of Chicago
                                                  August 1978

Abbreviations Used in the Sources and Notes

Abbreviation   *Full Reference*

CC   *Corpus christianorum. Series latina.* Turnhout: Brepols, 1954– .

CSEL   *Corpus scriptorum ecclesiasticorum latinorum.* Vienna: Hoelder-Pichler-Tempsky, 1866– .

MGH   *Monumenta Germaniae historica.* Hanover et al.: Hahn, 1826– . (The most frequently used series are the Scriptores, abbreviated *SS*.)

PL   *Patrologiae cursus completus. Series latina.* Paris: J. P. Migne, 1844–64.

RHC   *Recueil des historiens des croisades.* Paris: Académie des Inscriptions et Belles-Lettres, 1841–1906. (The most frequently used part is *Historiens occidentaux,* abbreviated *Hist. occ.*).

RIS   *Rerum italicarum scriptores.* New edition of G. Carducci and V. Fiorini. Città di Castello-Bologna: Zanichelli, 1900– .

RS   *Rerum britannicarum medii aevi scriptores* (Rolls Series). London: Longman et al., 1858–1911.

SC   *Sources chrétiennes.* Paris: Editions du Cerf. 1940– .

SS   See under *MGH.*

Visions of the End

Apocalyptic Traditions
in the Middle Ages

Introduction

Visions of the End—visions of terror and dread, visions of peace and of glory. Such is the stuff of the apocalyptic tradition.

For two thousand years Judaism and Christianity have contained strong elements of apocalypticism. The Book of Daniel in the Old Testament, sacred to both religions, and the Revelation of John in the New Testament, continue to be read, commented upon, and even today used to interpret the events of the times. While their hold upon contemporary religious beliefs is scarcely as widespread or as strong as it once was, present-day seers are still willing to announce the imminence of the End on the basis of their labors over biblical texts.

Daniel, John, and the other products of the earliest period of the apocalyptic tradition, the classical period from c.200 B.C. to A.D. c.100, were only the beginning. Apocalypticism, as a distinctive element in Judaism and Christianity, was an unfolding phenomenon of many centuries, a striking example of the interplay between tradition and innovation that all religions, but especially those with a strong historical commitment, display.

A vast literature exists regarding the classical period of Jewish and Christian apocalypticism from its origins in the first half of the second century before Christ. Despite the paucity of consensus on key issues, this literature is of profound interest not only to the student of ancient religions, but also to the contemporary Christian theologian. When the noted German New Testament scholar Ernst Käsemann proclaimed that "apocalyptic was the mother of all Christian theology,"[1] exegetes, historians, and theologians sprang to the task of testing the validity and significance of his claim. Modern biblical studies, indeed, began with the recognition of the centrality of the apocalyptic elements in Christian origins. From Reimarus in the late eighteenth century, through Weiss, Wrede, and Schweitzer at the turn of the present century, to the work of Bultmann and his followers today, apocalypticism has maintained a key role in biblical studies.

Unfortunately, the quest for origins can entail disadvantages. The con-

centration of religious scholars on the earliest period of Western apocalypticism has led to some neglect of the continuity of these traditions in later
ages.[2] This is not to say that a copious literature on later Jewish and Christian apocalypticism does not exist, and that there have not been scholars,
such as Wilhelm Bousset, who were not equally at home in both ancient and
medieval, Eastern and Western apocalyptic traditions. But division of labor,
perhaps necessary in dealing with such a complex field, has come close to
bringing about a separation of interest that cannot but render an adequate
and full understanding of the meaning of apocalypticism more distant as the
information at our disposal grows richer. It is my hope that this book may
begin to help in overcoming these separations.

The centuries between A.D. 400 and 1500 constitute half of the total
period during which apocalyptic traditions have been active in Western society. Despite the serious attention devoted to it, it remains the period least
known to the theologian, historian of religions, and the general reader. The
texts and commentary that make up this book are designed to present a
synoptic view of Christian apocalypticism during these centuries, but it is
obvious that to isolate this period from what went before and what came
after would be highly artificial. It is also obvious that to study Christian materials alone is to tell only a part of the story of Western apocalyptic traditions. I have not treated later Jewish apocalypticism, except for occasional
references to moments of interaction with Christianity. The works of Gershom Scholem and others have displayed the richness of Jewish messianism
in the centuries after the destruction of the Second Temple;[3] intensive studies of the morphology of Jewish and Christian hopes for the End offer a still
largely untapped area for comparative studies.[4]

While it would be impossible to include a detailed discussion of classical apocalypticism in this work, it would be an error to pay no heed to the
problems of the origin and meaning of apocalypticism in Judaism and in
Christianity. I make no pretense of solving the many serious difficulties that
continue to divide workers in this highly technical and difficult field; I rather
intend to set these questions within the wider historical framework which is
essential for their understanding as a chapter in Western religious history.

CLASSICAL APOCALYPTICISM (200 B.C. – A.D. 100)

The word *apocalypse* means "revelation," the unveiling of a divine secret.
Literary productions called apocalypses are well known in late testamental

and intertestamental Judaism, and the final book of the New Testament calls itself "the apocalypse given by God to Jesus Christ . . . to make known to his servant John." But there is variety of form and considerable difference in content among the texts that bear the name of apocalypse. If we elect to identify apocalyptic traditions in Western religious history with a concern for the structure and End of history, as will be done here, then it will be obvious that some intertestamental "apocalypses" are not a part of these apocalyptic traditions at all. Even the Book of Daniel, the only apocalyptic work admitted into the Old Testament canon, never calls itself an apocalypse, nor is it a pure apocalypse in form. Obviously, what constitutes the form of apocalypse and what is true apocalyptic content are not easy questions to determine.

Before turning to these questions, it is worthwhile to highlight something that may seem at first sight obvious. Apocalypticism, from its origins, is a highly complex phenomenon. Single-minded interpretations are immediately suspect. To reduce apocalypticism to a clear and distinct idea may well be to sacrifice understanding for illusory clarity. Apocalypticism throughout its lengthy and rich history fused together a variety of interests and was invoked for various purposes; the historian's task is to capture, to the best of his ability, the full range of the phenomenon under investigation. This, of course, does not excuse one from trying to set down, as clearly as possible, the components of what we have been calling apocalypticism; it may not even exclude a provisional or "working" definition, or list of characteristics; but it does provide a caution against too easy solutions to the issues involved. Perhaps the greatest challenge of comparative studies in this area is to try to vindicate sufficient community of content and purpose to allow this term to be applied to such diverse texts and authors during the course of so many centuries.

Apocalypticism in its Jewish origins is distinguishable from two related terms common in biblical theology and the history of religions: *eschatology* and *prophecy*. Apocalypticism is a species of the genus eschatology, that is, it is a particular kind of belief about the last things—the End of history and what lies beyond it. Scriptural scholars have used the term *apocalyptic eschatology* to distinguish the special teachings of the apocalypticists from the eschatology of the prophets. (Apocalyptic eschatology may be seen as equivalent to the frequently used term *Apocalyptic,* formed in imitation of the German *Apokalyptik.*) Valuable as the distinction may be in the realm of biblical studies, the picture will obviously become blurred in later Christian history when elements of both forms of eschatology will frequently be mingled. A more serious confusion has been caused by the fact that historians of Christian thought have sometimes used *eschatology* and *apocalypticism* as interchangeable terms. This is misleading. Every Christian view of history is in some sense eschatological insofar as it sees history as a teleological process and believes that Scripture reveals truths about its End. But it is possible to be orthodox and deeply eschatological and yet distinctly anti-apocalyptic, as the case of Augustine shows. It is true that the apocalyptic author frequently differs from the merely eschatological one more in degree than in kind, and it is not always easy to say when a particular writer or text is one or the other. But there is still an important difference between a general consciousness of living in the last age of history and a conviction that the last age itself is about to end, between a belief in the reality of the Antichrist and the certainty of his proximity (or at least of the date of his coming), between viewing the events of one's own time in the light of the End of history and seeing them as the last events themselves.[5]

Prophecy, a widespread religious phenomenon, also has an intimate relation to apocalypticism. From the viewpoint of the history of religions, the prophet may be defined as any "inspired person who believes that he has been sent by his god with a message to tell"; but in the later Christian tradition prophecy has usually been seen as a divinatory or occasionally reformative activity—the prophet as the man who foretells the future, or the one who seeks to correct a present situation in the light of an ideal past or glorious future.[6] One may say that during the centuries under review here most apocalypticists were in some way prophets, but that the medieval notion of prophecy as most properly the prediction of future events (see Thomas Aquinas, *Summa theologiae* IIa IIae, q.171, a.3) did not necessarily entail concern with the structure and imminent End of history. Later Christian apocalypticism is not coterminous with the history of prophecy in Christianity, but it is its most substantial component.

But what is this apocalypticism that cannot be separated, but can be distinguished from these related terms? The beginning of wisdom is a distinction between apocalyptic form and apocalyptic content. Apocalyptic form need not be restricted to those texts which explicitly identify themselves as apocalypses, because not only are there "apocalypses" which display almost nothing of the apocalyptic religious attitudes, but there are also apocalypses in the formal sense which do not announce themselves as such or which are embedded in compilations that are later in date and more eclectic in form. The variety of forms under which apocalyptic doctrines have been presented has led one foremost Old Testament theologian, Gerhard von Rad, to deny that it is possible to determine a genre peculiar to apocalyptic,[7] and is at the root of the procedure of a scholar like Walter Schmithals, who first defines the meaning of the apocalyptic movement and then uses his ideal construct as the basis for determining which of the works usually listed as apocalyptic actually convey the apocalyptic understanding of existence.[8]

Nevertheless, there have been many attempts, both old and new, to isolate the defining characteristics of the genre "apocalypse" and there are at least some features that many scholars have seen as basic.[9] These involve both the manner of revelation to the seer and also the way in which he in turn presents the received message to mankind. D. S. Russell, for instance, claimed there were "certain features which may be said to characterize the *literature* of the apocalypticists as distinct from their *teaching*. They are these: it is esoteric in character, literary in form, symbolic in language, and pseudonymous."[10] More central in recent study has been stress upon the manner of revelation as involving the disclosure of a secret through the action of an intermediary, usually an angel. The disclosure takes place either through a heavenly vision or dream, or through an actual journey to heaven on the part of the seer (frequently portrayed as deeply disturbed or perplexed by his experience).[11]

The seer is invariably a literary man—he writes down his message in a book. Although the Jewish prophets had frequently committed their oracles to writing, written form was not as integral to the essence of Jewish prophetism as it was to apocalypticism. "By the beginning of the second century B.C. divine revelation had come to be associated in people's minds not so much with the spoken as with the written word."[12] Later apocalyptic traditions were never to depart in substantive fashion from this characteristic: apocalypticism remained a learned, a "scribal" phenomenon.

From the very beginning, the apocalyptic message was presented in a rich and distinctive style, with abundant use of symbols, allegorical figures, and rhetorical devices. General evaluations concerning the language of apocalypticism are frequent, and usually difficult to maintain across the board. Many of the attacks on the artificiality of apocalyptic style spring from the modern division, introduced by Goethe, between "good" symbolism and "bad" allegory.[13] To the modern reader the variety of figurative devices used in apocalyptic literature may seem at times either highly artificial or richly meaningful—in either case, we should beware of our immediate reactions, at least before making an attempt to appreciate the intent of the original modes of literary presentation. It seems highly questionable to identify the apocalyptic use of symbols with what one modern literary critic has called "steno" symbols, that is, one-dimensional signs easily translated into a literal message, as against the "tensive" symbols which are marked with the manysidedness and transcendentality within which modern critics and philosophers have located the essence of the symbolic mode of presentation.[14] There are undoubtedly many "steno" symbols in the world of apocalyptic literature; but the existence of "tensive" symbols, or better, modes of presentation which fulfilled the same intention as the modern critic's "tensive symbol," has been defended by students of classical apocalyptic literature.[15] One school of modern investigation of early apocalyptic literature has been specifically concerned with the mode of rhetoric involved, and has made it the basic principle of its interpretation.[16]

Whether we wish to call it allegorical, symbolic, figurative, or confused, it will be obvious that apocalyptic presentation is usually highly dramatic in form. In its desire to present a picture of the conflict between good and evil, the apocalyptic text deliberately creates, if not a drama (spoken parts are usually lacking), at least a set of easily visualizable scenes and strongly-drawn characters that because of their imaginative power remain fixed in the reader's mind. The scenario of the events of the End has as its most basic structure a threefold pattern of crisis, judgment, and salvation essential to apocalypticism. This general script provides both a common basis and the possibility for subsequent enrichment.

The fact that the Jewish apocalypses of the first three centuries are invariably pseudonymous, that is, ascribed to authors who could not have written them, is a formal characteristic of some moment, not least because it was also to remain important during the centuries to come. Pseudonymity, to be sure, was a characteristic of a number of literary forms in an age when dissatisfaction with the present led to idealization of the wisdom of old.[17] The latter part of the Book of Daniel, written about 165 B.C., was issued under the name of a legendary wise man and prophet thought of as living at the time of the Babylonian captivity in the sixth century. Over fifteen centuries later, medieval prophecies of the time of the Great Schism were pseudonymously ascribed to the noted Calabrian abbot, Joachim of Fiore, who had died two centuries before. The Revelation of John is the great exception to the rule of pseudonymity among the formal apocalypses of the period of origins.

Numerous explanations for this pseudonymity have been given.[18] H. H. Rowley would have it that it grew out of the attempt by the author of Daniel to relate the visions of the second part of the work, advanced in the name of Daniel, to the stories about Daniel composed by the same author in the earlier chapters;[19] but in deriving everything from the Book of Daniel this explanation seems too inflexible. Pseudonymity is a corollary of what has been called the "scribal" character of apocalypticism. In the pre-modern world, written revelation was sacred not merely because it was written, but also because it was written long ago, ages before its accomplishment by someone famed as a favorite of God. The tally of approved apocalyptic authors was never a closed one—Daniel, John, the Sibyl, and later Merlin, Joachim, and a variety of saints was included—but the dynamics of pseudonymity remained constant for centuries.

Pseudonymity is at the root of that mark of apocalyptic literature which provides the most effective key for determining the date and frequently the milieu of individual texts, the technique of *vaticinium ex eventu,* or history disguised as prophecy.[20] A work like Daniel that purports to be written in the sixth century but was actually composed in the second usually contains recognizable details of recent history under the guise of prophecy. Specification of the transition from history disguised as prophecy to true prophecy, though not always an easy task because of the symbolic nature of apocalyptic language, is an invaluable tool in the investigation of apocalyptic texts.

Perhaps the most difficult question confronting the study of classical apocalypticism is that of the relation between the literary form of apocalypse and the various attempts to determine the nature of apocalyptic eschatology. German scholars, such as von Rad and Schmithals, have tended to concentrate on describing the religious outlook of apocalypticism and laid less stress on its relation to any single literary form. English-speaking scholars have generally tried to keep form and content more closely bound. Recent attempts to specify more exactly the content of the hope found in formal apocalypses have cast doubt on the centrality of the coming vindication within history as the chief message of apocalyptic eschatology. In the midst of such disagreement, a brief sketch of some characteristic approaches will help to frame the issues in the debate.

Laundry lists of the essential components of apocalyptic eschatology are many. For the sake of brevity, I mention only a few recent examples. For D. S. Russell the essence of Jewish apocalyptic involves the following: first, a systematic and deterministic view of the course of history conceived as a unitary process; second, a strongly highlighted (but not dualistic) conception of the conflict of good and evil, stressing the action of angels and demons; third, a sense of the imminence of the End of time and the transcendental character of the age to come; fourth, the hope for a messianic kingdom on earth, and at times a Messiah as well; fifth, the expectation of life after death, including belief in the last judgment, which he describes as "the most characteristic doctrine of Jewish apocalyptic.[21] Like many older authorities, Russell stresses the connection of apocalypticism with Old Testament prophecy, though he admits the influence of foreign, especially Iranian, elements.

Gerhard von Rad summarizes the characteristics of apocalyptic in succinct fashion:

> The characteristic of apocalyptic theology is its eschatological dualism, the clear-cut differentiation of the two aeons, the present one and the one to come. A further characteristic is its sheer transcendentalism—the saving blessings of the coming aeon are already pre-existent in the world above and come down from there to earth. . . . The early idea that the final events were determined far back in the past and foretold in detail to certain chosen men many centuries before they were to occur is also characteristic. This is linked in turn to the pseudonymity of apocalyptic writings. . . . This introduces us to another characteristic of apocalyptic writings, its esotericism and gnosticism. The last things can be known; indeed, they can be exactly calculated, but this is only possible for the initiated.[22]

Von Rad lays great stress upon the fact that the apocalypticists' view of history contains no special reference to Israel, but "gains its splendor" from the conception of the unity of world history objectified in allegorical and symbolic fashion. This conception of history is viewed as fundamentally pessimistic and deterministic. For these reasons von Rad sees "incompatibility between apocalyptic literature's view of history and that of the prophets,"[23] and traces its origins to the Wisdom literature of the Old Testament. In a similar vein, but more strongly etched, is the interpretation by W. Schmithals in *The Apocalyptic Movement*.[24] Schmithals' portrayal of the essence of apocalyptic piety highlights the understanding of history, especially the doctrine of the two aeons, as the central motif of the apocalyptic mentality.[25]

In 1970 K. Koch published an historiographical introduction to apocalypticism that advanced a deliberately eclectic approach. The eight motifs that he identifies as summarizing "generally accepted opinion today" are different in significant particulars from those of von Rad and his followers.[26] In recent American scholarship we may note the efforts of Paul Hanson and

John Collins. For the former, apocalyptic eschatology is defined as "a religious perspective which focuses on the disclosure (usually esoteric in nature) to the elect of the cosmic vision of Jahweh's sovereignty—especially as it relates to his acting to deliver his faithful—which disclosure the visionaries have largely ceased to translate into terms of plain history, real politics, and human instrumentality due to a pessimistic view of reality growing out of the bleak post-exilic conditions within which those associated with the visionaries found themselves." [27] Hanson's cumbrous definition is colored by his attempt to show that apocalypticism grows out of a fusion of Jewish prophecy's concern with history and the cosmic and mythological dimensions present in the royal cult of Israel. He holds that apocalypticism originates in the sixth century B.C. rather than in the early second.[28] Hanson has reemphasized the intimate relation between apocalypticism and the prophetic tradition denied by von Rad; but if one defines the essence of apocalypticism largely in terms of what it shares with prophecy, the reason for the birth and proliferation of Jewish apocalypticism as a distinct movement in the intertestamental period becomes quite problematic. J. Collins, on the other hand, holds to the traditional dating for the origins of Jewish apocalyptic, and finds its essence in the hope for individual transcendence of death. This hope is envisaged as having both horizontal, or future, and vertical, or heavenly, dimensions.[29] The same author expands upon these insights to construct a definition of apocalyptic genre as "a heavenly revelation, mediated by a heavenly being, disclosing a transcendent eschatology which involves the personal transcendence of death."[30] The genre includes two types, one in which the eschatological pattern of crisis–judgment–salvation is preceded by a review of history, and another which emphasizes the seer's heavenly journey and is more "mystical" than historical in accent.

Modern attempts to determine the historical and social context, the *Sitz im Leben,* of early apocalypticism vary widely. Hanson looks to a group of visionaries opposed to the Zadokite priesthood; Schmithals, in agreement with O. Plöger,[31] finds its creators among the heirs to the prophetic tradition in the period c.400–200 B.C., though for him the historical situation cannot really explain the new understanding of existence that became present in the apocalyptic movement.[32] The discoveries at Qumran have shown that the Essenes formed what one scholar has called an "apocalyptic community," and have reinforced the connections between apocalyptic eschatology and disaffected elements in Judaism in the period c.200 B.C. to A.D. c.135.[33]

When such quarrels exist among the family of biblical experts it would be rash for others to step in to attempt to solve the disputes. From a viewpoint whose primary interest lies in what became of apocalyptic motifs in the post-biblical period, it seems that the differences of opinion have been frequently exacerbated by being cast in too narrow a framework. Judaism did not exist in a cultural and religious vacuum; and apocalyptic teaching, even the apocalypse as a literary form, is in many senses a part of a more general phenomenon of the Hellenistic world. Students of the Hellenistic period have called for a wider treatment of apocalypticism and related phenomena, and such an endeavor can only be applauded by all who wish to understand apocalypticism as a general religious phenomenon as well as in its specifically Jewish forms.[34] This broader discussion should not restrict itself to the Hellenistic and Roman periods, but should also be open to later developments, Jewish, Christian, and Moslem.

What such a discussion might show is that while it may be possible to determine the literary genre of the Jewish apocalypse in fairly satisfactory fashion, this form is merely one in a spectrum of special revelations about the relation of history and the heavenly realm which have been widespread in Western religious traditions (I include the Iranian here) and which may still be legitimately grouped under the heading "apocalyptic." The very real differences that undoubtedly exist between the Jewish examples and their contemporaries and successors, as well as among the Jewish texts themselves, suggest that there is no *single* "apocalyptic understanding of reality," as W. Schmithals puts it. Rather, the content of apocalyptic eschatologies (the plural is surely more accurate) expresses a pattern of beliefs about time and eternity that are too complex to be reduced to any single essential notion. There are, to be sure, only a limited number of possible combinations of beliefs relating to the interaction of history, the End, and the heavenly realm that can be included under the rubric of apocalyptic without the term losing all meaning whatsoever; but apocalypticism should always be seen as a genus that includes a number of species.

Apocalyptic texts from various religious backgrounds and different ages display family resemblances in key areas that include: first, a sense of the unity and structure of history conceived as a divinely predetermined totality; second, pessimism about the present and conviction of its imminent crisis; and third, belief in the proximate judgment of evil and triumph of the good, the element of vindication. This vindication can take many forms—this-worldly or other-worldly, individual or collective, temporary or definitive, or a combination of some or all of these elements. I should not like to say that any one of these areas is more central than another, and I admit that my election of them is that of a medievalist seeking to find sufficient continuity between the Jewish apocalypses and their later influence to allow us to speak of an apocalyptic tradition;[35] but these three characteristics do seem to provide a way to conceive of the unity of the apocalyptic tradition in all its changing variety.

The problem of the unity of apocalyptic traditions becomes more complex when we reflect upon the relation of the earliest Christian apocalypticism to its Jewish heritage. Christianity was born apocalyptic and has remained so, not in the sense that apocalyptic hopes exhaust the meaning of Christian belief, but because they have never been absent from it.

Early Christian apocalypticism cannot be separated from the world of Jewish intertestamental apocalypticism. (There is even considerable doubt about whether some late first- and early second-century apocalypses are to be labeled Jewish or Christian.) Before reflecting upon the profound similarities and puzzling differences between Jewish and early Christian apocalypticism, it will be useful to survey the key New Testament texts involved since they are the first examples of the specifically Christian apocalypticism that is the center of our story.

The earliest datable witness to Christianity that we possess, the First Epistle of Paul to the Thessalonians (probably A.D. 51), is not an apocalypse in form but contains apocalyptic teaching of importance in 4:13 to 5:11, showing how strong expectation of the End was in the first Christian communities.[26] The specific literary form created by early Christianity, the Gospel, had intimate relations with apocalyptic, both in form and in content. Norman Perrin has shown how the earliest Gospel, that of Mark, occasioned by the crisis of the Jewish Wars and the fall of Jerusalem and written shortly after A.D. 70, is organized according to a three-act apocalyptic drama. The innovation of the first evangelist was to make use of realistic narrative descriptions to convey his message.[37]

The Gospels are books of the nascent church. They can tell us much about the apocalyptic beliefs of the early Christians, and even perhaps about the apocalyptic elements in the preaching of Jesus. The most important apocalyptic text ascribed to Jesus by the synoptics is the so-called Little Apocalypse or Apocalyptic Discourse of Mark 13, Matthew 24–25, and Luke 21. The theory that a written source, specifically a brief Jewish apocalypse, lies behind Mark 13 and its parallels was first advanced in 1864. (Such a theory implies that the Little Apocalypse has nothing to do with the actual preaching of Jesus.) An extensive controversial literature has developed on the problem of the Little Apocalypse.

One recent scholar, L. Hartman, has concluded that "an exposition or meditation on Daniel texts about the last days underlies the discourse."[38] The nucleus of the original meditation or "midrash" had two poles: first, the activity of the Antichrist involving "I am" sayings parodying the divine self-description, mention of the "Abomination of Desolation," and reference to false prophets performing signs and wonders; and second, the description of the Parousia, or glorious return, of the Son of Man and the gathering of the faithful into heaven.[39] The presence of these elements in the Epistles to the Thessalonians indicates that the "midrash" must have existed in Christian scribal circles prior to A.D. 50.[40]

Could the "midrash" have originated in the teaching of Jesus himself? Hartman recognizes that the answer to this question depends upon the image that we have of Jesus, as well as upon the criteria used to distinguish possible sayings of Jesus from the productions of the early community. In conclusion he presents some reasons for giving a positive answer to the question,[41] but the debate continues. Indeed, there is at present a strong tendency among many Scripture scholars to minimize the extent of apocalyptic influence detectable in what they hold to be the probably authentic fragments of the preaching of Jesus contained in the Gospels.[42] Whatever the future of this tendency, the importance of apocalypticism in the formation of the earliest Jewish Christian communities is undeniable.

The foremost witness to the strength of apocalypticism in Jewish Christianity is the Revelation (or Apocalypse) of John, a center of controversy in early Christianity. Widely accepted in the second century, its use by suspect authors appears to have provoked a negative reaction in the third century that continued in the East until about A.D. 500. It is not hard to see why Revelation should have aroused such debate, for the book is rich in lurid symbolism, contains teachings (such as chiliasm, the doctrine of the thousand-year reign of Christ and the saints on earth after the Second Coming, but before the End) that were subsequently condemned, and adopts a strong anti-Roman stance that must have been increasingly embarrassing to Christians of the third and fourth centuries. There is considerable disagreement over the authorship, composition, and significance of the work.[43] As A. Farrer has put it: "It is not only that the text is sometimes hard to explain; it is just as much that we do not always know what sort of explanation it calls for."[44]

Basically a series of visions prefaced by seven letters to early Christian communities, Revelation is striking in abandoning the pseudonymity that had been standard since Daniel. Later tradition claimed that the John who announces himself as the author in 1:1–2 was none other than the beloved disciple of Jesus and the author of the Fourth Gospel. This is highly unlikely, as Dionysius of Alexandria pointed out as long ago as the third century. Modern scholarship suggests that the awkward Greek and the Hebraic character of the book argue that Revelation has a better claim than the Gospel as a possible product of the pen of the apostle. Others have thought that the author was the mysterious Elder John mentioned in some second-century sources. Whoever he was, the author was certainly a Christian prophet living in Asia Minor toward the end of the first century. His eschewing the traditional pseudonymity of apocalyptic writers may be best explained by his sense that the Revelation of Jesus Christ needed no added authority to enhance it. The figure of the Risen Lord is at the center of the stage of early Christian apocalypticism.

John's prophetic consciousness is of special importance. As recent scholars have pointed out, prophetism experienced an important revival in late Judaism and in the early Christian communities, but with the exception of Revelation this new wave has left little literary remains. P. Vielhauer remarks: "Here [in the Christian prophecy of Palestine] we find for the first time the union of prophecy and Apocalyptic, a union which finds expression again and most impressively in the author of the Apocalypse of John. . . . Later Apocalyptic and prophecy again fall apart."[45]

The Revelation of John is so closely tied to the meaning of the entire Christian apocalyptic tradition that any simple characterization is impossible. The book is at once a summary of preceding literature, an appropriation of the genre on a new level, and the point of departure for much subsequent commentary and expansion. A. Wikenhauser has provided a summary characterization of three major currents of interpretation: Revelation has been read *eschatologically,* as dealing explicitly with the End of the world; *historically,* i.e., as reflecting contemporary events through the literary device of *vaticinium ex eventu* (though there is really not a great deal of this outside chapter 17); or in *mythological fashion* as a compendium of traditional legendary material.[46] One might add to this the *literary approach* of those who stress the creative symbolic mentality of the author as a key to the essential meaning.[47] Obviously, no single approach can suffice to capture the richness of the book.

Despite the fact that Revelation may be obscure and even tedious at times, there is no denying that it is the most powerful apocalyptic work ever written. The searing visions and majestic hymns (based in part on the early Christian liturgy) have continued to provide matter for inspiration as well as speculation throughout the history of Christianity. The Revelation of John is the apocalyptic book *par excellence*.

By the beginning of the second century, the Christian communities, themselves formed in the crucible of apocalyptic expectations and heirs to Jewish apocalyptic traditions, had been forced to confront the problem of the delay of the Parousia, the return of the Risen Christ. Some would have it that the solution to this problem entailed the end of any true Christian apocalypticism. This is far too simple an answer. Apocalyptic expectations went through many changes, both in terms of the manner of presentation and the nature of the content, but apocalypticism did not die out in Christianity.

PATRISTIC APOCALYPTICISM—A.D. 100–400

The most striking change found in Christian apocalypticism in the second century is the way in which formal apocalypses tend to lose interest in the historical concerns of classical apocalypticism while these concerns persist in the apocalyptic material present in other literary forms. There are at least twenty texts of the second and third centuries that share the literary characteristics of the apocalypses of the classical period, including the division into visions where the revelation entails a heavenly journey, such as the Ascension of Isaiah, and those where it does not, such as the Apocalypse of Peter.[48] According to the survey of Adela Collins, the systematic review of history dominant in many Jewish apocalypses is found in only one of the Christian examples, the text known as Jacob's Ladder. What interest there is in history tends to take a paradigmatic, or exemplary, form, in which certain key past events, especially those relating to Adam and Christ, are stressed, but without direct connection to the impending crisis.[49]

Stress upon the personal afterlife, more or less explicit, is found in all the early Christian apocalypses. This at times includes a detailed account of the pains of hell and joys of heaven, as in the influential Apocalypse of Paul, a work whose Greek original probably goes back to the mid-third century and whose Latin versions assured it an important role in later medieval literature. The heavenly revelation is always communicated through an intermediary, though the intermediary is sometimes Christ himself, as in the third-century text known as The Testament of the Lord. Although interest in history as a unitary structure is not strong in these formal apocalypses, the eschatological pattern of crisis, judgment, and salvation is found in many of them. Considerable interest in the career of the coming Antichrist is also present at times. This evidence shows a concern with the eschatological meaning of the present that is one of the themes of apocalyptic traditions.

A sense of the unity and structure of history conceived as a divinely predetermined totality is found in many early Christian works that do not possess the characteristics of apocalypse as a literary genre. What, then, are we to make of the bifurcation of the themes of classical apocalyptic that becomes evident as we move deeper into the Christian era? Visions of the world beyond the grave, in a wide variety of languages, were immensely popular in the Middle Ages. This vast literature includes the supreme literary creation of the period, the *Divine Comedy* of Dante.[50] These visions share in some of the characteristics of the classical apocalypses, such as intermediary revealing figures, interest in heavenly realities, and stress upon coming judgment; but looked at as a whole, it is obvious that they form a genre of their own.

Classical apocalypticism had a twin offspring, it seems. On the one hand, we have visionary literature increasingly centered on the fate of the individual soul; on the other, a variety of texts linked by more general historical concerns, especially a view of the present as a moment of supreme crisis, and a fervent hope of an imminent judgment that will vindicate the just. Texts of the latter sort frequently, though not invariably, incorporate concern with the structure of history, usually in terms of a theory of world ages.

The apocalypticism of the medieval period that will be our main concern will thus have a direct, but nonetheless ambiguous relation to the Jewish and Christian apocalypticism of the classical period. Direct, because so many (though by no means all) of its themes had their origin in the classical period; ambiguous, because what we have identified as the major components of the apocalyptic message will be conveyed through forms increasingly distant from the original notion of apocalypse.

No less important than the change in the form of presentation is the much-debated question of the effect of the loss of a sense of the imminent return of the Lord upon Christian beliefs. Did this mean that apocalypticism vanished? Some modern interpreters have made the problem of the delay of the Parousia, the gradual lessening of apocalyptic fervor, and the wide-ranging doctrinal and institutional changes furthered by these factors the center of their explanation of the early Church. In the words of Martin Werner, perhaps the foremost proponent of this interpretation of early Christian thought: "The delay of the Parousia of Jesus, which after his Death became increasingly obvious, must, in view of the non-fulfillment of the eschatological expectation, have grown into a problem which was conducive to the transformation of the original eschatological doctrine."[51]

Although the delay of the Parousia was certainly a crucial factor in the development of early Christian thought, the "consistent eschatological" interpretation, that is, the claim that the loss of a sense of the imminent return of the Lord was *the* major turning point in the life of the early Church, is open to serious distortion. That Christianity from the beginning shared some of the characteristics of the apocalyptic sects of Judaism cannot be denied, but this judgment does not mean that from these same early days the Christian communities did not have a rich identity of their own. The earliest Christian literature gives evidence of a number of interpretations of the meaning of the life of Jesus, the existence of the community, and the hope for the return of the Risen Christ.

The rapid expansion of the Christian communities throughout the Roman empire and the many accommodations necessitated by survival and success induced substantial changes. Many factors modified primitive Christian apocalyptic, even moved it away from its original central position; but they did not kill longing for and speculating about the last times. Many continued to hope for the triumphant Parousia; apocalyptic currents had important effects on Christian thought and history through and beyond the second century. As Jaroslav Pelikan remarks: "The impression seems unavoidable that the relation between 'already' and 'not yet' in Christian apocalyptic raised more problems for the philosophical theologians in the early church and for the proponents of 'consistent eschatology' among modern exegetes than it did for believers and worshipers in the second and third centuries."[52] The apocalyptic tradition continued to renew itself, not only through the study of texts of the classical period, but also by the creation of new scenes in the drama of the End.

The Antichrist

Rich development of three themes serves to show the vitality present in patristic apocalyptic. The first of these relates to the figure of the Antichrist already so prominent in John's Revelation and in other first-century texts. The early Church's rapidly evolving Christology seems to have stimulated the development of an obverse "Antichristology," that is, a more detailed and inflated account of the career and person of the final enemy. Myth, popular folklore, and current history all contributed to this evolution. Perhaps the most distinctive element of these evolving notions was the formation of a double view of the Antichrist. The Jewish and Jewish-Christian version of the Antichrist myth found in Revelation 13 and 17 was fundamentally anti-Roman, identifying the Antichrist with *Nero redivivus,* the resurrected persecutor. Elements in apocalyptic traditions that presented a picture of the Antichrist as a false Messiah were instrumental in producing another version of the myth stressing a Jewish Antichrist who was to be born from the tribe of Dan and to reign as a false prophet and Messiah from a rebuilt Jerusalem. Both traditions are found in some authors. This doubling could find scriptural warrant in the two beasts found in Revelation 13.[53]

The Duration of the World and the Thousand-Year Kingdom

The second and third themes are intimately connected. An interest in the number and duration of the ages of the world had been found in classical apocalyptic, but the schemas used were generally quite varied. The determination of ages does not play a large part in the New Testament texts,[54] but by the second century a number of patristic writings not only show a revived interest but also indicate a preference for a scheme based on seven periods of one thousand years each, or the "cosmic week" theme. The studies of J. Daniélou, A. Luneau, and others have made it clear that the doctrine of the world ages cannot be considered apart from the third major element in patristic apocalyptic, that of the thousand-year kingdom of Revelation 20:4–6.[55] The evidence of Eusebius (*Church History* 3:39) concerning the early second-century bishop Papias indicates that chiliasm was not only found in the Revelation, but was also received by many Christians as part of an oral tradition that went back to Jesus.[56] According to Daniélou, who has given the most convincing interpretation of the development of patristic ideas on the thousand-year kingdom, "Millenarianism is the form in which Jewish Christianity expressed the doctrine of the Parousia."[57] He discerns two major strands: a type that developed largely in Asia Minor and for which we have witness in Revelation and in Papias; and a type that developed in Syria and whose earliest witness is the pseudonymous Epistle of Barnabas (c.135). The first type stresses "the conception of an earthly reign of the Messiah which comes before the new creation and constitutes the 'repose of the saints.' " [58] It describes the kingdom in rich and concrete terms taken from the account of Paradise in Genesis chapters 2–3. In Syria and Egypt, on the other hand, "the messianic reign was related to the calculations of the astrologers on the cosmic week consisting of seven millennia," [59] and was thus based on speculations concerning the first chapter of Genesis. [60] Despite the vehement reaction against chiliasm at a later time, [61] both views are found in many patristic writers.

An indication of how influential these apocalyptic themes were in second-century Christianity can be found in the writings of Irenaeus, the most important Christian author of the period. He was born in Asia Minor, visited Rome, and finished his life as bishop of Lyons in France from A.D. 178 to about 200. His great work, *The Unmasking and Refutation of False Gnosis,* usually called *Against Heresies,* was a lengthy attack on the errors of the day, especially the various forms of Gnosticism. Although there is a systematic and even speculative character to his theology, especially his doctrine of Christ, Irenaeus is the great spokesman for the role of tradition in determining correct belief. The criterion for the discrimination between true and false gnosis, or wisdom, is the inherited teaching of the Church enshrined in the episcopal office.

Somewhat to the embarrassment of later theologians and commentators, in Book 5 of the *Against Heresies* Irenaeus includes a good deal of apocalyptic material, including a detailed account of the Antichrist and a strong chiliasm as a part of this inheritance. [62] Daniélou points out that 5:25–35 contains "a whole mass of traditional material which makes these chapters the most important source of information on Asiatic millenarianism." [63] But Irenaeus is not a mere reporter; his apocalypticism shows real originality. He is the first to seek to combine the two strands of patristic chiliasm: the materialistic paradisiacal hope of the Asian tradition, and the more refined speculation of the Syriac background. [64] The materialistic stress in Irenaeus, particularly in his account of the thousand-year kingdom, may have been designed to counter the excessive spiritualization of the Gnostic accounts of salvation. [65]

The Sibylline Oracles

The second century also saw the beginnings of Christian use of another genre of literature whose history is intimately tied to that of apocalypticism, the Sibylline Oracles. Although Irenaeus does not cite the Sibyl, a contemporary apologist, Theophilus of Antioch, was deeply influenced by the Sibylline verses. During the same century, Christians began to imitate their Jewish predecessors in composing Sibyllines. Apocalyptic reviews of world history and prophecies of imminent destruction ascribed to the Sibyl will continue to proliferate during the Middle Ages; hence it is necessary to survey in brief fashion the background to the history of Christian Sibyllinism.

The existence of a female seer known as the Sibyl probably goes back to the Greek colonies of Asia Minor in the eighth century B.C.[66] The philosopher Heracleitus (c.500 B.C.), in a fragment preserved by Plutarch, gives us our earliest literary witness: "The Sibyl with frenzied lips, uttering words mirthless, unembellished, unperfumed, penetrates through the centuries by the powers of the gods."[67] As a special vessel of divine madness or inspiration the Sibyl was spoken of with reverence by Plato (*Phaedrus* 244b).

During the Hellenistic period Sibyls spread throughout the ancient Mediterranean world. Nowhere were they more popular than in Rome. According to legend, King Tarquin the Proud in the late sixth century bought three books of prophetic verses from the Sibyl for the price originally demanded for nine.[68] Whether such an overtly Greek element in Roman religion really goes back so far is disputable, but we do know that the Sibylline books, kept on the Capitol and guarded by a special priesthood, were frequently consulted during the republic in times of crisis or upon the appearance of unusual omens. It was by means of the consultation of the Sibylline books that Rome expanded her religious horizons and allowed the entry of Greek and Eastern deities into the city.[69] When the books were destroyed by a fire in 83 B.C., new material was gathered and installed on the Capitol.[70] Learned antiquarians, such as Varro (d. 27 B.C.), discussed the history of the Sibyls and enumerated ten in all, the most important being the Erythraean Sibyl from Asia, who was supposed to have lived at the time of the Trojan War and was thought by some to have migrated to Cumae near Naples. The poet Virgil used the Cumaean Sibyl not only as the guide of his hero Aeneas through the underworld, but also as the prophetess of the return of the Golden Age:

> Now is the last age of the song of Cumae,
> The great line of the centuries begins anew.
> (Eclogue 4:4–5)

Under the Emperor Augustus the collection of Sibylline verses was purged of spurious oracles and placed in the Temple of Apollo on the Palatine.[71] They came to be less and less consulted in imperial times, though notable catastrophes, such as the great fire in Rome in A.D. 64, still sent frightened Romans off to the Temple of Apollo to take their advice.[72] Use of the oracles never quite died out; it appears that in the late fourth and early fifth centuries they were a part of the polemic of the pagan die-hards against the Christians—the probable reason for their destruction by Stilicho around A.D. 408.[73]

Only fragments of the pagan Sibyllines remain,[74] but this is enough to indicate that their form was frequently acrostic and their meaning wrapped in customary prophetic obscurity. The Sibylline books that have come down to us, fourteen in all,[75] are of Jewish and Christian origin, though they undoubtedly contain pagan material as well. They represent an interesting fusion between pagan and Judaeo–Christian notions of prophecy and, as one author puts it, are the apocalyptic of Hellenistic Diaspora Judaism.[76] The existence of a native Egyptian apocalyptic literature still popular in Hellenistic and Roman times demonstrates the missionary appeal that these productions had in the Alexandrian context in which some were produced.[77] From the mid-second century B.C., the date of the earliest Jewish productions, they played an important role in propagating "to this wider, Sibylline audience the rudiments of the Hebrew faith, especially her monotheism and moralism."[78] Within Diaspora Judaism, and later within Christianity, they played a role similar to that which they had enjoyed in early Roman religion, that of an authoritative voice ideally suited to expanding traditional religious wisdom by countenancing the introduction of exotic and foreign elements. They were also a witness to the universality of revelation: the Sibyls were thought to have performed the same functions for the pagan world that the prophets had in the case of Israel—to testify to the true God, to call sinners to penance, and to announce God's plans for the coming age. *Teste David cum Sibylla,* "with the witness of David and the Sibyl," as a thirteenth-century poet put it, was no idle remark.

Jewish use of the Sibyl had a deep influence throughout the early Christian world, not only in Jewish–Christian circles. P. Vielhauer claims: "Christianity took over the genre of the Apocalypse from Palestinian Judaism and that of the Sibyllines from Hellenistic Judaism."[79] Almost all the Jewish Sibylline books were utilized and reworked by Christian authors to such an extent that it is sometimes difficult to say whether a particular section is actually Jewish in origin or not.[80] Books I and II, originally Jewish, were reworked by a Christian redactor in either the second or the third century.[81] Books VI to VIII are more properly Christian and appear to date from the second half of the second century.[82] Book VIII, the most important of the Christian Sibyllines, is a confusing mixture of material, some of it Jewish and pagan, put together by perhaps three separate redactors. It reflects the age of the Emperor Marcus Aurelius (A.D. 161–80) and is written from a decidedly anti-Roman point of view. The Book is frequently cited by later Christian authors, and its famous acrostic poem referring to Christ (lines 217–50) was known to the Middle Ages through the translation in Augustine's *City of God*.[83]

The Sibylline Oracles were treated with great respect by the Christian Fathers from the second century, a respect that was not to decline until the time of the Enlightenment.[84] Indeed, Christianity's wholehearted adoption of the Sibyl led to criticism from pagans like Celsus.[85] Tertullian, suspicious of any commerce between Athens and Jerusalem, apparently thought differently about the association of Cumae and Jerusalem.[86] The early fourth-century writer Lactantius cited the Sibyls extensively and thus transmitted knowledge of the early Sibylline tradition to the Latin West. Augustine himself, generally so opposed to any form of apocalypticism, not only quoted the Sibyl but also included her among the members of the City of God.[87]

Later Patristic Apocalypticism

The teaching of theologians like Irenaeus and the production of the Christian Sibyllines argue that apocalyptic elements continued to be strong in second-century Christianity, despite the delay of the expected return of Christ. An important dissident movement of the time, that of Montanus and his followers, active in Phrygia in Asia Minor from around 172, has been frequently seen as a reaction against the loss of apocalyptic fervor.[88] The Montanists undoubtedly emphasized a number of traditional Jewish–Christian apocalyptic elements, especially the hope for the descent of the heavenly Jerusalem, which they thought would come down on Pepuza, an obscure Phrygian town; but a survey of the authentic fragments of their teaching, as well as their emphasis on oral rather than written teaching, has convinced one investigator that "early Montanism seems to have been a prophetic, but not a strictly apocalyptic movement."[89] Whether primarily prophetic or apocalyptic, Montanism attracted important converts like Tertullian in the third century and continued to exist into the era of the Church's recognition.

R. M. Grant has pointed to a renewal of apocalyptic expectations, par-

tially triggered by persecutions, about the year 200.[90] Tertullian of Carthage
(c.160–c.220), the first major Latin Christian author, shows an acquaintance
with such notions, especially the chiliastic traditions of Asia (e.g., *Against
Marcion* 3:24), although he prayed for the continuance of the Roman empire
that he identified with the force restraining the Antichrist (the *Katechōn*)
mentioned in 2 Thess. 2:6–7 (*Apology* 32).

His contemporary Hippolytus (d. 235) is an even more important
witness to apocalypticism. In the learned Roman presbyter we find a fairly
complete theological sketch of apocalyptic themes, though he himself was
in many ways an enemy of apocalypticism. The occasion of his *Commentary
on Daniel,* the earliest complete Christian exegetical work that has come
down to us, was apparently the upsurge in expectations of the End at the
beginning of the third century.[91] Hippolytus is principally interested in prov-
ing that the study of Daniel shows that the End is not immediate. He uses
the theme of the cosmic week to demonstrate that Christ was born in the
middle of the sixth millennium rather than at its end.[92] His view of the
earthly kingdom of the returning Christ belongs to the milder Syriac variety
rather than the more radical Asiatic form.[93] Even if he is not a strict apocalypticist, Hippolytus' *Treatise on Christ and the Antichrist,* written about
200, is the most complete summary of early patristic traditions on the final
enemy of man.

The third century saw further growth and consolidation of traditions
concerning the Antichrist. The Testament of the Lord, purporting to give the
instructions of the Risen Christ to his disciples,[94] is really a combination of
two works: an apocalyptic discourse, probably mid-third century in date,
and a fifth-century church order of a fairly developed type. It contains a remarkable physical description of the Antichrist:

And these are the signs of him: his head is as a fiery flame; his right eye shot with
blood, his left eye blueblack, and he hath two pupils. His eyelashes are white; and
his lower lip is large; but his right thigh slender; his feet broad; his great toe is
bruised and flat. This is the sickle of desolation.[95]

The Latin poet Commodian has been dated anywhere from the mid-
third to the mid-fifth century. J. Martin, his most recent editor, contends
that he was born in Syria and wrote probably at Rome about the middle of
the third century,[96] thus vindicating for him the title of the oldest Latin
Christian poet. His two main works, the Instructions and the Song of the
Two Peoples, both evidence a strong apocalypticism that may have been influenced by the Gothic invasions and the imperial persecutions of the time.

Commodian was a convinced chiliast (Instructions 1:44) and fervently anti-Roman in the tradition of the Book of Revelation. He taught that there would be two Antichrists—a revived Nero in the West who would be killed by the final Antichrist arising from Persia and ruling over the Jews.

> For us Nero is the Antichrist, for the Jews he is. . . .
> Nero is the destruction of Rome; he of the whole world. . . .[97]

Formal scriptural commentary was an increasingly important vehicle for the dissemination of apocalyptic ideas during the patristic period. Reflection upon received texts, such as Daniel, had already been an influence upon the authors of the New Testament. From the time of the formation of the canon, or list of accepted books, of the New Testament (a process well advanced by the end of the second century), one of the most acceptable ways to advance applications of traditional apocalyptic images to current events was by means of scriptural exegesis. Just as Hippolytus' *Commentary on Daniel* is the earliest surviving work of its kind in Greek, the oldest preserved Latin commentary is on the Book of Revelation.

John's Revelation had come in for criticism both in the East and in the West. In the last quarter of the second century the so-called Alogi had attacked the book, claiming it was the product of the heretic Cerinthus; in the early third century the Roman priest Gaius also denied its authenticity. Bishop Dionysius of Alexandria (d. 265) claimed that it was not written by John the Disciple.[98] In the early fourth century, opposition to Revelation is found in some parts of the *Church History* of Eusebius,[99] and this theme was echoed at least to the end of the fifth century. But these were minority views, especially in the West. Even Dionysius admitted: "I would never dare to reject the book, of which many good Christians have a very high opinion."[100] A witness to this Western popularity is found in the *Commentary* of Victorinus, a Greek who was bishop of Pettau in modern Yugoslavia and died a martyr under Diocletian in 304. Much influenced by the thought of Irenaeus, Hippolytus, and Origen, he is most like the first in his pronounced, though moderate, chiliasm.[101] Victorinus is the earliest of the long series of Western commentators on the greatest of apocalyptic texts. His popularity was such that Jerome was induced to undertake an orthodox revision of his work in the late fourth century.[102]

The most striking proponent of apocalypticism among the early Latin Fathers was Lucius Caecilius Firmianus Lactantius, a Roman rhetor and Christian convert active at the courts of Diocletian and Constantine in the early fourth century. He might well be described as the most inventive Christian apocalyptic author since the John of Revelation. The genre that he used was not that of apocalypse as such, but rather the doctrinal treatise. The seventh book of his *Divine Institutes,* which were composed between 304 and 313, summarized his teaching concerning the ages of the world (chs. 14–15), the coming and defeat of the two Antichrists (chs. 16–19), and the thousand-year kingdom (ch. 24).

What was most remarkable about his treatment was the catholicity of the witnesses he invoked. He firmly believed the testimonies to Christian truth regarding the End were not restricted to the canonical scriptures. God had revealed his message, at least in part, to Egyptians, Persians, and Greeks as well as to the Jews. Lactantius made extensive use of the Sibylline Oracles (in 1:6 he summarized traditional lore about the Sibyls in a form that was to be a major source for most later medieval acquaintance). Book VII showed extensive knowledge not only of Jewish and Christian apocalypticism, but also of Iranian and Egyptian materials.

In several places Lactantius referred to Hystaspes whom he called "a very ancient king of the Medes" (7:15). Besides the explicit references, he also made silent use of the so-called Oracle of Hystaspes (a text known to some other Christian authors) in the *Institutes.* The Oracle has not survived, but the fragments that we possess suggest that it was of authentic Iranian origin written no later than the first century B.C. and representing a form of Zoroastrian eschatology known to us through later Persian texts.[103] If this hypothesis is correct, the *Institutes* have the unusual distinction of representing a direct Iranian influence on Christian apocalyptic.

Lactantius also made use of the Hermetic treatise known as the Asclepius. Supposedly the production of Hermes Trismegistus, "Thrice-Great Hermes" (the Hellenistic version of the Egyptian god Thoth), the work was written in the late third century in Egypt. Aside from a few Greek fragments, it survives in a Latin translation made about the mid-fourth century, used by Augustine, and widely read in the Middle Ages and the Renaissance. Heavily influenced by late classical thought and showing traces of Jewish and Christian themes, the Asclepius contains a brief apocalypse (9:24–26) that was also known in Gnostic circles.[104] This text shows affinities to earlier Egyptian apocalypses such as the "Prophecies of a Potter," originally written in the late second century B.C. but re-edited at later periods.[105] Lactantius, the "ecumenical" apocalypticist among the Fathers, summarized his intent as follows:

Wherefore since all these things are true and certain, being foretold by the unanimous annunciation of all the prophets, since Trismegistus, Hystaspes, and the Sibyls have all foretold the same things, it cannot be doubted that all hope of life and salvation rests solely in the worship of God.[106]

Opposition to Apocalypticism

The apocalypticism of Lactantius was fostered by some later fourth-century authors, such as Cyril of Jerusalem (d. 386), the fifteenth instruction of whose *Catechetical Lectures* contains a full account of the career of the Antichrist. But in the fourth and early fifth centuries powerful theological forces, both in the East and in the West, reacted against apocalypticism. There were many factors at work in this attack, not least the conversion of the Emperor Constantine to Christianity. The empire had generally played a negative role in earlier Christian apocalyptic writings. With Tertullian we have seen the beginnings of a more positive evaluation. When Rome adopted Christianity, the destinies of *Imperium* and *Christianitas* seemed to have been providentially united; many Christians felt that any expectation of the downfall of the empire was as disloyal to God as it was to Rome. Even more, on an exegetical level apocalypticism appeared to many to be a throwback to an outmoded, "Jewish," literal reading of the Scriptures. The Revelation of John was not to be understood as prophecy of the last events of history, but rather as an allegory of the conflict between good and evil in the present life of the Church. Attempts to determine the time of the End of the world were ruled out with an appeal to "It is not for you to know the times or dates" (Acts 1:7).

In the East, Bishop Eusebius of Caesarea (263–339), the court theologian of Constantine, was one of the leaders in the rejection of apocalyptic ideas. As an heir to the thought of the great third-century exegete Origen,[107] he adhered to a strongly allegorical reading of Revelation and even came to doubt its authenticity. The doctrine of the world ages found in the bishop's *Chronicles* (the source of most of the universal histories of the Middle Ages) is concerned with the antiquity of Christian truth and not with its future. As one author remarks, Eusebius was not troubled overmuch to distinguish Constantine's reign from the time of the messianic kingdom.[108]

At the end of the fourth century, the two most important Latin theologians also reacted against overt apocalypticism. The biblical translator and exegete Jerome (347–420) had little sympathy with the cruder forms of apocalyptic interpretation of the canonical texts. He edited Victorinus' *Com-*

mentary to remove its chiliasm and wrote a *Commentary on Daniel* designed to drown apocalypticism in pedantry.[109] Although the savant Jerome was important in conveying elements of earlier apocalyptic views to later ages, his own approach was notably cautious. Despite his best efforts, there were times when the great exegete's methodical attempts to solve scriptural problems helped rather than hindered later apocalypticism. As R. Lerner has shown, Jerome's desire to account for a surplus of forty-five days between two reckonings in Daniel for the time of the Antichrist led him to project a brief period of peace immediately prior to the End that would in later times be used to encourage new strains of millenarian hope.[110]

Augustine of Hippo (354–430), the greatest of the Latin Fathers, was the most incisive opponent of the apocalyptic interpretation of history in the patristic period. At an early stage in his career he accepted much of the Eusebian theology of history with its linking of the destinies of Rome and the Church,[111] and even held to a mild form of chiliasm.[112] His later writings, especially after the sack of Rome by Alaric in 410, break with both positions in decisive fashion. Pagans were quick to point out that the sack of Rome had given the lie to Eusebius and his followers—if the safety of the city and the continuation of the world depended upon divine protection, then the Christian God seemed to have achieved a worse job-rating than his pagan predecessors. Augustine argued that the basic premiss of both Eusebius and his opponents was wrong: there was no essential relation between God's plan for salvation and the destinies of secular kingdoms and empires.[113] External history needed to be secularized so that the inner history of the City of God could shine forth.[114]

Augustine's shift in the understanding of history entailed a new attitude toward the interpretation of apocalyptic texts. As R. A. Markus has put it: "The apocalyptic prophecies are not to be read as referring to any particular historical catastrophe, but to the final winding up of all history; and the time of that no man can know."[115] The bishop of Hippo shied away from any reading of canonical apocalyptic texts that would attempt to find in them a source of information about current events (*City of God* 18:52–53); rather, he tried to interpret them as a message about the perennial struggle between good and evil in the souls of men (e.g., 20:7 and 19). While he did not deny the historical veracity of the scriptural message concerning Antichrist and the End (20:30), he spurned any attempt to determine the time of his advent or to read the signs of the final consummation. Although Augustine is the fountainhead of all anti-apocalyptic eschatology in the Middle Ages, his writings, like those of Jerome, incorporate many themes of earlier patristic apocalyptic speculation, most notably the theories of the ages of the world. Luneau has shown that Augustine was the first to integrate the traditional six-thousand-year pattern with the Pauline four eras of grace.[116] In this he is the prototype of much later medieval thought.

A study of Augustine's important exegetical treatise *On Christian Doctrine* indicates how deeply dependent he was upon a fellow North African, the Donatist scholar Tyconius (c.330–390) for his hermeneutical theory. Tyconius was the author of the most influential *Commentary* on Revelation (composed c.385) in the early medieval period.[117] Although the original text has perished, much of it can be reconstructed from later witnesses.[118] Despite his conviction of the near approach of the Antichrist, the importance of Tyconius lies primarily in the moral and typological vein: apocalyptic symbolism is to be understood in terms of the constant struggle between the forces of good and evil within the Church in every age. The solidarity of the two opposing camps with their respective heads Christ and the Devil is the primary concern of the Donatist. Tyconius, like his two better-known contemporaries, was an anti-apocalypticist who was frequently to be put to quite a different use in the centuries to come.

This brief survey of the development of apocalyptic themes in early Christianity shows that hopes for an imminent End did not die out after the delay of the Parousia became evident. Even the attacks on overt apocalypticism of the writers of the fourth century are witnesses to its continued strength. Ironically enough, Jerome, Augustine, and Tyconius, far more widely known to medieval authors than true apocalypticists like Irenaeus, Commodian, and Lactantius, could be used as sources of information for views with which they were not sympathetic. Even more important than the ambiguous witness of the theologians, however, was the revival of apocalypticism evident in the latter part of the fourth century, especially in the case of the Sibylline tradition. It is with this material that properly medieval apocalyptic literature may be said to begin. As in so many other areas, the conversion of Rome marked the end of one world and the beginning of another.

Before turning to the medieval story, however, it is worthwhile to consider the phenomenon of apocalypticism from the perspective of recent social scientific studies that attempt to place Jewish and Christian apocalypticism in a wider framework.

MESSIANISM, MILLENARIANISM, AND APOCALYPTICISM

Much work has been done in recent years by historians, anthropologists, and sociologists on messianism and millenarianism, related and frequently over-lapping areas of study. Investigations of classical Jewish and Christian apo-calypticism have been conducted under these rubrics, and they have also served as key terms for the most popular account in English of medieval apocalypticism, Norman Cohn's *The Pursuit of the Millennium*.[119] It is im-portant at this point to explain why I have chosen to present this history under the heading of *apocalypticism* rather than under the more current terms of *millenarianism* or of *messianism*. To some extent this may seem like a purely semantic question, but there are also issues of substance at stake.

My choice was not by any means due to the difficulty involved in get-ting some sense of what the alternative terms meant, though there are ob-viously considerable differences among the authors who make use of them. "Hard" definitions seem as inadequate for both *messianism* and *millenar-ianism* as they are for *apocalypticism*,[120] but from our point of view this can be seen as an advantage. The major difficulty is that *messianism* and *mille-narianism* as currently used by most social scientists bear connotations that I find misleading when applied to medieval materials.

Christian apocalypticism is certainly messianic, but *messianism,* even when used in the broad sense, tends to suggest only the optimistic and ne-glects the pessimistic aspects of medieval apocalypticism. Used in the narrower sense, in terms of hopes for a coming savior figure or as indicating a certain type of religious leadership, it captures some but not all of the val-ues found in the pattern of apocalyptic beliefs. While messianic figures, ei-ther the returning Christ or sundry secondary characters, are of great impor-tance in Christian speculation about the End of history, they by no means exhaust the full scope of these hopes. The action of messianic figures always takes place within a scenario of events, and this scenario is the product of a total vision of history that theories of messianism do not always compre-hend. Furthermore, messianic leaders of groups or sects, while not unknown in the Christian tradition, are far less important for it than they are for later Jewish apocalypticism. With good reason there is no historical Christian messianic figure as potent as Sabbatai Sevi. *In fine,* then, later Christian apocalypticism involves messianism, but cannot be adequately contained under this heading.

The inadequacy of *millenarianism* as a blanket term to elucidate these chapters in Christian history is even more fundamental.[121] According to N. Cohn, the author usually cited in these connections, millenarianism is a particular type of salvationism which always pictures salvation as collective, terrestrial, imminent, total, and miraculous.[122] Many medieval beliefs about the End do fit these categories, but others lack at least the note of terrestriality. It is my contention that the notion of apocalyptic as used here is a more precise description of a wider range of materials than the sociological understanding of millenarianism.

The inadequacy of the usual understanding of millenarianism is most evident when we advert to the social and political functions that it is said to have possessed. It is true that in the revised edition of his work Cohn notes a variety of functions, emphasizing that millenarian sects come in all stripes, from "the most violent aggressiveness to the mildest pacifism and from the most ethereal spirituality to the most earthbound materialism,"[123] and that he suggests that in dealing with the millenarianism that flourished among the rootless poor of Western Europe between the eleventh and the sixteenth centuries he is really concerned with only the most violent segments. He also admits that millenarian beliefs originate among "would-be prophets or would-be messiahs many of them former members of the lower clergy," thus suggesting the dispossessed poor had learned leaders whose beliefs were frequently modified by their ignorant followers. All of this is an improvement over the cruder picture presented in the earlier edition of *The Pursuit of the Millennium,* upon which, unfortunately, most of the sociological generalizations of Cohn's users are based. But a fundamental problem still remains. This approach is almost totally blind to those manifestations of apocalyptic traditions that were intended to *support* the institutions of medieval Christianity rather than to serve as a critique, either mild or violent.

The sociological stereotype of the millenarian movement sees it as an agent of social change, a pre-political phenomenon, at times a proto-revolutionary one. This picture, supported by anthropological studies of millenarianism in primitive societies, such as those of P. Worsley and M. Burridge,[124] and by a few historical works, like E. J. Hobshawm's *Primitive Rebels,*[125] and Cohn's book, has been summarized by Y. Talmon under the rubric: "Most millenarian movements were subterranean and amorphous popular revolt movements."[126] Such a generalization does fit a number of patristic and medieval apocalyptic movements, and is partially helpful for understanding a few others; but it is quite misleading in the case of many medieval texts and sects, as will become evident below. To cover the full range of medieval beliefs about the imminent End we must find a more adequate model than that provided by current social scientific understandings of millenarianism.

Beliefs about the coming age—whether ideas of salvation that in Cohn's terms were "collective, terrestrial, imminent, total, and miraculous," or related teachings that lack some of these characteristics—were as important for social continuity as they were for social change. Better understood as forms of political rhetoric rather than as pre-political phenomena, they were as often designed to maintain the political, social, and economic order as to overthrow it. Their interest in the structure of history, their sense of the present as crisis, and the variety of their hopes for the vindication of the just, can be more easily contained under the broad range of characteristics of apocalypticism given above. It is at least clear that these hopes differ from the usual social-scientific understandings of messianism and millenarianism in enough ways to discourage the use of such terms to encompass the full range of medieval hopes regarding the imminent End. The following typology of the negative and positive functions of apocalyptic beliefs is advanced as a more adequate and nuanced way to understand the role of such hopes in the history of medieval religion. From this perspective imperial propagandists and papal publicists were no less important than Taborite radicals. Neither side exhausts the full story of medieval apocalypticism.

The apocalypticist is one who seeks, in Frank Kermode's phrase, "to be related to a beginning and an end."[127] The structure and meaning of time, the meeting place of this age and eternity, are consistent concerns of the medieval apocalyptic visionaries and scribes. The desire to understand history—its unity, its structure, its goal, the future hope which it promises—is not a passing interest or a momentary whim, but a perennial human concern. A sense of belonging in time, as well as the need to understand the special significance of the present, is the anthropological root of apocalyptic systems of thought.

Moments when the sense of belonging in time is threatened or disrupted have an important, but by no means univocal, relation to apocalypticism. A. N. Wilder holds that "the rhetorics of apocalyptic are peculiar in that they dramatize the group hierophany in a situation of broken continuities," a time of crisis when all is forfeit to chaos.[128] Much sociological study has concentrated on the relation of millenarianism and messianism to crisis situations,[129] yet the connection with crisis can be used to explain too much.

There are, after all, crises and crises. Almost every generation has been tempted to see itself as undergoing a unique crisis. Even if we accept that the crises are real, the variety in reactions provokes thought. No one would want to deny that apocalypticism is frequently literature of consolation, but it would be erroneous to think that it is only that.

I would agree then with W. Schmithals that the crises experienced by the Jewish communities in the Hellenistic period cannot really "explain" the meaning of Jewish apocalypticism, though they may be said to provide the occasion or situation in which it came to birth. Similarly, crisis situations are always apt moments for the invocation of apocalyptic rhetoric, but any survey of the major crises in the history of Western Christianity disproves any simple one-to-one relation. How are we to explain the great disasters, for example the Black Death of the 1340s, which had at best a minor effect upon the history of apocalypticism, at least in comparison with other less troubled times? How are we to account for the important new stages in the apocalyptic tradition that were not a reaction to a shattering crisis, but rather an accommodation to a new positive situation, such as the conversion of the Roman empire or the rise of the Reform papacy? It is not so much crisis in itself, as any form of challenge to the established understanding of history, that creates the situation in which apocalyptic forms and symbols, either inherited or newly minted, may be invoked. These challenges may be positive as well as negative, unexpected strokes of good fortune as well as terrible disasters. They may be major or minor—the apocalypticist maintains as much freedom as the next man in the way he reacts to events.

The concern for the meaning of the present explains why the political context of apocalypticism provides a useful key for its understanding.[130] Apocalypticism was a way in which contemporary political and social events were given religious validation by incorporation into a transcendent scheme of meaning. This insight enables us to coordinate the variety of ways in which apocalyptic beliefs were used in medieval history into a coherent framework and to construct a tentative typology of their functions. The apocalyptic traditions inherited from the classical and patristic eras formed a paradigm, a framework, a language that could provide meaning. Historians and political philosophers have already begun to recognize this fact;[131] theologians and students of the history of religions should also be prepared to admit how inextricably apocalypticism is intermingled with the "political" sphere at all times.

The social type to which most medieval apocalyptic propagandists con-

form was not that of the lonely prophet on the mountain top, or even that of
Norman Cohn's renegade members of the lower clergy leading bands of the
uprooted poor (though there are a few of these), but rather the well-educated
and well-situated clerical intelligentsia—the court official, scribe, or pamph-
leteer. Even those apocalypticists who led more private lives of separation
from the seats of power were frequently potent political figures, like Joachim of Fiore, or were at least intensely interested in political questions, like
Telesphorus of Cosenza. As the recent work of J. Z. Smith suggests, a similar social group were largely responsible for the production of apocalyptic
texts in the classical period.[132]

This form of leadership suggests that Christian apocalypticism during
the centuries presented here was not primarily a movement from below, a
manifestation of popular religion, a protean enthusiasm forcing its way like
molten lava up through the hardened sediment of institutional religious and
political forms. It was, for the most part, an attempt by a group of educated
religious *literati* to interpret the times, to support their patrons, to console
their supporters, and to move men to pursue specified aims at once political
and religious in nature. It took its unique power from an ability to locate
current events within a schema of universal meaning, to eranscendentalize
the present by viewing it from the aspect of the End.

The potent symbols and strong rhetoric of the apocalyptic drama could
be used in a variety of ways by its proponents. The rhetoric could be
directed against the present evil order in the name of some proximate millennial state. The Revelation of John is intensely anti-Roman, and the seer's picture of the thousand-year kingdom is a hope for what would come after God
had destroyed the Great Whore, Babylon, and vindicated his saints. But it
must be noted that John nowhere recommends active resistance to the hated
Roman regime. It is the lot of the saints to wait and to suffer, to be prepared
to rejoice when God comes to avenge them on their foes. This *negative* political use (that is, apocalyptic beliefs as directed *against* the established
order) is much more frequently passive than active in its attitude toward the
actual means of bringing about the transition to a better state or to the End of
history. There are a few cases in the history of Jewish and Christian apocalypticism, such as the Bar-Kochba revolt of A.D. 132–135 and the Hussite
Taborites, in which we do find active negative apocalypticism, something
very close to revolution; but these are exceptions. Most negative apocalypticists cannot even be described as reformists, since their passive attitude
toward change and their expectation of divine destruction of the old order

left them with little desire to ameliorate its structures or to advance concrete plans.[133]

Even before John had issued his flaming condemnation of Rome, the Second Epistle to the Thessalonians had spoken of the mysterious restrainer or restraining force that was holding back the appearance of the Antichrist (2:6–7). Modern biblical scholars still do not agree what this means, but the commonly accepted interpretation during most of Christian history has been that which saw in the "restraining force" a reference to the Roman empire destined to last until the End of the world.[134] This shows that from the beginning the seeds of a *positive* political use of apocalypticism were present in Christianity. The true extent of the positive mode and its many variations will become clear as this history unfolds.[135]

It is possible to specify broad ways in which the rhetoric of apocalypticism has been used in support of the political and social order. The two most fundamental approaches during our period might be described as the *a priori* and the *a posteriori:* the one making use of the already established apocalyptic scenario to interpret current events and thus to move men to decision and action, the other reacting to political and social change by expanding the scenario to include transcendentalized versions of recent events, thus giving final validation to the present by making a place for it at the End. It is this latter function which shows medieval Christian apocalypticism at its most creative.

The major additions to the apocalyptic scenario during these eleven centuries can be seen as attempts to provide such final validation for three of the most significant developments of the period—the conversion of the Roman empire, the onslaught of Islam, and the emergence of the high medieval papacy.

There is no mention anywhere in Scripture of a good Christian emperor who would come at the End of time to defeat the enemies of the Cross and usher in a period of peace and plenty before the advent of the Antichrist. Such a figure would have been inconceivable before the conversion of Constantine and the development of the "imperial theology" linking the fates of Christianity and the empire. After the event, however, it became a most effective way to validate the trans-historical significance of this change and to provide a hope in times of imperial crisis. No matter what reverses the empire might suffer, it would last until the End. No matter what defeats or difficulties individual emperors might undergo, a reign of universal triumph would finally come. What stronger support could be given to any emperor than to hail him as the long-awaited last ruler, as many emperors and kings were for over a thousand years of Christian history? The Last Emperor myths that formed such an important part of medieval apocalyptic hopes were decidedly positive in their relation to the structure of Christian society. Optimism about the future glory of the Christian empire was inextricably mixed with pessimism concerning the approach of the Antichrist in the newly expanded scenario, but the message was clear: support of the emperor put one on the side of the angels.

Similar types of *a posteriori* incorporation of social and political changes into apocalypticism can be found in the way in which Islam was given the role of the apocalyptic enemy *par excellence,* and in the creation of another new apocalyptic figure, the *pastor angelicus,* or Angelic Pope, who would come to restore the Church at the End of time.

The positive evaluation given the empire since the time of Constantine made it easy to identify her enemies as the enemies of God, at times even to make use of apocalyptic rhetoric in describing them. But no foe of the Christian empire prior to Islam had the proper eschatological weight in terms of continuity, success, and violent opposition to the Christian religion to be so directly identified with the forces of evil. The sudden appearance of this new foe in the seventh century, at a time when Christianity seemed to have achieved almost universal domination, obviously invited an apocalyptic explanation. The identification of the Moslems either with the army of Antichrist himself or with his immediate predecessors (variably symbolized by the beasts and plagues of the Revelation of John) introduced a whole new chapter in the history of Christian apocalyptic traditions. Above all, this identification could be used as a powerful stimulus for concrete political and military action against Islam.

Although the Christian Emperor early assumed a role in the drama of the last days, it was not until the thirteenth century that the papacy achieved a similar apocalyptic stature. It is obvious that the creation of the figure of the Angelic Pope was made possible by the new universal role in Christian society given the papacy during the Great Reform movement. Indeed, the Last Pope was both an apocalyptic validation of the universal significance of the papacy, and thus an example of positive apocalypticism, and also a critique of the papal government of the time, as made clear in the contrast between the worldliness of present popes and the holiness that would characterize the *pastor angelicus.* The element of critique was further heightened by the fears for a present or proximate Papal Antichrist.[136] The fundamental message of these additions to the apocalyptic scenario was similar to that of the Last Emperor: the adaptability of apocalypticism to political, social, and religious change, and its flexibility as a mode of political and religious rhetoric. Again, we must note that there is no evidence that these potent new creations were in any way the product of popular revolutionary movements. They were attempts of the educated clerks to make sense of major changes in society within the universal scheme of history provided by apocalypticism. Only after their creation in the pamphlets of the polemicists were they diffused to a broader audience.

The *a priori* use of apocalypticism also has a variety of modes of application. Inherited apocalyptic language was a readily available, or *a priori,* way of interpreting contemporary events, especially conflict situations. Hence apocalyptic language was frequently invoked to support one position, program, or individual against another. Although the most usual form that the *a priori* use took was the damning of an opponent, especially by identifying him with one of the evil symbolic figures of the canonical apocalyptic texts, paradoxically this can be seen as an essentially positive or sustaining use of apocalypticism. First of all, in the vast majority of cases such language was invoked by a part of the established order in support of the total medieval notion of a divinely ordained society. If a pope accused an emperor of being the Antichrist or one of his minions, as both Gregory IX and Innocent IV accused Frederick II, this was not an attack on the Christian empire as such, but a denial that a particular occupant was really emperor because of his manifest wickedness. The *a priori* use was also positive in that it was designed to move men to take sides in a struggle rather than to abstain from conflict. Granted that in the apocalyptic drama it is always God and not man who takes the major role, it is still required of man that he act out his part, that he come to recognize which party is actually God's and cast in his lot with those whom divine aid has guaranteed eventual winners whatever their temporary misfortunes. Hence, according to the *a priori* use political conflicts were given apocalyptic significance not to expand the scenario, but to show that the final confrontation of good and evil had already begun and there could be no middle ground. The textbook case for the *a priori* mode was the confrontation between Frederick II and the papacy, but other examples will be seen in the pages that follow.

My specification of these *a posteriori* and *a priori* functions of apocalypticism in Christian history is meant to be general and suggestive rather than exhaustive. It should be clear that I have no intention of reducing the complex phenomenon of apocalypticism to a simple expression of political, social, or economic conditions. Reductionism of any sort is a grave danger, whether it is the reductionism that would see every expression of apocalypticism/millenarianism as an ideology born in crisis and despair, or the reductionism that would see in it nothing more than a language of political hacks without sincere religious dimensions.

The most fundamental appeal of apocalypticism is the conviction it holds forth that time is related to eternity, that the history of man has a discernible structure and meaning in relation to its End, and that this End is the product not of chance, but of divine plan. Obviously, such beliefs are incapable of rational demonstration; they can only be revealed, that is, presented or manifested in symbolic and dramatic forms. That over many centuries these beliefs answered deep religious needs and performed important social and political functions is the message of this study. Many may claim that the apocalyptic modes of apprehending reality are now things of the past, dead relics popular only among the ignorant. Have we really given them up, or have we merely found surrogates which we blandly conceive to be more scientific?

Part One: A.D. 400–1200

Introduction

Despite the attacks of Augustine and the indifference of others, apocalypticism did not die out at the end of the fourth century; rather, the year 400 may be taken as a decisive turning point in the history of apocalyptic traditions. About this time the inherited themes concerning the End of the world were enriched in a number of ways that were to continue to be of influence for many centuries. It is true that the apocalyptic understanding of history was rarely, if ever, the dominant interpretation during the succeeding centuries, nor had it been prior to 400. Apocalypticism continued to be *one* of the options open to believing Christians, as it had been to devout Jews of the time of Daniel or of Jesus, in their attempts to understand the meaning of history.

The characteristics that distinguished the apocalyptic literature produced between A.D. 400 and 1200 may, for the sake of simplicity, be divided into those of form and of content. Formally speaking, the genre of apocalyptic vision or revelation by no means died out during this time. In keeping with earlier practice, it maintained its pseudonymous nature. Sometimes such productions were ascribed to biblical figures, as in the case of the Pseudo-Johannine Revelation and the various Visions of Daniel; sometimes they were issued under the authority of a patristic name, e.g., Methodius or Ephraem. On the whole, pseudonymous visions were more an Eastern than a Western phenomenon, though in translation texts like the Pseudo-Methodius were very widespread in Latin Christianity.

Western authors were more prone to express their apocalyptic theories through the medium of homilies, scriptural commentaries, or theological treatises. Jerome's classic *Commentary on Daniel* made further major efforts to comment on this text superfluous for centuries; precisely the opposite was the case for the Book of Revelation, one of the most popular subjects for exegesis in the Latin West. These commentaries may be grouped into three periods: late Roman (350–550), with Jerome's revised version of Victorinus, Tyconius, Apringius, and Primasius; Carolingian (700–900), includ-

39

ing Bede, Ambrosius Autpertus, Beatus, Alcuin, Berengaudus, and Haymo; and twelfth-century, with Bruno, Anselm of Laon and the *Glossa ordinaria,* Rupert, Richard of St. Victor, and Joachim of Fiore. Although the moralizing Tyconian tradition was dominant until the twelfth century, it was not a stifling block to exegetical originality. The study of the earlier medieval commentaries is an important avenue to the understanding of the apocalypticism of the time, just as the revolution in hermeneutics effected by Joachim's *Exposition* was central to later medieval apocalyptic.[1]

Homiletic use of apocalyptic themes is found both in Byzantium and in the West. More distinctive of Latin apocalyptic is the continuation of the doctrinal treatments we have already mentioned in the patristic period with Irenaeus and Hippolytus. *The Book of the Promises and Predictions of God* (c.450), Adso's *Letter on the Antichrist* (c.950), and a number of twelfth-century works are examples of a genre not popular in the East.[2]

Some experiments in form are found during the period in question. Beginning in the Carolingian period, we find a number of apocalyptic poems in Latin and even, in the case of the famous *Muspilli* (c.850), in the vernacular. These do not appear to be dependent on earlier metrical treatments of the last events.[3] The poetic rendition of the career of the Antichrist, central to these works, may be seen as the forebear, if only in indirect fashion, to the *Play of Antichrist,* the twelfth-century metrical drama that is the most distinctive of apocalyptic plays. Also to be noted is the new life and in some instances new form given to the Sibylline tradition. The Sibyl became a figure of authority almost equal to the prophet and evangelist, one ideally designed to serve as an access point for the incorporation of new elements into the scenario of the last times. The Tiburtine Sibyl, a Greek production of the late fourth century, became the paradigm for a whole new stage in the centuries-old history of the Sibyls. Closely tied to imperial legends and hence subject to constant revision due to political changes, the strength of the Sibylline tradition was one of the most notable features of these six centuries.

Any division between form and matter in this area is bound to be somewhat artificial, and the complex interaction between tradition and innovation in the history of apocalyptic texts precludes any simple outline of the changes in content. Although most of the authors responsible for the texts we shall investigate thought they were doing little more than recording immemorial truths, few failed to leave some mark of their own, however nugatory, on the finished product. Innovation, of course, is most evident in the constant updating of prophetic texts.[4] A study of this process discloses once again a fundamental law of the apocalyptic tradition that we have adverted to before—the responsiveness of apocalypticism to political change taken in the broadest sense of the word.

Much apocalyptic literature was an attempt by groups of *literati* to make sense of political change or to advance political programs in the light of a strict teleological view of history. The six centuries of texts presented here reflect at least three such changes, as pointed out in the Introduction. The first of these was the conversion of the Roman empire and the role that this suggested for a messianic imperial figure in the last events. The second was the rise of Islam and the manner in which Christianity's great rival was given apocalyptic meaning. Finally, from the end of the eleventh century apocalyptic authors had to confront the changes brought about by the reformed papacy and the ferment in the religious life of the time that accompanied it. What was the apocalyptic function of the universal head of Christendom? Were religious *virtuosi* to have a role in the time of the End? These selections are designed to introduce the reader to these developments in the tradition and to explore something of the background that formed them.

1. The Tiburtine Sibyl

The Tiburtine Sibyl is the earliest and most cogent proof of the revival of apocalypticism in the Christian Roman empire of the fourth century. The importance of the Latin versions of this text have been known to scholars since the edition of E. Sackur in 1898; in 1949, S. Mercati's announcement of the discovery of a Greek text opened up a new field of investigation.[1] The admirable edition of the Greek text by P. J. Alexander has unlocked some but by no means all of the problems connected with the history of the work.[2]

The Tiburtine Sibyl was obviously written by someone well-versed in traditional apocalyptic lore, not least of all that of the earlier Sibyllines; but the text was a new departure, at the very least in its attempt to tie the events of the Christian empire to a new version of apocalyptic vision. The concern for universal history evident in the dream of the nine suns provided a stronger validation for the trans-historical significance of the Christian emperors than that of any other fourth-century author, even the imperial apologist Eusebius of Caesarea.

According to Alexander's reconstruction, it was around A.D. 380, during the reign of Theodosius, that the original Greek text was written (Σ). Based in part upon Egyptian apocalyptic themes such as those found in the fourth-century Coptic Apocalypse of Elijah,[3] the Tiburtine Sibyl was intended as a response to the military disaster of Adrianople (378) where the Emperor Valens had been killed by the Goths. The Greek original was soon translated into Latin (W^a), but both texts have been lost. The three surviving Greek manuscripts witness to an expansion of the Theodosian Sibyl composed in the region of Baalbek in Phoenicea shortly after 500. This version, Alexander's Oracle of Baalbek, does not contain the reference to a Last World Emperor found in the medieval Latin versions, though there is a good deal of speculation on the role of good and bad emperors in the time before the coming of the Antichrist.[4]

The lost fourth-century Latin version was reworked in the late tenth or early eleventh century, probably in northern Italy, and this text (W^b) was twice revised (W^1, W^2), the former being the text edited by Sackur. There is in addition another family of medieval Latin versions. This complicated history, visually clarified by means of Alexander's chart,[5] is convincing proof of the continued topicality of the work.

The surviving Latin versions include a brief but forceful account of the career of the Final Emperor. Since this is not found in the Oracle of Baalbek, there is no reason to suppose that it was in the Greek original. Where and when was it introduced? Sackur, unaware of the Greek text, thought the reference was present from the beginning;[6] Alexander is inclined to think that the conception of an imperial war of liberation and the subsequent abdication of the Last Emperor are too much involved with later Byzantine experience and ideology to be earlier than the time of the Arab invasions of the seventh century, and hence suggests that the Latin versions derive the myth from the late seventh-century Pseudo-Methodius, which already contained a full account of the new apocalyptic figure.[7] Recently M. Rangheri, noting the differences between the portrait of the Last Emperor found in the Pseudo-Methodius and that in the Latin Tiburtine Sibyl, asserts that the one cannot have been derived from the other, but that the myth must have been already present in the earliest Latin version.[8] Given our present information, no final conclusion is possible. Rangheri's solution has several points in its favor, notably the appearance of details in the Latin text that would have been more understandable in the fourth rather than in the tenth century;[9] but at present the weight of evidence suggests that the fully formed myth of the Last Emperor was not present until the later period.

The exact date of the origin of the myth is not the central question. The presence of a number of versions of the stories regarding the Last Emperor in both the East and the West suggests that the formation of this significant apocalyptic figure was a gradual process.[10] The image of the returning hero was widespread in many cultures; in specifically Western traditions, the stories connected with Alexander the Great were undoubtedly a factor.[11] The Coptic Apocalypse of Elijah has a number of features in common with the Oracle of Baalbek, and though it contains no single Last World Emperor, it does mention two important good rulers of the last times—a "King of Peace" from the West,[12] and a Persian King from the East. The latter is described as: "A just king . . . whom the Lord hath sent us, in order that the Land not become desert. . . . In the fourth year of that king shall the Son of Lawlessness show himself."[13] This ruler, who in some ways is like the king of Heliopolis in the Oracle of Baalbek, suggests that a fourth-century base for a final ideal ruler preceding the coming of the Antichrist is at least possible.[14]

The formation of this potent myth must always be viewed within the context of the christianization of the imperial office.[15] Only a Christian Roman emperor could have aspired to a role of such significance. As H.-I. Marrou has said: ". . . in the measure that one has a more exalted idea of God, the Emperor invested by Him, defined as His lieutenant, His representative, His visible manifestation (*theophaneia*), is found to receive a sacred character which elevates him all the more above the human community as the God whom he reflects is conceived of as radically transcendant."[16] The vast popularity of the myth undoubtedly was a major reason for numerous copies that survive of this new example of Sibylline literature.[17]

THE ORACLE OF BAALBEK[18]

By the Sibyl, who by revelation interpreted the vision of the
one hundred judges of the great city of Rome

When the Sibyl had come to Rome, there came to meet her the entire city, both great and small. The one hundred judges came to meet her and said: "The wisdom and sagacity of Your Majesty is great. Do now interpret for us the vision which we, the one hundred judges, saw today. We cannot interpret it and cannot discover its meaning." The Sibyl answered them and said: "Let us go to the *Capitolium* of the great city of Rome, and let the tribunal take place." And it was done as she had ordained.

And she said to them: "Report to me the vision which you saw, and I shall interpret for you the meaning." And the Sibyl sat down on the *Capitolium* among the olive trees[19] and answered them and said; "Report to me what you saw." And the one hundred judges answered and said to her: "We saw nine suns shining upon the earth." And the Sibyl answered and said to them: "The nine suns are nine generations." They say to her: "So be it, our lady. We shall report to you all that we have seen in the vision." And the Sibyl answered and said: "So be it." And the judges say to her: "We shall report to you the vision just as we saw it." The Sibyl says to them: "What did you see?" They say to her: "This is what we saw. The first sun was many-colored, shining with rays, very bright, very large, very shining. The second sun was exceedingly bright, very large, many-colored, shining with rays. The third sun was bloodlike, like Tartarus, very large, a blazing fire.

The fourth sun was bloodlike, like Tartarus. The fifth sun was bloodlike, very bright, flashing forth as during a thundershower. The sixth sun was like a cloud, like snow, like blood. The seventh sun was like Tartarus, like blood, terrifying. The eighth sun was shining with rays so that it had hands in the middle. The ninth sun was like Tartarus beyond the others and had a radiance."[20]

And the Sibyl answered and said: "The nine suns are nine generations. The first sun is the first generation, men who are innocent, long-lived, free, truthful, gentle, mild, and they love the truth. The second sun is the second generation; they too are truthful men, gentle, hospitable, innocent, and they love the generation of the Free. The third sun is the third generation. Kingdom will rise against kingdom, nation against nation, there will be wars, but men will be hospitable and merciful in the city of the Romans. The fourth sun is the fourth generation. The son of the godhead will appear in the south; for there will arise from the Hebraic land a woman named Mary and she will give birth to a son, and they will call him Jesus by name. And he will destroy the law of the Hebrews and establish his own law, and his law will be king. And the heavens will be opened for him, and he will hear a voice, and hosts of angels will carry his throne, and the six-winged creatures will worship the tracks of his feet. And he will take men from Galilee and will give laws and say to them: 'The word which you have received from me, preach it to the peoples of the seventy-two languages.' "[21]

And the priests of the Hebrews say to her: "Most awesome mistress of ours, we wish to pose a question to you." And the Sibyl answers and says to them: "Tell me what you wish." And they say to her: "From the Gentiles we have heard a report that the god of heavens will beget a son. Do you believe that this will happen, our lady?" The Sibyl says to them: "Do you who are priests of the Hebrews not believe it?" They say to her: "We do not believe that God will beget a son; for he made a promise to our fathers that he would not lift his hand from us." The Sibyl says to them: "This Law is a thorn to you." And they say to her: "And what do you say, our lady, concerning this question?"[22]

The Sibyl answered and said to them: "The god of heaven will beget a son who will be like his father and will assume the likeness of a child. And Kings will arise against him, Alexander, Seleucus, and Herod, who cannot save themselves. They will carry out many persecutions in the land of Judaea and will slay children with their parents so that the river Jordan will be commingled with blood; and they will not benefit. And after this he who will be crucified on the wood of the cross will perform many healings. And when they will sacrifice . . . . her altars, they will hear of his miracles which he performed in the land of Judaea. And from Phrygia, there will arise a king named Augustus and he will rule in Rome and the entire inhabited world will be subjected by him. And every king of the Romans will be called by his name, Augustus. The thrice blessed cross upon which Christ will be stretched out. . . .[23] And after this the mobs of the Jews will be assembled, and he who will be hung on the wood of the cross will do miracles and will heal many people. And they will hang three men alongside him on the cross; and they will pierce his side with a stake and will not harm him.

In the fifth generation three kings will arise, Antiochus, Tiberius, and Gaius, and they will carry out many persecutions because of him who was crucified on the wood of the cross. And they will build up the temples of Heliopolis and the altars of Lebanon; and the shrines of that city are very large and shapely beyond any other temple in the inhabited world.

In the sixth generation there will arise two kings with short reigns, and they will carry out many persecutions against the Christians. And their officials will judge and destroy the ranks of the men of the senatorial order and will kill them because of the name of Christ; and they will not benefit. And after that there will arise a king named Constantine, a terrible and mighty warrior, and he will destroy all the temples of the Gentiles and the altars of Lebanon and their sacrifices, and he will humble the pagans. And a sign will appear to him in the sky, and his mother Helen will seek in the land of Judaea the wood of the cross where Christ, the son of the living god, will be crucified. And he will build up Byzantium, and the name of that city will be changed, and she will be named Eudocopolis-Constantinopolis. And all the tribes of the seventy-two languages will inhabit her. Do not boast, city of Byzantium, thou shalt not hold imperial sway for thrice sixty of thy years![24]

And after this there will arise three kings, Valens, a grandson of Constantius (Constantine?), Valentinian, and Jovian, and they will carry out many persecutions; and one of them will be consumed by fire.[25] And the barbarians will not harm the cities of the Roman Empire. And after this there will arise two kings, Marcianus (Gratianus?) and Theodosius, mighty dynasts, warriors and righteous judges, teachers of the faith, and they will destroy the forsaken temples of the pagans, and the temples of the Gentiles will be transformed into tombs of the saints. . . .

And after[26] that men will be rapacious, greedy, rebellious, barbarian, they will hate their mothers, and in lieu of virtue and of mildness they will assume the appearance of barbarians. They will raid their own ancestral cities, and there is none to resist their works and deeds; they work their land because of their great avarice. In the ninth generation the years will be shortened like months, and the months like weeks, and the weeks like days, and the days like hours. And two kings will arise from the East and two from Syria, and the Assyrians will be countless like the sand of the sea, and they will take over many lands of the East unto Chalcedonia. And there will be much shedding of blood, so that the blood will reach the chest of horses as it is commingled with the sea. And they will capture and set on fire the cities and despoil the East. And after that another emperor will arise from the East, whose name is Olibos.[27] He will seize the four kings who preceded him and will slay them. And he will grant an exemption from paying a public tax and will restore all the people of the entire East and of Palestine. And after that there will arise another king who has a changed shape and he will rule thirty years and will rebuild the altars of Egypt. And he will wage war upon the king from the East and will kill him and all his army and will seize children from the age of twelve.[28] And people will seize poisonous asps and suck milk from women with new-born babes and draw blood for the sake of the poison of arrows and the violence of wars.[29] Woe to women with child and to those who suckle their babes in those days! And the cities of the East will become deserts. And he ("the king who has a changed shape") will be established by the foul nation of the Cappadocians and he will hiss and say: "Was there ever a city here?" And after that there will arise a woman. She will run from the setting to the rising of the sun and will not see a man; and she will long for the track of a man and will not find it. And she will find a vine and an olive-tree and say: "Where is he who planted these?" And she will embrace these plants and give up her spirit, and wolves will eat her. And after that there will arise another king from Heliopolis and he will wage war against the king from the East and kill him. And he will grant a tax-exemption to entire countries for three years and six months, and the earth will bring forth its fruits, and there is none to eat them.[30] And there will come the ruler of perdition, he who is changed, and will smite and kill him. And he will do signs and wonders on earth. He will turn the sun into darkness and the moon into blood. And after that the springs and rivers will dry up, and the Nile of Egypt will be transformed into blood. And the survivors will dig cisterns and will search for the water of life and will not find it. And then there will appear two men who did not come to know the experience of death, Enoch and Elijah, and they will wage war upon the ruler of perdition. And he will say: "My time has come," and he will be angered and slay them. And then he who was crucified on the wood of the cross will come from the heavens, like a great and flashing star, and he will resurrect those two men. And he who was hung on the cross will wage war upon the son of perdition and will slay him and all his host. Then the land of Egypt will burn twelve cubits deep, and the land will shout to God: "Lord, I am a virgin." And again the land of Judaea will burn eighteen cubits deep, and the land will shout to God: "Lord, I am a virgin." And then the son of God will come with great power and glory to judge the nine generations. And then Christ will rule, the son of the living God, with his holy angels. Amen, so be it, amen."

The translation is that of the late Paul J. Alexander, *The Oracle of Baalbek,* pp. 23–29. It is reprinted here with the kind permission of Mrs. Alexander and the Dumbarton Oaks Center.

THE LATIN TIBURTINE SIBYL

Then will arise a king of the Greeks whose name is Constans.[31] He will be king of the Romans and the Greeks. He will be tall of stature, of handsome appearance with shining face, and well put together in all parts of his body. His reign will be ended after one hundred and twelve years.[32] In those days there will be great riches and the earth will give fruit abundantly so that a measure of wheat will be sold for a denarius, a measure of wine for a denarius, and a measure of oil for a denarius.[33] The king will have a text before his eyes that says: "The king of the Romans will claim the whole Christian empire for himself." He will devastate all the islands and the cities of the pagans and will destroy all idolatrous temples; he will call all pagans to baptism and in every temple the Cross of Christ will be erected. "Then Egypt and Ethiopia will be eager to stretch their hands to God."[34] Whoever does not adore the Cross of Jesus Christ will be punished by the sword. When the one hundred and twelve years have been completed, the Jews will be converted to the Lord, and "his sepulchre will be glorified by all."[35] In those days Judah will be saved and Israel will dwell with confidence.

At that time the Prince of Iniquity who will be called Antichrist will arise from the tribe of Dan. He will be the Son of Perdition, the head of pride, the master of error, the fullness of malice who will overturn the world and do wonders and great signs through dissimulation. He will delude many by magic art so that fire will seem to come down from heaven. The years will be shortened like months, the months like weeks, the weeks like days, the days like hours, and an hour like a moment. The unclean nations that Alexander, the Indian king, shut up (i.e., Gog and Magog) will arise from the North. These are the twenty-two realms whose number is like the sand of the sea.[36] When the king of the Romans hears of this he will call his army together and vanquish and utterly destroy them. After this he will come to Jerusalem, and having put off the diadem from his head and laid aside the whole imperial garb,[37] he will hand over the empire of the Christians to God the Father and to Jesus Christ his Son.[38] When the Roman empire shall have ceased,[39] then the Antichrist will be openly revealed and will sit in the House of the Lord in Jerusalem. While he is reigning, two very famous men, Elijah and Enoch, will go forth to announce the coming of the Lord. Antichrist will kill them and after three days they will be raised up by the Lord. Then there will be a great persecution, such as has not been before nor shall be thereafter. The Lord will shorten those days for the sake of the elect, and the Antichrist will be slain by the power of God through Michael the Archangel on the Mount of Olives.[40]

Translated from the edition of E. Sackur, *Sibyllinische Texte und Forschungen,* pp. 185–86.

2. Antichrist in the Fifth Century

The six-thousand-year scheme of history as revised by Hippolytus indicated that the End of the world would come about the year 500. Barbarian onslaughts and the partial collapse of Roman governmental structure, especially in the West, seemed to confirm this in the eyes of many writers of the late fourth and early fifth centuries. When Rome, "the restraining force," was dissolving before men's eyes, could the final enemy be far off?

Sulpicius Severus (d. c.430) was the friend and biographer of Martin of Tours, the Father of Western monasticism. His popular *Life of St. Martin* was written shortly after the saint's death in 397. Within a few years he supplemented the *Life* with a mass of material about Martin, partly legendary, in three letters and two books of *Dialogues*. Whether or not the teaching on the Antichrist at the end of the first *Dialogue* goes back to the saint himself, its omission from later copies indicates that such views were popular enough to be considered dangerous by Church authorities in the later fifth century.[1]

Quintus Julius Hilarianus, an African bishop, composed two chronographical works in 397. One of these, *The Progress of Time,* shows a strong adhesion to the Hippolytan tradition and gives evidence of the strength of chiliasm at the end of the fourth century. More than a half-century later, a comparable expectation of the imminence of the End is found in *The Book of the Promises and Predictions of God,* long thought to be the work of Prosper of Aquitaine, but more recently ascribed to Quodvultdeus, a pupil of Augustine who became bishop of Carthage, fled the Vandals, and died in Italy about 453.[2] This summary of salvation history consists of three books arranged according to the Pauline–Augustinian scheme of three ages (*ante legem, sub lege, sub gratia*), and a fourth book in two divisions: the "Half-Time with the Signs of the Antichrist,"[3] and the "Glory and Kingdom of the Saints."

From the Eastern Empire comes the pseudonymous Revelation of John, first cited in the ninth century, though H. Weinel and others would date it to the fifth.[4] The work is arranged in question and answer form. It contains a detailed description of the coming events of the End and of the fate of the good and the evil in the afterlife. The form is that of the earlier Apocalypse of Peter—a post-Resurrection discourse of the Lord.

SULPICIUS SEVERUS, *DIALOGUES* 1:41[5]

When we asked him about the End of the world, he told us that Nero and the Antichrist were to come first. Nero will rule in the western region after subduing the ten kings. He will conduct a persecution to compel worship of the pagan idols. Antichrist will first seize the Eastern empire and will have Jerusalem as the seat and capital of his kingdom. He will rebuild the city and the Temple. His persecution will be to compel denial that Christ is God, rather setting himself up as the Anointed One. He will order all circumcized according to the Law. Then Nero himself will be destroyed by the Antichrist so that the whole world and all nations may be drawn under his power until that wicked one is destroyed by the coming of Christ.[6] There is no doubt that Antichrist, conceived by an evil spirit,[7] has already been born. He is now a child and will take over the empire when he comes of age. We heard all this from him seven years ago. Ponder how close these coming fearful events are!

Translated from the edition of C. Halm, *Sulpicii Severi Libri Qui Supersunt* (*CSEL* 1), p. 197.

QUINTUS JULIUS HILARIANUS, *THE PROGRESS OF TIME*

17. Concerning the 470 years from the Passion of the Lord,[8] on March 24th in the Consulate of Caesarius and Atticus,[9] 369 of them have passed. There remain 101 years to complete the six thousand. The six thousand years will not be completed before the ten kings first go forth into the world near the End and remove from the midst of the world the daughter of Babylon who now stands firm.[10] Immediately the One who has power over them will march against them; he is called the Dragon in Revelation. He will gain power over the ten kings—some he will destroy, others will remain under his control. "Then the impious one will be revealed, the Son of Perdition, who is lifted up against all that is called God or worshiped as God, so that sitting in the Temple he will show himself as though he were God" (2 Thess. 2:8, 4). This is the true Antichrist. The very powerful Dragon to

whom the ten kings yielded will give over his power and might to him, and all men will be in awe of him. The times of the Antichrist will be necessarily deadly, like the times when Antiochus tried to make one people commit apostasy under his reign. The Antichrist will attempt to do what Antiochus could not, since he had not the time. When he comes, he will come for the destruction of the faithful.[11] His time will be harsh and evil, "he whom the Lord Christ will slay with the breath of his mouth and destroy by his coming" (2 Thess. 2:4).

18. When the Antichrist has been overcome and killed at the completion of the six thousand years, the resurrection of all the saints will take place while the world still stands. . . . To the saints the resurrection will be one day, but this day of the saints will be prolonged so much that to the evil who will be living with pain in the world it will number a thousand years.[12] This is the seventh day, the eternal and true Sabbath whose image and figure was that temporal Sabbath written in the Law of Moses, as was said to the Jews: "Six days do the works of the world, but on the seventh day which is called the Sabbath rest from your works" (Exod. 23:12). So when the six days, i.e., the six thousand years of labor and pain for the saints, have passed, the seventh day, the true Sabbath, will come for all of them who have existed from the beginning of the world.

19. . . . After the seven-thousandth year, Satan will be loosed from his prison and will go forth to seduce the nations of Gog and Magog. He will bring them together as if ready to fight at the Camp of the Saints. Fire will descend from heaven and all men will be consumed, and then will be the second resurrection for all flesh and all will be judged by the just judgment of God because they have not believed, but have done justice pleasing to themselves.

Translated from the edition in *PL* 13, cc. 1105–06.

THE BOOK OF THE PROMISES AND PREDICTIONS OF GOD, "HALF-TIME"

Chapter 13. The Promise to be Fulfilled in the Mission of Elijah and Enoch

Here also we find a triple division of witnesses. Against Pharaoh two spokesmen of God were sent, Moses and Aaron; and there were two magicians of Pharaoh, Jamnes and Mambres, who resisted Moses and perished along with their king. Against Nero there were also two, the apostles Peter and Paul;[13] in opposition was Simon Magus who destroyed himself and deceived Nero. Against the Antichrist there will be two prophets, Enoch and Elijah, against whom the three false prophets of the Antichrist will rise up. If there is one more in this case, it is because in the last case there was one less, and so the number six is complete on both sides because of the six days of creation and the six angels sounding the trumpets that introduce the six plagues into the world.[14] The seventh trumpet signifies the end of labors and the repose of the saints, as does the seventh day which is morning alone for it has no evening.[15] Divinity itself enjoins this sabbath rest to be observed with every command, so that abstaining from all evil we may stand upright in the morning and behold Him "Who crowns in compassion and mercy" (Ps. 102:4), judging all with equity and damning no one unjustly. Tyconius has written much on these subjects.[16]

The Revelation of John and Daniel the Prophet prove that the consummation and perfection of the times is to be completed in three years and six months (said to be 1,260 days or to make forty-two months). In these times, as it is thought, the Holy City will be trodden down by heretics, especially by the Arians who will be very powerful then.[17] Gog and Magog, as some say, are the Goths and the Moors,[18] the Getes and the Massagetes, through whose savagery the devil himself already lays waste the Church and will then persecute it more fully, even making the "perpetual sacrifice" (Dan. 11:31) to cease. For this reason the Lord warns: "I am coming quickly; blessed be he who is wakeful and preserves his garments lest he walk naked" (Rev. 16:15). The following chapter will show what the vestments are that are to be preserved.

Translated from the edition of René Braun, *Quodvultdeus* (*SC* 102), pp. 632–34.

THE REVELATION OF THE HOLY THEOLOGIAN JOHN

I spent seven days praying and after these things a bright and shining cloud caught me up from the mountain and set me before the presence of heaven, and I heard a voice saying to me, "Look up John, servant of God, and understand." And when I looked up I saw heaven opened and the scent of many sweet spices came from within, and I saw a golden lamp shining much brighter than the sun. And again I heard a voice saying to me, "Behold, O righteous John." And I lifted up my eyes and saw a book lying there which seemed to me to be as thick as seven mountains, but its length no human mind would be able to grasp. It had seven seals.[19] And I said, "O Lord my God, reveal to me what is written in this book." And I heard a voice saying to me, "Hear, O righteous John, in this book which you have seen is written the things in heaven, and on earth, and in the Abyss and the judgments and righteousness of the whole human race." And I said, "O Lord, when are these things to be and what will distinguish these times?" And I heard a voice saying to me, "Hear, O righteous John, in that time there will be an abundance of grain and wine, such as has never been on the earth nor will be until those times come. The one ear of corn will bear a half measure and one twig on a branch will produce a thousand clusters and one cluster will yield a half a jar of wine.[20] But when the year is over there will not be found one half measure of grain or one half jar of wine on the face of the whole earth."

And again I said, "O Lord, what will take place after this?" And I heard a voice saying to me, "Hear, O righteous John, at that time the Denier shall be manifest, the one banished in darkness, the one called Antichrist." And again I said, "Lord, reveal to me what he is like."

And I heard a voice saying to me, "The appearance of his face is gloomy; his hair like the points of arrows; his brows rough; his right eye as the rising morning star and the left like a lion's. His mouth is a cubit wide, his teeth a span in length, his fingers are like sickles. His footprints are two cubits long, and on his forehead is the writing 'The Antichrist.'[21] He will be lifted up to heaven and he will be brought down to the Abyss, working falsehood. And then I will make the heavens like copper, so that there will be no moisture on the earth; and I will hide the clouds in the secret places so that they will not supply rain on the earth, and I will restrain the horns of the winds so they will not blow upon the earth."

The text was edited by K. von Tischendorff, *Apocalypses Apocryphae* (Leipzig: Mendelssohn, 1866), pp. 70–94. I owe this translation of vv. 2–8 to James Tabor.

3. The Legend of Alexander

Few men have ever changed the history of the world as decisively as Alexander the Great (356–323 B.C.). The world that he created provided the context for the birth of apocalypticism, and legends concerning his superhuman career reentered the apocalyptic tradition in the fifth century of the Christian era to provide new motifs and inspiration for the next thousand years.[1]

Historical accounts of Alexander's life were well known in the ancient world, but it was a legendary romance whose original version was composed in Greek at Alexandria probably in the third century A.D. which was the ancestor of the apocalyptic Alexander.[2] The Greek original of this text, the so-called Pseudo-Callisthenes, has been lost; it was the remote source for some eighty later versions composed in twenty-four languages.[3] Some early versions close to the Greek, like the fifth-century Armenian text, disclose no overt apocalyptic message.[4] The Syriac versions, based on one of the four recensions of the Greek text, are the earliest witnesses to the fusion of the Alexander legends with late classical apocalypticism. They were translated into Latin in the tenth century by a Neapolitan priest.[5]

A striking legendary episode provided the entry for the apocalyptic interest, the story of Alexander's construction of a wall or gate in a mountain pass of the Caucasus to exclude from the civilized world the wild barbarian tribes he encountered there.[6] The story finds its earliest appearance in Josephus, where the excluded tribes are identified with the Scythians.[7] It was present in at least one of the versions of the Pseudo-Callisthenes. After the Huns had pierced the Caucasus barrier in 395, the incident received greater importance in the spread of the Alexander legends,[8] and in the fifth century it was given an apocalyptic interpretation when the excluded tribes were identified with the Gog and Magog of Ezekiel and the Book of Revelation in the "Syrian Christian Legend concerning Alexander."[9] The most complete version is to be found in the metrical homily ascribed to the great Syrian ecclesiastical writer Jacob of Serugh (c.451–521).[10]

THE DISCOURSE OF JACOB OF SERUGH

The Lord spake by the hand of the angel, saying, "I will magnify thee
More than all the kings and governors in all the world.
This great gate which thou hast made in this land
430 Shall be closed until the End of times cometh.[11]
Jeremiah also prophesied concerning it and the earth hath heard,
"The gate of the north shall be opened on the day of the End of the world,
And on that day shall evil go forth on the wicked.
There shall be woe to those who are with child and to those who give suck"
      (Jer. 1:14).
435 The Lord says, "In that the seven thousandth year
Shall there be rumors and dire quakings in all countries.
Sin and wickedness and all evil things shall increase in the world,
Envy, craftiness, adultery, murder, and all hateful things,
Lying and slander of the children of wickedness.
440 Fraud and pride shall increase in the earth,
And haughtiness and lasciviousness and infidelity,
And schisms and contentions shall fall among the children of men.
The heavens shall be like darkness and the earth shall quake,
And the love of many shall wax cold in these days (Matt. 24:12).
445 And wars and captivities and death shall increase among the children of men.
And there shall be famines and cruel wars in various countries,
And there shall be also tumults in the islands that are in the sea.
And the sun and the moon and the stars shall be dark in their risings,
And the earth shall be devoured by fire and locusts and mighty hail,
450 The ends of the earth shall tremble with the noise of the thundering in all lands,
And winter and winds and storms and lightnings and mighty earthquakes.
The heavens shall become like smoke through darkness,
The sea shall be troubled, and wickedness shall increase in all the world.
Towns and cities and villages shall dwell in mourning,
455 Through the terrible quakings of all the horrible signs.
And when these things have come to an end and passed away before the End
The earth shall quake and this door which thou hast made be opened.
At the End of times creatures and men shall make evil to increase,
And wickedness shall wax strong in all quarters of the earth, and the Lord shall
      be grieved,
460 And anger with fierce wrath shall rise up on mankind.
And the earth and vineyards and oliveyards and all plants shall be laid waste,
And woods and gardens; and the earth and mankind shall dwell in mourning,
And destructive winds shall go forth against creation;
And the Lord shall visit evil upon the world, upon the fertile lands.
465 And the nation that is within this gate shall be roused up,
And also the hosts of Agog and of the peoples of Magog shall be gathered
      together.
These peoples, the fiercest of all creatures,
Of the mighty house of Japhet are they of whom the Lord spake, saying, "They
      shall go forth on the earth
And cover all creation like a locust. . . ."[12]

And when all these things had been spoken by the angel
540 To the wise king Alexander, the son of Philip,
The angel, in the spirit of the revelation of prophecy, told him
To write down these things and teach the world that these things would happen.
And when all these things had been said by the angel,
The Spirit of the Lord rested upon the king as upon Jeremiah,
595 And he wrote down hidden things like Daniel and like Isaiah.
He wrought mighty deeds and destroyed kings in their wars,
He destroyed idols like Hezekiah and like Josiah.
The just king who served truth and righteousness.
The earth shone through his wisdom full of beauties,
550 And he wrote and showed everything that was to come like Daniel.[13]
Alexander the king, the son of Philip, said,
"Let the kings and their ranks and their dominions tremble,
On the day on which these people go forth over the earth at the End of times.
And men and all the quarters of the earth will anger the Lord of Hosts,
555 And His anger will rise and blot out the earth with an evil desolation.
Mighty Rome from her greatness He shall throw down to the depths,
The seas shall roar, the earth shall cry out, and the mountains shall shriek,
The valleys shall fear, and towns and villages shall be desolated.
The vineyards shall be destroyed and stupor shall fall upon the planters thereof,
560 Joy shall come to an end, and the power of all mighty men shall fall.
Beautiful things shall perish, riches shall fail and power shall vanish,
Fountains shall fail, streets shall be destroyed, and the valleys shall be useless.
The hosts and filthy assemblies of the children of Magog shall stand up,
And all creation shall become and remain a ruin. . . .
617 The prophet says "Woe to thee, O earth, what is this nation
Harsh of speech which slays and destroys without sparing?
The keepers of vineyards shall weep over the vineyards through sorrow,
620 And all the dwellings of the shepherds shall dwell in mourning."
The earth shall say, "Woe is me, for I have seen all revolutions
With evil quakings and disturbed horrible things full of misery."
For to them will the Lord cry in anger at the End of times,
And as with a broom will the Lord sweep and purge it,
625 And He will overturn it and rend it and destroy it.
Gloomy and sorry and full of darkness shall be the days and months,
Before the coming of the sinful people of the children of Magog.
In those days the living will ascribe happiness to the dead,
By reason of the disturbance and quaking and slaughter and blood.
630 They shall not, however, enter into Jerusalem, the city of the Lord.
For the sign (*i.e.,* the Cross) of the Lord shall drive them away from it, and they
shall not enter it.
All the saints shall fly away from them to mount Sanir
All faithful true ones and the good and all the wise.
They shall not be able to approach mount Sinai, for it is the dwelling place of
the Lord,
635 Nor to the high mountains of Sinai with their shame.
By Jerusalem shall fall by the sword the hosts
Of the children of Agog and of the house of Magog with great slaughter.

After these things shall the days full of trouble decrease,
And evil shall come and stand in the world with great trembling.
640 And the earth shall be drunk with the blood and slaughter of their ranks,
For the sword of a man shall fall upon his fellow with great amazement.
And if it were possible for the mountains and the earth and the stones
And the sea and the dry land to weep, they would weep for the whole world.
O how much more bitter than the slaughter of the sword and the blood of the
spear,
645 Is the affliction of the cursed children of the great family of Japhet!
For they shall lead away captive and subdue the earth and all people.
Then the hosts of Agog and of the house of Magog shall go forth,
And man shall fall upon his fellow, and nation upon nation,
And the quaking of the earth and the sword of anger shall be there.
650 On the skirts of Zion shall the bodies of the dead lie in heaps.
And after these things the earth shall be desolated of mankind,
Villages shall be destroyed and all towns and cities;
The scattered ones only remain in the earth as a remnant.
Then shall Antichrist rise upon the whole earth,
655 Through that gate shall go forth and come that rebel;
That lying one shall Christ overthrow as is promised.[14]
There shall stand up before him demons and spirits and wicked devils,
And they shall gather together all creation to their cursed master.
The earth shall cry out, "I entreat Thee, O Lord, in Thy mercy to spare me,
660 For, behold, I am sick and persecuted with all wounds."
These things which I have spoken shall come to pass before the End of the
world,
And let him that hath an ear of love listen to them.
These beautiful things did king Alexander interpret,
That they should all take place before that day at the End.

The translation is taken from E. A. Wallis Budge, *History of Alexander the Great,* pp. 186–88, 193, 196–98, which also includes an edition of the Syriac text.

4. Pseudo-Ephraem

Ephraem was born in Nisibis about 306 and fled to Edessa when his native city was conquered by the Persians in 363. The final ten years of his life at Edessa established this city as the intellectual center of the Syrian Church. Ephraem is the most important and prolific of the Syrian Church Fathers, though there is still a good deal of uncertainty regarding the authenticity of much that has been ascribed to him. His numerous treatises, homilies, and hymns, many in metrical form, were soon translated into Greek and Armenian. Later translations in Latin, Slavonic, and other Eastern languages also exist.[1]

The apocalyptic sermons in Syriac, Greek, and Latin handed down under his name are particularly problematic. Most authorities think that some of the material in these addresses goes back to the concerns of the historical Ephraem, but it is difficult to say just what, given the current state of scholarship. According to E. Beck, the Syriac apocalyptic sermon ascribed to Ephraem dates to the second half of the seventh century, since it refers to the Heraclius legend and to the Arab invasions and rule.[2] The legend of Alexander's Gate and the identification of the Huns with Gog and Magog are found in both the Syriac and Greek versions of the sermon.[3] There is a Latin "Sermon on the End of the World" found in three eighth-century mss. under the name of Ephraem and one of the ninth century under that of Isidore of Seville.[4] W. Bousset thought that portions of the source of this work, though not by Ephraem, could be dated to near the time of his death;[5] but most scholars have sided with the editor, C. Caspari, who though he admits the use of a document from the late fourth century, assigned the original composition to the Byzantine period between 565 and 628.[6] The Sermon makes use of some of the material found in the slightly later Pseudo-Methodius and is an important witness to the transmission of Eastern apocalyptic materials to the Frankish West.

SERMON ON THE END OF THE WORLD

Dearly beloved brothers, believe the Holy Spirit who speaks in us.[7] We have already told you that the End of the world is near, the consummation remains. Has not faith withered away among mankind? How many foolish things are seen among youths, how many crimes among prelates, how many lies among priests, how many perjuries among deacons! There are evil deeds among the ministers, adulteries in the aged, wantonness in the youths—in mature women false faces, in virgins dangerous traces![8] In the midst of all this there are the wars with the Persians,[9] and we see struggles with diverse nations threatening and "kingdom rising against kingdom" (Matt. 24:7). When the Roman empire begins to be consumed by the sword, the coming of the Evil One is at hand. It is necessary that the world come to an end at the completion of the Roman empire.

In those days two brothers will come to the Roman empire who will rule with one mind; but because one will surpass the other, there will be a schism between them.[10] And so the Adversary will be loosed and will stir up hatred between the Persian and Roman empires. In those days many will rise up against Rome; the Jewish people will be her adversaries.[11] There will be stirrings of nations and evil reports, pestilences, famines, and earthquakes in various places. All nations will receive captives; there will be wars and rumors of wars. From the rising to the setting of the sun the sword will devour much. The times will be so dangerous that in fear and trembling they will not permit thought of better things, because many will be the oppressions and desolations of regions that are to come.[12]

Translated from the edition of C. P. Caspari, *Briefe, Abhandlungen,und Predigten,* pp. 208–10.

5. Gregory the Great

Gregory I, pope from 590 to 604, was a key figure in the development of the medieval papacy. As the *servus servorum Dei*, "Servant of the Servants of God," he stressed the pastoral nature of his office and sought to mediate between the eastern and western portions of the empire. As *consul Dei* he moved the papacy into the gap created by the collapse of imperial authority in most of the West and sought to enhance the place of Peter's See among the new barbarian kingdoms.[1] Monk, liturgist, scriptural commentator, spiritual master, preacher, sponsor of missions, administrator and diplomat, Gregory was a man of remarkable talents.

Although Gregory did not compose any works specifically devoted to apocalyptic themes, his letters and sermons are filled with a pronounced conviction, almost an obsession, with the imminence of the End of the world.[2] Although he did not completely abandon Augustine's moral reading of Revelation, Gregory's use of apocalyptic material passes beyond that of a purely spiritual and moral interpretation. The collapse of Roman government in the West and the terrors of the Lombard invasions brought the pope to a position of deep pessimism about the future course of history. It is ironic that one whose influence was to have such pronounced effect on the future of Western society did not think that that society had any future at all.[3]

HOMILY ON EZEKIEL 2:6

What is there now, I ask you, which might give pleasure in this world?[4] Everywhere we see grief, on all sides we hear groans. Cities are destroyed, armed camps overturned, districts emptied of people, the earth reduced to solitude. Not a native remains in the countryside, nor scarcely an inhabitant in the cities; nevertheless, these small remains of humankind are still being slaughtered daily and without cease. The scourges of heavenly justice have no end because even in their midst there is no correction of the faults of our

actions. We see some led away in captivity, some beheaded, some slaughtered. What is there then in this life, my brothers, that might give pleasure?
If we still love such a world, we now love wounds, not delights. We see
how she who once seemed to be the queen of the world, Rome, has been
left—trodden down in many ways by immense pains, by loss of citizens, by
assault of enemies,[5] by spread of ruins, so that we seem to see fulfilled in
her what through this same prophet was said long ago against the city of
Samaria, "Put the pot, put it, I say, on the fire, place water in it and gather
pieces of meat in it" (Ezek. 24:3–4). And a little later: "Its cooking has
boiled over and its bones are boiled to pieces in its midst" (v. 5). And
again: "Gather the bones which I will burn with fire. Let the flesh be consumed, the whole mixture burnt up and the bones dissolved. Place it empty
over live coals that it might grow hot and its bronze melt away" (vv. 10–
11).[6]

The pot has been placed in our case, since this signifies the city. Then
water was put in it and pieces brought together when people flowed together
to it from all sides. They grew hot like boiling water by the deeds of the
world and were melted like pieces of meat in their burning. Of this it is well
said: "Its cooking has boiled over and its bones are boiled to pieces in its
midst" (24:5), for previously worldly glory grew vehemently hot in her, but
then that glory and its followers failed. Through the bones the powerful of
the world are meant, through the flesh the people, because just as the flesh is
carried by the bones, so the weakness of the people is ruled by the powerful.
But behold all the powerful of this world are already taken away from her;
therefore the bones are burned to pieces! Behold the people have failed; her
flesh is melted! . . . Therefore be it said, "Let her be set empty upon the
burning coals." Since the Senate is not here, the people are perishing; and
yet in the few that remain pains and groans are daily multiplied—yes, empty
Rome is now burning. . . . Where are their pomps, their pride? Where their
repeated and excessive joy?

What we have said about the destruction of the city of Rome we see in
all the cities of the world. Some places are desolated through slaughter,
others consumed by the sword, others tortured by famine, others swallowed
up by clefts in the earth. Let us despise with all our being this present—or
rather extinct—world. At least let worldly desires end with the End of the
world. Let us imitate those deeds of good men that we are able to.

Translated from the edition found in *PL* 76, c. 1010.

TWO LETTERS[7]

Gregory to the Emperor Maurice (June, 597)[8]

    . . . About this matter the good will of the bishops in their ordinances has commanded me that scandal ought not be aroused among us for the sake of the use of a frivolous title. I ask that the Imperial Goodness consider that some frivolous titles are quite harmless and others are exceedingly harmful. Isn't it true that when Antichrist comes calling himself God that this will not be harmless but rather very dangerous? If you regard the length of the utterance, there are only two syllables in "Deus," but if you look at the weight of the evil, there is total destruction. I say with all confidence that whoever calls or desires to call himself "universal priest" in self-exaltation is a precursor of the Antichrist because he places himself before others in his proud bearing and by like pride is led to error. Just as the Perverse One wishes to seem as God, above all men, so whoever he may be who wishes to be called "sole priest" wishes to be above other priests. Since Truth says, "He who exalts himself will be humbled" (Matt. 23:12), I know that the further any self-exaltation is inflated, the more quickly it will be burst. Let Your Goodness then command those who have fallen into pride and vanity lest through the use of a frivolous title they give rise to scandal. As for myself, a sinner, I keep to humility with God's help and don't need to be advised about it.

Gregory to Ethelbert, King of the Angels (June, 601)[9]

    Further, we also wish Your Majesty to know, as we have learned from the words of Almighty God in Holy Scripture, that the End of the present world is already near and that the unending kingdom of the Saints is approaching. As this same End of the world is drawing nigh, many unusual things will happen—climatic changes, terrors from heaven, unseasonable tempests, wars, famines, pestilences, earthquakes. All these things are not to come in our own days, but they will all follow upon our times.[10] If you are aware of some of them happening in your land, do not be disturbed, for these signs of the End of the world are sent ahead so that we may have a concern for our souls. Awaiting the hour of death, by our good actions may we be found ready for the Judge Who is to come. I put this down in brief fashion, Most Glorious Son, so that as the Christian faith grows in your realm, our conversation with you may broaden. The more our joy multiplies

over the complete conversion of your people, the more we shall we be able
to speak freely to you.

These two letters are translated from the edition of P. Ewald and L. Hartmann, *Gregorii I Papae Registrum Epistolarum* (*MGH*. Epist. Sel. I), 1:478, and 2:309–10.

6. *Byzantine Apocalyptic*

The rich apocalyptic literature of the Byzantine empire is in need of further work to clarify important problems of the dating, transmission, and interpretation of many texts, as well as questions of their significance for Byzantine history in general.[1] Recent studies by Paul J. Alexander have shown how important Byzantine apocalyptic texts are as neglected historical sources;[2] their influence upon the Slavic world, and also in many cases on the Latin West, is indisputable.

We have already noted the strength of the Antichrist tradition in Byzantium as seen in such texts as the Pseudo-Johannine Revelation. The political use of the Antichrist myth, as directed against the Emperors Nero and Domitian, had been strong in early Christian apocalypticism. Later emperors and rulers, such as Commodus, possibly Decius, Odenathus of Palmyra, Constantius, and Gaiseric the Vandal, had also been identified with the dread last enemy. This tradition was carried on in one of the most lurid works of Byzantine literature, the *Secret History* of Procopius of Caesarea, written about 550. B. Rubin has shown that the malicious portrait of Justinian contained there is based upon the centuries-old traditions about the Antichrist. "It is true that Procopius does not use the word 'Antichrist' as a characteristic of Justinian, yet in such an incontestably Christian time and environment no other meaning of his 'Prince of demons' is possible."[3]

The use of traditional apocalyptic themes, however, was more frequently invoked in defense of the imperial office and the Byzantine state than in its condemnation. G. Podskalsky's recent study of Byzantine interpretations of Daniel 2 and 7 and Revelation 20 shows how the four empires motif and the millennial kingdom were used to uphold the existing order. Byzantium, the new Rome, would last until the End of time.[4] The ninth-century Visions of Daniel, studied by P. J. Alexander, demonstrate another use—the ability of apocalyptic ideas to be applied to the interpretation of current crises in the life of the empire.[5]

PROCOPIUS, *SECRET HISTORY*

Chapter Eight

It will not be out of place, I think, to describe his [Justinian's] personal appearance. He was neither tall nor too short, but of a medium height, not thin, but inclined to be fat. His face was round and not ill-favored, and showed color, even after two days' fast. In a word, he greatly resembled Domitian, Vespasian's son, more than anybody else. This was the emperor whom the Romans detested so much that they could not slake their hatred for him, even when they had him torn to pieces, but a decree of the Senate was passed to remove his name from all documents, and that all statues of him should be destroyed.[6]

Chapter Twelve

For the reasons which I have stated, I, and many of my position, never believed that they were really two human beings, but evil demons, and what the poets called scourges of mankind,[7] who laid their heads together to see how they could fastest and most easily destroy the race and the works of man, but who had assumed human forms, and become something between men and demons, and thus convulsed the whole world. One can find proofs of this theory more particularly in the superhuman power with which they acted.

There is a wide distinction between the human and the supernatural. Many men have been born in every age who, either by circumstances or their own character, have shown themselves terrible beings, who became the ruin of cities, countries, and whatever else fell into their hands. But to destroy all men and to ruin the whole earth has been granted to none save these two, who have been helped by Fortune in their schemes to destroy the whole human race. For, about this time, much ruin was caused by earthquakes, pestilences and inundations of rivers, as I shall immediately tell you. Thus it was not by mere human power, but by something greater, that they were enabled to work their evil will.

It is said that Justinian's mother told some of her intimates that Justinian was not the son of Sabbatius, her husband, or of any human being; but that, at the time when she became pregnant, an unseen demon companied with her, whom she only felt as when a man has connection with a woman, and who then vanished away as in a dream.[8]

Some who have been in Justinian's company in the palace very late at night, men with a clear conscience, have thought that in his place they have beheld a strange and devilish form. One of them said that Justinian suddenly arose from his royal throne and walked about (although, indeed, he never could sit still for long), and that at that moment his head disappeared, while the rest of his body still seemed to move to and fro. The man who beheld this stood trembling and troubled in mind, not knowing how to believe his eyes. Afterwards the head joined the body again, and united itself to the parts from which it had so strangely been severed.

They say, too, that a certain monk, highly in favor with God, was sent to Byzantium by those who dwelt with him in the desert, to beg that favor might be shown to their neighbors, who had been wronged and outraged beyond endurance. When he arrived at Byzantium, he straightaway obtained an audience of the emperor; but just as he was about to enter his apartment, he started back, and, turning round, suddenly withdrew. The eunuch who was escorting him, and also the bystanders, besought him earnestly to go forward, but he made no answer, but like one who has had a stroke of the palsy, made his way back to his lodging. When those who had come with him asked why he acted thus, they say that he distinctly stated that he saw the chief of the devils sitting on his throne in the midst of the palace, and that he would not meet him or ask anything of him.

Taken from the anonymous translation, *Procopius* (Athens: The Athenian Society, 1896), pp. 67, 103–6. The Greek text may be found in H. B. Dewing, ed., *Procopius*. Vol. VI. *The Anecdota or Secret History*. Loeb Classical Library (Cambridge, Mass.: Harvard University Press, 1954).

THE VISION OF THE PROPHET DANIEL[9]

. . . And the emperor[10] will send envoys to the western lands which in a similar fashion are faithful to him. When they will have reached the western lands, the inhabitants of the so-called Rebel City having rebelled, will sally forth and begin to insult him. And afterward men who are in that place will arise and they will kill them with the sword. They will arise against each other and fight each other. There will arise two rebels, the first from the east of that city, and the other from the west. And they will encounter each other in a place called Akrodunii[11] and will slay each other so that the sea will be mixed with their blood. A woman who is with child will come from the territory of that city where there stood in those days a sign. And she will see her brother lying dead and will beat her breast, and she will give birth to her child and grief will overcome her for a long time. The Ishmaelites will go forth into the extremity of the island and will take many prisoners until they will come to a place called Marianii, and the rebel will install them in that place. And they will come to a place called Ienna, and they will come to her aid, and they will not capture her.[12]

Translated by Paul J. Alexander, "Medieval Apocalypses as Historical Sources," p. 1013, note 47. Reprinted by permission of the American Historical Association.

7. Pseudo-Methodius

The crown of Eastern Christian apocalyptic literature is the treatise attributed to Methodius of Patara, a martyr bishop who died in the early fourth century. After the Book of Daniel and the Revelation of John it was among the most widespread of medieval apocalyptic texts.[1]

The creation and diffusion of the work display the kind of complications we have come to take for granted in the case of major apocalyptic texts. Despite the hesitations of earlier scholars, M. Kmosko showed that the work was originally written in Syriac.[2] There is still some dispute over the date and the place of composition. E. Sackur, the editor of one of the Latin versions, dated it to about 680;[3] Kmosko, however, suggested a date not long after 660,[4] and has been followed by P. J. Alexander.[5] Kmosko thought that the author was an Orthodox (Melchite) Syrian who had left eastern Syria for Palestine in the wake of the conquests of Heraclius.[6] Alexander thinks that the author was a Monophysite and wrote in Arab-controlled Mesopotamia near the ancient city of Singara.[7] In any case, through the Pseudo-Methodius the traditions of Syria, and even of Persia, once again were to fertilize Western apocalypticism.

Both Kmosko and Alexander agree on the basic meaning and political nature of the treatise. In the words of the latter:

Pseudo-Methodius' tract was thus a politico-religious manifesto, rejecting every kind of defeatism or collaboration with the Moslems, warning against reliance on the weak and distant ruler of Ethiopia as a will-o-the-wisp, calling for war to the finish against the conquerors, and preaching that salvation from the Moslem yoke could come from only one source, the most powerful Christian monarch of the time, the *basileus* at Byzantium.[8]

This passage highlights two of the most important contributions of the Pseudo-Methodius to the apocalyptic tradition. To these a third must be added.

The *Revelations of the Pseudo-Methodius* is the earliest surviving witness to the legend of the Last World Emperor. It may well be that the anonymous Syrian author was himself responsible for drawing together strands of imperial myths, as well as elements of late messianic Judaism, into this new and potent form, as some have claimed. At least it is evident that "the abdication scene on Golgotha is deeply rooted in the eschatological, theological, and ideological conceptions of Byzantine Christianity,"[9] and hence presupposes a more advanced and integrated imperial ideology than that available in the fourth century.

The Methodian picture of the Last Emperor directs our attention to the main lines of imperial Byzantine apocalypticism. Byzantium had become the new Rome, Daniel's fourth kingdom, identified with that force which restrained the coming of the Antichrist. Any general theory of history, such as that found in the Pseudo-Methodius, must explain how the empire was to come to an end so that the Antichrist might be released.[10] Paradoxically, it was a Syrian author who provided the most convincing explanation of the end of the empire, and the situation in late seventh-century Syria helps to explain why. Many of the author's compatriots had been long opposed to the anti-Monophysite theology of the emperors and hence had welcomed the Moslem liberation from the Byzantine yoke. Such eschatological hopes as they had seem to have been placed in the Monophysite ruler of Ethiopia. The response of the Pseudo-Methodius to these brethren was to show that the text from Psalm 68:31 on which they based their claims (". . . let Ethiopia hasten to stretch out her hands to God") would be fulfilled in a Byzantine ruler, the descendent of the legendary marriage between Philip of Macedon and Chuseth, the daughter of the king of Ethiopia.[11]

Like many great apocalypses, the Pseudo-Methodius was born in the midst of crisis. In the *Revelations* for the first time a foe worthy of the fully formed imperial apocalyptic myth steps upon the scene. It may even be that the two protagonists were born together—the Cain and Abel of later Christian accounts of the events before the End. The sudden onslaught and remarkable success of the Islamic conquests which almost overnight deprived the Christian empire of the land of its birth and many of the proudest monuments of its early history had cast into question the easy optimism of many of the traditional schemes of history. The Pseudo-Methodius offered hope in this dark hour. His vision of a coming Emperor who would defeat the Ishmaelites, the enemies of Christ, and restore Roman glory incorporated the rise of Islam, the most important historical event since the conversion of the empire, into the Christian apocalyptic scheme of history.[12]

Not only did the Pseudo-Methodius provide a meaning for the Islamic threat, but by a unique stroke of luck the text also could be used to explain the apocalyptic significance of enemies that seemed even more terrible than these, Gog and Magog and the twenty-two nations who were to burst the barrier of Alexander's Gate at the End of time to harass the world. These too, however, were to be defeated (by direct divine intervention) before the Last Emperor would proceed to Jerusalem to give over his crown to God and usher in the time of the Antichrist. Through the inclusion of this element from the Alexander Romance (originally probably related to the incursions of the Huns in the fifth century), the Methodian scheme of history could be used at later times as a consolatory prophecy at the time of the Mongol invasions of the thirteenth century.[13]

No wonder the Pseudo-Methodius was so widely read. Its vision of history not only gave hope for the future but, in a significant reversal of most earlier apocalyptic literature, it at least implicitly encouraged active resistance against the forces of evil. To fight for any Byzantine, and later Western emperor could be seen as fighting for God's chosen vessel of glory of the last days. Though the Methodian scheme of history, like all apocalyptic literature, is in the last analysis pessimistic about the course of history, the negative moment of the last act, (i.e., the brief and unoriginal account of the career of the Antichrist) is outshone by the dramatic picture of the epic struggle between God's chosen emperor and the forces of evil. We should not be surprised that in 1683, a thousand years after its origin, excerpts from the Pseudo-Methodius printed on broadsheets were used to encourage the Christian defenders during the last siege of Vienna.[14]

The Syriac original of the *Revelations* was soon translated into Greek.[15] The existence of later translations in Russian, Armenian, Arabic, and Old Slavonic testify to its importance in Eastern Christianity.[16] By the beginning of the eighth century the text had been translated into Latin under the lengthy title, "A Sermon on the Kingdom of God and Sure Demonstration of the Last Times."[17] Many problems still surround the history of the Latin Pseudo-Methodius. D. Verhelst has identified at least four versions,[18] and until further work is done the relation of these variants remains obscure. The Preface of Peter the Monk, the easterner who fled to Merovingian Gaul and was responsible for Sackur's text, is found in only a few of the early witnesses.[19]

The influence of the Pseudo-Methodius in the West was immense. The text itself was later translated into a number of the vernacular literatures, including Middle English,[20] and was printed early and often.[21] Although the question is still disputed (see Section 10), it is possible that Adso was familiar with the *Revelations.* The use of the text in the twelfth and thirteenth centuries, not only in the service of imperial propaganda, but also in connection with the legend of the ten lost tribes of Israel (sometimes identified with the nations cast out by Alexander), the confrontation with Islam, and the threat of the Mongol invasions gives sufficient evidence of its paramount importance.[22]

THE ALEXANDER LEGEND[23]

8. Hear now then in true fashion how these four empires were joined, the Ethiopian with the Macedonian and the Greek with the Roman. They are the four winds that move the great sea (Dan. 7:2). Philip the Macedonian was the father of Alexander and took to wife Chuseth, the daughter of King Phol of Ethiopia. From her was born Alexander, who was made ruler of the Greeks. He founded Alexandria the Great and reigned nineteen years. He went to the East and killed Darius, king of the Medes. He was the ruler of many regions and cities and he destroyed the earth. He even went as far as the sea which is called the region of the sun[24] where he beheld unclean races of horrible appearance. . . . He gave orders and gathered them all together with their women and children and all their villages. Leading them away from the East, he restrained them with threats until they entered the northern lands where there is no way in or out from East to West to visit them. Alexander prayed to God without interruption and He heard his prayer.[25] The Lord God gave a command to the two mountains which are called the "Breasts of the North,"[26] and they came together to within twelve cubits. Alexander built bronze gates and covered them with unmixed bitumen,[27] so that if anyone wished to force them open by steel or to melt them with fire, he would be able to do neither, but immediately every fire would be extinguished. . . .

Who are the nations and the kings that Alexander concealed in the North? Gog and Magog, Anog and Ageg, Achenaz, Dephar, and the Potinei, the Libii, Eunii, Pharizei, Declemi, Zarmatae, Theblei, Zamartiani, Chaconii, Amarzarthae, Agrimardii, the Anuphagii (who are called Cynocephali),[28] the Tharbei, Alanes, Phisolonici, Arcnei, and the Asalturii. These twenty-two kings live enclosed within the gates that Alexander made.[29]

Translated from the edition of E. Sackur, *Sibyllinische Texte und Forschungen,* pp. 72–75.

THE MOSLEM CRISIS

11. In the final seventh millennium the Persian empire will be wiped out. In this seventh millennium the seed of Ishmael[30] will begin to go forth from the desert of Ethribus. When they have gone forth, they will all assemble at the great Gabaoth and there will be completed the saying of Ezekiel the prophet: "Son of man," he said, "call the beasts of the field and the birds of the air and exhort them saying, 'Gather yourselves together and come since I will give you a great sacrifice, to eat the flesh of strong men and drink the blood of the mighty' " (Ezek. 39:17). . . . And so the Lord God will give them (i.e., the sons of Ishmael) the power to conquer the land of the Christians, not because he loves them, but because of the sin and iniquity committed by the Christians. Such sins have not nor shall be committed for all generations. Men will get themselves up as false women wearing prostitutes' clothes. Standing in the streets and squares of the cities openly before all they will be adorned like women; they will exchange natural sex for that which is against nature. As the blessed and holy Apostle says, "men have acted like women" (Rom. 1:26–7).[31] A father, his son, his brothers, and all the relatives will be seen to unite with one woman. . . .

For this reason they will be given over by God into the hands of the barbarians from whom they will sink into all uncleanness and stink of pollution. Their women will be contaminated by filthy barbarians and the sons of Ishmael will cast lots for their sons and daughters. The land of the Persians is handed over to corruption and destruction, its inhabitants led away to captivity and death. They also attack Armenia and those who dwell there fall into captivity by the sword. . . . The land of Syria will be empty and reduced; those dwelling in her will perish by the sword. . . . Egypt and the East and Syria will be under the yoke and hemmed in by great tribulations. They will be constrained without mercy; weight of gold and silver beyond their strength will be eagerly desired of them. The inhabitants of Egypt and Syria will be in trouble and affliction, seven times the greater for those in captivity. The Land of Promise will be filled with men from the four winds under heaven.

Translated from E. Sackur, *Sibyllinische Texte*, pp. 80–83.

THE LAST WORLD EMPEROR

13. . . . Then suddenly tribulation and distress will arise against them. The king of the Greeks, i.e., the Romans, will come out against them in great anger, roused as from a drunken stupor like one whom men had thought dead and worthless (Ps. 77:65).[32] He will go forth against them from the Ethiopian sea and will send the sword and desolation into Ethribus their homeland, capturing their women and children living in the Land of Promise.[33] The sons of the king will come down with the sword and cut them off from the earth. Fear and trembling will rush upon them and their wives and their children from all sides. They will mourn their offspring, weeping over them and all the villages in the lands of their fathers. By the sword they will be given over into the hands of the king of the Romans—to captivity, death, and decay.

The king of the Romans will impose his yoke upon them seven times as much as their yoke weighed upon the earth. Great distress will seize them; tribulation will bring them hunger and thirst. They, their wives, and their children will be slaves and serve those who used to serve them, and their slavery will be a hundred times more bitter and hard. The earth which they destituted will then be at peace; each man will return to his own land and to the inheritance of his fathers—Armenia, Cilicia, Isauria, Africa, Greece, Sicily. Every man who was left captive will return to the things that were his and his fathers', and men will multiply upon the once desolated earth like locusts. Egypt will be desolated, Arabia burned with fire, the land of Ausania burned, and the sea provinces pacified. The whole indignation and fury of the king of the Romans will blaze forth against those who deny the Lord Jesus Christ. Then the earth will sit in peace and there will be great peace and tranquillity upon the earth such as has never been nor ever will be any more, since it is the final peace at the End of time. . . .[34]

Then the "Gates of the North" will be opened and the strength of those nations which Alexander shut up there will go forth. The whole earth will be terrified at the sight of them; men will be afraid and flee in terror to hide themselves in mountains and caves and graves.[35] They will die of fright and very many will be wasted with fear. There will be no one to bury the bodies. The tribes which will go forth from the North will eat the flesh of men and will drink the blood of beasts like water. They will eat unclean serpents, scorpions, and every kind of filthy and abominable beast and reptile which crawls the earth. They will consume the dead bodies of beasts of burden and even women's abortions. They will slay the young and take them away from their mothers and eat them.[36] They will corrupt the earth and contaminate it. No one will be able to stand against them.

After a week of years, when they have already captured the city of Joppa, the Lord will send one of the princes of his host and strike them down in a moment. After this the king of the Romans will go down and live in Jerusalem for seven and half-seven times, i.e., years. When the ten and a half years are completed the Son of Perdition will appear.

14. He will be born in Chorazaim, nourished in Bethsaida, and reign in Capharnaum. Chorazaim will rejoice because he was born in her, and Capharnaum because he will have reigned in her. For this reason in the third Gospel the Lord gave the following statement: "Woe to you Chorazaim, woe to you Bethsaida, and to you Capharnaum—if you have risen up to heaven, you will descend even to hell" (Luke 10:13,15). When the Son of Perdition has arisen, the king of the Romans will ascend Golgotha upon which the wood of the Holy Cross is fixed, in the place where the Lord underwent death for us. The king will take the crown from his head and place it on the cross and stretching out his hands to heaven will hand over the kingdom of the Christians to God the Father. The cross and the crown of the king will be taken up together to heaven. This is because the Cross on which our Lord Jesus Christ hung for the common salvation of all will begin to appear before him at his coming to convict the lack of faith of the unbelievers. The prophecy of David which says, "In the last days Ethiopia will stretch out her hand to God" (Ps. 67:32) will be fulfilled in that these last men who stretch out their hands to God are from the seed of the sons of Chuseth, the daughter of Phol, king of Ethiopia. When the Cross has been lifted up on high to heaven, the king of the Romans will directly give up his spirit. Then every principality and power will be destroyed that the Son of Perdition may be manifest. . . .[37]

Translated from E. Sackur, *Sibyllinische Texte,* pp. 89–94.

8. Beatus of Liébana

The confrontation with Islam does not seem to have provided a source for major new apocalyptic speculation in the eighth and ninth centuries in the West.[1] Influential authors, especially the widely read English monk the Venerable Bede (c.672–735),[2] while expressing general pessimism about the age and conveying many important traditional themes, were scarcely innovators in the area of apocalypticism.

Among the most important conveyors of tradition during these centuries was the Spanish monk Beatus of Liébana (c.750–798). From Visigothic times the church in Spain had had close ties with North African Christianity, and as in Africa, the Book of Revelation was paid particular reverence. It should not surprise us then that the most influential commentary on Revelation from this era was that of Beatus. Issued in three editions between 776 and 786, the *Commentary* is not an apocalyptic work as such. It makes no reference to current historical situations and tends to adhere closely to the Tyconian line.[3] It is possible, however, that in his preaching Beatus showed himself to be more daring, since arguments regarding the Antichrist were involved in the polemics between the Asturian monk and Elipandus of Toledo, the primate of Spain.[4]

Though not overtly apocalyptic, the *Commentary* of Beatus deserves note in the history of the apocalyptic tradition not only because of its importance as a source for the lost text of Tyconius,[5] but also because of its place in the history of apocalyptic iconography.[6]

BOOK IV (REV. 7:4)

For the first age was from Adam to Noah and occupied 2,242 years; the second, from Noah to Abraham, was 942 years. The third, from Abraham to Moses, was 505 years, and the fourth, from the departure of the sons of Israel from Egypt until their entrance into the promised land, was 40 years.

From the entrance into the promised land to Saul, the first king, the Israelites had Judges for 355 years. Saul reigned 40 years, and from David to the beginning of the Temple there were 43 years. The fifth age, from the first building of the Temple to the Babylonian captivity, took 446 years. There were 70 years in which the people were captive and the Temple desolate. The Temple was restored by Zorobabel in 4 years, and from the restoration until the Incarnation of Christ there were 540 years.[7]

The whole time from Adam to Christ makes 5,227 years, and from the coming of Our Lord Jesus Christ to the present Spanish era of 824,[8] there are 786 years. Therefore, compute the time from Adam to the present Spanish era and you will find 5,986. There are then only 14 years left in the sixth millennium, and the sixth age will end in the Spanish era 838.

The time remaining to the world is uncertain to human investigation. Our Lord Jesus Christ rejected every kind of question on this matter when he said: "It does not belong to you to know the times or the moments which the Father has put in his own power" (Acts 1:7); or again: "No one knows the day nor the hour—neither the angels of heaven, nor the Son, but only the Father" (Mark 13:32). Because he said "day and hour," sometimes they are to be taken for general time spans, sometimes to be understood directly. You should know in truth that the world will end in 6,000 years; but whether these years are to be completed or to be shortened is known only to God.[9]

Translated from H. A. Sanders, *Beati in Apocalypsin Libri Duodecim,* pp. 367–68.

BOOK XI (REV. 20:3).

One thousand is said as a manner of speaking, just as that passage which reads, "That which he commanded for a thousand generations" (Ps. 104:8) is to be understood not as a thousand but openly signifying the whole. Therefore do not listen to those who say that from the Nativity of the Lord to his Second Coming there are a thousand years—they think the same as the heretic Cerinthus.[10] Nor should we listen to those who say that all the baptized and all those who die without penance will not be judged guilty of sin or offense because they remained in the faith, or if they be buried in Hell, after a thousand years they shall be freed. These do not understand that the Lord will say to sinners, "Go into everlasting fire" (Matt. 25:41), since it has no end. Such men are of one mind with Eunomius and Origen the heretics.

Translated from H. A. Sanders, *Beati in Apocalypsin Libri Duodecim,* p. 601.

9. Muspilli

The mysterious poem usually called the *Muspilli* has caused considerable debate, much of it still unsettled. We are not even certain what *muspilli* means, though it appears to signify something like "the End of the world." The text as we have it, a fragment of about a hundred lines written in a Bavarian dialect of Old High German and surviving by accident in a single manuscript, appears to date from about 850.[1]

The Germanic tribes that had been gradually converted to Christianity over a period of some five centuries had a rich eschatology of their own. Claims have been made that the *Muspilli* may enshrine some elements of pagan doctrines of the End; but even if this be true, they have been recast in a Christian fashion. Nevertheless, there are peculiarities to the apocalypticism of the poem, especially in the treatment of the conflict between Elijah and the Antichrist, that are not found in Western apocalyptic texts and that have led some to see a strong Eastern influence in the *Muspilli*.[2] This too is difficult to prove.

The fragment consists of two intermingled parts, M I, a poem on the fate of the soul, and M II, an adaptation of an ancient lay on the destruction of the world by fire. The properly apocalyptic elements are three: the battle between Elijah and the Antichrist, an account of the signs preceding the End, and a description of the Last Judgment. A recent attempt at a political reading of the fragment, interpreting Elijah as Louis the German and the Antichrist as Charles the Bald, goes far beyond anything that can actually be proven from the text itself.[3]

MUSPILLI

37 This is what I heard the wise men in the law of this world relate,[4]
    that Antichrist shall fight with Elijah.[5]
    The evil one is armed and then a battle will take place between them.
40 The warriors are so powerful, the issue is so great.
    Elijah fights for eternal life,

and wishes to ensure the kingdom for those who seek righteousness,
for this reason he will be helped by the one who rules over heaven.
Antichrist stands side by side with the Old Enemy,
45 stands at the side of Satan who will destroy him.
For he will fall down wounded on the battleground,
and will be the loser in that place.
But many men of God believe that Elijah will be wounded in the battle,[6]
so that his blood will drip down to earth;
50 then the mountains will catch fire,[7] no tree at all will be left standing
on earth, the waters will dry up,
the marshland will swallow itself up, the sky will be aflame with fire,
the moon will fall, and the earth will burn,
no stone will be left standing, then the day of judgment will drive through the
land,
55 traveling with fire as a visitation on the people.
Then can no relative help another in the face of the "Muspilli,"
for the widespread rain will burn up everything,
both fire and air will purge it all:
where then the march where one fought constantly with one's kin?

Translated for this volume by Kenneth J. Northcott. The Old High German text may be found in standard readers, such as F. von der Leyen, *Deutsche Dichtung des Mittelalters* (Frankfurt: Insel, 1962), pp. 58–60.

10. Adso's Letter on the Antichrist

For all its originality, the *Revelations of the Pseudo-Methodius* had not done much with the figure of the Antichrist.[1] Nonetheless, speculation on the Antichrist had remained popular both in the East and the West during the centuries from A.D. 500 to 900. The corporate interpretation of the Last Enemy was common, with the Antichrist usually being identified with heretics or sometimes with the Jews.[2] Belief in a final individual Antichrist was also known. The new life given to learning, education, and theology in the Carolingian period inspired Agobard of Lyons in a letter written to Louis the Pious in 826 to suggest that someone should compose a treatise summarizing traditional teaching on the Son of Perdition.[3]

The hope was not fulfilled for over a century. Adso was born about 910 and entered the monastic life during the time of the great reforms associated with the houses of Cluny and Gorze. He became abbot of the reformed monastery of Montier-en-Der and died in 992 while on pilgrimage to the Holy Land.[4] A noted hagiographer and confidant of the West Frankish royal family, Adso composed his *Letter on the Origin and Life of the Antichrist* about 950. It was dedicated to Gerberga, the sister of Otto the Saxon, the future renewer of the empire, and wife of the young Louis IV (ruled from 936 to 954), one of the last descendents of the Carolingians.

Adso's *Letter* was published by E. Sackur from four mss. in 1898. This edition has served as the basis for most modern treatments, but D. Verhelst in an unpublished thesis based upon an exhaustive study of 170 mss. of this popular work cautioned against overreliance on Sackur's text. Verhelst's recent critical edition of Adso's work and its subsequent versions clearly supersedes that of Sackur and provides a new and more solid basis for study.[5] Recently, a good deal of work has also been done on Adso's sources.[6] The monk was a learned man for his day, but in the tenth century even scholars traveled with light academic baggage.[7] It is certain that Adso depends ultimately upon patristic teaching on the Antichrist,[8] though his access to this material seems to have been largely through summaries dating from the eighth and the ninth centuries. M. Rangheri has shown the close dependence of parts of the *Letter* on the *Computation of Time* of Bede (d. 735) and Haymo of Auxerre's (d. c.860) *Commentary on Second Thessalonians.* Rangheri has also criticized R. Konrad's claims for direct patristic contacts found in the text.[9]

The question of sources is not unimportant because it directly touches on the more significant issue of the originality of the Adsonian work. The author admits to being a compiler of the opinions of others, but this confession was neither the first nor the last time that such a *topos* has been used as a mask for a considerable degree of creativity. In one area at least, that of form, there can be no question of Adso's innovation. Relying on his background as a hagiographer, as Konrad has pointed out,[10] the monk modeled his account of the Antichrist on a typical saint's life. The relative simplicity and the immense popularity of the genre undoubtedly contributed greatly to the widespread use of the text. But was Adso also original in the way in which he adapted the Antichrist legend to his own time? On the balance, the answer must be yes. While his sketch of the life of the Last Enemy is very traditional, it is personal and historical rather than collective and moralized as in the Tyconian tradition so popular at the time. Furthermore, the author's melding of this history with the theme of the permanence of the empire and the attendant legend of the Last Emperor seems to have been a stroke of genius, both within his own political context and during the centuries to come.

Scholars are now agreed that Adso did not know the Tiburtine Sibyl and hence did not depend upon it for his version of the Last Emperor myth.[11] Did he then make use of the Latin Pseudo-Methodius? The question remains open. There are significant differences between the Emperor of the Methodian *Revelations* and Adso's ruler. On the basis of this some students are inclined to think that the monk did not know Methodius;[12] others hold that he did, but changed the myth to suit his own purposes.[13] In any case, the future abbot's use of the Last Emperor figure is the first distinctively western adaptation of the Byzantine myth that has survived to us. For Konrad this adaptation is among the most important claims to Adso's originality;[14] Verhelst and Rangheri think that the myth may have already been westernized in Carolingian times though no explicit texts are presently extant.[15] This argument may seem strained, but we must remember that not only was the Pseudo-Methodius well known in the Carolingian period, but that the notion of the endurance of Rome to the End of time as the last of the four world empires was also a subject for speculation.[16] There appear to have been two attitudes to this complex of apocalyptic ideas in the Carolingian age—one jettisoned the traditional exegesis which identified Rome with the restraining power of 2 Thess. 2;[17] the other attempted to update the traditional teaching by showing how the reality of Roman rule had passed from East to West during the course of history.[18] Adso is among the most influential exponents of the latter option in early medieval thought.

As in the case of the Pseudo-Methodius, one must note the thoroughgoing political tone of the *Letter*.[19] As Konrad points out, in his desire to support the claims of the West Frankish line against both powerful local barons and the rising Saxon power to the east, Adso transformed the Last Emperor from a "rex Romanorum et Grecorum" to a "rex Francorum."[20] This westernized version of the myth and its current of optimism regarding victory over present enemies of the empire were potent forces in a number of later apocalyptic texts. In a manner similar to other key texts in the history of apocalypticism, Adso's *Letter* was edited, adapted, and revised extensively in the succeeding centuries. Verhelst's new edition presents no less than seven subsequent Latin versions of the text dating from the eleventh and twelfth centuries.[21]

THE ORIGIN OF THE ANTICHRIST

Since you want to know about the Antichrist, the first thing to observe is why he is so named. It is because he will be contrary to Christ in all things and will work deeds against Christ.[22] Christ came in humble fashion; he will come as a proud man. Christ came to raise up the humble, to justify sinners; he, on the other hand, will cast out the humble, magnify sinners, exalt the wicked and always teach the vices contrary to virtues. He will destroy the Law of the Gospel, call the worship of demons back into the world, seek his own glory, and call himself almighty God. This Antichrist will have many ministers of his evil: many of them have already gone forth into the world, such as Antiochus, Nero, and Domitian.[23] In our own time we know there are many Antichrists. Any layman, cleric, or monk who lives in a way contrary to justice, who attacks the rule of his order of life, and blasphemes the good, he is an Antichrist, a minister of Satan.[24]

Let us see about the origin of the Antichrist. What I say is not thought out or put together on my own; I have found all these things in written works that I have diligently studied. As our authorities say, Antichrist will be born from the Jews, namely, from the tribe of Dan, as the prophet says: "Let Dan be a snake on the wayside, an adder in the path." [25] He will sit like a serpent on the wayside and in the path to wound those who walk on the paths of justice and to kill them with the venom of his malice. He will be born from the union of a father and mother, just as other men are born, and not, as some say, from a virgin alone. Nevertheless, he will be conceived wholly in sin, generated in sin, born in sin. The devil will enter the womb of his mother at the very instant of his conception. He will be fostered by the power of the devil and protected in his mother's womb. The power of the devil will always be with him. Just as the Holy Spirit came into the Mother of Our Lord Jesus Christ, overshadowed her with his power, and filled her with divinity, so that she conceived of the Holy Spirit and what was born of her would be divine and holy, so too the devil will descend into the mother of the Antichrist and completely fill her, surround her completely, possess her completely both inside and out, so that she will conceive through a man with the cooperation of the devil, and what will be born will be totally inimical, evil, and lost. So this man will be called the "Son of Perdition," or destruction, because he will destroy the human race as far as he can and he himself will be destroyed at the End. [26]

Translated from the edition of D. Verhelst, *Adso Dervensis,* pp. 22–23. Compare with the text in E. Sackur, *Sibyllinische Texte,* pp. 105–7.

THE LAST EMPEROR

He will stir up persecution everywhere against the Christians and the elect. He will raise himself up against the faithful in three ways—by terror, by gifts, and by miracles. [27] He will give hoards of gold and silver to those who believe in him. Those he cannot corrupt with gifts he will overcome with terror; those he is not able to terrify he will attempt to seduce with signs and miracles; those he cannot tempt by signs he will put to death in the sight of all after cruel torture. Then there will be such tribulation as has never been on earth from the time that the nations began until then (Dan. 12:1; Matt. 24:21). Those who are in the field will flee to the mountains, and he who is on the roof will not go down into his house to take anything from it (Matt. 24:16–17). At that time every faithful Christian who is discovered will either deny God, or, if he persevere in faith, will perish, whether through sword or fiery furnace or serpents or beasts or through some other kind of torture.

This terrible and fearful tribulation will last three and a half years throughout the world. Then the days will be shortened for the sake of the elect, for unless God shortened the days, no flesh would be saved (Matt. 24:22). The Apostle Paul discloses the time when the Antichrist will come and when the Day of Judgment will begin to appear in his Epistle to the Thessalonians where he says: "I ask you through the coming of Our Lord Jesus Christ . . . ," down to ". . . unless the falling away first comes and the Man of Sin and Son of Perdition be revealed" (2 Thess. 2:1-3). We know that after the Greek empire and even after the Persian empire, each of which in its day throve in great glory and flourished in very great strength, finally, after all the others, began the Roman empire, which was the strongest of all and had the whole world under its sway. All nations were subject to the Romans and served them as tributaries. Hence the Apostle Paul says that Antichrist will not come into the world unless first comes the falling-away, i.e., unless first all kingdoms fall away from the Roman empire to which they were long subject.[28] This time has not yet come, because, though we see the Roman empire destroyed in great part, nevertheless as long as the kings of the Franks who hold the empire by right shall last, the dignity of the Roman empire will not totally perish, because it will endure in its kings.[29]

Some of our learned men say that one of the kings of the Franks who will come in the last time will possess anew the Roman empire.[30] He will come at the last time and will be the last and the greatest of all rulers. After he has successfully governed his empire, at last he will come to Jerusalem and will put off his scepter and crown on the Mount of Olives.[31] This will be the end and the consummation of the Roman and Christian empire. Immediately, according to the opinion of Paul mentioned above, they say that the Antichrist will be at hand. Then the "Man of Sin" will be revealed, Antichrist who, although he is a man, will nonetheless be the source of all sin, and the "Son of Perdition," that is, the son of the devil, not through nature but through imitation, because he will fulfill the devil's will in all things, and because the fullness of diabolical power and of every evil disposition will dwell bodily in him in whom will be hidden all the treasures of malice and iniquity.[32]

Translated from D. Verhelst, *Adso Dervensis*, pp. 25–26. See also E. Sackur, *Sibyllinische Texte*, pp. 108–10.

THE DESTRUCTION OF THE ANTICHRIST

Because we have spoken of his beginning, we ought to say what kind of an end he will have. This Antichrist, the son of the devil and the totally wicked agent of all evil, for three and a half years will torment the whole world with a great persecution and torture the whole people of God with various punishments, as foretold. After he has killed Elijah and Enoch and has crowned with martyrdom those holding fast in the faith, finally the judgment of God will come upon him, as St. Paul writes: "The Lord Jesus will slay him with the breath of his mouth" (2 Thess. 2:8). Whether the Lord Jesus will kill him by the power of his might, or whether the Archangel Michael will slay him, he will be killed through the power of Our Lord Jesus Christ, and not through the power of any angel or archangel. The learned say that Antichrist will be killed on the Mount of Olives in his pavilion and on his throne, opposite that place where the Lord ascended to heaven.[33]

You should know that after Antichrist has been slain the Day of Judgment will not come right away, nor will God immediately come to judge; but, as we understand from the Book of Daniel, the Lord will grant forty days to the elect to do penance because they were led astray by the Antichrist.[34] No man knows how great a space of time there may be after they have finished this penance until the Lord comes to judge. It remains in the disposition of God, who will judge the world at that hour which he predestined for judgment before the ages.[35]

Translated from D. Verhelst, *Adso Dervensis*, pp. 28–29. See also E. Sackur, *Sibyllinische Texte*, pp. 112–13.

11. Apocalyptic and Non-Apocalyptic Themes of the Eleventh Century

The eleventh century has frequently been seen as an age of strong apocalyptic expectations. Basing themselves upon two wide-spread historical myths, the legend of the year 1000 and the claim for the apocalyptic motivation of the crusading movement, many accounts, both old and new, stress the revival of apocalypticism at this time. Both myths contain germs of truth, but in the forms in which they have generally been presented they are more misleading than helpful. The eleventh century did not produce anything new in the history of apocalypticism, and in comparison with the following centuries it should not be singled out as an era of especially fervent hopes of the End of the world.

On the basis of a handful of texts, some nineteenth- and twentieth-century French historians created a picture of widespread terror in Christendom at the approach of the year 1000, the final year of the sixth and last millennium.[1] We must remember, however, that the tradition of the centuries since Augustine had been against the literalistic treatment of the final thousand-year period. That there were some preachers and writers of the time who expected the imminent End is a sign of the continuity of apocalyptic expectations rather than a mark of any special florescence.

The posthumus work of Paul Alphandéry (edited by his pupil A. Dupront), *La Chrétienté et l'idée de la croisade* (Paris: Albin Michel, 1954–59), is largely responsible for recent stress on apocalyptic elements in the motivation of the great onslaught that captured Jerusalem (1095–1099).[2] Such claims have been exaggerated, as a study of the careful work of C. Erdmann indicates.[3] It is impossible to exclude apocalypticism from the range of motives present among the first crusaders; after all, Jerusalem was the apocalyptic city *par excellence*.[4] Prior to the crusade the pro-imperial writer Benzo of Alba used the Sibylline theme of the Jerusalem journey of the Last World Emperor as a focus for his prophecies regarding Henry IV, but such a claim was scarcely welcome to Gregory VII and his successors.

One of the accounts of the famed speech given by Urban II at Clermont in 1095 stresses apocalyptic themes, but it is a late product from a notably imaginative pen and is not corroborated by other witnesses.[5] Alphandéry and Cohn have placed special emphasis on the role of apocalyptic and messianic hopes among the masses of poor who took part in the expeditions of 1096, but we really know very little about how large a place these hopes played in the popular enthusiasm. Ekkehard of Aura and Guibert of Nogent, writing after the event, mention the influence of apocalyptic signs on the populace, and the semilegendary Tafurs are thought by some to have been primarily motivated by their hope for the establishment of the millennial kingdom in Jerusalem.[6] In neither case are our sources reliable enough evidence for the actual expectations of those who set off for the East at the end of the eleventh century.[7]

The Great Crusade was fundamentally a papal plan for the reestablishment of the Mediterranean Christian empire under the leadership of the pope.[8] Insofar as it formed a part of Gregory VII's plans for the realization of an ideal of world order, it might be described as having important eschatological, but not directly apocalyptic, implications. As a major form of organized lay piety, the crusade was not so much the result of apocalypticism as it was a notable stimulus to the revival of apocalyptic themes. Jerusalem became a concrete historical place as well as an apocalyptic ideal, and changes that affected the political situation of the city were bound to suggest apocalyptic implications after 1100.

THE YEAR 1000

Abbo of Fleury, *Apologetic Work*[9]

When I was a young man I heard a sermon about the End of the world preached before the people in the cathedral of Paris. According to this, as soon as the number of a thousand years was completed, the Antichrist would come and the Last Judgment would follow in a brief time. I opposed this sermon with what force I could from passages in the Gospels, Revelation, and the Book of Daniel.[10] Finally my abbot of blessed memory, Richard, wisely overthrew an error which had grown up about the End of the world after he received letters from the Lotharingians which he bade me answer. The rumor had filled almost the whole world that when the feast of the Annunciation coincided with Good Friday without any doubt the End of the world would occur.[11]

Translated from *PL* 139, cc. 471–72.

Ralph Glaber, *History of His Times,* 4:6[12]

When some of the more truthful of that time were asked by many what might be the meaning of such a great flocking together of people to Jerusalem, unheard of in previous centuries,[13] they cautiously responded that it presaged nothing else but the coming of the Lost One, the Antichrist, who according to divine authority stands ready to come at the End of the age. Then the road to the eastern region from which he was to come was opened to all nations, so that all might go forth to meet him without delay. Truly that prophecy of the Lord will be fulfilled which says: "Then even the elect, if it be possible, will fall into temptation (Matt. 24:24)."

Translated from *PL* 142, cc. 681D–682A.

APOCALYPSE AND THE ORIGIN OF THE CRUSADE

Benzo of Alba, *Panegyrikus* 1:15[14]

Title: She spoke of Christ and also wrote down the lists of rulers,
      The ancient prophetess of Cumae, with inner rejoicing.

For a long road still remains to him [Henry IV] as the prophecy of the Sibyl testified.[15] When Apulia and Calabria have been put in order and brought back to the former state, Bizas will see him crowned in his own land.[16] Then he will lead an expedition to Jerusalem and having rescued the Sepulcher and the other sanctuaries of the Lord he will be crowned to the praise and glory of the One who lives forever and ever. Babylon in amazement will come to Sion desiring to lick the dust of his feet. Then will be fulfilled what is written: "And his sepulcher will be glorious" (Isa. 11:10). Caesar, why do you wonder about this? He who created you has decided without you what he will do in your case. You should say: "O Lord, my God, you have done many wonders; in your deep thoughts there is none like you" (Ps. 39:6). The Lord lives and ". . . He is my illumination" (Ps. 26:1). These things will take place as the song of the Sibyl foretells.[17] You, fellow priests of the emperor's ear, do not think the Sibyl's words the voice of a screeching crow! Where you hear that the sea is to be crossed, you should think upon deep things. If you are doubtful in any way ". . . ask in Abel. . . ,"[18] and when the veil has been rent those things that were hidden will be clear.[19]

Translated from the corrected text given by C. Erdmann in "Endkaiserglaube und Kreuzzugsgedanken," pp. 405–6.

Guibert of Nogent, *The Deeds of God through the Franks,* chapter 4[20]

You ought to consider with deep deliberation whether, as a result of your pains, with God acting through you, it should happen that the mother church of all churches begins to bloom again to the Christian religion. You ought also consider whether perhaps he may not wish other parts of the East restored to the faith against the approaching times of the Antichrist. For it is clear that Antichrist will not wage war against Jews and pagans, but, according to the etymology of his name,[21] he will attack Christians. If he finds no Christians there (as today there are scarcely any), there will be no one to oppose him or whom he may legally overcome. According to Daniel and his interpreter Jerome, he will fix his tents on the Mount of Olives,[22] and it is certain, as the Apostle teaches, that at Jerusalem he will sit "in the Temple of God, as if he were God" (2 Thess. 2:4). According to the same prophet, there can be no doubt that he will first slay three kings, namely those of Egypt, Africa, and Ethiopia, for the sake of the Christian faith.[23] This could not happen at all unless Christianity be found where now there is only paganism. If then you are forward in waging holy war, just as you once received the seed of the knowledge of God from Jerusalem, so now you will return a repayment of borrowed grace there, so that the Catholic name will be propagated, that name which is opposed to the perfidy of Antichrist and his followers. Who cannot imagine that the God who surpasses the hope of all by the abundance of his power will consume such great thickets of paganism by your fire that Egypt, Africa, and Ethiopia, separated from the fellowship of our belief, will be included within the first principles of this Law? Who cannot imagine that the "Man of Sin," the "Son of Perdition" (2 Thess. 2:3) will find some to oppose him?

Lo, the Gospel calls out: "Jerusalem is to be trodden down by the nations until the times of the nations are fulfilled" (Luke 21:24). "The times of the nations" can be understood in two ways. First, either because the nations have dominated the Christians at will, and for the satisfaction of their passions have chased after the sloughs of every shamefulness and found no obstacle. (For they who have everything at their pleasure are said to "have their time," as the text: "My time is not yet come, but your time is always ready" [John 7:6], and as we say to voluptuaries, "You're having your time!") Or second, "the times of the nations" are the fullness of those nations that will steal in before Israel will be saved. Dearly beloved, these times will now perhaps be fulfilled while you repel the pagan powers with God's cooperation. The End of the world is already near, even if the pagans are no longer being converted to God, for as the Apostle says, there must first come a falling-away from the faith (2 Thess. 2:3). According to prophecies, before the coming of the Antichrist it is first necessary that the Christian empire be renewed in those parts, either through you or through those whom God pleases, so that the head of all evil who will have his imperial throne there may find some nourishment of faith against which he may fight. Think then that the Almighty has perhaps prepared you to rescue Jerusalem from such subjugation! I ask you to consider what hearts could conceive the joys when you have seen the Holy City raised up by your aid, and the prophetic, nay divine, oracles fulfilled in our times!

Translated from the edition found in *RHC*. Hist. occ. 4:138–39.

Ekkehard of Aura, *Jerusalem Journey,* chapter 10 [24]

After the sign in the sun that had been foretold was seen, many portents appeared in the sky as well as on the earth and excited not a few who were previously indifferent to the Crusade. We thought that some of these signs could be usefully inserted here: to give all of them would be very tedious. About the fifth of October we saw a comet in the south, its tail extending sideways like a sword. In the third year after these events, on February 24, we saw another star in the east changing its position by leaps and bounds after a long interval. [25] We and many witnesses attest to have seen blood-red clouds rising from the west as well as the east and rushing together in the center of the sky, as well as brilliant fires from the north in the middle of the night, and frequently even sparks flying through the air. Not many years before, a priest of venerable life by the name of Siger one day at about three in the afternoon saw two knights charging against each other in the sky and fighting for a long time. The one who was carrying a good-sized cross with which he struck the other turned out the victor. At the same time the priest

G. (now a monk with us, paying the humble service of a proud man to Christ for the sins of our first parents) was walking in the woods with two companions about noon. He saw a sword of marvelous length, arising from an unknown source, borne off into the heavens in a whirlwind. Until the distance hid it, he heard its din and saw its steel. Others who kept watch feeding horses reported that they saw the likeness of a city in the air and that they beheld various crowds hurrying to it from different places both on horseback and on foot.[26] Some showed the sign of the cross stamped by divine influence on their foreheads or clothes or on some part of their body, and by that mark they believed themselves to be ordained for the army of God. Others who were converted by a sudden change of heart or instructed by a vision in the night sold their manors and household possessions and sewed the sign of mortification on their clothes. In the midst of all of this, more people than can be believed ran to the churches in crowds, and the priests blessed and handed out swords, clubs, and pilgrim wallets in a new ritual. Why should I report that at that time a woman, pregnant for two years, gave birth to a son already speaking when her womb finally opened?[27] Why should I speak of the infant born with two members in all parts, or of another with two heads, or of the lambs with two heads, or of the foals who at birth put forth the large teeth which are commonly called "equine," and which nature grants only to three-year-olds?

Translated from *RHC*. Hist. occ. 5:18–19.

12. Apocalypticism and the Great Reform

The central event of the late eleventh and early twelfth centuries was the prolonged struggle between the popes and emperors over the leadership of Christian society. From about 1050 a group of reform-minded prelates gathered around a succession of popes had attempted to purify the Church from the evils of the time: the corrupt life of the clergy, simony (the buying of ecclesiastical offices), and especially lay investiture (the investing of a churchman with the symbols of office by a secular ruler). In 1073, the monk Hildebrand, one of the most vehement of the reformers, was elected pope as Gregory VII. By 1075 he was locked in a mighty struggle with Henry IV, a struggle which N. F. Cantor has described as one of the great world revolutions.[1]

It is not my purpose to detail the history of this encounter nor the battle of the books that accompanied it. The struggle proper was ended by the compromise reached at the Concordat of Worms in 1122 and confirmed by the First Lateran Council the following year; its ramifications were to be felt for centuries. The Great Reform engendered by the investiture controversy brought about the most far-reaching political changes that Latin Christendom had seen since the conversion of the Roman Empire. It called into question not only the theocratic dream of the Christian emperors, both East and West, with the attendant immersion of sacral power in the lay world, but also challenged the theory of history and version of the apocalyptic scenario connected with it. The success of the reformers in elevating the papacy to a position of truly effective universal authority in the Western Church could not help but provoke a serious reconsideration of traditional eschatology and apocalypticism. Schemes of history based upon the succession of empires and the view of the End that stressed the role of the Last Emperor as the predecessor of Christ were called into question in an age when the sacrality of both empire and emperor was challenged by many. The rise to power of the papacy made it possible to begin to wonder what role the popes would play in the last times.

The full implications of these momentous changes for the history of the apocalyptic tradition will become more evident as our account proceeds. Here the task is a more limited one: first, to ask how far the motivations of the original reformers themselves, and especially Gregory VII, might be described as apocalyptic; and second, to sketch the apocalyptic interpretations given to these events by representative twelfth-century thinkers.

Gregory VII made heavy use of Antichrist rhetoric in the course of his struggles. Guibert, the archbishop of Ravenna and imperial Antipope, is called "Antichrist and archheretic";[2] other opponents are spoken of as precursors, heralds, members, or limbs of the Antichrist.[3] But this kind of language was by no means novel—all of these uses appear in previous authors, though perhaps not in the profusion present in Gregory. The pope is also more inclined than most of his predecessors to provide a concrete political interpretation to the opposition between the followers of Christ and the servants of the Antichrist, but he does not seem to have held that the End itself was at hand.[4] The closest Gregory comes to an imminent sense of the Last Things is found in a remark he made to explain the conflict his views had brought forth: "the nearer the day of Antichrist approaches, the harder he fights to crush out the Christian faith."[5] This is a familiar eschatological *topos,* not necessarily a real apocalyptic one.

It seems more correct to describe Gregory's program as involving important eschatological claims but not directly apocalyptic ones. In a brilliant short paper on "The Problem of Medieval World Unity," E. Kantorowicz has claimed that "the medieval Myth of World Unity has a predominantly messianic or eschatological character."[6] From this point of view, any attempt to realize world order—a convincing explanation of the fundamental intent of the Gregorian program[7]—implied the establishment of an eschatological situation in which the approach of the End was hastened though not necessarily made proximate. Whether or not this realization was consciously in Gregory's mind, it is a convincing interpretation of the logic of his plans.

The Great Reform had its most profound repercussions in Germany, the home of the empire. Hence we should not be surprised at the pride of place that speculation about the meaning of history found among German authors of the twelfth century.[8] In their struggle to wrest meaning from the great revolution of their times, these writers made use of a wide variety of eschatological and apocalyptic themes.

Rupert of Deutz (c.1070–1129) was one of the most prolific authors of the time.[9] In his opposition to the early Scholastic masters such as Anselm of Laon and William of Champeaux he is the prototype of the anti-Scholasticism of most of the twelfth-century theorists of history. His concern for the structure and meaning of history is evident in his major works, including the *Commentary* he wrote on Revelation.[10] As a young monk and upholder of the Gregorian party, Rupert and his abbot had been compelled to flee from their monastery of St. Lawrence at Liège. The poem "The Calamities of the Church of Liège," most likely an early product of his pen (c.1095),[11] is notable for its full and concrete application of apocalyptic imagery to the events of the investiture controversy.[12] Like his hero, Gregory VII, Rupert did not expect the immediate End of the world;[13] he did, however, carry Gregory's general use of apocalyptic rhetoric a step further toward full historical realization.

Otto of Freising (c.1110–1158), monk and bishop, reformer and imperial propagandist, Scholastic and symbolist, is one of the more complex figures of the twelfth century. Born into the highest levels of German nobility (he was an uncle of Frederick Barbarossa, the early years of whose reign he enshrined in his *Deeds of Frederick Barbarossa*), he was no simple imperialist. His major work, *The Two Cities,* written prior to the panegyric for Frederick, is unique in the Middle Ages in combining a profound Neo-Augustinian theology of history with a skillful and critical analysis of recent events.[14] Otto's universal history does give over its eighth and final book to the consideration of the events of the End, but there is little originality in the treatment. His profound historical pessimism, evident in the reflections he gives on the investiture controversy, as well as the use that he makes of the *translatio* theme,[15] are more cogent proofs of his apocalyptic interests.

The writer for whom the struggle between *regnum* and *sacerdotium* played the most important role as a key to the course of history was the bellicose Bavarian canon, Gerhoh of Reichersberg (1093–1169).[16] Unlike Rupert and Otto whose writings he knew, Gerhoh survived to witness the second major clash between the papacy and the empire, the long schism of 1159–1177 between Frederick Barbarossa and Alexander III. The reformer's reflections upon these events strengthened his deep sense of opposition to the empire and convinced him that the career of the Antichrist named Henry IV had begun the final catastrophic age of history. Gerhoh's first major apocalyptic work written during the schism was entitled *On the Investigation of the Antichrist.*[17] The treatise is notable for its highly spiritualistic view of the Antichrist as the collectivity of all who have opposed the Church since the time of Cain. R. Manselli has suggested that by his break with the fantastic and legendary accounts of the Final Enemy, Gerhoh opened up the way for a more immediate application of antichrist language to current events.[18]

The events of the Great Reform also played a role in the speculations of the visionary and prophetess Hildegard of Bingen (1098–1179), one of the most remarkable religious leaders of the time.[19] Hildegard's striking visions mark her as one of the most original apocalyptic thinkers since the intertestamental period. Her writings display a wide variety of themes both cosmological and historical. The central production, the *Scivias* completed in 1151, shows this Benedictine abbess as conservative and monastic in outlook, and primarily moralizing in intent. Hildegard was not particularly papalist; indeed, she predicted that both the universal powers of Christendom, the empire and the papacy, would fail as the age of crisis unfolded. According to her thought, this time of trouble, the *tempus muliebre,* began at the end of the eleventh century with the attacks of Henry IV upon the Church.[20] Although the German abbess tends to be less concerned with the details of the great controversy than some of her contemporaries, it is obvious that her view of history can only be understood within the context of the Great Reform movement.

"THE CALAMITIES OF THE CHURCH OF LIÈGE"

I. Now the bellicose dragon wages war.[21]
Woe to me! The tail of the dragon laden
With such great spoils drags a third of the
Stars in bondage . . . .[22]

IX. . . . Now the ancient enemy arises from the sea,[23]
And rules as victor over the seven hills.[24]
He fights and with a huge millstone
Strikes the already broken head.
Do you not see where Simon sits,
Relying on Nero, so like a king?
His lambs are fashioned like horns
And become like dragons.[25]
They have put to flight the six guardians
Who had protected your city;
They have put false prophets in their place,
Dragging away everything sacred for a price.
The Supreme Pontiff who persecuted crimes
And dared to attack the "kingly disease"
Fled from the See of Rome
And was buried in exile.[26]

The Bishop of Metz,[27] a long-time exile,
Followed the pope and suffered many things.
But he performed worthy deeds
Who did not suffer his house to be burned
When Attila burned the French cities
With flames. . . .[28]

Translated from the edition in *MGH*. Libelli de lite, 3:624.

OTTO OF FREISING, *THE TWO CITIES*,
BOOK 6, CHAPTERS 35 TO 36

35. In the one thousand and sixty-sixth year from the incarnation of the Lord, a star of the sort that is called a comet is said to have been seen and failed not to have its effect.[29] In the same year William, count of Normandy, conquered Greater Britain, which is now called England, killing Harold, its king, and, after reducing the entire province to slavery and settling the Normans there, ruled there himself as king. In the following year the emperor[30] took to wife Bertha, the daughter of the Italian margrave Otto, celebrating the wedding at Tribur. The Roman pontiff excommunicated the emperor after frequently summoning him to appear before him to do penance, and upon the pontiff's advice and authority (so tradition says) Rudolf, duke of Alemannia, was made emperor by certain nobles. Not long afterwards Rudolf was killed in open and public war and Herman, prince of Lorraine, was chosen in his stead; he too was killed not long afterwards by loyal supporters of the emperor. I have read and reread the history of the Roman kings and emperors, but I nowhere find that anyone of them was excommunicated by a Roman pontiff or deprived of his kingdom before this emperor—unless perchance one is to consider as equivalent to excommunication the fact that Philip was for a short time placed among the penitents by the bishop of Rome and that Theodosius was barred by the blessed Ambrose from the portals of the church on account of a bloody and murderous deed.[31]

36. At this point I think I ought to relate what above I postponed, the fact that the Roman empire—compared in Daniel to iron—had feet "part of iron and part of clay" (Dan. 2:33) till that it was struck and broken to pieces by a stone cut out of the mountain without hands. For, without the prejudgment of a better interpretation, how can I interpret "the stone cut out without hands" (Dan. 2:34) as anything other than the Church, the body of its Head, a body that was conceived by the Holy Spirit without carnal admixture, was born of a virgin and reborn of the Spirit and of water—a rebirth in

which mortal man had no part. . . . It was clearly the Church that smote the kingdom near its end (that is the meaning of "the feet"). The kingdom was of iron on account of its wars and of clay on account of its condition. The Church smote the kingdom in its weak spot when the Church decided not to reverence the king of the City as lord of the earth but to strike him with the sword of excommunication as being by his human condition made of clay. All can now see to what a mountainous height the Church, at one time small and lowly, has grown. What great calamities, how many wars and perils of wars followed in consequence of the weakness of the kingdom; how often unhappy Rome was besieged, captured, laid waste; and how pope was placed over pope even as king over king, it is weariness to record. In a word, the turbulence of this period carried with it so many disasters, so many schisms, so many dangers of soul and of body that it alone would suffice to prove the unhappy lot of our human wretchedness by reason of the cruelty of the persecution and its long duration. The aforesaid Pope Gregory was driven out of the City by the emperor and Guibert, archbishop of Ravenna, was thrust into his place. Gregory abode at Salerno and, as the time of his summons drew near, he is said to have remarked, "I have loved righteousness and hated wickedness; therefore I am dying in exile" (Ps. 45:7). Not only, then, was the kingdom severely smitten in the case of its emperor, who had been cut off by the Church, but the Church also suffered no little sorrow in being bereft of so great a shepherd, who had been notable among all the priests and bishops of Rome for his zeal and force of character. With so great a transformation, as the times were passing from perfection to overthrow, let us put an end to the sixth book that, with God's guidance, we may hasten on to the seventh and to that rest of souls which follows the wretchedness of this present life.[32]

Taken from the translation of C. C. Mierow, *The Two Cities: A Chronicle of Universal History to the Year 1146 A.D.* (New York: Columbia University Press, 1928), pp. 400–1, with minor verbal changes. The Latin text may be found in A. Hofmeister, *Cronica sive Historia de duabus civitatibus* (Hanover and Leipzig: Hahn, 1912), pp. 304–6.

GERHOH OF REICHERSBERG, *THE INVESTIGATION OF THE ANTICHRIST* 1:19

Many of the faithful and prudent believed that what was thus prophesied in the Revelation of John was fulfilled or began to be fulfilled from that time.[33] "When the thousand years have been completed, Satan will be loosed from his prison and will go forth and lead astray many nations that are at the four corners of the world, Gog and Magog'' (Rev. 20:7). Until that time, as we have said before, the same Satan had been bound through the Angel of Great Counsel in the abyss of the hearts of the very evil and by the huge chain of his deep malice. He was enclosed and ''sealed over for a thousand years so that he might not seduce the nations any more until the thousand years be finished.'' For ''after this,'' as the same passage says, ''it is necessary that he be released for a brief time'' (Rev. 20:1–3). At that very time at which the devil was freed as it were through King Henry (of whom we have spoken and will speak again), a thousand years had already passed from the Passion, when the devil was put in prison and sealed over. The devil, when truly free, began to rule as a tyrant. From that time began the split in the papacy and the conflict between *sacerdotium* and *regnum* which surely contributed to the loosing of Satan.

For as long as the priesthood remained strong, shining and burning through unity and devotion to religion, and as long as kingship with the co-operation of the priesthood was strong in good fear of evil works and not fear of good ones, Satan and evil men, his ministers, were bound in their lairs by these luminaries, like beasts, far from the presence of God. From the time when these two luminaries were moved against each other and failed in their devotion to religion, Satan was loosed. From that time one pope stood against another, the one attempting to loose what the other would bind and vice versa. From that time the priesthood was made like a smoking cloth through the evil of simony and the wickedness of incontinence so that in many it was evident as a fear not of evil works but of good ones. The rare bishop who wished to correct his clergy did not dare to do so through fear of the Roman curia, with whom even the wicked could find judgment for a price. Then ''it was night'' in which ''all the beasts of the forest wandered about, the whelps of the lions roaring to lay waste and to seek their meat from God'' (Ps. 103:20–21). Under a disguise of piety they hid their purpose, so that what they did in an evil and bestial manner might seem to be done at God's inspiration, that is, ''to seek their meat from God.''

Translated from the edition in *MGH*. Libelli de lite, 3:328–29.

HILDEGARD OF BINGEN, *SCIVIAS* 3:11

Then I looked to the North,[34] and there were five beasts standing. One was like a fiery hound, though not burning, one like a lion of tawny color, another like a pale horse, another like a black pig, another like a gray wolf. They were all turning to the West.[35] In the West before the beasts something like a hill with five peaks appeared so that a single cord was stretched from the mouth of each of the beasts to each peak of the hill. The cords were all somewhat blackish, especially the one which came from the mouth of the wolf and seemed part black and part white.[36]

Behold in the East I again saw above the cornerstone that youth whom I had previously seen clothed in a purple tunic above the corner of the shining wall and the stone wall of the building.[37] Now he appeared to me from the navel down so that you might see him gleaming like the dawn from the navel to the groin. There was at that place something like a lyre with its cords lying crosswise. From there to the bottoms of his feet, that is, to a measure of two fingers set across from above touching the heel, he was shaded. From the two-finger measure through the whole of his feet he appeared brighter than milk.[38]

The image of the woman before the altar in front of the eyes of God that I saw earlier was now also shown to me again so that I could also see her from the navel down. From the navel to the groin she had various scaly spots. In her vagina there appeared a monstrous and totally black head with fiery eyes, ears like the ears of a donkey, nostrils and mouth like those of a lion, gnashing with vast open mouth and sharpening its horrible iron teeth in a horrid manner.[39]

From that head to the knees the image was white and red, bruised as with many a beating. From the knees to the two white transverse zones which crosswise seemed to touch the bottoms of the feet from above, the image appeared to be bloody.[40] Lo, the monstrous head removed itself from its place with so great a crash that the entire image of the woman was shaken in all its members. Something like a great mass of much dung was joined to the head; then, lifting itself upon a mountain, it attempted to ascend to the height of heaven.[41] A stroke like thunder came suddenly and the head was repelled with such strength that it both fell from the mountain and gave up the ghost. After this a stinking cloud suddenly enveloped the whole mountain. The head was surrounded with such great filth in the cloud that the people standing by were struck with the greatest terror as the cloud stayed upon the mountain somewhat longer. The people standing there beheld it and struck with much fear said to each other: "Woe! Woe! What is this? What does that seem to be? Who will help us, unfortunate as we are? Who will deliver us? We are ignorant of how we have been deceived. Almighty God, have mercy on us. Let us, oh let us return. Let us prepare the covenant of Christ's Gospel, since we have been bitterly deceived.'' [42] Behold, the feet of the aforementioned female image appeared to be white, giving out a brightness above that of the sun. I heard a voice from heaven saying to me: ''Even though all things on earth are tending toward their end, so that the world with all its powers now weakened and oppressed by many hardships and calamities is bowed down to its End, nevertheless, the Spouse of my Son, though much weakened in her children, will never be destroyed either by the heralds of the Son of Perdition or by the Destroyer himself, however much she will be attacked by them. At the End of time she will arise more powerful and more secure; she will appear more beautiful and shining so that she may go forth in this way more sweetly and more agreeably to the embraces of her Beloved. The vision which you saw signifies all this in mystic fashion.'' [43]

Translated from the edition in *PL* 197, cc. 709A–710C.

13. Gerhoh of Reichersberg

Mention has already been made of the life of Gerhoh and the way in which his writings reflect the crisis of *regnum* and *sacerdotium*. In many ways the canon of Reichersberg is the most interesting of the twelfth-century apocalypticists before Joachim of Fiore, particularly due to the manner in which his vision of the End foreshadows some apocalyptic themes of the later Middle Ages.

Gerhoh's interests centered upon the historical significance of the Church and the stages of its history, though the scheme of the succession of empires is also found in his works. Patterns of history based upon the three Persons of the Trinity, the seven gifts of the Holy Spirit, and the four horsemen of the sixth chapter of Revelation are found in his writings; but most interesting of all is a four-age pattern of the Church symbolized by the four watches of the night in the Synoptic account of the miracle of Jesus' walking upon the water.[1] This scheme dominates his most overtly apocalyptic work, *The Fourth Watch of the Night*.

Gerhoh was much influenced by the Tyconian tradition of scriptural exegesis—the concept of the Antichrist as the historical continuum of those who have attacked true religion throughout history is a characteristic of his work.[2] The canon distances himself from earlier adherents of the Tyconian tradition, however, in the way in which he is eager to make use of apocalyptic themes to interpret the events of his own times, as well as in the expectation of the imminent End found in his last works.[3] He also broke with the Augustinian tradition that denied the validity of parallels between the Old and the New Testaments to stress the concordances between aspects of the history of Old Testament times and events in the current life of the Church.[4] While the reformer was not the first to indulge in this type of historicizing interpretation, his extensive use of it bears striking affinities to the concordances of Joachim, though there is no evidence that the Calabrian Abbot had direct knowledge of the German canon's works. Finally, as B. Töpfer has pointed out,[5] it is with Gerhoh that we begin to get the first hints of a unique

role for the papacy in the last times, though there is no precise figure of an
"Angelic Pope" present in his writings. The Bavarian canon's stress upon
the witness of poverty in the future papacy as a contrast to the avarice that is
the characteristic sin of the fourth age and his optimistic hope for a future
triumph of the Church form a glimmer of the new set of characters and new
scenes soon to take their place in the apocalyptic scenario.

THE FOURTH WATCH OF THE NIGHT

The third watch is believed to have been brought to an end and fulfilled by
means of a continual struggle of this sort waged by the Roman pontiffs from
Gregory I to Gregory VII of holy memory.[6] He struck the head from the
house of the wicked when he condemned King Henry who forced in Guibert
the schismatic and all those agreeing with him, especially the married and
simoniacal clergy.[7]

From then it appears that more dangerous times began, because then
there arose a new avarice in the city of Rome.[8] Previously, the Roman people used to pay their pastor free loyalty with due obedience, but when the
struggle between the priesthood and the kingdom arose, the citizens of
Rome who adhered to the pope did not wish to fight in such a war for
nothing. They demanded much money as a kind of salary owed for their
military service, and even when such service ceased in time of peace,
through noisy disturbance they claimed it as hereditary for themselves and
their children. For this reason they compelled the Roman pontiffs to gather
gold and silver from everywhere to satisfy their avarice which, like a fire,
never says "Enough!" In this fourth watch widespread avarice swollen with
desire for gain rules the whole Body of Christ from head to foot. A tasteful
poet has said of this:

> Immoderate love of possession still vexes Rome.
> Only the wrath of the fearful Judge will extinguish it.[9]

This is true. In the other watches men triumphed through divine aid—in the
first watch through the martyrs, in the second through the confessors, in the
third through the holy fathers, the teachers of moral discipline, among
whom was Pope Gregory. In this fourth watch the entire sea is disturbed
down to the depths by a strong wind violently opposed to the disciples of
Christ. Since to be a disciple of Christ is so defined that he who does not
renounce all he owns is not able to be his disciple, the spirit of avarice,

which not only strongly holds on to its own but with desire pants to obtain what does not belong to it, is a most strong wind opposed to this teaching. So it comes about that soldiers are not content with their wages nor clerics with theirs, namely, that those who serve the altar should live from the altar and have from it food and clothing with which they ought to be content. From avarice, this root of all evil (1 Tim. 6:10), many evils are born. Whatever sane and true doctrine is opposed to them is despised as a phantasm. For in the first watch he who disputed against idolatry was seen to have a foundation of firm truth through the witness of accompanying miracles. Likewise in the second watch the defenders of the Catholic faith were seen and found to rest upon a solid foundation of Scripture. So in the third watch the teachers of morals were seen to speak the truth, since each man's conscience reproved him with thoughts either accusing or defending conscience itself.

Now in vain does one pour out a sermon where there is no hearing, in the sight of men who think that gain is goodness. Anything said against the gain which is held to be goodness is thought to be an empty phantasm. In the midst of this, "Blessed is he who understands about the poor and needy man" (Ps. 40:2), that is, he who understands about the needy Roman pontiff, since he requires much in the face of Roman avarice, not indeed to sate it, insatiable as it is, but to mitigate it in any way whatever, since it is intolerable. In the midst of the avaricious the pope is as a poor man, not having what they demand from him. When he sees the strong wind of such great avarice he is afraid lest he be deserted or attacked by the Romans if he does not satisfy their thirst. From this point he begins to sink by expecting, though not demanding, gifts during the judgments that he gives freely, since the power of judging was freely given to him. Were he to sell his judgments not only by expecting something but even by demanding what is not owed, either through himself or through some Jezites,[10] he would not only begin to sink through hidden desire of gain, but he would be altogether sunk through open profit. Alas for such profit! . . . Because the abbot of Clairvaux of holy memory in his work *On Consideration*[11] clearly noted such mutilations of the Church we can forbear any exaggeration of the fact. We desire that all the successors of Peter, even if with God's permission they begin to sink, will not be totally submerged. May they walk upon the sea with the right hand of Christ holding them up, and, being received by Christ into the ship committed to him, may they hasten to the shore.

Translated from *De quarta vigilia noctis,* ch. 11 (*MGH. Libelli de lite,* 3:509–10).

The Approach of the End

We can say something sure about past times and events that we know about through trustworthy histories, but about things in the future we are better able to conjecture than to assert, as when we read something prophesied before our time. Many affirm that Antiochus Epiphanes was a forerunner of the final Antichrist,[12] which is quite credible since he, greedy and avaricious beyond the usual, despoiled and profaned the Temple of God that had been enriched and adorned by Seleucus, the king of Asia, and other kings when the Holy City as yet was at peace. . . .

From the proliferation of such simoniacs, so prevalent in the last times, will come the final Antichrist. Like another Antiochus he will grow strong against the few elect. Although like the Maccabees they are few, they will prevail against him when Christ comes to their aid. Christ will destroy Antichrist without a hand being raised, just as we read that Antiochus, somewhat humiliated by the Maccabees, was struck by God with an incurable disease . . . (2 Macc. 9:5 sqq.). So struck down and made humble, that wicked man showed first in his person the kind of disease by which the final Antichrist will be humbled when the Lord Jesus slays him with the breath of his mouth and destroys him by the brightness of his coming (2 Thess. 2:8). At the time when the first coming of Christ was drawing near, the ancient serpent (already a great dragon) in the person of the precursor of the Antichrist attacked more cruelly than before the people from whom Christ was expected to be born. More than he had previously, he also polluted, despoiled, and profaned the Temple in which Christ was to be presented with sacrificial victims, lest the prophecy be fulfilled which says: "The ruler whom you seek will soon come to his Temple" (Mal. 3:1). (A Temple polluted with such filth might seem to be not his but the devil's!) So today, when the Second Coming of Christ himself is approaching or already soon imminent, [13] that same dragon, destined to be sent into the abyss, in the person of the final Antichrist rages against the Holy Church in the cruelest fashion, the Church which is the living Temple of God in which Christ himself is immolated every day and offered to his Father in mystery.

Surely the Temple of God is polluted through the forbidden sacrifices of the simoniacs and nicolaites, as is said: "O God, the gentiles have entered your dwelling place, they have defiled your holy Temple" (Ps. 78:1). When this happens, Satan, more avaricious in the person of the final Antichrist than in all the preceding Antichrists, shows himself as God, indeed is even lifted up above everything that is termed God, or worshiped as God

(2 Thess. 2:4). It will go so far that God, offended by simony and by the shamelessness of his ministers, will say to those who no longer serve him but Mammon and Beelphegor in the house of the Lord: "Behold your house is left you as a desert" (Matt. 23:38), just as during the reign of Antiochus, his very unclean and greedy predecessor, the house of the Lord was deserted in the destroyed city of Jerusalem.

We trust in the mercy of God. Through the holy Maccabees and their faithful assistants the house of the Lord was then purified from the uncleanness of idols, so that the Temple front was adorned with gold crowns. When the altar that had been profaned by the gentiles was destroyed, a new altar was dedicated and gave great joy to the people. So now before the Lord comes in open fashion the Church of God will be thus purified from the pollutions of filth and simony and will be adorned with gold crowns as it were. And so there will be great joy among the Christian people at the destruction of the final Antichrist through the brightness of the Lord's coming which like the dawn of the sun is thus believed to come before the Lord himself will rise to judge. He who then did wonders in Israel, giving victory to his people, is now also able to do great things among his people against the people of the Antichrist, as we have recently heard has happened at Rome.[14] Many princes along with the emperor, the patron of schismatics, had gathered together there against the Lord and his anointed (Ps. 2:2). There were also schismatic bishops with the leader of the schism, Guido, the successor of Octavian.[15] They did their will, crowning the empress[16] in the emperor's presence, and consecrating, or rather execrating, the intruding bishops. The anger of God suddenly came upon them in terrible fashion and killed their fat ones and hindered their elect (Ps. 77:31). Many of them died suddenly and the rest withdrew in confusion when God openly showed that he cursed those that Guido blessed. As he said of such men: "I will curse your blessings" (Mal. 2:2). Thus will the people of Antichrist be cursed when the justice of God triumphs in the people of God.

Translated from *De quarta vigilia noctis*, ch. 16 (*MGH*. Libelli de lite, 3:522–23).

14. The Ages of the Church

Speculation on the succession of ages had formed a part of the apocalyptic tradition from the very beginning. There are numerous schemata, both from the intertestamental period and from the early centuries of the Christian era. The most popular were the six-age theory based upon the six days of creation and the four ages rooted in the Pauline understanding of the history of salvation. Many symbolic presentations of these divisions were passed on to later authors by the Fathers.[1]

Given the interest in the theory of history present in the twelfth century, the extent of concern with the division of ages should come as no surprise. Not all authors who indulge in such speculation are overtly apocalyptic. Nevertheless, the concern with the determination of the stages of history is always a near neighbor to expectations of the End—the desire to locate one's own time in the grand scheme of history frequently serves to show its proximity to the final events.

Especially evident in the twelfth-century authors is the shift of emphasis toward the determination of the ages of the history of the Church in the time of the New Covenant. For patristic authors, Christ had come at the beginning of the last age of history. They showed little interest in subdividing what for many of them could at best be a time of brief duration. By the twelfth century men looked back upon a millennium of the Church's existence with all its great upheavals and changes. Some felt that the peace of the Church established by Constantine in the fourth century marked the beginning of the final millennial age of the binding of Satan, an age rapidly drawing to a close. Various authors looked upon the changes of their time— the conflict between the Church and the empire, the crusades, the growth of new forms of religious life, the spirit of avarice that seemed to characterize the new economy—and sought to find an explanation for them in the light of God's salvific plan for history. Such concerns were central to the historical theorists and apocalypticists of the twelfth century.

Rupert of Deutz, in the Prologue to his vast *The Holy Trinity and Its*

Works, sketched a threefold division of history, not the traditional Pauline one of *ante legem, sub lege, sub gratia,* but one that was Trinitarian in structure. Rupert's division differed from the later threefold pattern of Joachim of Fiore, however, in that the age of the Spirit was a present reality, not one to be awaited in the future. The abbot of Deutz was concerned with the total character of salvation history and showed no overt apocalyptic interests here.[2] Hugh of St. Victor (c.1090–1141) spent many years teaching in Paris as one of the foremost thinkers of the early Scholastic period. His wide-ranging interests were pervaded by a concern for the history of salvation; he thought that the End was near, though his writings are not notably apocalyptic. In Hugh's symbolic writings on the ark of Noah we note the appearance of the *translatio* theme found in Otto of Freising and others,[3] a notion frequently connected with the scheme of the four monarchies of the second chapter of Daniel.

Even more famous than Hugh was the Cistercian abbot Bernard of Clairvaux (1090–1153), the foremost spiritual leader of his time and the greatest of monastic authors. Bernard made frequent use of Antichrist rhetoric in the many quarrels in which he was involved, most notably against the Antipope Anacletus II[4] and against Peter Abelard,[5] but an important letter indicates that the Cistercian disagreed with his friend and contemporary St. Norbert, who thought that the final Enemy would come in the current generation.[6] Bernard proposed a four-age division of the Church's history. In most texts this is tied to an exegesis of the four temptations described in Psalm 90:5–6,[7] but in one *Sententia* the four ages are symbolized by the four horses of Revelation chapter six.[8] The saint's increasing pessimism after the failure of the Second Crusade may have moved him to more openly apocalyptic views toward the end of his life.[9]

Another contemporary of Bernard has bequeathed us what is perhaps the most original early twelfth-century thoughts on the meaning of the history of the Church. Anselm of Havelberg (c.1100–1158) was one of the first disciples of Norbert, the reformer of the canonical life. Although he was made bishop of the frontier diocese of Havelberg in 1129, he spent much of his career outside the see, serving on a wide variety of missions for a succession of popes and emperors. In 1149 at the request of Pope Eugene III he composed the *Dialogues,* whose first book gives us his progressive views on meaning of sacred history. The three books of the *Dialogues* are primarily concerned with polemics with the Eastern Church (Anselm had twice been on embassy to Constantinople). In the first book, however. the bishop was also concerned to defend the new forms of canonical orders against conservative critics troubled by the "novelties" of the time. Anselm's dynamic conceptions of growth (*incrementum*) and diversity (*varietas*) in the life of the Church, and the optimism that this brought to his historical outlook, make him in many ways unique among early twelfth-century authors.[10] Anselm fleshed out this view by evolving a pattern of seven states in the life of the Church, which he found symbolized in the seven seals of the Book of Revelation. While he was not the first to use the seven seals as a basis for a division of ages,[11] and while his determinations are not as historicizing in intent and execution as those of Joachim were to be, Anselm's concentration on this apocalyptic pattern is very much a prelude of things to come.

RUPERT OF DEUTZ, *THE HOLY TRINITY:* PROLOGUE

Seeking to adore the glory of the Holy Trinity in this pilgrimage, let us bring the mirror of its works to our understanding, so that even though we cannot fix our weak eyes on the splendor of its majesty due to our mortal condition, we may at least walk without error by beholding its works to a small degree in its light. The work of the Trinity has three parts from the founding of the world to its End. The first is from the rise of the first light to the fall of the first man. The second from the fall of the same first man to the Passion of the second man, Jesus Christ, the Son of God. The third from his Resurrection to the End of the world, that is, to the general resurrection of the dead. The first work is proper to the Father, the second to the Son, the third to the Holy Spirit.[12] Plainly the Trinity is inseparable and the one God works in undivided fashion; but in the case of each of these Persons, that is of Father, Son, and Holy Spirit, just as there exists a personal property, so too there is a proper action to each to be considered in the perfection of the world, namely, creation pertains to the Father, redemption to the Son, and the work that is the renewal of creation to the Holy Spirit. . . .

This three-part book is for the honor of the Father, the Son, and the Holy Spirit. The first part deals with the first week of days;[13] the second concerns the week of the following ages of the world;[14] the third deals with the double resurrection of the dead.[15] For this reason each week is completed and perfected in the eighth day.

Translated from *PL* 167, cc. 198D-200B.

HUGH OF ST. VICTOR, *THE MYSTICAL ARK OF NOAH* 4:9

The works of restoration [16] are all those things that have been done or will be done for the salvation of man from the beginning of the world to its End. Among these we must consider the deeds themselves, the persons through whom, for whose sake, and among whom they were done, as well as the places and times where and when they were performed. Three types of order can be seen in the works of restoration: place, time, and dignity. According to place, we consider whether a thing happened near or far; according to time, whether before or after; according to dignity, whether lower or higher. This final type has many divisions. . . .

The order of place and the order of time seem to agree almost completely in the course of events. Thus it appears to be established by divine providence that what was done at the beginning of the ages, at the outset of the world, took place in the East, and finally, as time runs along to its End, the completion of events should penetrate even as far as the West. Hence we may acknowledge that the End of the world approaches because the sequence of events has reached the geographical end of the world. [17] The first man was placed in the East, in the Garden of Eden already prepared, so that from this source his posterity might spread throughout the world. After the Flood, the chief realm and head of the world was in the East with the Assyrians, the Chaldaeans, and the Medes. Then it came to the Greeks, and finally, nearly at the End of time, the highest power came to the Romans, who dwelt in the West, almost at the edge of the world. Thus by a course of events running in a straight line from East to West, anyone who has inquired diligently can see that everything that was done on the right hand or on the left, that is, to the North or the South, agree so completely in meaning that the action of Divine Providence cannot be doubted. . . .

Therefore, the order of dignity pertains to the height of the ark, the order of time to its length, the order of place to both together. To the length of the ark belongs the text: "The kingdom of heaven is like the head of a household who went out early in the morning to hire workers for his vineyard, and again at the third hour, the sixth hour, and the ninth hour. And going out at the eleventh hour he saw others standing by and sent them into his vineyard" (Matt. 20:1–7). [18] The text, "Their sound has gone forth into the whole world by their word unto the ends of the earth" (Ps. 18:5), pertains to the breadth. To the height belongs: "The tribes, the tribes of the Lord, go up there, the testimony of Israel to confess the name of the Lord"

(Ps. 121:4). I will briefly tell you what is left rather than delay over each point. The whole of Sacred Scripture is contained in these three measurements. History measures the length of the ark because the order of time is discovered in the course of events. Allegory measures the breadth of the ark because the cohesion of the faithful depends upon participation in the mysteries, and tropology measures the height of the ark because the dignity of merits grows with the increase of virtues. . . .

Translated from *PL* 176, cc. 677B–678D.

BERNARD OF CLAIRVAUX, *ON THE SONG OF SONGS* 33:7

I can still try to assign these four temptations in their order to the Body of Christ, that is, the Church, if the length of the sermon does not prove wearisome. I will run through it as briefly as I can. Regard the primitive Church. Was it not at the beginning very fiercely penetrated by the "fear at night"? (Ps. 90:5) For it was night when everyone who killed the saints thought that he was paying homage to God. When this temptation was overcome and the tempest stilled, the Church became glorious, and according to the promise made to her was briefly placed on high as the pride of the ages. The Enemy, in sorrow at being frustrated, craftily changed himself from the "fear at night" to the "arrow flying in the day" (Ps. 90:6), and by that wounded some members of the Church. Vain men desiring glory and wishing to make a name for themselves arose. They left the Church and for a long time afflicted their Mother in different perverse doctrines. But this pest was also expelled by the wisdom of the saints, just as the first one was by the patience of the martyrs.

Look at these times, free indeed by God's mercy from either of these evils, but plainly foul with the "thing that walks in darkness" (Ps. 90:6). Woe be to this generation from the leaven of the Pharisees which is hypocrisy. (If that ought to be called hypocrisy which is now unable to hide because it is so prevalent and so impudent that it does not even try!) Today the stinking corruption slowly spreads throughout the whole Body of the Church, both more desperate as it is more widespread and more dangerous as it is more internal. Were an open heretic to arise, he would be cast outside and wither away. Were a violent enemy to come, the Church might hide herself from him. But now whom will she cast out or from whom will she hide herself? All are friends, all are enemies. All are supporters, all are adversaries. All of the household, but none peaceful. All are neighbors, but each one seeks his own advantage. They are ministers of Christ and serve the Antichrist. . . .[19]

Translated from the edition of J. Leclercq, *Sancti Bernardi Opera* 1:243–44.

THE LETTER OF GERARD TO EVERMORD

The priest Gerard sends an offering of prayer and brotherly love to Evermord, beloved father.[20] Look upon the conditions of this time and you will find it full of dangers. In Revelation John prophesied that Satan would be freed after a thousand years (Rev. 20:3). Eight hundred and nine years have passed from the time of Constantine and Silvester when, in heavenly fashion, peace was granted to the Holy Church after the triumphant struggle of the martyrs. Thus Satan, meditating on the long-desired end of this peace now almost completed, shakes the chains binding him with such great force that he seems to have been already loosed in the present time rather than to be freed in the near future. Charity, the strongest of bonds, has grown cold; the sacraments of the Church are considered worthless, and the justice that looked down from on high has left earth behind and gone back to heaven. The direction of all prelates is spurned, virtue has become silent, every vice falsely usurps the name and mantle of virtue. In summary fashion I have thus described to you the bonds with which Satan was bound.

Again, because John saw two beasts (Rev. 13), the one signifying the forerunners of the Antichrist, the other the Antichrist himself, in my fearful conjectures I have a presentiment of the attack and onslaught of the former beast. I then ask, supplicate, and beg you to meet with Margrave Albert before the conference of the princes at "The Wood" and carefully to persuade him to show himself a spokesman of Christ and defender of the monasteries with faithful devotion. . . .[21]

The peace of the Church is the barrier against those evil ones whom John foretold as the beast coming out of the sea. Just as no time has lacked attackers of the Church, no time has been without those who devoutly defended her. . . .[22] If Albert does not give you a favorable hearing after supplications and exhortations, you should boldly say to him, just as if Christ were speaking through you and in you, that Christ will not desert the

Church for which he has suffered. . . . You should also say to him that it would be better for the man who through schism or destruction of the peace opens the door through which the former beast may enter (the one still excluded from the Church by the bars of peace) that he had never been born. You should also say to him that the world has already sworn itself to peace, but let that peace not be turned into war against Holy Church! Above all, persuade him to be careful that innumerable evils do not surface at this time.

Translated from G. Hertel, *Urkundenbuch des Klosters Unser Lieben Frauen zu Magdeburg*, pp. 17–19. I owe my acquaintance with this text to W. Froese.

ANSELM OF HAVELBERG, *DIALOGUES*, BOOK I

Diversity in the Life of the Church

It clearly appears that the one Body of the Church is given life by the one Holy Spirit. He is both unique in himself and diverse in the manifold distribution of his gifts. The Body of the Church, vivified by the Holy Spirit, distinct and discrete in its different members in various times and ages, began with Abel, the first just man, and will be consummated in the last of the elect.[23] It is always one in faith, but diversified in many ways by its multiple variety of life. . . .

From the coming of Christ to the day of judgment, the period that distinguishes the sixth age and in which one and the same Church is renewed by the presence of the Son of God, it is never found in a single uniform state, but the states are many and diverse. . . .

Translated from the text of G. Salet, *Anselme de Havelberg, Dialogues I (SC 118)* chs. 2 and 6 (pp. 44, 64).

The Seven Seals

Truly the seven seals which John saw as he tells us in his Revelation are seven successive states of the Church from the coming of Christ until all things will be consummated at the End and God will be all in all. "When the Lamb opened the first of the seven seals, lo, there was a white horse. He who sat upon it had a bow and was given a crown. He went forth to conquer" (Rev. 6:2). The white horse is the first state of the Church, gleaming and very beautiful in the brightness of miracles. All admired and praised it in its newness. The one who sat upon the horse and held a bow is Christ ruling the Church and humiliating and casting down the proud with the bow of apostolic teaching. . . .

"And when he opened the second seal, a red horse went forth. He who sat on him was given the power to take peace from the earth so that men might kill each other, and he was given a great sword" (Rev. 6:3). Behold the second state of the Church is openly revealed to the disciple that Jesus loved. For what is the going forth of the second horse except the blood of the martyrs poured forth as a testimony of Christ when peace was taken from the earth and a great sword was given to persecute the Church? This state of persecution began with the glorious proto-martyr Stephen, whom the Jews stoned. After his triumph, such a great persecution blazed forth that the Church was no longer able to remain in the sole location of Jerusalem; but the apostles, having dispersed throughout the whole world, preached the faith of Christ and by preaching ended their lives in martyrdom. . . .

"When he had opened the third seal, there was a black horse and he who sat upon him had a scale in his hand" (Rev. 6:5). Behold the third state of the Church in which the black horse emerges. The black horse is the dark teaching of the heretics whom the great dragon we mentioned raised up against the Church of God so that what he was not able to swallow up earlier when the blood of the martyrs was poured out he might now disturb by the most wicked dogma of the heretics. . . .

"When he had opened the fourth seal, lo, a pale horse appeared and he who sat on him was named Death, and Hell followed after him" (Rev. 6:7–8). This truly is the fourth state of the Church in which the most serious and deadly danger is in false brethren. Just as a pale color is a mixture of white and black and does not show itself a straightforward white but has both colors in a false fashion, so indeed false Christians or false brethren of whom there is now an innumerable multitude, confess Christ publicly but deny him by their deeds. . . .

In this state of the Church religious men appear, lovers of truth, restorers of the religious life. . . .[24] And so it happens that by the wondrous dispensation of God, as from generation to generation one always sees the growth of new forms of religious life, the youth of the Church is renewed like that of the eagle (Ps. 102:5). By this it is both able to fly higher in contemplation and with almost unblinded eyes can behold the rays of the true sun more plainly.

So do you think it possible that in so great a multitude of good men there should be no scandal found in false brethren? Would that it were so, would that it were truly so. . . . We grow up together in one field, but at the time of the harvest we will not all be gathered together in one storehouse (Matt. 13:30). They are with us and we are with them. We run the race together, though with different paths and with different intention, until this fourth state of the Church is ended and the saints follow the Lamb wherever he goes (Rev. 14:4), and those who carry the name of pallor and death will be buried in hell.

"When he had opened the fifth seal I saw under the altar the souls of those killed for the Word of God . . ." (Rev. 6:9–11). This is the fifth state of the Church. The Church has labored in persecution and grown in patience; labored in the subtle falseness of heretics and grown in wisdom; labored in false brethren and hypocrites and grown in toleration. Now the souls of the saints under the altar that is Christ, although they have already merited rest in the spilling of their blood, seeing the endless miseries of the Church in her labor cry out for it in a loud voice of compassion. . . .[25]

"When he opened the sixth seal there was a great earthquake" (Rev. 6:12). This is the sixth state of the Church in which there will truly be a great earthquake, that is, the very strong persecution which will come in the times of the Antichrist. . . . "When he opened the seventh seal there was a silence in heaven of the space of about a half hour" (Rev. 8:1). The seventh seal is the seventh state of the Church in which there will be silence. After the tribulations of the Church which brought forth the sons of God in great sadness, after the judgment that will be at the coming of the Son of God, in a moment, in the flicker of an eye, all things will be brought to conclusion. Then there will be the silence of divine contemplation, the renewal of the year of jubilee, and the celebration of the eighth day of infinite beatitude.

Translated from the text of G. Salet, *Anselme de Havelberg: Dialogues I* (*SC* 118), chs. 7–13 (pp. 68–114).

15. *Imperial Apocalyptic*

Despite the growth of forms of apocalyptic centering on the life of the Church, the twelfth century did not witness the demise of imperial apocalyptic expectations. At the beginning of his *Deeds of Frederick Barbarossa,* written 1156–1158, Otto of Freising somewhat scornfully recounts a prophecy that had circulated in France in 1146 while Louis VII was preparing to embark on crusade. This obscure text, also known through other sources,[1] appears to be a French variant of the Last Emperor myth.

Like many twelfth-century German authors, Otto himself had no place for a Final Emperor in his scheme of the Last Things. But there is one important text from Hohenstaufen Germany that shows that there were those for whom the imperial revival under Barbarossa called up the memory of old traditions. The *Play of Antichrist,* which survives in a single manuscript from the Benedictine monastery of Tegernsee in Bavaria, appears to have been composed about 1160 at the court of Frederick. Whether the drama was ever actually staged is not known; it is the earliest and the most impressive of the Antichrist plays that proliferate in the following centuries.[2] Heavily dependent on Adso and the Pseudo-Methodius, the play is a conservative, pro-imperial account of the End, in which the papacy plays a very secondary role and in which there are clear criticisms of the reformed church.[3]

In order to understand the selection given here it is necessary to read a brief outline of the drama. After the introduction of the characters, the first part recounts the German Emperor's subjection of the world to his sway through his conquering the haughty French King and recalling the King of the Greeks and the King of Jerusalem to obedience. The King of Babylon attacks Jerusalem and is defeated by the Emperor, who then fulfills the traditional role of the Last World Emperor by giving up his crown. Unlike earlier accounts, however, the Emperor does not die but resumes his role as King of the Germans. The second part is devoted to the career of the Antichrist, whose appearance is triggered by the Emperor's abdication.[4] Antichrist's companions, Hypocrisy and Heresy, effect his victory. Hypocrisy helps him triumph over the leaders of the Church (a clear swipe at the reforming party);[5] the Kings of Jerusalem and of the Franks also agree to become his men. The King of the Germans defeats the forces of the Antichrist in battle but is then converted by his miracles. The King of Babylon is defeated; but the Jews, at first converted by Antichrist's preaching, are convinced by Enoch and Elijah of their error. After the Antichrist kills the two prophets, he is immediately destroyed by Christ. While the pro-German *Play of Antichrist* ends in fairly conventional fashion, its author displays considerable originality not only in adopting a new genre for the promulgation of his message but also in many of the details of his presentation.

OTTO OF FREISING, *THE DEEDS OF FREDERICK BARBAROSSA*

Now as to my saying that at that time the western peoples were inspired by the spirit of the pilgrim God,[6] let no one interpret this to mean that we believe in some pilgrim God, but let him know that we borrowed this term from the document which was read repeatedly in those days in many parts of Gaul. It goes like this: "I say to you, L, shepherd of bodies, whom the spirit of the time of the pilgrim God has inspired, addressing you by the first letter of the sum total that makes up your name." In the course of this writing, under a certain husk of words concerning the storming of the royal city and also of ancient Babylon, a triumph over the entire Orient, after the manner of Cyrus, King of the Persians, or of Hercules, was promised to the aforesaid Louis, King of France. Hence such words as these are found therein:

When you have arrived at the side of the eternal seated square and come the side of the eternal standing squares and to the product of the blessed number through the first actual cube,[7] raise yourself to her whom the Angel of your mother promised to visit and did not visit.[8] You shall extend from her even to the penultimate—when the promiser ascends her first, the promise fails on account of the best goods.[9] Then plant your rose-colored standards even as far as the uttermost labors of Hercules, and the gates of the city of B will open before you. For the bridegroom has set you up as a mainsail, he whose bark has almost foundered and on whose peak is a triangular sail, that he who preceded you may follow you.[10] Therefore your L will be turned into a C, who diverted the waters of the river, until those who toil to procure sons have crossed the stream.[11]

This document was then considered by the most excellent and pious personages of the Gauls to be of so great authority that it was declared by some to have been found in the Sibylline books, by others to have been divinely revealed to a certain Armenius. But whosoever that prophet or charlatan was who spread this abroad, let him determine whether its fulfillment may yet be expected in the future, or if (being scorned as already having failed of fulfillment) the fact that it gained some credence may be attributed to Gallic credulity.

The translation is that of C. C. Mierow, *The Deeds of Frederick Barbarossa* (New York: Columbia University Press, 1953), pp. 25–26, with some minor corrections. The Latin text may be found in G. Waitz, *Ottonis et Rahewini Gesta Friderici I Imperatoris* (Hanover: Hahn, 1884), pp. 8–9.

THE PLAY OF ANTICHRIST

The Last Emperor Lays Down his Crown.

In the meantime, while the Emperor gathers his army, an Angel of the Lord suddenly appears and sings: [12]

> Judea and Jerusalem have no fear,
> Knowing that tomorrow you shall see God's help!
> For your brethren are at hand who will free you,
> And will overcome your enemies in power.

Then the chorus:

> Judea and Jerusalem have no fear; tomorrow we will go forth and the Lord will be with you. Alleluia! [13]

In the meantime, the Emperor and his men go out to battle, and when the responsory is finished they fight with the King of Babylon. When they have overcome him and he begins to flee, the Emperor and his men enter the Temple. After he has worshiped there, taking the crown from his head and holding it along with the scepter and imperial globe before the altar he sings: [14]

> Receive what I am offering! With a bounteous heart
> I resign the empire to You, King of Kings,
> Through whom all rulers reign. You alone can
> Be called Emperor and are ruler of all things.

Having placed them on the altar, he returns to the throne of his ancient realm, [15] *while Ecclesia, who went to Jerusalem with him, stays on in the Temple. . . .* [16]

The Appearance of the Antichrist

Then, while Ecclesia, Gentilitas, and Synagoga sing in turn, as above, the Hypocrites come forth in silence with the semblance of humility, bowing down on all sides and winning the favor of the laity. Finally, all come before Ecclesia and the throne of the King of Jerusalem, who receives them fittingly and submits himself totally to their advice. Immediately, Antichrist enters clothed with a breastplate under his other garments. Accompanying him are Hypocrisy on the right and Heresy on the left. He sings to them:

> The hour of my kingdom is come! [17]
> Without delay, through your activity
> I will ascend the throne of the realm.
> The world will adore me and no other!
>
> I know that you are prepared for this;
> I have nourished you for it thus far.
> Behold! Your labor and your hard work
> Are now necessary to me in this effort.
>
> The nations honor Christ;
> They venerate and adore him.
> Therefore, blot out his memory,
> And transfer his glory to me!

To Hypocrisy:

> I place the foundation on you.

To Heresy:

> Through you will come the growth.

To Hypocrisy:

> Build up the laity's support of me!

To Heresy:

> Tear down the clergy's teaching!

Then they sing:

> Through us the world will believe in you;
> The name of Christ will yield to you.

Hypocrisy:

> Through me the laity will give support.

Heresy:

> Through me the clergy will deny Christ.

Then they go before him, and he follows a little way back. After they have come before the throne of the King of Jerusalem, Hypocrisy whispers to the Hypocrites and tells them of the coming of the Antichrist. They immediately go to meet him singing:

> Holy religion has already long faltered.
> Vanity has seized Mother Church.
> Why this waste through these adorned ones?
> God does not love worldly priests.
> Climb to the height of kingly power!
> Through you the remnants of old age will be changed! [18]

Then the Antichrist:

> How shall this be? I am a man unknown.[19]

Then they sing:

> By means of our counsel the whole world will support you.
> We have won the support of the laity.
> Now do you corrupt the teaching of the clergy!
> With our help you will take this throne,
> By your deserts you will complete the rest.

Then Antichrist comes before the throne of the King of Jerusalem and sings to the Hypocrites:

> Me whom you conceived in the womb of the Church
> You have finally brought forth after long efforts.[20]
> Therefore, I will ascend the throne and subject all realms;
> I will put away the old laws and give forth new ones.

Then they lay down their outer garments before him, go up with drawn swords, and deposing the King of Jerusalem, they crown the Antichrist and sing:

> May thy hand be strengthened and thy right hand exalted! (Ps. 89:13)

Then the King of Jerusalem goes alone to the King of the Germans and sings:

> I have been deceived by those who appeared to be good;
> I have been robbed by the fraud of the dissemblers.
> I thought that the condition of the Kingdom was favorable
> If it was ordered by the laws of such men.
> While you were the defender of the high dignity of Rome,
> The state of the Church was honorable.
> Now that the evil of your withdrawal is exposed,
> The law of destructive superstition flourishes.[21]

Translated from the edition of K. Langosch, *Geistliche Spiele* (Basel-Stuttgart: Schwabe, 1957), pp. 206, 214–16.

16. The Erythraean Sibyl

Another late twelfth-century text testifies to the importance of imperial apocalyptic at the same time as it demonstrates further dependence of Western
prophecies upon Eastern forbears. The *Vaticinium Sibillae Erithraeae* survives in a number of manuscripts from the late thirteenth to the sixteenth
centuries.[1] As it presently stands, the text dates from the second half of the
thirteenth century; but Evelyn Jamison has convincingly argued that the information given in the preface is not literary fiction but historical fact and
that the core of the work is older than the surviving versions.[2] The
Erythraean Sibyl, like her Tiburtine sister, proved to be such a popular
prophetess that her predictions were subject to frequent later revisions.

The preface tells us that the work was originally composed in "Chaldaean," that is, Syriac, and translated into Greek by Doxapater. No such
Syriac text survives, but C. H. Haskins was the first to note that Nicholas
(later Nilus) Doxapatres was a well-known Byzantine scholar and monk who
took refuge in Sicily in the 1140s after falling from imperial favor.[3] In any
case, the number of Greek forms and the existence of passages praising the
glory of Constantine's city argue that our Latin text is based upon a Greek
original. There is no reason to doubt that it was brought to Sicily from the
treasury of the Emperor Manuel Comnenus (1143–80),[4] where it was translated by the noted scholar Eugenius of Palermo (c. 1130–1203), a high official under King William II (1154–1160), later appointed admiral, or highest minister of the realm, under Tancred in 1190. The strongly theocratic
character of the Sicilian kingdom whose rulers had adopted many aspects of
Byzantine statecraft and ceremony argues that a text which gave such an important place to imperial prophecies would find a warm welcome.

Like the Tiburtine Sibyl, the work is a sketch of world history purporting to have been given to the Greeks after the conquest of Troy. It contains
three sections, a division reflected in some of the manuscripts.

The first part begins with the history of Greece and Rome, briefly
sketches the rise and triumph of Christianity, recounts the appearance of a

beast who will attack Christianity (probably Mohammed), and concludes with an account of a "most mighty lion" who will check the beast—almost certainly a reference to the Last World Emperor.[5] It is quite possible that the core of this part goes back to a Syriac source,[6] a simplified parallel to the Pseudo-Methodius.

The second part (originally the third, but later transposed) deals with events in Sicily and Byzantium from the 1180s to the 1250s, including long accounts of the careers of Frederick II and his sons. Whether the earlier parts of this go back to Eugenius or not, in its present form it is the work of a Sicilian Joachite writing sometime after 1250.

Finally, the third or properly apocalyptic section describes the combat with the Antichrist and the End of the world. Jamison holds that it is Eugenius' reworking of the Greek text, since among other signs of the End it contains an account of the natural disasters that struck Sicily in 1169 to which the admiral refers in other works. In terms of both its complicated textual history and its later influence, the Erythraean Sibyl is one of the most important witnesses to the continued alliance between the Sibylline tradition and imperial apocalyptic.

SELECTIONS FROM PARTS I AND III

Part I

This book is taken from the book called *Basilographia,* that is the "Imperial Writing," which the Erythraean Sibyl of Babylon made at the request of the Greeks in the time of Priam the king of Troy. Doxapater,[7] a father of extraordinary skill, translated it from Syriac into Greek, then it was taken from the treasury of Manuel, emperor of the Greeks, and translated from Greek into Latin by Eugenius, admiral of the king of Sicily.[8]

You have asked me, most famous tribe of Danaans,[9] to record in writing the fate of the Greeks and the ruin of Troy—what has been foreordained for the most noble offspring of Laomedon, what for Diomedes that very mighty leader, what for the Teucrian halls, what for the heifer of contention.[10] Nor am I to omit what after the dust of Ilion will come to pass in the world and in the case of the noble generations of the goats,[11] so that they may be wary in the future. You have sent the Pellidean and Calchas off to Delphi,[12] you have consulted a work of man, sought out a clay god. How can the divine mind be known from such a source? Now you have disturbed

my womanly rest so that my deepest judgment may be forced out in an unusual manner. After the deepest contemplation I respond. . . .[13]

There will be a horrible beast coming from the East.[14] His roaring will
be heard as far as the nations of Africa; he will have seven heads,[15] un-
counted scepters, and six hundred and sixty-three feet.[16] He will oppose the
Lamb so that he may blaspheme his covenant, enhancing the waters of the
dragon. The kings and nobles of the world will sweat profusely, and his feet
will not be lessened. Two entirely similar stars[17] will first arise against him
and will not prevail until the Abomination comes and the will of the Most
High is consummated, as we make clear below.

A most mighty lion of heavenly color, spotted with gold, with five
heads and fifty feet will roar from the West. He will make an attack on the
beast and crush his power. He will devour the tail of the beast, but will not
harm his head or feet at all. After this the lion will die and the beast will be
strengthened; he will live and reign until the Abomination comes.[18] After
the Abomination the Truth will be revealed and the Lamb will be known; the
lions and kingdoms will bow their necks to him. All the inhabitants of the
earth will come together so that there may be one flock (John 10:16) and
they may be ruled by one rod. And there will be a short space of time.

Part III

The Last Judgment will follow the Abomination. Signs will precede.
There will be four kinds of unusual color in the elements and a change of
course in the heavenly bodies. There will be a celestial sign in that the air
will appear at times yellow, at times pitch-black, now green, now clear red.
Apollo will be split, now in ten, now in four, now in two parts; the moon
will run together with the sun. Those dwelling on earth will be struck with
fear when they see the stars all bloody. At the same time the earth will give
forth sweat, bloody fountains will well up in different places, and there will
be a fearful sign of commotion. There will be collision of kingdoms, seizure
of thrones, earthquakes, and famines. Out of desire for food mothers will
abase their sons and daughters in debauchery. . . .[19] All these things are indications of the Abomination for whom there is no rule.

When three signs come the inhabitants of the earth should know that he
is near. In the city of Aeneas a one-hundred-year-old woman will bear twins
with the aid of the faithless.[20] A burning river will issue from Mt. Etna and
devour the inhabitants. After this two peaks will crash together in the snowy

mountains, the earth there will be opened in an abyss, and a snowy mist will ascend to heaven.[21]

After these things, there will be a gathering together of many nations bestial in their manner of life and a division of the world into ten scepters. The vilest forms of copulation will precede pregnancies, the worst of all being that of the Abomination. He will then kill many kings whom he has put under his yoke. The Spouse will be silent, the cock will grow hoarse, and there will be abuse of the Lamb.[22] Heaven, the sun, and the elements will seem to be a testimony to the Abomination in that he will do wonders, make the stars dark, weaken the perfect, regain the Jews. All this will happen so that he may renew what was old and cast out what has been renewed. . . .[23]

The Last Judgment will be imminent; the signs will precede it.[24] The sun will be frequently eclipsed and stretching out in vast fashion will destroy the inhabitants of Egypt.[25] The Euphrates will be dried up to a mere trickle; Etna will be laid open on two sides, Avernus will roar, and three parts of the inhabitants of Sicily will perish.[26] Pharos will swell up most horribly and flood the nearby areas.[27] After this the sea will sink to the depths and the fish gathered together will give forth a roar. Then the heavens will open in four parts, there will be thunder, and the inhabitants of the earth will hear threats of Judgment. Ineffable things will blare forth on the trumpet. Blameless heralds will announce the destruction of all things saying: "Let there be humility and repentance!" . . .[28]

Then all the kings and princes will appear and behold the Lamb who pays back all men upon his throne of terror. No discrimination of wealthy or poor will take place there, but only the weighing of merits. Then crimes will be made evident, fear and trembling and horror of the abyss set out for punishment will strike all so that there will be weeping and gnashing of teeth. They will stretch out their hands in prayer, but the Lamb will be inflexible; he will be fearful in punishing. In his sight there will be lightning and thunder, merits along with sins. Blessing will be on his right; curses will come from his left. He will judge the good and the evil to lift the former on high and allow hell to swallow the latter to the fate of the demons. This is the end of the book of the Erythraean Sibyl of Babylon.

Translated from the longer text edited by O. Holder-Egger, "Italienische Prophetieen des 13. Jahrhunderts," *Neues Archiv* (1890), 15:155–56, 162–63, 170–73.

17. Joachim of Fiore

Joachim of Fiore (c.1135–1202) is not only the most important apocalyptic author of the Middle Ages, but one of the most significant theorists of history in the Western tradition.[1] His writings are extensive—some still are unedited, others are available only in defective early printings.[2] The secondary literature about the Abbot and his thought is not only vast, but also filled with marked divergencies of opinion on central issues.[3] The following sketch is selective and in part controversial.[4]

Born in Calabria and in early life an official in the Sicilian court at Palermo, Joachim experienced a conversion, traveled to the Holy Land, and returned to Calabria where he entered the Benedictine monastery of Corazzo about 1171.[5] He soon became abbot of the house, and in his desire to strive for the most perfect realization of the monastic life (a constant theme in his career), worked to have Corazzo incorporated into the Cistercian order. It was on this task that he journeyed to the important monastery of Casamari south of Rome about 1183. Here he had the visions that launched him on his writing career and changed the course of Christian apocalypticism.[6] As an early biographer tells us, "He remained at work in Casamari about a year and a half, dictating and correcting at the same time the *Liber Apocalypsis* and the *Liber Concordiae*. At the same time he there began the *Liber Psalterii decem chordarum*."[7] In May 1184 he was called before Pope Lucius III to expound a mysterious prophecy attributed to the Sibyl and was given papal encouragement for his projects.

For the remaining eighteen years of his life Joachim was not just a monastic prophet speculating on some distant mountain top, but also a figure of international repute. Besides the three major treatises, he produced more than a dozen other writings. His meetings with the popes of the time and the undoubted approval of his works by several pontiffs argue that he served as something like an apocalyptic adviser to the peace party in the Roman curia (the group seeking compromise with the empire) in the period between the death of Alexander III in 1181 and the accession of Innocent III in 1198.[8]

Joachim himself was by no means pro-imperial, but his consciousness of an imminent crisis in history led him to believe that the Church must assume the role of a suffering servant rather than that of a belligerent in the face of imperial attack. During the same period Joachim became dissatisfied with the Cistercian order of his time. By about 1190 he had founded a new house of his own at Fiore in the remote fastnesses of the Sila plateau of Calabria, an action for which he was condemned by the Cistercian General Chapter in 1192. The house was the source from which spread the Florensian order.[9]

The Abbot met with many of the important personalities of the day, including Richard the Lionhearted, the Emperor Henry VI, the Empress Constance, Pope Innocent III, and the young Frederick II.[10] Innocent's election marked a definite victory for the anti-imperial party in the curia, and it seems no accident that the Fourth Lateran Council held under his auspices in 1215 condemned Joachim's views on the Trinity, though even this condemnation was tempered by personal praise for the Abbot.

Joachim's thought revolves around three central issues: the interpretation of Scripture, the mystery of the Trinity, and the meaning of history. The Abbot of Fiore's view of Scripture is in one sense conservative, in another radical in the extreme.[11] Like many of the theorists of history of his century, he protested against the rise of Scholasticism,[12] believing that theology could not be distinguished from the interpretation of Scripture, the *divina pagina*. But Joachim broke with the traditional theory of the four senses of Scripture to create an idiosyncratic scheme of twelve in which seven "typical" senses manifest the action of the Trinity throughout the course of history.[13] The "concordance," or "letter to letter" comparison between the Old and the New Testaments are at the root of the gift of understanding by which the Abbot claimed to be able to find the events of past, present, and future clearly manifest in the Scriptures—a thought that would have horrified Augustine.

The Abbot's theology of the Trinity was also both conservative and radical in the context of his time. On the one hand, it was an archaizing protest against the technical distinctions of Scholastics such as Peter Lombard;[14] on the other, it spoke to an issue that Scholastic theology neglected to its detriment: the involvement of the Trinity in history. For Joachim the inner meaning of the historical process could not be understood apart from the mystery of the Trinity.

Joachim's thought about the meaning of history is difficult to reduce to any simple formula, not least of all because the Abbot, like many other apocalyptic writers, expresses himself in symbolic rather than in discursive ways. From this perspective, the *figurae,* or illustrated diagrams, which he added to his works and which in expanded fashion were put together, probably at his direction, into the famous *Book of Figures* are of special importance. As Marjorie Reeves puts it: "Joachim's was a mind wonderfully fertile in imagery and one has the sense that his strange and intricate patterns of thought convey themselves more immediately today through these powerful *figurae* than through the endless repetitions of his somewhat turgid Latin."[15]

A study of the Book of Figures and the major works reveals Joachim's obsession with the ordering of the patterns of history. A bewildering variety of patterns emerges from his works—the course of the Two Testaments, each divided into seven parallel periods creating what Marjorie Reeves has called the "pattern of double sevens"; the distinctive division of history into three overlapping "states" (*status*—given debates about the meaning of the term, the Latin will be used here) respectively attributed to the Father, the Son, and the Holy Spirit; and the use of the pattern of twelve built out of five representing the second *status* and seven representing the third. It is obvious from the *Book of Figures,* most of whose drawings are concerned with presenting aspects of the order of history, that Joachim saw these patterns as complementary and not as opposed. The secret of their complementarity, however, is not always evident.[16]

What is unique about Joachim's attempts to synthesize the symbolic patterns of historical order is the dynamic and organic character of his vision. Trees are the most frequent images chosen to present the patterns,[17] the interrelations of ages are a key factor, and organic metaphors of germination and fructification come constantly to his mind. Alone with Anselm of Havelberg in his time Joachim shares an organic and partially optimistic view of the course of history.

Joachim's optimism, of course, was a tempered one. In apocalyptic fashion he saw his own age as one of unique crisis. The Abbot's historicizing interpretation of Scripture enabled him to see in the events of the day— the continuing conflict between *regnum* and *sacerdotium,* the resurgence of Islamic power under Saladin, etc.—signs of the advent of the Antichrist. There is good evidence that Joachim believed that the Antichrist had already been born and would soon come into his power.[18] In line with thinkers like Rupert, Gerhoh, and Hildegard, there is no place in Joachim's system for a Last Emperor—his gaze is fastened on the Church. Two potent forces will carry the banner of God in the dark days ahead, a holy pope who will preach to the pagans at the time of the Antichrist,[19] and the *viri spirituales,* two groups of religious, one of preachers, the other of contemplative hermits, who will resist his onslaught. Joachim played a key role in the development of the myth of the pope of the last days, and was the ultimate source of the intense apocalypticism found in certain circles of religious orders who came to identify themselves with his hoped-for "spiritual men."[20]

Both of these important innovations were part of a wider framework, the myth of the third *status,* Joachim's most powerful creation. For the Abbot of Fiore the defeat of the Antichrist at the end of the second *status* would usher in a new stage of history,[21] the *status* of the Holy Spirit, in which a renewed Church would reign in peace and contemplation. It seems likely that Joachim thought of the coming time of the *ordo novus,* or "new people of God," as a real historical period, though he was hesitant to speculate about its length. His scheme was in one sense a revival of early Christian millenarianism; but it was also much more, a distinctive form of utopianism that sought not only to give ultimate historical validation to the institutions to which Joachim was most devoted, especially monasticism, but which also represented an original viewpoint on the theme of *reformatio* conceived of as a new divine irruption into history rather than as a return to the past.

Perspectives on the significance of Joachim's vision of history are almost as many as the interpreters. Older debates centered around the question of the orthodoxy of the Abbot's ideas concerning the third *status.* Did the concept of a coming time of the Holy Spirit destroy the centrality of Christ in the history of salvation? What would happen to the institutions of the present Church in the time to come?[22] Answers differ regarding particulars, but as I have elsewhere remarked:

Joachim's stress on the domination of the spiritual and charismatic over the institutional and rational in the future church was diametrically opposed to the forces that triumphed in the thirteenth century. . . . In this sense the concept of the third age in the writings of Joachim of Fiore was a radical critique of the thirteenth-century church.[23]

The Joachite tradition was a quasi-revolutionary element in the later Middle Ages, and though his would-be disciples went far beyond the Abbot of Fiore in many ways, he cannot be absolved of all responsibility for what was to come.

Even more complex are the philosophical debates over Joachim's significance. The ideological spectrum ranges from interpretations which see him as "the spirit of *revolutionary Christian social utopianism*" who "set a date . . . for the communist kingdom"[24] to those who find him at the origin of the Gnostic spirit that dominates "the self-interpretation of modern political movements."[25] In any case, the Abbot's organic and melioristic vision of history was to have many heirs in the West, even if few of them were in any sense direct. Joachim marks the beginning of a new stage in the history of the apocalyptic tradition and in European philosophy and theology of history.

JOACHIM'S VISION OF THE MEANING OF REVELATION[26]

Having gone through the preceding verses of the Book of Revelation to this place (Rev. 1:10), I experienced such great difficulty and mental constraint beyond the ordinary that it was like feeling the stone that closed the tomb opposed to me. . . . Since I was involved in many things,[27] forgetfulness led the matter far away. After a year, the Feast of Easter came round. Awakened from sleep about midnight, something happened to me as I was meditating on this book, something for which, relying on the gift of God, I am made more bold to write. . . .

Since some of the mysteries were already understood, but the greater mysteries were yet hidden, there was a kind of struggle going on in my mind. . . . Then, on the above-mentioned night, something like this happened. About the middle of the night's silence, as I think, the hour when it is thought that our lion of the tribe of Judah rose from the dead, as I was meditating, suddenly something of the fullness of this book and of the entire agreement of the Old and the New Testaments was perceived by a clarity of understanding in my mind's eye.[28] The revelation was made when I was not even mindful of the chapter mentioned above.

Translated from *Expositio in Apocalypsim*, f. 39r–v (see note 2).

COMMENTARY ON AN UNKNOWN PROPHECY[29]

In the year of Our Lord 1184, in the month of May, the second indiction, when the Lord Pope Lucius was staying at the city of Veroli, inspired by the example of such a great man,[30] I, Joachim, the abbot of the monastery of Corazzo located in Calabria in the province of Cosenza, thought to unravel the words found this year in the Roman curia . . . and in a true interpretation to explain what in them seems to me to be in agreement with the divine authorities. Their content is thus:

Rome will be aroused against the Roman, and the Roman who was put in the place of the Roman will threaten Rome. The staffs of the shepherds will be removed, and their consolation will be in repose. The zealous will be disturbed and will pray, and repose will be in the tears of many. The humble one will sport with him who rages, and destroying rage will be flattered. A new flock will slowly proceed to the mass, and those who were given a title of old will be fed on short rations. The hope of those who hoped has been frustrated because consolation rests in the one who provides security. Those who walked in darkness will come to the light, and what was divided and dispersed will be made one. A substantial cloud will start to rain since he who will change the world has been born. The lion will be substituted for by lambs and lambs will ravage lions. Rage will rise up against the simple, and a weakened simplicity will draw breath. Honor will be changed to disgrace and the joy of many will be sorrow.[31]

These words were found in the year of our Lord 1184 among the books which belonged to Master Matthew of Angers, the venerable cardinal priest of San Marcello.[32] While we carefully weigh their content to explore its mysteries we unaffectedly adopt a mournful style, noting before everything else that mystery contained in the prophecy of Micah as a type of the Church. "Bewail," he says, "and be troubled daughter of Sion, because now you will go forth from the city and live in the country to be led as far as Babylon" (Mic. 4:10).

For we should remember that the Hebrew people bore seven special persecutions in which without doubt the seven special tests of Christians are signified. The Apostle testifies to this when he says that "all things happened to them in figure" (1 Cor. 10:11). Just as in the Old Testament, when the seven tribulations were finished, the Savior who was to redeem the human race came into the world, so when just as many persecutions against the Church have been completed, the punishing Judge of this world will make his appearance.[33]

The first persecution against Israel was that of the Egyptians, the second that of the Midianites, the third of the other nations, the fourth of the Assyrians, the fifth of the Chaldaeans, the sixth of the Medes and Persians, the seventh immediately following that of the Greeks under Antiochus. If there was time and place, a long discussion might be had of these; but in order to proceed as quickly as possible, contracting something important in summary fashion, let us return to the material to be treated.

Those seven tests which the sons of Israel underwent are the seven persecutions of the Church. They are partly manifested by the course of history and partly by the sayings of the prophets. The first persecution of the Church was that of the Jews, the second of the Pagans, the third of the Arians (this is that of the Goths, Vandals, Alemanni, Lombards). At the same time Rome was violently shaken in the four parts of the world so that the vision of Daniel would be fulfilled which said: "The third beast was like a leopard having four heads" (Dan. 7:6). The fourth persecution, that of the Saracens takes the place of that of the Assyrians, so that this persecution devastated many Greek churches, just as the former had devastated the ten tribes. Therefore in the times of Gregory the Syrian pope and of Zachary his successor this persecution rather severely hemmed in the eastern and southern zones, as one can read, so that the emperor of Constantinople was scarce able to defend his metropolis against the Saracens.[34] Just as the Lord, moved by loving kindness at the tears of Hezekiah added fifteen years to his life and promised that he would protect and defend the city of Jerusalem from the Assyrian kings (Isa. 38:1–6), so, having heard the prayers of the Roman Church, he raised up to faith the Church which had despaired of its own safety. She who in fear of the Saracens (who were like the swelling sea) used to tremble at being devoured on all sides, during the reign of the devout Charles, king of the Franks, was given courage by many victories and rejoiced that she enjoyed the protection of Christ. Therefore, from the time of Pope Zachary, in whose days Italy enjoyed widespread peace, these words began to be fulfilled. . . .

There remains for us that other and worse Babylonian persecution, the fifth. In it mother Sion is led away to Babylon. The days are at hand of which the Savior said: "Days will come when you will desire to see a single day of the Son of man" (Luke 17:22). "There was then an abundance of peace until the moon was taken away" (Ps. 71:7), that is, until the Roman Church, borne away in exile, lost the splendor of its brilliance. Since it is already in the cloud of darkness, there are persecutions left, the first of which will especially injure the clergy, while two following not long after will be against all in general . . .

The mystical manifestation of past events explicitly suggests that this threatens. Therefore, as it is said in those words written down earlier and recently found: "Rome will be aroused against the Roman." What was done some time ago openly proclaims it. For Rome was aroused against the Roman Pope Alexander, and because she condemned the special glory divinely paid to him, by quite a just judgment it happened in heaven that "the Roman who was put in the place of the Roman will threaten Rome." [35] But before this threatening of Rome the approaching day of the Lord will declare those things which are to come when the time is favorable. Since it is necessary that Antichrist appear before the great day of the Lord, it is also required that tyrants precede Antichrist as Daniel and John in Revelation testify. Among the other things that he heard through angelic revelation was: "The fourth beast will be the fourth kingdom in the world, and will destroy the whole earth and crush it. Furthermore the ten horns which you saw on the beast were ten kings of its kingdom. And another king will arise after them who will be stronger than the former ones and will humble three kings; and he will speak against the most High and crush his saints, etc." (Dan. 7:23–25, Rev. 17:12). Lo, he is the Antichrist preceded by the ten terrible tyrants of whom we read in Revelation: ". . . the ten horns which you saw on the beast, these hate the fornicator called Babylon and will make her to be desolate and stripped; they will eat her flesh and burn it with fire" (Rev. 17:16). Which Babylon? Could it be the metropolis of the Chaldaeans? Of course not, but the one which it signifies. "For the letter kills, but the spirit gives life" (2 Cor. 3:6). I think you understand that I know which Babylon this is, which the Chaldaean Babylon is, who the king of Babylon is; but I prefer in the meantime merely to mention them, rather than give an explanation. [36]

Translated from the edition in McGinn, "Joachim and the Sibyl," lines 10–81, 91–114.

THE THREE *STATUS*

The first of the three *status* of which we speak was in the time of the Law when the people of the Lord served like a little child for a time under the elements of the world. They were not yet able to attain the freedom of the Spirit until he came who said: "If the Son liberates you, you will be free indeed" (John 8:66). The second *status* was under the Gospel and remains until the present with freedom in comparison to the past but not with freedom in comparison to the future. [37] For the Apostle says: "Now we know in part and prophesy in part, but when that which is perfect has come that which is in part shall be done away with" (1 Cor. 13:12). And in another place: "Where the Spirit of the Lord is, there is liberty" (2 Cor. 3:17). Therefore the third *status* will come toward the End of the world, no longer under the veil of the letter, but in the full freedom of the Spirit when, after the destruction and cancellation of the false gospel of the Son of Perdition and his prophets, those who will teach many about justice will be like the splendor of the firmament and like the stars forever.[38] The first *status* which flourished under the Law and circumcision was begun with Adam. The second which flourished under the Gospel was begun by Uzziah. The third, insofar as we can understand from the number of generations, was begun at the time of St. Benedict. Its surpassing excellence is to be awaited near the End, from the time Elijah will be revealed and the unbelieving Jewish people will be converted to the Lord.[39] In that *status* the Holy Spirit will seem to call out in the Scripture with his own voice: "The Father and the Son have worked until now; and I am at work."[40] The letter of the Prior Testament seems by a certain property of likeness to pertain to the Father. The letter of the New Testament pertains to the Son. So the spiritual understanding that proceeds from both pertains to the Holy Spirit. Similarly, the order of the married which flourished in the first time seems to pertain to the Father by a property of likeness, the order of preachers in the second time to the Son, and so the order of monks to whom the last great times are given pertains to the Holy Spirit. According to this, the first *status* is ascribed to the Father, the second to the Son, the third to the Holy Spirit, although in another way of speaking the *status* of the world should be said to be one, the people of the elect one, and all things at the same time belonging to Father, Son, and Holy Spirit. Nor is this to be thought contrary to the authority of the Fathers when they speak of the time before the Law, the time under the Law, and the time under Grace. Each one is said to be necessary in its own class.[41]

Translated from *Expositio in Apocalypsim*, f. 5r–v.

THE PAPACY AND THE SPIRITUAL MEN

The Book of Concordance
    The end of the solemn mystery is also numerically given when David says in the Book of Psalms: "For forty years I was with this generation and

I have said that they always erred in their hearts" (Ps. 94:10). And if the sixfold number of perfection requires that the labor of the Church be completed as if in six weeks,[42] then the forty-second generation in the Church will begin in a year or hour which God knows.[43] In this generation first of all the general tribulation will be completed and the wheat carefully purged of all tares, then a new leader will ascend from Babylon,[44] namely a universal pontiff of the New Jerusalem, that is, of Holy Mother the Church. His type is found written in Revelation: "I saw an angel ascending from the rising of the sun having the sign of the living God" (Rev. 7:2).[45] With him are the remnants of those who were driven out.[46] He will ascend not by speed of foot nor change of place, but because full freedom to renew the Christian religion and to preach the word will be given to him. The Lord of hosts will already begin to reign over the whole earth.

Translated from *Liber Concordiae novi ac veteris Testamenti,* f. 56r (see note 2).

Treatise on the Four Gospels [47]

Therefore when such a child had been manifested in the Church of God, he was indeed contemplative, just, wise, and spiritual. Hence he was able to succeed the order of bishops established by the Lord to follow him in the active life, as Solomon succeeded King David, as John the Evangelist succeeded Peter, the prince of the apostles, or rather as Christ himself succeeded John the Baptist. Joyful and strengthened, the pope will withstand these things with equanimity and will suffer the torments of the Antichrist knowing what the Lord said to him in the person of Peter, "When you are old, another will bind you and lead you where you do not wish" (John 21:18). The aged Simeon will receive the child in his arms when the successors of Peter to whom the privileges of the faith and discernment between sacred and profane are given will see that order which follows Christ's footsteps in virtue and will support it with the protection of his authority.[48] He will confirm it by the words of his testimony, announcing that the oracle of the prophets is fulfilled in it in saying: "The kingdom which is under the whole heaven will be given to the people of the Most High" (Dan. 7:27). Nor will the pope be able to grieve over his own dissolution since he will know that he will remain in a better succession.[49]

We know that one order designated by the predecessor and another by the successor does not bring about difference of faith but the proper character of the forms of religious life. When any order begins to exist in solemn fashion it keeps the same name as long as it continues in the same form; but if some depart from it, and, having taken up another, better, form are changed for the better, they are not now said to be of the same order, but of another proceeding from it.[50] Can he who sees that he will be succeeded in such fruit grieve that partial perfection in him will cease when it is followed by universal perfection? No, no! Let such a thought be far from Peter's succession! Let not envy languish over the perfection of the spiritual order which he will see to be one spirit with his God and walking according to his doctrine in all the paths of his commandments.[51]

Translated from E. Buonaiuti, *Tractatus super quatuor Evangelia di Gioacchino da Fiore* (Rome: Tipografia del Senato, 1930. Fonti per la Storia d'Italia, No. 67), pp. 86–88.

Exposition on the Apocalypse

We think that in him who was seen sitting on the white cloud and was like the Son of Man (Rev. 14:14) there is signified some order of just men to whom it is given to imitate the life of the Son of Man perfectly . . . and nevertheless to have a tongue learned in preaching the Gospel of the Kingdom and in collecting the final harvest of the Lord's granary. . . .

Now we must see about the man who went forth from the Temple which is in heaven and had a sharp sickle (Rev. 14:15–16). . . . He went forth from the Temple that is in heaven . . . because that life which is signified by the cloud is lower than that which is signified by heaven. . . . Although he who ascended upon the white cloud of the contemplative life presses forward in comparison with those who are involved in worldly cares, he who went forth from the Temple which is in heaven seems to be of a higher form of life. The freedom of teaching and spiritual doctrine signified in the cloud is one thing, the freedom of the love of divine contemplation another. Wherefore, just as in him who was like the Son of Man there is to be understood a future order of perfect men preserving the life of Christ and the apostles, so in the angel who went forth from the Temple in heaven is to be seen an order of hermits imitating the life of the angels. . . .

An order will arise which seems new but is not. Clad in black garments and girt with a belt from above, they will increase and their fame will be spread abroad. In the spirit of Elijah they will preach the faith and defend it until the consummation of the world. There will also be an order of hermits imitating the angels' life. Their life will be like a fire burning in love and zeal for God to consume thistles and thorns, that is, to consume and extinguish the wicked life of evil men so that they do not abuse the patience of God any longer. I think that in that time the life of the monks will be like rain watering the face of the earth in all perfection and in the justice of brotherly love. The life of the hermits will be like a blazing fire. . . . The former order will be milder and more pleasant in order to gather in the crop of God's elect in the spirit of Moses. This order will be more courageous and fiery to gather in the harvest of the evil in the spirit of Elijah.[52]

Translated from *Expositio in Apocalypsim*, ff. 175v–176r.

THE ANTICHRIST

After that wound [to the sixth head of the dragon][53] which has already in some part begun, there will be victory for the Christians and joy for those who fear the name of the Lord at the casting down of that head of the beast over which the sixth king reigns and at its being brought almost to destruction and annihilation. Then after a few years its wound will be healed,[54] and the king who is over it (whether it be Saladin if he is still alive or another in his place)[55] will gather together a much larger army than before and will wage general war against God's elect. Many will be crowned with martyrdom in those days.

In that time the seventh head of the dragon will also arise, the king who is called Antichrist and a multitude of false prophets with him. We think that he will arise from the West and will come to the aid of the king who will be at the head of the pagans.[56] He will perform great signs before him and his army, just as Simon Magus did in the sight of Nero. . . . The Lord will shorten those days for the sake of the elect so that they will not be longer than forty-two months.

It is not to be thought, as the holy Doctors say, that the End of the world will come soon after he is judged, just because he is said to come at the End of the world.[57] The End of the world and the last hour are not always to be taken for the very last moment, but for the time of the End, as John, who wrote a thousand years ago, openly teaches: "Little children, this is the last hour, and as you have heard that Antichrist will come, there are now many Antichrists. And so we know this is the last hour" (1 John 2:18). We should note that John and John's Master say many Antichrists will come, but Paul predicts one Antichrist. Just as many pious kings, priests, and prophets preceded the one Christ who was king, priest, and prophet, so many unholy kings, false prophets, and Antichrists precede the one Antichrist who will pretend to be king, priest, and prophet.

After the destruction of this Antichrist there will be justice on earth and an abundance of peace. "The Lord will rule from sea to sea, from the river to the ends of the earth" (Ps. 71:8). Men will turn their swords into ploughshares, their spears into sickles. One nation will not lift up the sword against another; there will be no more war (Isa. 2:4). The Jews and many unbelieving nations will be converted to the Lord,[58] and the whole people will rejoice in the beauty of peace because the heads of the great dragon will be crushed. The dragon himself will be imprisoned in the abyss (Rev. 20:2–3), that is, in the remaining nations which are at the ends of the earth. The number of years, months, and days of that time are known only to God. When they will have been completed and led to their end, Satan again will be released from his prison to persecute God's elect since there will still be that remaining Antichrist signified by the tail of the dragon.

Translated from L. Tondelli, M. Reeves, and B. Hirsch-Reich, *Il Libro delle Figure* (Turin: SEI, 1953), plate XIV, lines 9–55 *passim*.

THE NEW PEOPLE OF GOD

Title. The Arrangement of the New People of God in the Third State after the Model of the Heavenly Jerusalem.[59]

I. The Oratory of St. Mary, the Holy Mother of God, and of Jerusalem the Holy. The Dove. The Seat of God. The Spirit of Counsel. The Nose.[60]

This house will be the mother of all and in it will be the Spiritual Father who will govern all.[61] All will obey his direction and will. The brothers of this house will live according to order in all things so that the example of their patience and sobriety may be able to inform the others. In fasting let them follow the Cistercian model. At the will of the Spiritual Father who will live in that house the brethren of the lower orders can pass to the stricter life. . . .

II. The Oratory of St. John the Evangelist and all the Virgin Saints. The Eagle. The Spirit of Wisdom. The Eye.

In this oratory there will be approved and perfect men who aflame with spiritual longing wish to lead a contemplative life. They will have individual cells to which they may quickly retire when they wish to pray. These cells will not be where each one might wish, but near the cloister according to the arrangement and will of the Spiritual Father who is over all. . . .

III. The Oratory of St. Paul and all the Holy Doctors. The Man. The Spirit of Understanding. The Ear.

In this oratory there will be learned men as well as those who are being taught and are teachable in divine things. These are men who both desire and are able to devote themselves to reading and to spiritual teaching more than the rest. . . .

IV. The Oratory of St. Stephen and all the Holy Martyrs. The Calf. The Spirit of Knowledge. The Mouth.

In this oratory will be those brethren who are strong in manual labor, but who are not able to grow in spiritual discipline as much as is required. . . .

V. The Oratory of St. Peter and all the Holy Apostles. The Lion. The Spirit of Fortitude. The Hand.

In this oratory will live the elderly and delicate brothers who, possibly because of weak stomachs, are not able to bear the full austerity of the Rule in fasting. . . .

Between this monastery and the place of the clerics there ought to be a distance of about three miles.[62]

VI. The Oratory of St. John the Baptist and of all the Holy Prophets. The Dog. The Spirit of Piety. The Foot.

In this oratory will be gathered priests and clerics who wish to live a chaste and common life, but not to abstain completely from the eating of meat and warm clothing. . . . They will obey their prior according to the direction and will of the Spiritual Father who is over all . . .

Between these two oratories there ought to be a distance of about three stadia.

VII. The Oratory of St. Abraham the Patriarch and of all the Holy Patriarchs. The Sheep. The Spirit of Fear. The Body.

Under the name of this oratory will be assembled the married with their sons and daughters in a common form of life. They sleep with their wives for the sake of procreation rather than for pleasure. At assigned times and days they will abstain from them by consent in order to be free to pray (1 Cor. 7:5), taking into consideration the constitution and age of the youths lest they be tempted by Satan. They will have their own homes and guard themselves against every accusation. Their food and clothing will be in common, and they will obey the Master according to the direction and will of the Spiritual Father whom all these orders will obey as a new ark of Noah perfected to the cubit. . . . Let there be no idle among these Christians, those who do not work for their bread, so that each may have that from which to provide something for those who are in need. Each one shall work at his own craft and the individual trades and artisans shall have their own superiors. Therefore, whoever is able to work and does not is to be compelled by the Master and censured by all. Their food and clothing should be simple as befits Christians. Worldly clothing is not to be found among them nor dyed cloth. Honest and approved women will work wool for the benefit of the poor of Christ, and they will be like mothers of the others, instructing the young women and the girls in the fear of God. They will give tithes to the clerics of all that they possess for the support of the poor and strangers, as well as for students. They should do this so that if they have an abundance and a few of the others do not, according to the will of the Spiritual Father the surplus shall be taken from those who have more and given to those who have less. Thus there may be no one needy among them, but all things held in common possession.[63]

Translated from Tondelli, Reeves, and Hirsch-Reich, *Il Libro delle Figure,* plate xii.

JOACHIM'S TESTAMENT[64]

Brother Joachim, called Abbot of Fiore, wishes eternal salvation in the Lord to all to whom this letter may be shown. As can be known from the letters of the former Pope Clement which we have,[65] and from the orders of Pope Lucius and of Pope Urban,[66] I have composed certain works and I am still writing to the extent that this labor recommends itself to the glory of God and the profit of readers. Insofar as God inspired me and I was able, I have completed the *Book of Concordance* in five volumes, the *Exposition on the Apocalypse,* divided by titles into eight sections, and the *Ten-Stringed Psaltery* in three volumes, besides other things I included in the minor works, the *Against the Jews,* and the *Against the Enemies of the Catholic Faith.*[67] If I am allowed while still in this body something further for the instruction of believers in Christ, and especially of monks, I will take care not to postpone it. Due to lack of time, I have thus far not been able to present my works, with the exception of the *Book of Concordance,* to papal judgment for correction, in case there are some things in them which I do not reject or which I do not realize are in need of correction. Man is uncertain of the number of his days. It may happen that I should die before I would be able to present them to the Apostolic See in conformity with the commands I have received. I undertook these compositions on the condition that my labor be his and his teaching authority be in them in every way. By almighty God I ask my fellow abbots and priors and the other brothers who fear God, and I command by that authority which I seem to have, that those who possess this letter or a copy as a form of will, may collect as quickly as possible all the works I have written up to the present and anything new which it may happen I compose to the day of my death. Leaving the originals in safekeeping, let them present them to papal scrutiny. Let them receive correction from that same Seat in my place and explain my faith and devotion to it. I have always been prepared to hold what it commanded or will command. I would defend no view of mine against its holy faith, fully believing what it believes, receiving its correction in morals as well as in doctrine, rejecting whom it rejects, accepting whom it accepts, and firmly believing that the gates of hell will not prevail against it. If it be disturbed for an hour and blown about by storms, its faith cannot fail until the End of the world. I, the Abbot Joachim, have caused this to be written and signed it with my own hand in the year of Our Lord 1200. I pledge that I hold as is contained herein. Signature. I, Joachim, Abbot of Fiore.

Translated from *Expositio in Apocalypsim,* Epistola prologalis (unnumbered folio).

Part Two: A.D. 1200–1500

Introduction

The bewildering mixture of traditions, the number of surviving texts, and the notorious difficulty of generalizing about the history of the three centuries in question make it difficult to introduce this second section of our history. The sheer extent of material has suggested an organization based more upon themes and periods than upon famous authors and texts. I am particularly conscious of the many omissions that I have been forced to make. If at times less well-known works have been chosen, it is because they illustrate significant themes so well.

From the point of view of form, there are some important shifts and interesting innovations made during this period. Perhaps the most important of the new forms in Latin apocalyptic are the Papal Prophecies, short obscure predictions of future popes with accompanying illustrations. Admirable teaching devices, similar combinations of text and image had already been foreshadowed in Joachim's *figurae* and were to be used in other contexts in the centuries to come.[1] The immediate prototypes of the popular Papal Prophecies are to be found in twelfth-century Byzantium, a sign that the interchange between East and West was not dead during the final age of the life of the Eastern empire.

To some degree there is a more "Scholastic" aspect to many late medieval apocalyptic works. Most of the *literati* who wrote the texts had been trained in the procedures of the Schools—the practice of commentary on a text, the citation and concordance of discordant authorities, the articulation of a logical structure for the presentation of an argument. Probably as a result of this, the commentary method came to be applied to non-scriptural texts with increasing regularity. Not only Daniel and John, but other vatic authorities old and new—the Sibyl, Merlin, Methodius, the Oracle written on silver tablets and delivered by an angel to the Carmelite hermit Cyril— were all the subject of learned commentaries. But the logical, discursive procedures of the Schools did not drive out the visionary element from the apocalyptic tradition. Texts containing new revelations proliferated in the late Middle Ages. Sometimes the obscure products of pedantic littérateurs, sometimes the direct and seemingly artless presentations of naive visionaries, such material is rarely lacking in the period.

The history of these three centuries must be viewed at least in part under the star of Joachim. While it would be an error to restrict the history of apocalypticism from 1200 to 1500 to the story of the influence of Joachim, there are only a few important authors or texts untouched by the Calabrian and the tradition he initiated. This is why the rich work of Marjorie Reeves, while not technically a history of late medieval apocalyptic as such, provides a wealth of information on almost all the figures and movements portrayed here.

A central problem, however, dogs any evaluation of the influence of Joachim in the three centuries after his death. How far was the Calabrian actually responsible for the broader Joachite tradition? It is no secret that this tradition, if not truly revolutionary in itself, formed a powerful critique of the Church of the time and served as grist for the mill of at least some of the proto-revolutionary ideologies of the later Middle Ages. Joachim was not the author of many of the most popular works that circulated under his name, nor could he be in any way accused of their very real departures from—even contradictions of—his own cherished hopes and beliefs. Nevertheless, in a real sense, Joachim *was* responsible for the Joachites. His differences with the Church of Innocent III, though respectfully put, were real; his dissent from Augustine's view of history, while not fully explicit in his own mind, was profound. The Abbot's optimistic hope for a new and better Church on earth was neither early Christian millenarianism revived, because it was the hope for a renewed Church and not for the scriptural Kingdom of God, nor was it the medieval papacy's canonization of the status quo as the best thing available within the framework of the pessimistic Augustinian theology of history. In his apocalyptic optimism, and in the fecundity of the new symbols and myths he introduced into the apocalyptic scenario, Joachim began what the Joachite tradition was to advance.

The other significant change in late medieval apocalyptic involves the social context in which apocalyptic literature was produced and found its support. If such texts usually tended to be attempts by an educated class to make sense of historical change and to move others to certain courses of action, as I have argued, it is not too much to say that there is a further degree of specialization evident in the concerned *literati* of the late Middle Ages as compared to earlier periods. Joachim's potent myth of the coming "spiritual men'' was perhaps the most effective of all his prophecies, because almost from the moment of his death, various groups found in this image a transcendental justification for their own historical importance. Although the Spiritual Franciscans are the most noteworthy example, many other religious bands identified themselves at one time or another with the hoped-for remnant of spiritual men who would form the seed of the rulers of the age to come.[2] Spiritual virtuosi dedicated to perfection and seeing themselves as the harbingers of the future provided the milieu for many of the most important productions of late medieval apocalyptic.

In the period from A.D. 400 to 1200, most forms of literary production had been the exclusive preserve of the clergy. After 1200, the educated laity took on an increasingly active role in European society, and it should not surprise us that this was also true in the apocalyptic tradition. Did this interest of the laity have a real effect upon the content of apocalyptic warnings? The answer must be a guarded one. Criticism of the vices of the clergy has a large role in many of the texts that follow, and lay authors, such as Fra Dolcino and the savage "Revolutionary of the Upper Rhine," were among the most bitter opponents of the clerical state; but such criticisms were not produced solely by the laity. Criticism of the medieval Church began within the clerical establishment itself and continued to find a home there.

In terms of the doctrine of the ages of the world, what is most significant is the way in which Joachim's pattern of threes comes to dominate the consciousness of the age. With few exceptions, late medieval apocalypticists looked forward to a better time to come, a *renovatio* of the Church and the world, whether they spoke in terms of a third *status* or of some variation of the pattern of the seven ages of the Church. From Joachim too came the speculation regarding the interrelation or concurrence of ages which was a feature of the thought of some of the Franciscan thinkers.

In the scenario of the last events there is a distinctive mixture of the old and the new. Joachim's detailed vision of the End had no place for a Messiah-like Last World Emperor, but had rather exalted a future Holy Pope along with the "spiritual men." The later Middle Ages saw the full development of an apocalyptic understanding of the papacy, and it is a sign of the increasing distance of the occupants of the throne of Peter from suspect religious currents that they themselves made almost no use of these hopes in furthering papal political programs. Thirteenth-century popes invoked Antichrist rhetoric against Frederick II and his seed, but the Joachite vision of a coming Angelic Pope who would reform the Church appears in no official papal document. The *pastor angelicus* was the consolation of those who labored under the persecution of quite another kind of pope—worldly, carnal men, that they eventually came to identify with the Antichrist.[3]

The Last Emperor myths continued to enjoy great popularity during these centuries, even entering the Joachite tradition in the thirteenth century. Much of the material out of which the accounts of the coming Emperor were formed was ancient; new versions were much influenced by contemporary events. A notable factor was the increasingly nationalistic interpretation of the Final Emperor—the Second Charlemagne versus the Third Frederick. This clash between the French and German versions of Christendom's ultimate savior was characteristic of the fourteenth and fifteenth centuries. The figure of the Emperor was not always a beneficent one. Primarily as a result of the tracts emanating from the fierce struggle of the popes against Frederick II, the emperor as persecuting Antichrist (an interpretation with much scriptural warrant) served to make yet more complex the centuries-old imperial component of Christian apocalypticism.

Finally, it was during these centuries that medieval apocalyptic traditions began to serve as an ideology for revolutionary groups, that is, as at least a partial justification for violent attempts to overturn the existing social, economic, political, and religious structure in the name of a better time to come. Perhaps not since the days of Bar-Kochba's revolt in second-century Palestine had there been such revolutionary apocalypticism. Even in intertestamental and Jewish apocalyptic it was the exception rather than the rule—ancient apocalypticism, like its medieval successor, tended more toward a passive rather than an active role when it took a negative stance toward the establishment. For those who wish to see apocalypticism before 1500 as primarily a proto-revolutionary phenomenon this may come as a disappointment. For others, the fact that apocalypticism can at times also be such is yet another proof of its fecundity.

18. Moslems, Mongols, and the Last Days

Conflict between Christendom and Islam remained a nurturing ground for the production of apocalyptic texts during the thirteenth century. As the reality of Christian power grew more tenuous in the East, and as the crusading expeditions became more desperate and less successful, men increasingly turned to prophecies of the imminent end of Moslem rule for solace and hope. Some East Christian apocalyptic texts of anti-Moslem nature, such as the Pseudo-Methodius, had long been known in the West. It is possible that others, such as the Syro-Arabic Apocalypse of Sergius-Bahira, may have been translated in the thirteenth century.[1] A new element in the anti-Moslem apocalyptic of the time was that the revelations were frequently ascribed to Moslem rather than to Christian sources, as if to heighten the objectivity of predictions that might otherwise be thought to spring from forlorn hopes. Such prophecies were also at times confirmed by astrological speculation. Both of these features were foreshadowed in a late twelfth-century text of ultimately Jewish origin, the so-called Toledo Letter, widely popular in Western Europe at the time of the fall of Jerusalem in 1187 and frequently revived in the following centuries.[2]

Another example is found in the thirteenth-century author Caesarius of Heisterbach who records a supposed interview between a Christian knight and Nur-ad-Din in the year 1187. The Moslem is made to claim: "We fear none of your kings, not even your Emperor Frederick. But as we read in our books, a Christian emperor named Otto will soon arise who will restore this land along with the city of Jerusalem to the Christian religion."[3]

The Fifth Crusade (1217–1221), perhaps because it had promised so much by the capture of Damietta and yet in the end had resulted in an utter defeat, was a fountainhead of these prophecies. R. Röhricht edited Latin and vernacular versions of a supposed Arabic Prophecy of the Son of Agap discovered while the crusaders were besieging Damietta and later sent to Rome by the cardinal legate, Pelagius.[4] The purport of the text is clear—after a short sketch of Christian–Moslem conflicts, a "thin man" and then a ruler from Calabria will come to defeat the Turks, destroy Jerusalem, and usher in the time of the Antichrist.

In 1239, the treaty between Frederick II and the sultan of Egypt came to an end, and the city of Jerusalem, in Christian hands for a decade, was once again taken by Moslems. Within the context of these events, two English chronicles record a brief astrological prophecy promising the destruction of the enemy:

The lofty cedar of Lebanon will be cut down. Mars will prevail over Saturn and Jupiter, and Saturn will lie in wait for Jupiter in all things. There will be one God, that is, one bishop. The second God will depart. The sons of Israel will be freed from captivity within eleven years. A wandering people considered to be without a leader will come. Woe to the clergy—a new order will grow strong! Woe to the Church—should it fail! There will be changes of belief, of laws, of kingdoms. The whole land of the Saracens will be overturned.[5]

The prophecy was reworked in more dramatic fashion in the shadow of the fall of the kingdom of Acre, when it became known as the "Tripoli Prophecy."[6] In the early 1270s Pope Gregory X had collected a series of reports on hopes for a new crusade. The most interesting of these came from the Dominican William of Tripoli, who had little faith in the success of a crusade, but expressed belief in Arabic prophecies of the approaching end of Islam.[7]

The mélange of apocalyptic prediction and astrology that provided some hope in the face of the successes of Islam is not to be separated from the thirteenth century's new chapter in what has been called the history of "The World against the West," the encounter between Christendom and the Mongol empire. Looked upon at times as the hope for the destruction of Islam, at others as the dread incursion of Gog and Magog, the Mongols were a dramatic new element in the apocalyptic tradition.

The rise of the Mongol empire is inseparably connected with the name of Jenghiz Khan (1167–1227), the man who formed the clans of the far Asiatic steppe into an unrivaled instrument of conquest. The new power first came to European notice as a result of Jenghiz Khan's spectacular defeat of the Moslem Khwarismian empire in Central Asia between 1218 and 1221. This defeat of the Moslem foe, and knowledge of the fact that there were Nestorian Christians among the nomadic tribes that made up the Mongol army, led to hopes that the mysterious new force might be an important ally in the crusade, perhaps even the fabled Prester John.[8] By 1222 Jenghiz' generals had penetrated into the Caucasus and the Crimea and shown that they would massacre Christians as readily as Moslems. As David Bigalli has pointed out, from this time we have the development of two conflicting interpretations of the significance of the Moslem expansion:

Where the Tartars are immediately presented as the invaders of the West which is considered the object of their expansionistic program, that is in Slavic and in Central Europe, the typical reaction became the crusade. . . . But there is also another aspect of Mongol expansion, that of a force that presses on the shoulders of Islam, places its structures in crisis and therefore alleviates the pressure on the Latin Kingdoms of the Near East, becoming an objective ally of the crusade enterprise.[9]

After the dynastic quarrels following the death of Jenghiz, Batu began the invasion of Russia in 1237. By 1241 he had defeated the Poles, the Hungarians, and other Central European powers, penetrating into Germany and even to the shores of the Adriatic. The death of the Great Khan Ogodai and Batu's return to take part in the quarrel over the succession saved Western Europe from the fate of the East—the Mongols were never again to threaten Christian Europe in quite the same fashion. The revived expansionism under Mongka as Great Khan concentrated on Kubilai's conquest of China and new attacks on the Moslem states of the Near and Middle East under another brother, Hulagu.

Nestorian Christians were especially powerful at the court of Mongka, and a number of European rulers attempted to ally themselves with him.[10] Though the Mongols could never form true alliances, since the only forms of relation to their empire they recognized were subjection or enmity, Hulagu's destruction of the Abbasid caliphate of Baghdad in 1258 was welcomed by the Christians of the East as an act of divine deliverance. Hulagu next conquered the Moslems of Syria, but the death of Mongka in 1259 brought with it another dynastic quarrel during which a reduced Mongol force was defeated by the Mameluke sultan of Egypt at Ain Jalud. Mongol hopes to destroy Islam did not survive this disaster of 1260.

The remote Asiatic origin of the Mongols and the irresistibility of their onslaught could not but raise specters of the approach of the End. A Hungarian Dominican named Julian, who had traveled in neighboring lands, thought they were actually the Ishmaelites or Midianites of the Old Testament;[11] others thought they were Gog and Magog (sometimes identified with the Lost Ten Tribes), the dread predecessors of the Antichrist.[12] It is no surprise that Christian concern with the Mongols was intense. In the wake of the reform ideals of the First Council of Lyons in 1245, Pope Innocent IV sent the Franciscan John of Piano Carpino to the court of the khan in an attempt to convert him. The noted English Franciscan Roger Bacon (d. c. 1292) also reflected much on the meaning of the Mongols and found in them an important key for his apocalyptic hopes.

THE TOLEDO LETTER

The Astrologer Corumphiza's Letter Concerning the Conjunction of the Planets

In the name of the Father, and of the Son, and of the Holy Spirit, Amen. The all powerful God knows and the meaning of the number demonstrates that the higher as well as the lower planets will come together in Libra in September in the year of our Lord Jesus Christ, eternal and true God, 1186, of the Arabs 582. In that year a fire-colored, partial eclipse of the sun will occur before the conjunction in the first hour of the twenty-second day of the month of April. A total eclipse of the moon will occur before the eclipse of the sun on the fifth day of that same month of April in the first hour of the night preceding Tuesday. This shall happen if God wills it—or rather since he wills it, will will it, has willed it, and will not stop having willed it. Therefore, in this year, when the planets are drawn together by God's command in Libra, in a windy and airy sign, with the Dragon's tail also present, a marvelous earthquake will take place, especially in those regions in which it is accustomed to happen. It will destroy the areas used to earthquakes and vulnerable to destructive calamities.[13] A strong and very powerful wind will arise in the western regions, blackening the air and corrupting it with a poisonous stench. Then death and infirmity will seize many, and clanging and cries will be heard in the sky, terrifying the hearts of the listeners. A wind will lift sand and dust from the face of the earth and will cover the cities located on the plain, especially in desert areas. In the fifth climatic zone, Mecca, Barsara, Baghdad, and Babylonia will be utterly destroyed; nor will any land be left without being covered with earth. The regions of Egypt and Ethiopia will be destroyed by sand and dust so that they will scarcely be habitable. This calamity will extend from the West into the regions of the East.

In the West discord will also arise and insurrections will occur among the people. There will be one among them who will gather innumerable armies and will make war along the seashore; [14] in this war such a massacre will take place that the force of the spilled blood will be equal to the rising waves. It is held for certain by some that the future conjunction signifies the change of kingdoms, the pre-eminence of the Franks, the destruction of the Saracen nation, greater charity and the greatest exaltation of the law of Christ, and a longer life for those who will be born afterward. Whatever others say, it means this to me—if God so wills it.

Translated from the version of Roger of Howden, *Chronica* (*RS* 51, 2:290–91).

THE PROPHECY OF THE SON OF AGAP [15]

Hearken to the things which are to come at the end of the kingdom of the caliphs, that is, the followers of that accursed Mohammed. After the setting of the sun a star with a long tail like a lance will ascend; it will have a circular appearance like a shield. [16] At that time, with the appearance of that sign, the kingdom of the caliphs will be reduced and weakened. . . . [17]

After this will come a great king. He will come down about Acre and tarry over it; he will be a lord of counsel and insight, born of a race of kings. An army like a flame will be with him; all things will be beneath his command. Another king will give him aid, will capture Acre with his sword, slay its people, and lead them away captive, but will not be able to free Jerusalem from the hand of the king with the golden standard. [18] I would that my eyes might behold that time, so that I might give you good counsel were God to command it. But after twenty-nine years the Turks will lose that land which the lord of counsel, that is, the lord of the golden standard, allowed them to gain. [19] This will be the sign—immense armies gathered together of their own volition will come from across the sea like locusts over the land of Egypt. Their assault will be like thunder, clashing and terror. They will not fear death as their banners go forth. A man thin of face and tall of stature will lead them, at his command all will stand fast. His command will be over kings and all will obey his orders—nor should this be marvelled at since the whole army will stand fast at his command. This is the judgment of God, because victory always accompanies him as he overcomes all his foes.[20] Woe to the Turks in the days of the thin man! Their kingdom will be scattered at that time, because it has thus been established by God. . . .[21]

A man of noble race will come and seize Damascus and will enter and capture Tadmor which is beyond Damascus, as well as the adjoining lands. He will hold them for a year and two months. . . .[22] A king from Calabria will go forth.[23] He will come and destroy Mecca on a cruel day and will draw near to battle. A grazing camel heavy with offspring will appear and the people seeing her will say: "She belongs to the Parthians. She will go to the water of Zamzam (the name of a well) and will find no clear water to drink."

After this Mexadeigen,[24] that is, the Antichrist, will appear and will overthrow as many nations as had previously existed. The river Nile will flow but little; evil men will be mixed with good, as water is mixed with wine. For four years and four months will this endure, and a single star will be born at the setting of the sun. Other words beyond these will not be had. Afterward, the Day of the Lord upon those outside his path will take place. O my fine friends, hear the words I have spoken about the good teachers and about those who say good things! It will take place as we have heard.

Translated from the edition of R. Röhricht, *Quinti Belli Sacri Scriptores Minores,* pp. 214–15, 217–18, 220–22

WILLIAM OF TRIPOLI, *TREATISE ON THE CONDITION OF THE SARACENS*

XXIV. The Saracen Religion Will Fall

One of the articles of belief among them goes this way: The Saracen religion arose through the sword of Mohammed and will fall through the sword which will be God's, that is to say, it began through the sword and through the sword will end. There is another argument to the same point. Another article says: The Jews had their time and state and fell, and so also the state and realm of the Saracens will fall; but the belief and state of the Christians will endure until Christ again descends from heaven where he now lives, makes all things straight and level, and slays the Antichrist.

Another argument to the same. There is another article, and this one written in the Koran: The Romans have been conquered, but those who were conquered will yet conquer and be victorious. (By the Romans understand the Latins, though others understand the Greeks, who lost the Holy Land in the time of the Emperor Heraclius, as mentioned above.)[25] Another argument. Yet another article which no one denies says that when the generation and the offspring of the line of Mohammed ceases, something which was always awaited in the house of those called caliphs of Baghdad, the Saracen religion and people will fail. But this house collapsed completely when the Tartar Prince Hulagu took Baghdad and killed its caliph in 1254, as mentioned above.[26] So they say that their end is near and at the gates.

Translated from the edition of H. Prutz, *Kulturgeschichte der Kreuzzüge,* pp. 589–90.

ROGER BACON, *THE LONGER WORK*[27]

They speak with precision and certainty about the destruction of the law of Mohammed. For according to what Albumazer says in the eighth chapter of the second book,[28] the law of Mohammed cannot last longer than six hundred and ninety-three years. It can endure and will endure this long unless the time is shortened by some intervening cause (as touched on previously), a shortening that can be large or small depending on the different causes. It is now the six hundred and sixty-fifth year of the Arabs from the time of Mohammed, and therefore it will soon be destroyed by God's grace—something which ought to be a great consolation to Christians. Therefore God is to be praised. He gave philosophers the light of wisdom through which the law of truth is confirmed and strengthened, and through which we understand that the enemies of the faith will be destroyed. The thirteenth chapter of Revelation agrees with this position, for it says that the number of the beast is six hundred and sixty-three, thirty years less than the number above. But Scripture in many places removes something from the full number, for this is its custom as Bede says. Perhaps God wished that here it should be hidden a bit and not totally expressed, just as in the case of many other things written in Revelation. Hence, before the final time set down for that sect, according to its principal cause as Albumazar determined it, it may happen that the Saracens will be destroyed either by the Tartars or by the Christians. Already the larger part of the Saracens has been destroyed by the Tartars, along with their capital, Baghdad, and the caliph who was their pope. This was done twelve years ago. . . .[29]

Since we do not believe that another sect will come after the law of Mohammed, except for the law of the Antichrist, and the astronomers agree with this, viz., that after Mohammed there will be a powerful figure who will set up an unclean and magical law that will suspend all other laws, it is most useful for the Church of God to ponder the time of this law, whether it will come soon after the destruction of the law of Mohammed or much later. Aethicus the philosopher in his *Cosmography* expressly says that the race shut up within the Caspian Gates will rush out into the world, meet the Antichrist, and call him "God of gods." [30] Without doubt, the Tartars were within these Gates and issued forth. We know for certain that the Gates are already broken, [31] for Franciscans whom Louis, the present king of France, sent forth, passed through the midst of the Gates and went far on into the mountains along with Tartars who had been shut up there. [32] Not only do all the nations of the East know that the Tartars have gone out from their regions, but it is also known to those who understand the disposition of the world, its habitable parts, and the diversity of its regions, either through astronomy, through authors like Pliny, Martianus, and others, who describe the regions of the world, or through histories. I do not wish to be haughty here, but I do know that if the Church wished to study the sacred text and the holy prophecies, as well as the Sibylline prophecies, those of Merlin and Aquila, of Seston, of Joachim, and of many others, [33] and furthermore, also histories and the books of the philosophers, along with the paths of astronomy, she would find a sufficient conception and greater certitude about the time of the Antichrist.

Translated from the edition of J. H. Bridges, *The Opus Majus of Roger Bacon* (Oxford: At the Clarendon Press, 1897), 1:266, 268–69.

II. Near these mountains there is a city which was very large before the Tartars destroyed it. There were once eight hundred Armenian churches in it, but in the time of Friar William there were only two small ones when he passed through. Sts. Bartholomew, Jude, and Thaddaeus were martyred near there. There are two prophecies there. The first is of St. Methodius, who belonged to that race and plainly prophesied concerning the Ishmaelites, a prophecy fulfilled in the Saracens. Their other prophet is called Akaton. He prophesied about the Tartars and their destruction. He said: "A race of archers will come from the North and will subjugate all the nations of the East. They will come to the western realm, that is to Constantinople, and there they will be destroyed by the western rulers. Then all nations will be converted to the faith of Christ, and there will be such great peace every-where that the living will say to the dead, 'Woe to you who did not live this long!' And the Christian Emperor will place his throne in Tabriz in Persia." The Armenians hold this prophecy to be gospel-truth. . . .[34]

We must pay careful heed to these places.[35] Gog and Magog, concerning whom Ezekiel and Revelation prophesied, are inclosed in these places, as Jerome says in his second book on Ezekiel. The Scythian race of Gog stretches across the Caucasus and the Maeotic and Caspian Seas to India. From the name of the ruler Gog all subject to him are called Magog. They are also the Jews, whom Orosius and other saints said would go forth.[36] Alexander, as Aethicus states, shut up twenty-two tribes of the stock of Gog and Magog that are to go forth in the days of the Antichrist. They will first devastate the world, will then meet the Antichrist and will call him "God of gods," as St. Jerome confirms. How necessary it is for the Church of God that prelates and good men should pay attention to these places, not only for the sake of the conversion of the races in them and for the consolation of the Christian captives there, but also for the sake of the persecution of the Antichrist so that whence and when he will come may be known through this consideration and through many others.

Translated from Bridges, ed., *The Opus Majus,* 1:363–65.

19. The Joachite Movement before 1260

The influence of the Abbot Joachim is among the most important new elements in late medieval apocalyptic, as noted above. Other currents of expectations about the End maintain their identities during the centuries to 1500, but few remain untouched by the thought of the Calabrian seer. By about 1250, it was almost as difficult to ignore Joachim as it was to neglect Daniel or the Book of Revelation.

Sketching the history of Joachim's influence is complicated by the rapid growth of the literature pseudonymously ascribed to him. This is a phenomenon we have often met in the history of apocalyptic traditions, but one that is nowhere more marked than in the case of Joachim.[1] A century of scholarship has provided us with an accurate list of what can legitimately be said to have come from Joachim's pen, but it has not solved all the difficult questions regarding the relation of the Joachite movement to the real views of the Abbot. Was the Joachite movement fundamentally a development from certain radical themes present in the authentic works? Or was it a perversion of the pious Abbot's theology of history? Any general answer depends on the interpretation of all the texts in question, as well as upon the view that one takes of Joachim. Fortunately, we are not completely in the dark, because at least the broad lines of the history of the Joachite movement are well known and some sketch of the characteristics of the movement, at least in its early stages, is possible.

Joachim's reputation did not perish with his death in 1202; rather, as the research of Marjorie Reeves has shown, it remained alive, certainly in southern Italy, but also in England and even in Germany, from the early thirteenth century.[2] The references to Joachim outside southern Italy at this time indicate that he was best known as a prophet of the imminence of the Antichrist.[3] It was in the circles of the Florensian order that Joachim's texts continued to be copied, special interest being given to the *Book of Figures,* as the earliest pseudonymous work, a Letter explaining the figures, seems to indicate.

The first grave crisis in the history of the Joachite movement was the Fourth Lateran Council's condemnation of the Abbot's attack on Peter Lombard's trinitarian theology.[4] Ardent Joachites sought to assure themselves, either by visions prophesying the eventual triumph of the Calabrian over the Lombard,[5] or by the production of works expanding on Joachim's critique of the Scholastic,[6] that this had been a misunderstanding or an error. It was a fateful moment, for the seeds of the Joachite reaction against the papacy had been sown. After 1215 Joachim was to continue to be a paradoxical figure. Judgments about him were rarely balanced—prophet or heretic, saint or deceiver—which was the real Joachim?

Among the most widely read works that passed under the Abbot's name was the *Commentary on Jeremiah,* supposedly addressed to Emperor Henry VI (d. 1197) and accepted as authentic until the mid-nineteenth century.[7] Older scholars thought that the work came from Franciscan circles; Reeves has reopened the question by claiming that it was the product of Florensian–Cistercian groups in southern Italy.[8] Others have not been convinced by her arguments,[9] and until we are in possession of a critical edition of this work, definitive judgment is not possible. In any case, there is agreement that the *Commentary* was written in the early 1240s and that it marks the beginning of a new stage in the Joachite movement. In its stress upon the importance of the coming third *status* and on the role of the two orders of spiritual men, the *Commentary* picks up on real themes of Joachim, but it carries them forward in ways beyond those present in the authentic works. In its virulent attack on the worldly Church of the second *status* and in its willingness to assign a definite date for the critical transition to the new age (the end of the forty-second generation, that is, the year 1260),[10] it marks the onset of the Joachite misunderstanding of the Abbot's complex and subtle views. The explicit references to the quarrel between Emperor Frederick II and the papacy (see Section 20) are also a new factor.

Whether the *Commentary on Jeremiah* was written by a Franciscan or not, it does seem likely that southern Italy, possibly Naples,[11] saw the first entry of Joachite ideas into the Franciscan order. The two key figures in the first stage of Franciscan Joachitism were Hugh of Digne (d. c.1257) and John of Parma, minister general of the order from 1247 to 1257. Hugh, a Provençal by birth, may have picked up his interest in Joachim from his friend John. By 1247, when he was in residence at Hyerès on the Riviera, he had become a key figure in the diffusion of Joachite ideas in the order. John of Parma had been a lector at Naples before he was called upon to teach at Paris in 1245. His ten-year rule over the order was devoted to restoring the Franciscans to the original ideals of the founder, and the Joachite standpoint he took toward the historical significance of the Friars Minor was an important part of his motivation. John was apparently the first to identify Francis with the Angel of the Sixth Seal of Revelation 7:2.[12] He made use of Joachite themes in some of his most important documents, and looked with favor upon the fervent Joachites in the order.

Gerardo of Borgo San Donnino, an enthusiastic young friar, was sent to Paris to study theology about 1250. In 1254 he issued a work called the *Introduction to the Eternal Gospel,* an interpretation and summary of Joachim's three major works that made claims from which the Abbot would have fled in horror.[13] For Gerard the third *status* that was to arrive in 1260 signified the total abrogation of the Church of the second *status,* even down to the substitution of Joachim's writings for the Old and the New Testaments. The scandal engendered by Gerardo was to prove the first major crisis of the Joachite movement.

The increasing presence of the friars at Paris had not been to the liking of many of the secular masters. Disaffected elements, centered around the person of Master William of St. Amour, using Gerardo's radical views as a handle for attack, issued a series of scurrilous diatribes against both mendicant orders.[14] Had not the papacy been behind the friars at this crucial moment, the crisis might have been a severe check in their growth. The orders marshaled their forces in retaliation—two rising young theological stars, Thomas Aquinas for the Dominicans and Bonaventure for the Franciscans, were drawn into the fray. The Franciscans, more infected by the virulent Joachite strain than the Dominicans, were compelled to clean house. A papal commission held at Anagni under Alexander IV in 1255 condemned Gerardo's *Introduction,* though not Joachim himself. The young friar was imprisoned for life, and the respected John of Parma had to step down from his position, to be succeeded by Bonaventure as minister general in 1257. Franciscan Joachitism had been curbed, but by no means abandoned, as the later thought of Bonaventure himself was to show.

The final event that marked the end of the first period of Joachitism was the failure of the year 1260 to usher in the third *status.* Doubts about the timetable had already been expressed since 1250 when the death of Frederick II, who had ten years yet to fulfill his role as the Antichrist, had disconcerted many. The year 1260 passed without event.[15] Although many Joachites abandoned their beliefs, in the manner of so many apocalyptic movements, discomfiture was to lead others to a more intense adherence.[16]

THE LETTER EXPLAINING THE FIGURES

. . . . Forty-two carnal generations are contained in the first tree from its root to Christ. From the root of the second tree to Christ the Judge there are forty-two spiritual generations, even though the middle ones that are the end of the first tree and the root of the second are partly spiritual.[17] The lower generations are marked with the names of the Fathers, the higher with the multiples of thirty. They think that the Church will endure through just as many spiritual generations as the Synagogue did carnal ones. Since from the Nativity, or better from the Passion of Christ, forty generations, that is, twelve hundred years have been completed in our time, there remain only two generations to be fulfilled, that is, sixty years from the Passion or ninety from the Nativity—two thirty-year periods in which everything said about the Antichrist and the End of the world must be fulfilled. Hence the verses:

> When one thousand and two hundred years are done
> And six times ten after the delivery of the Good Virgin
> Then will be born Antichrist filled with the devil.[18]

Translated from the edition of L. Tondelli, *Il "Libro delle Figure," I. Introduzione e Commento: Le Sue Rivelazioni Dantesche,* pp. 41–42.

COMMENTARY ON JEREMIAH

The Two Orders [19]

"Learn this parable from the figtree" (Matt. 24:32). Concerning this coming tempest it is said: "The time has brought a tumult" (Jer. 46:17). And so the young man has raised an uproar against the old man, the preacher against the pastors, and the insignificant against the important, that is, the one despised against the famous leader.[20] In the figure of the insignificant young man the two orders to come are portrayed. They are also signified in Caleb and Joshua,[21] in Manasseh and Ephraim, in Moses and Aaron, in John the Baptist and Christ, in Elijah and Elisha, in Paul and Barnabas. . . .[22]

All these figures are strong in faith and able to bear tribulation. They differ in varieties of preaching and form of religious life, just as the crow and the dove differ, because the former is completely black and the latter is all varied, that is mixed. "The voice of one singing on the window; the crow upon the lintel" (Zeph. 2:14). The crow, that is the order of preachers sent out of the Ark of the Church by the High Priest Noah through obedience, does not return, because it is sent forth so that it should not fear the flood but abide in the waters.[23] It certainly does this that it might snatch the bodies of sinners from the waters, that is, from the tribulations to come over the whole earth, and perhaps also to hide them from the face of the persecutor. This order will sing by preaching on the Christian people's window which lets in the light of Christ's faith. . . .

"The crow is upon the lintel." It is sent not only to the underlings signified by the window, but also to the prelates signified by the lintel, of which it is said: "The lintels of the hinges are moved" (Isa. 6:4). Something similar is found in the Gospel, where Herod was disturbed and all Jerusalem with him. There has arisen or will arise in the Church a form of preaching that is like the star when Christ was born. The prelates will be disturbed by an order of preachers; the underlings will also be upset because they will lose temporal rule, carnal priesthood, and worldly reward. For this reason many will enter stealthily by fraud in their desire to snuff out the light of the star, as if preaching could be wiped out. . . . Many of them will be punished by a future Herod, without doubt the Antichrist. Like a pope he will sit in the Church as though he were God; and some will be saved in Egypt, i.e., among the unbelievers up to now left in the blindness of ignorance. . . .

After the crow, a differently clad dove is sent forth (Gen. 8:8 sq.). Note that the crow is black, loves corpses, and has a loud voice. The nimble and changeable dove shuns corpses, has a groan for a song, and is different in all things. The former preachers were black with sadness of heart, not the sadness of the world. They were serious in manner of life, eloquent in doctrine, kind in their compassion for their fellow man. The dove is more fruitful in its offspring. It is diverse with wings of virtues, nimble in obedience, and is fed with the food of the elect, namely the Scriptures. In place of the song of preaching, it has sorrow for sins and the desire for the heavenly country. . . . Here note that for this reason the crow is of one color, the dove of different colors. In themselves we can understand that the orders signified by them are different in dress, but not in spirit. They strive toward one food and agree in a single vow and resolute desire. . . . Spiritually, Peter signifies the order of preachers, James their lay brothers, and John the other order of minors,[24] made a little lower than the angels themselves because it is the final order. . . .

Translated from *Interpretatio preclara Abbatis Ioachim in Hieremiam Prophetam* (Venice: B. Benalius, 1525), ff. 12v–13r.

Joachim's Unjust Condemnation [25]

Caiaphas the High Priest hints at the truth of the events to come when he says: "One doctor[26] must be condemned, that is, killed for the people, so that the entire race does not perish in error" (John 11:50). Thus Zedechiah rose up against Jeremiah—he condemned the book; he separated the Trinity from the Divine Unity, by the scribe's knife cutting away the opinion of the doctor.[27] I do not know, but God knows, whether these events are to be brought to completion in us or are to be consummated in the order to come.

Accordingly, since Christ lay dead in the heart of the earth for three days, now the spirit of life is to be hidden beneath the letter as the soldiers, doctors, and masters are summoned to guard the deadly letter as if it were a tomb. This will continue until the tribulation of the new republic (that is, Babylon) passes, the tribulation of an unfaithful people, the tribulation of the heretical synagogue.[28] The first of these is signified by the capture of Christ, the second by his scourging, the third by his death. Afterwards, whether the world wishes it or not,[29] the seventh angel (Rev. 10:1 sq.), that is, the Sevenfold Spirit of God, will raise up the spiritual understanding by which the blind will see and understand the mysteries of the Trinity.

Herod signifies a pope to come after Celestine,[30] whoever he may be, under whom, because the star has disappeared,[31] the spiritual understanding will be snuffed out by fraud and betrayed through envy. He will think to destroy it. When the bishops of the churches and the Pharisees, that is, the abbots, priors, and Cistercian religious, envious of Christ, have gathered together, perhaps in a general council,[32] everything will be blamed on that doctor of truth. The sixth angel describes this (Rev. 9:13); indeed under this person is also demonstrated the open book of truth in the hand of the other angel (Rev. 10:2). Even though Scripture indicates one man, many faithful will die for others. Signed with the sign of the cross, by common consent they are destined to go forth to the barbarous nations.

There follows: "Go to the men of Anathoth who seek your life" (Jer. 11:21–3). This evil arose from some Cistercians, namely, the claim that the doctor did not prophesy in the name of the Lord.[33] He died, that is, was condemned by their hands, that is, through their efforts and advice. Then follows: "Their young men will die by the sword; their sons and daughters by famine. Not one of them will be left" (Jer. 11:22). The young men are the Cistercian priors, the sons are the monks, the daughters are the monasteries and domains. The first will perish by the sword of the new republic, the second by the lack of catholic teaching, the remaining powers of the order by neglect of monastic obedience. . . .

Translated from *In Hieremiam* (Venice: Benalius, 1525), f. 23r.

THE JOINT ENCYCLICAL OF 1255[34]

To the most dear and beloved in Christ Jesus Brother Preachers and Friars spread throughout the world. Brother Humbert, Master General of the Preachers,[35] and Brother John of Parma, Minister General of the Friars, send greetings to all. May you walk worthily and praisefully in your holy calling.

The Savior of the world who loves souls and wishes no one to perish has ceaselessly raised up remedies through different ministries in each generation for the varied repair of the human race after its first ruin. In the last days at the End of the world, as we believe without any doubt, he raised up our two orders in the ministry of salvation, calling many to himself and enriching them with celestial gifts through which they are effectively able to work salvation by word and by example not only for themselves but also for others. These orders are—to speak to God's glory and not our own—two great luminaries which by celestial light shine upon and minister to those sitting in darkness and the shadow of death.[36] These are the two trumpets of the true Moses, of Christ our God, by whose ministry a multitude of peoples has already been called to the source (Num. 10:2). These are the two Cherubim full of knowledge, gazing at each other while they behold the same object, spreading out their wings to the people while they protect them by word and example, and flying about on obedient wing over the whole people to spread saving knowledge (Exod. 25:18). These are the two breasts of the spouse from which Christ's little ones suck the milk by which they are nourished and receive saving increase (Song of Sol. 4:5). These are the two olives of the Son of Splendor that stand near the ruler of the universe ready for his command wherever his will might lead them to fulfill his mission (Zech. 4:14). These are the two witnesses of Christ who, clad in sackcloth, are already preaching and bearing testimony to the truth (Rev. 11:3). These are the two shining stars that according to the Sibylline prophecy have the appearance of the four animals and in the last days will cry out in the name of the Lord in the way of humility and voluntary poverty. . . .[37]

Translated from the text found in L. Wadding, *Annales Minorum* (Rome: R. Bernabò, 1732), 3:380–81.

THE PROTOCOL OF ANAGNI

We have extracted and noted these things from the *Introduction to the Eternal Gospel* that was sent to the pope by the bishop of Paris and by him given to the three of us to inspect, i.e., to Odo, the cardinal bishop of Tusculum, to Stephen, the cardinal bishop of Palestrina, and to Hugh, the cardinal priest of Santā Sabina.[38]

Item. That about the year 1200 the spirit of life left the two Testaments, so that the "Eternal Gospel" could come into existence. This is proved in chapters 15d and 23b.

Item. That the *Book of Concordances,* or the *Book of the Concordance of Truth,* should be called the first volume of the "Eternal Gospel" is proved in chapter 17g. That this *Book of Concordance* is Joachim's is held throughout the chapter.

Item. That the book which is called *The New Revelation* should·be called the second volume of the same Gospel is proved in chapter 20c and especially g. Similarly, that the book which is called *The Ten-Stringed Psaltery* is the third book of the same Gospel is proved in a and g of the twenty-first chapter and throughout. . . .[39]

In the year of our Lord 1255, the eighth day before the Ides of July, in the presence of Odo, bishop of Tusculum, and Brother Hugh, cardinal priest, both established as papal investigators, together with our reverend father Stephen, the bishop of Palestrina (who excused himself through his chaplain and permitted us to act in his place), Master Florence, the bishop of Acre, presented certain passages taken from the books of Joachim that he thought were suspect.[40] He thought they should not be publicly taught, preached, or copied (as might happen), unless the teaching, or Joachim's book, be condemned in the areas that seemed objectionable to him. In order to hear and investigate these matters we called others to join us, Brother Bonavaletus, the bishop of Banias, and Brother Peter, the Dominican lector at Anagni. One of them possessed original texts of Joachim from the monastery of Fiore, and examined them in our presence to see if the things which the bishop of Acre read and had read by our secretary were in them.

He began in the following way: First must be noted the foundation of the teaching of Joachim. He proposes three *status* of the world in the fourth chapter of the second book, the one that begins, "But that understanding, etc . . ."[41] Joachim's whole doctrine is based on this foundation. He predicts many things in varying ways concerning the faith of the second *status* and of the third, and also about a religious order that is to rule in the third *status* down to the End of the world. . . .

Item. In the *Treatise on the Four Gospels,* in expounding on the passage concerning Simeon, when the Christ Child was presented in the Temple on the Day of Purification, he says, "So the just and God-fearing old man signifies the leaders of the Roman Church. . . ."[42] So far the words of Joachim. In marvelous and incredible fashion he attempts to exalt I know not what future order and says that it is to come at the end of the second *status* of which only five years remain, as is clear from the above. I say that he exalts it, not only above other orders, but also above the whole Church and the whole world, as is clearly said in many places cited above. We should carefully note, however, that his insecurity and uncertainty begin to be demonstrated from his own words, for he sometimes says that these things are to be completed in the fortieth generation, sometimes in the forty-second. The first of these is false because the fortieth generation is already past in this fifty-fifth year of the century.

Translated from the edition of F. Ehrle, "Das Evangelium aeternum und die Commission zu Anagni," *Archiv für Literatur-und Kirchengeschichte* (1885), 1:99–100, 102–5, 110–12.

SALIMBENE OF PARMA, *CHRONICLE*[43]

Brother Hugh lived in that walled town more than in any other place.[44] There were many notaries, judges, doctors, and other lettered men who used to come to his cell on feast days to hear him discourse and expound on the Abbot Joachim's teaching, explaining the mysteries of Sacred Scripture and predicting the future. He was a great Joachite and had all the books of the Abbot Joachim in large letters. I too was involved in that teaching for the sake of hearing Brother Hugh. Previously, when I lived at Pisa,[45] I had been instructed in it by an abbot of the order of Fiore, a holy old man who had placed all his books by Joachim under protection in the convent of Pisa, being afraid that the Emperor Frederick would destroy his monastery, which was between Lucca and Pisa on the road that leads to Luni. He thought that at that time all the mysteries were to reach fulfillment in Frederick since he was in conflict with the Church. Brother Rudolph of Saxony, the lector at Pisa, a great logician, theologian, and disputer, left the study of theology when these books of the Abbot Joachim were placed in our house. He became a great Joachite.

Another time, when I lived at Ravenna,[46] Brother Bartholomew Calarosus of Mantua, who was lector and minister at Milan and Rome, but at that time was living at Ravenna as a private person, said to me: 'I tell you, Brother Salimbene, that John of Parma upset himself and his order because he was of such great knowledge, holiness, and excellence of life that he was able to correct the Roman curia and they would have believed him. But later on he followed the prophecies of insane men, brought censure on himself, and injured his friends not a little. . . .'' I responded: ''I agree, and it saddened me not a little because I loved him deeply. . . .'' When he heard all this, Brother Bartholomew said: ''And you also were a Joachite.'' I said, ''You speak the truth, but after the death of the Emperor Frederick and the passing of the year 1260, I completely left that teaching behind and propose to believe only what I see.''

Translated from *MGH*. SS. XXXII, pp. 236–38, and 302–3.

20. Frederick II versus the Papacy

We have already had occasion to note the role of the Emperor Frederick II Hohenstaufen (1194–1250) in the early stages of Joachite speculation.[1] The abundant hopes surrounding the man whom his contemporaries called the "Wonder of the World" are wider than those of Joachitism alone. They form one of the clearest examples of the *a priori* political uses of apocalypticism in the centuries under discussion.

Frederick's personality and genius seem at times larger than life. He himself was not unconcerned with the growth of his legend; indeed, he deliberately encouraged forms of messianic adulation toward his person that went beyond the usual patterns of sacral kingship. As E. Kantorowicz in his biography of Frederick has claimed: "The whole life of Frederick could be interpreted either in the Messianic or in the Anti-Christian spirit."[2]

Pope Gregory IX (1227–41) had excommunicated the emperor in 1227, supposedly for his hesitation to embark upon his pledged crusade, but actually for the threat that his policies offered to the security of the Papal States. This was only a preliminary to the bloody conflict that began in 1236 when Frederick moved to return the north Italian cities to the control of the empire and thus surround the papal domains. In 1239 Gregory launched his second excommunication, the point of no return in the quarrel between the papacy and the House of Hohenstaufen. It was to last beyond Frederick's death in 1250 down to the execution of Conradin in 1268.

The intensity of this third and most savage of the struggles between *sacerdotium* and *imperium* in the Middle Ages is indicated by the force of the apocalyptic rhetoric used on both sides.[3] It was, of course, to be expected that the pope would see in Frederick at least a precursor of the Antichrist—this had been a traditional accusation in such circumstances. Gregory VII had spoken of his enemies in such fashion, as we have seen, though it is significant that he refrained from any direct identification of Henry IV with the Antichrist. An important circle in the Roman curia, dominant under Gregory IX and still active to some degree under his successor, Innocent IV (1243–1254), was far more explicit in its invocation of apocalyptic rhetoric.[4]

Frederick's immediate protest against the second excommunication featured an attack on the abuses of the thirteenth-century papacy, especially its abandonment of the ideal of poverty. Gregory's response, issued on June 21, 1239, the Letter "Ascendit de mari bestia," marked the beginning of the overt apocalyptic dimensions of the confrontation. Frederick's polemicists were not slow to introduce apocalyptic elements into their own propaganda. The Hohenstaufen was, after all, king of Jerusalem and, as the messianic ruler, were not his enemies part of the entourage of the Evil One? Thoughts such as these were at the root of the Letter of July 1239, in which the emperor responded to the pope in kind.

A war of letters and pamphlets continued for the next year. In answer to a famous open letter of 1240 penned by the imperial adviser Piero della Vigna, Gregory again called upon apocalyptic themes: "What other Antichrist should we await, when as is evident in his works, he is already come in the person of Frederick? He is the author of every crime, stained by every cruelty, and he has invaded the patrimony of Christ seeking to destroy it with Saracen aid."[5] After the defeat of the papal fleet and the capture of the prelates in May 1241, Frederick came to look more and more like the persecuting Antichrist. In his declining days, Gregory again turned to an apocalyptic outburst in his Letter "Vox in Rama."[6]

Gregory died in August 1241. After the brief pontificate of Celestine IV a long vacancy followed until the election of Cardinal Sinibaldo Fieschi as Innocent IV in 1243. He proved to be an even more determined opponent of Frederick than Gregory had been. The new pope fled to the safety of southern France where, in 1245 at the Council of Lyons, he deposed the emperor. This dramatic event had been prepared for by a new round of apocalyptic rhetoric. The foremost polemicist on the papal side was the aged and devious Cardinal Rainer of Viterbo, a Cistercian protégé of Innocent III, confidant of the late Gregory, and inveterate foe of the emperor.[7] He had been responsible for the apocalyptic missives issued under Gregory's pontificate, and he now returned to the attack with virulence in a series of letters and pamphlets in the spring and summer of 1245.[8] In the most noted of these, the letter "Iuxta vaticinium Isaiae," the cardinal's language speaks for itself: "Since Frederick has in his forehead the horn of power and a mouth bringing forth monstrous things, he thinks himself able to transform the times and the laws and to lay truth in the dust, and hence he blasphemed against the Most High and uttered outrages against Moses and God." [9]

We possess two short treatises from the camp of Frederick thought to have been written in the period after the Council of Lyons when the emperor was willing to make use of anything that might cause difficulties for the pope. The first, the work of a Dominican named Arnold, called for imperial reform of the Church within an eschatological context. The second, anonymous treatise, was more overtly apocalyptic in its interpretation of the name *Innocencius papa* as equal to 666, the dread number of the Antichrist found in Revelation 13:18. [10]

Perhaps the most popular product from this apocalyptic battle of the books was the set of prophetic verses supposed to have been exchanged between the emperor and the pope and known in at least eight versions:

The Emperor to the Pope:
> The fates warn, the stars teach, and so do the flights of birds
> That I will soon be the hammer of the world.
> Rome, a long time wavering, having committed various errors,
> Will collapse and cease to be the capital of the world.

The Pope to the Emperor:
> Your reputation relates, Scripture teaches, and your sins announce
> That you will have a short life and eternal punishment.

O. Holder-Egger, the editor, thought that the four lines of the emperor might have been originally composed by an imperial propagandist after Frederick's victory over the Lombards at Cortenuovo in 1237. His hypothesis was that during the pontificate of Innocent they came to the attention of a papal supporter who took them as addressed to the pope and added Innocent's reply. [11] H. M. Schaller, on the other hand, thought that they reflected the fervid atmosphere after Frederick's great naval victory off Monte Christo in 1241. [12] The later additions and changes in these verses testify to the degree to which this poetic presentation of the epic struggle captured the imagination of many. [13]

Frederick was an Antichrist figure not only in official curial circles, but also among the followers of Joachim. [14] Indeed, the picture of Frederick as the persecuting imperial Antichrist developed among the Joachites was to be far more influential in the subsequent growth of the Frederick legends than were the papal bulls. The widely diffused *Commentary on Jeremiah* is the earliest literary monument to this identification, and the one-time Joachite Salimbene gives us valuable evidence in his *Chronicle* about the Franciscan

Joachites who believed that the Antichrist Frederick would continue his persecution of the Church until the fateful year 1260, when the forces of evil would be overcome by God and the third *status* would be ushered in.[15] In 1250 the success of the determined emperor, once again in an advantageous military position, might well have seemed confirmation of the worst fears of the Joachites. Frederick's unexpected death in the same year relieved the papacy but brought temporary confusion to the ranks of the apocalypticists.

Frederick dead was as much a wonder as Frederick alive. Like Nero before him, the emperor became the focus of a mass of legends. Perhaps he was not really dead; or if dead, he would be brought back to life to complete his role as the Antichrist. The unexpected character of his death and the possibility of his survival were early noted in widespread prophetic verses:

> His death will be hidden and unknown.
> Among the people will resound: "He lives," and "He does not live." [16]

Even if the dread Frederick was finally out of the way, his seed, the talented and energetic Hohenstaufen heirs to the imperial throne, might well be seen as having inherited the mantle of the persecutor. One of them, or perhaps a third Frederick to come, might be the Antichrist of the second *status*.

Frederick's life and the various predictions regarding his seed played a large role in the luxuriant Joachite literature produced between 1250 and 1270, most of it in Franciscan circles.[17] Among these texts are the two Joachite reworkings of the Erythraean Sibyl, which Reeves dates to c.1251–1254, and which give much attention to Frederick and his successors. There is also an *Exposition on the Sibyls and on Merlin* ascribed to the Calabrian prophet and most probably produced during the same decade. The *Commentary on Isaiah* probably dates to the 1260s, when the papal pursuit of the Hohenstaufen was entering its last phase.[18] Although this text identifies Frederick as the seventh head of the dragon, his death does not spoil the system, since his seed is understood as the tail of the dragon that marks the final moment of persecution (see selection "Frederick and His Seed in the Joachite Tradition: *Commentary on Isaiah*"). The later history of the third Frederick as either an Antichrist or a Messiah has been amply reviewed by Reeves and others and need not detain us now.[19]

In their savage vendetta against the last of the Hohenstaufen the popes after Innocent did not totally abandon the use of apocalypticism to further their aims. Against the hopes of Manfred, Frederick's bastard son, the papacy called in the power of Charles of Anjou, younger brother of Louis

IX of France, a man as unscrupulous in his treatment of the Church as ever Frederick had been. Manfred was killed at the battle of Benevento in 1266; and Conradin, young grandson of the emperor, was defeated at Tagliacozzo and executed at Naples in 1268. Curial propaganda may have hailed Charles as the Last Emperor, the second Charlemagne, as suggested by the prophecy ascribed to John of Toledo, the cardinal of Porto, a text probably dating from the 1260s.

Nor did the protagonists of the House of Hohenstaufen surrender their claims to apocalyptic glory. Shortly after Frederick's death, the pro-imperial city of Tivoli greeted his son Conrad IV as the Last Emperor in terms dependent on the Tiburtine Sibyl.[20] A Ghibelline text from the Veneto dated by its editor to about 1264 goes so far as to predict the end of the papacy itself: "After Celestine will reign a proud pope; after the proud pope a Catholic pope; after him a heretical pope; and after the heretical one, no pope at all."[21] Finally, mention must be made of what was perhaps the most influential of the late Hohenstaufen prophecies, the text beginning "Regnabit Manfredus bastardus," which also appears to date from about this time. With this text, and its later addition, the "Veniet aquila," we pass into the realm of the hopes for a third Frederick.[22]

No one would claim that apocalyptic expectations were at the origin of the quarrel between Frederick and the papacy—there are more than enough evident causes. What does deserve highlighting is the way in which the polemicists on both sides seized upon elements of the apocalyptic drama to further their cases. It is a prime example of the peculiar force that apocalypticism could give to current events by placing them within the sphere of history at its most universal and critical moment. Both sides were calling for allegiance in terms designed to stress the ultimacy of the choice in the most effective fashion known to them. Not a little of the intransigency that marked this encounter of *sacerdotium* and *imperium,* not a little of the ferocity with which the papacy pursued the last of the line of Frederick to the grave, come from the apocalyptic tenor of the debate.

NICHOLAS OF BARI, SERMON[23]

It is said that the scepter will not be taken from the hand of the Lord Frederick nor a leader from his thigh (that is, the empire from his heirs), until he who is to be sent comes (that is, Christ comes to the Last Judgment).[24] This race will rule to the End of the world because the Origin is with it in the day of his power (Ps. 109:3), which means that Christ is in all his vicars.[25]

Concerning such matters it has been said through the prophet: "Justice and an abundance of peace will arise in the days of the Lord, until the moon is lifted up and rules from sea to sea and from the great river to the ends of the earth. The Ethiopians will go before him and his enemies will lick the dust."[26] All the days from Christmas to Epiphany are especially called days of the Lord, since on or within these days, that is on the Feast of St. Stephen following the Nativity, justice was born, namely the justice of the Lord Emperor Frederick which is so great in this world and which renders to each his due[27]—to God three things, fear, honor, and love; to kings, friendly alliance; to subjects, grace and mercy. This has been done by the Lord and is wonderful in our eyes (Ps. 117:23), that the emperor was born on St. Stephen's day. Stephen means "crowned," and on his day was born the Lord who was to be crowned with many a diadem so that the meaning of the name might allude to his dignity and earthly things might agree with divine. . . .

Therefore, dearly beloved, let us salute him with the Angel Gabriel: Hail, Lord Emperor, full of the grace of God. The Lord is with you, that is, was, is, and will be. . . . (Luke 1:28)

Translated from the edition of R. Kloos, "Nikolaus von Bari, Eine Neue Quelle zur Entwicklung der Kaiseridee unter Friedrich II," in *Stupor Mundi: Zur Geschichte Friederichs II von Hohenstaufen* (Darmstadt: Wissenschaftliche Buchgesellschaft, 1966), pp. 373, 375.

GREGORY IX, LETTER "ASCENDIT DE MARI BESTIA"

Gregory, Bishop, Servant of the Servants of God, sends health and apostolic blessing to his venerable brothers the Archbishop of Canterbury and his suffragans.[28] The beast filled with the names of blasphemy has risen up from the sea. With the feet of a bear, a mouth like a lion, and the rest of his limbs like a leopard, in his rage he has opened his mouth to blaspheme the divine name (Rev. 13:1–2). He even hurls like darts against God's tabernacle and against the saints who dwell in heaven. He desires to break all things to pieces with his iron hooves and teeth and to tread everything underfoot. At one time he prepared secret battering rams against the faith; now he constructs the war machines of the Ishmaelites in the open, he arranges stratagems to carry off souls, and he rises up in his true form against Christ, the

Redeemer of the human race, the tables of whose Law he has already tried to abolish with the pen of wicked heresy.[29] Therefore, let all to whom have come the scandals of blasphemy sent forth against us by this beast cease to be surprised that we who are subject to God in every service are attacked by the arrows of detraction, since even the Lord himself is not free from his reproaches. Cease to be surprised that he who now arises to destroy the name of the Lord from the earth directs an injurious sword against us. Rather, so that you may be able to resist his lies with open truth and to confute his fallacies with pure argument, carefully consider the beginning, middle, and end of this beast Frederick called emperor. . . .[30]

Translated from J. Huillard-Bréholles, *Diplomatica Friderici Secundi* (Paris: Plon, 1857), vol. 5, part 1, p. 327.

FREDERICK II, LETTER "IN EXORDIO NASCENTIS MUNDI"[31]

In the very beginning of the world, the wise and ineffable providence of God, whose counsels are secret, set up two lights in the firmament of heaven, a greater and a lesser: the greater to rule the day and the lesser to rule the night. These two are set up in such a manner in their own places in the zodiac that even if they are often placed side-by-side, the one does not interfere with the other; rather, the higher shares his brightness with the lower. By means of a similar eternal provision God wished there to be two powers in the firmament of the earth, the priesthood and the empire, the one for security, the other for protection, so that man, who was for too long separated into the two components of body and soul, should be restrained by double bonds, and the world have peace when all excesses have been curbed.[32]

The Roman pontiff of our time, a Pharisee sitting in the seat of false doctrine and anointed with the oil of evil beyond all his fellows, has stopped following the heavenly order and strives to abolish all this. Perhaps he thinks he can exhort those higher bodies that are governed by nature and not by human will. He intends to bring the radiance of our majesty into eclipse while turning truth to falsehood in papal letters full of lies sent out to various parts of the world attacking the purity of our faith from sophistry and not from true reason.[33] He, who is pope in name alone, has said that we are the beast rising from the sea full of the names of blasphemy and spotted like a leopard. We maintain that he is the monster of whom we read: "Another horse arose from the sea, a red one, and he who sat thereon took away peace from the earth so that the living slaughtered one another" (Rev. 6:4). From the time of his election he has been not a Father of mercy, but of discord, an eager promoter of desolation rather than consolation. He has scandalized the whole world. Construing his words in the true sense, he is that great dragon who leads the world astray (Rev. 12), Antichrist, whose forerunner he says we are. . . . He is the angel coming from the abyss bearing vials full of bitterness to harm the sea and the earth (Rev. 16:1–3).

Translated from Huillard-Bréholles, *Diplomatica*, vol. 5, part 1, p. 348.

INNOCENT IV AS ANTICHRIST

It should be known and firmly held by all Christ's faithful that since the Antichrist is said to be contrary to Christ, he will come in that state of life in which he will be most directly opposed to Christ and from which his fall will be the greatest. . . . Therefore since state in life increases the gravity of sin, the same kind of sin is graver in the clergy than in the laity because of their greater knowledge, and graver in a bishop than in a simple priest because of his higher position, and most serious of all in the case of the pope because he possesses the highest state. Hence it is necessary that Antichrist appear in the place of the Supreme Pontiff, in which state his avarice and other vices will be most directly opposed to Christ and in which the Church will be most scandalized and corrupted in him. . . .

In the Second Epistle to the Thessalonians it says: "He will be lifted up and extolled above everything spoken of or worshiped as God, so that he will sit in the Temple of God," that is, the Church," showing himself as if he were God" (2 Thess. 2:4), that is, as the Vicar of Christ, so that whatever he does is thought to be an act of God and even in his worst deeds he is not said to sin. . . . In the thirteenth chapter of Revelation we read: "Let him who has understanding compute the number of the beast," namely what is contained in his mark, "and his number is 666" (Rev. 13:18). This number is found in the new Bull. "Innocencius papa" signifies 666 according to the *Gloss* and to reason.[34] *I* equals 1, *N* equals 50 and 50 again, *O* is 70, *C* a 100, *E* 5, *N* 50, *C* another 100, *I* 1, *V* 5, *S* 200. *P* is not in the *Gloss*, but according to the meaning of the number it equals 16 because *P* is the sixteenth letter according to the Greeks and Revelation in which the number of the beast is found was written by John in Greek. *A* equals 1, another *P* is 16, and another *A* 1. When the number is fully added up, the name of the mark of the beast, that is, of the Antichrist who is Pope Innocent, equals 666. This number surpasses the fivefold number of the law and of the senses and does not attain the sevenfold perfection of grace, because the Antichrist and his members will be the complete transgressor of every law and every curb on the senses and will in no way attain to the remission of sins of the Holy Spirit. . . . All these signs, which the saints applied to the Antichrist according to the Sacred Scripture, spiritually understood, that is, as completely contrary to Christ and his teaching, apply to Pope Innocent. There is no doubt that he is the true Antichrist.

Translated from E. Winkelmann, *Fratris Arnoldi De Correctione Ecclesiae et Anonymi de Innocentio IV P.M. Antichristo,* pp. 20–22.

FREDERICK AND HIS SEED IN THE JOACHITE TRADITION

Commentary on Jeremiah [35]

The Temple is the Roman, or Universal Church, which is to be trodden down in general like the holy city for forty-two months from the time of Christ to the end of the second *status.* The forty-two months are forty-two generations in which the Christian people are to be afflicted. They will end in the year 1260. . . .

In sixty years the affliction of the Church will end. In the more particular sense, in three and a half years a more serious hardship will come. According to Ezekiel,[36] it can come about that new Chaldeans, that is, Germans, will come upon Tyre, that is, the kingdom of Sicily, laying it waste and bringing it into disorder because its king made his heart like the heart of God (Ezek. 28:6). They will destroy him from the midst of the live coals (Ezek. 28:16).

Hear, Lord Emperor, and attend to what is said: "From the root of the serpent will arise a basilisk, and his seed will swallow the bird" (Isa. 14:29). You are the serpent on the roadside, your successor is the horned basilisk in the road.[37] Under him the empire will be stung, that is, will be divided, and any rider coming to it will fall. Like a winding snake you will be led forth from the kingdom; your successor, whose glance will scatter all, will spring out of his cave. He is called a horned serpent perhaps because he will stand up to many kingdoms. We should fear lest he bite the hooves of the horse by wounding the Church, that is, in his last hours he will cause the rider, the pope, to fall, or render the prelates, the princes of his dishonor, inactive.[38] He might do this because they reproached him with his evil, or perhaps because he encroaches on the worship of the Church, employing the power of unclean nations.[39] Thus he knows that it is not of his own power that he does this, but by the power of strangers that he devastates all things. Two horns are mentioned on the beast that ascends from the earth (Rev. 13:11), because the Roman empire rests upon heretics and tyrants as its agents. The other beast, the one from the sea with the ten horns, will be joined to the empire, so that the Church will be almost submerged between Scylla and Charybdis, enduring false nations on top of heretics. When it is said that the water was higher than the mountains (Gen. 7:19), incredibly high, it means that it will destroy all things so that there will be nowhere that will escape its flood. . . .

Doubtless the basilisk himself will fly higher and farther so that he will afflict the Church throughout the whole breadth of the empire. As if to swallow the bird, he will sit like God in the Temple (2 Thess. 2:4), either in his own person or in his seed.[40] For thus it is written: "Because you have said, 'I am God and dwell in the heart of the sea,' I will destroy you from the midst of the live coals" (Ezek. 28:2, 16). . . .[41]

Hence the Lord will restore the Church to life with a sword hard, large, and strong. The German empire has always been hard, cruel, and alien to us: hard in its yoke, cruel in its rod, alien in its scepter. It is necessary that the Lord destroy it with the sword of the Spirit and of fury so that all the kings of the earth may tremble at the crash of its ruin.

Translated from *In Hieremian* (Venice: Benalius, 1525), ff. 45v–46r.

The Erythraean Sibyl

An eagle with one head and sixty feet will come.[42] In color like a leopard, with a breast like a fox, and a tail like a lion,[43] he will say "Peace!" that he may be able to take captives without a struggle. He will be fed at the breasts of the Spouse of the Lamb while he grows a second larger head at Rome and a third smaller one.[44] There will be whisperings from Germany to Tyre.

He will be given one hen from the Moors, another will be from the

East. He will have two chicks and devour one, though that one will come back to life as we will show below.[45] The third hen will be British, and she will bear one chick, another, and another.[46] The fourth will be German and will bear two chicks; the fifth French of whom we will speak below. . . .[47]

Hence the eagle will rest in Sicily until the French hen comes. She will close his eyes in death and hidden away she will outlive him. There will sound forth among the people: "He lives; he does not live!" One of the chicks and one of the chicks of the chicks will survive him. The crow of the cock will be heard as far as Sicily. . . .[48]

Translated from the longer text edited by O. Holder-Egger, "Italienische Prophetieen," *Neues Archiv* (1890), 15:165–68.

Commentary on Isaiah

It is necessary that the more widely the kingdom of France spreads out its branches, the more lightly it will bend the shoulders of its arrogance to the nod of the Church at the sign of the cross.[49] As Jeremiah says: "The daughter of Egypt is thrown into confusion and betrayed into the hands of the people of the North" (Jer. 46:24). The public is not ignorant of how much the power of the German empire wore down that same kingdom in past days. Yet, under the seed of the seventh head of the beast or dragon (Rev. 17:8–12), that power will rise up a bit and be brought to the nursery. Within Italian territory it will shave the tail and head of the dragon with its modest forces, both in the case of the college of Peter the fisherman and in that of the "Summit" of the kingdom of France.[50] The barbaric remnants of the kingdom of Sicily can be humbled or destroyed, partly by baptism and partly by steel.[51] Nevertheless, he will be a hazard to French fierceness, because whichever chick from the third nest shall set up the burden of the realm after the others, he will be so enkindled against insane rivals that what was written must be understood anagogically: "The Beast that was and is not" (Rev. 17:8), as though he had been led down to destruction at the End of time.[52] He is the eighth beast and yet belongs to the seven, for which reason he stands among the successors of the Eagle and in the multitude of Gog, the final false prophet. The rest of chapter seventeen is to be considered under another type of understanding. If the beast with the seven horns is the eighth beast and yet belongs to the group of seven, he shall certainly have been destroyed among the remnant, at least for the duration of the threatening sixth age. Nevertheless, he will again rise up alive and will disturb both those within and without.[53]

Translated from *Abbatis Joachim Florensis Scriptum super Esaiam Prophetam* (Venice: L. de Soardis, 1517), f. 59r–v.

A CURIAL VERSION OF THE LAST EMPEROR[54]

A new king will come and will prostrate the whole world
To vanquish with horror of war the farthest region.
He hastens from the high and craggy mountains,
From an unhoped-for source, a mild man without guile.
Poor in resources, rich in goodness, richest in his
Bountiful understanding. Because of his merit God will be his seer.
He will conquer the Sicilians and the evil tribe of the
Savage Frederick. They will not be named any more.
He will rebuild all the things which the harsh Frederick,
His savage shoot, and its successor overthrew.
Under the guidance of the pope he will put the Romans in sore straits;
They will strengthen Rome and thus bear the burden.
After that, by battle they will drag the followers of Mohammed to Christ
So that there will be one flock and one shepherd.[55]
You, my companions, have confidence that all these things
Were revealed to me by the science of the moving heavens.
One thousand two hundred and fifty-six years
Had gone by when the work was completed.

Translated from O. Holder-Egger, "Italienische Prophetieen," *Neues Archiv* (1905), 30:383–84.

21. Merlin, the British Seer

In any late medieval list of prophetic authorities three names are unavoidable—the Sibyl, Joachim, and Merlin. The historical Joachim we have already seen, as well as the beginnings of the pseudonymous Joachim. The revival of the Sibylline tradition in the twelfth century was to suffer no diminution during the next three hundred years, though interpretation rather than the creation of new texts was the order of the day. But how did Merlin, the legendary sixth-century British seer, come to occupy such an important place in the apocalyptic tradition?

The impetus behind the beginning of Merlin's fame as prophet was due to the genius of Geoffrey of Monmouth (c.1100–1155), a Breton-Welsh ecclesiastic and littérateur. Geoffrey's masterpiece, *The History of the Kings of Britain* (c.1136), wove together a mass of legendary material, much of it Celtic in origin, into a narrative of truly epic dimensions.[1] Central to Geoffrey's glorification of the kings of Britain was his account of the reign of King Arthur. The story of Arthur's immediate forebears is interwoven with that of the prophet Merlin Ambrosius, the child of a princess and a demon *incubus,* the magician who brought Stonehenge from Ireland to Salisbury Plain.[2] Geoffrey was undoubtedly aware of Welsh traditions about the poet and seer Myrddin, but in name and in character Merlin contains the unmistakable cast of originality as well as the use of tradition. The author's fascination with the character is shown by the fact that the section devoted to Merlin's prophecies of the dooms of Britain (VII, 1–4) formed an earlier and independent work. To compound further the problems relating to Geoffrey's views and sources, he later wrote a *Life of Merlin,* a poem of some 1,500 lines completed about 1150. In this work he makes use of Celtic mythic materials about a wild man of the woods to create a somewhat different and more authentic picture of the Celtic Merlin—a king struck with madness who flees to the wood of Calidon in Scotland (hence called Merlin Calidonius) and there acquires prophetic powers.[3] Although Geoffrey attempts to reconcile both Merlins in the *Life,* the identification is strained.

What is of real significance is that a potent figure had been launched into the prophetic consciousness of coming ages—a seer famed for his ability to foretell the future, especially the fate of kings and their realms. Throughout the later Merlin materials, it is political prophecy rather than speculation about the End which is central.[4]

Merlin's fame spread rapidly in the twelfth and thirteenth centuries; the mass of material devoted to him is impressive in scope.[5] Although the figure of Merlin the seer and adviser to Arthur was of some significance in the development of the Arthurian Romances,[6] Merlin the prophet maintained a distinct reputation.[7] Paul Zumthor's survey of the evidence shows that over one hundred different texts from five countries in the period between 1135 and 1750 are witnesses to the fame of the prophet.[8] Many new productions came to be ascribed to the Celtic seer, and it should not surprise us that the largest and most interesting body of this material comes from thirteenth-century Italy—the Italian hunger for prophetic messages could scarcely have neglected to make use of a name whose reputation was European-wide.

Both Latin and vernacular Merlin texts were produced in thirteenth-century Italy, many of them having some connection with the epic quarrel between the House of Hohenstaufen and the papacy.[9] One key text appears to have perished. The pseudo-Joachite *Book of Fiore,* composed about 1304, says: "Because I am concerned to fulfill the prophetic message in other matters, I do not make any mention of kings. The same Merlin, perhaps at the request of Arthur, who was then reigning in England, described kings more seriously than anything else in the time to come."[10] A number of fourteenth- and fifteenth-century authors also refer to the *Book of Kings* of Merlin, thus leading H. Grundmann to postulate the existence of a work by this name produced in Italy, perhaps in Venice, sometime in the second half of the thirteenth century.[11] More important than the hypothetical *Book of Kings* was the brief text known as The Sayings of Merlin, obscure lines describing the careers of the first and second Frederick and cited by Matthew of Paris and Salimbene among others.[12] They appear to be the work of first-generation Joachites, especially in their opposition to Frederick II. Among the works ascribed to Joachim was the *Exposition on the Sibyls and on Merlin,* a Franciscan Joachite commentary on the Erythraean Sibyl and an expanded version of The Sayings of Merlin. It was probably composed in the early 1250s.[13] This text, still unedited, is interesting for its combination of the three most potent names in thirteenth-century apocalyptic. Other Latin Merlin texts exist, notably the prophetic verses on the Italian cities.[14] The surviving texts are undoubtedly but a part of the mass of material available in Italy in the centuries to come.

The vernacular Merlin prophecies are best represented by *Les Pro-phécies de Merlin,* a lengthy mixture of prose romance and prophecy that was originally written in French of the Franco-Venetian dialect, but also survives in Italian translations. L. A. Paton has shown that *Les Prophécies* was probably composed in Venice by an anti-imperial Franciscan about 1275.[15]

Fourteenth-century apocalyptic authors, notably Cola di Rienzo, John of Rupescissa, and Telesphorus of Cosenza make reference to the British seer; but there seems to have been little new creation under the name of Merlin after about 1300. Fifteenth- and sixteenth-century witnesses are also found throughout Europe, but the strictures of the Council of Trent against the sayings ascribed to Merlin spelled an end to his prophetic career outside the British Isles.

GEOFFREY OF MONMOUTH, *HISTORY OF THE KINGS OF BRITAIN*

I had not yet reached this place in the history when, since everybody was talking about Merlin, my contemporaries, especially Alexander, the bishop of Lincoln, a man of deep religion and prudence, persuaded me to publish his prophecies.[16] No other person among the clergy or laity had so many noble friends as Alexander; his gentle devotion and kind generosity attracted many to his service. Having decided to please him above all others, I translated the prophecies and sent them to him with the following letter.

"Bishop Alexander of Lincoln, love of your nobility compels me to translate the prophecies of Merlin from the British into Latin before I complete the *History* I began of the Kings of Britain.[17] I had proposed to finish the *History* first and develop the other work later, lest involving myself in both labors, my mind would be less apt for each."

While Vortigern, king of the Britons, sat on the edge of the empty pool, two dragons appeared, one white and one red.[18] They approached each other and engaged in a savage fight, breathing fire. The white dragon prevailed and chased the red one to the edge of the pool. But the red dragon, bewailing the fact that he was driven out, made an attack on the white dragon and compelled him to withdraw. While they were fighting like this, the king bade Merlin Ambrosius to say what the battle of the dragons portended. He straightaway burst into tears, called up his prophetic spirit and said:

"Woe to the red dragon for his destruction is nigh. The white dragon who signifies the Saxons you have called in will take his caves. The red dragon is the British people who will be oppressed by the white dragon— their mountains and valleys will be leveled and their river valleys will run with blood. Religious worship will be destroyed, the churches will be ruined. He who is oppressed will finally prevail and will resist the savagery of the strangers. . . .[19]

Translated from the edition of E. Faral, *La légende arthurienne* (Paris: H. Champion, 1929), 3:189–91.

MERLIN IN ITALY

The Sayings of Merlin

The first F, a lamb in his shorn hair, a lion in his mane, will be a destroyer of cities. In the midst of a just resolve he will die between the crow and the crow.[20] He will survive in H who will die at the gates of Milazzo.[21]

The Second F will be of unhoped-for and miraculous origin.[22] The lamb will be torn to pieces among the goats, but not devoured by them. His marriage bed will swell and will prove fruitful in the neighbors of the Moors, and he will be relieved in them.[23] After that he will be enveloped by his own blood, but not dipped in it for long; nonetheless, he will nest there.[24] In the third nest will be lifted up the one who will devour the preceding sons like a lion raging among his own.[25] He (i.e., the second F) will have great confidence in his own prudence. He will plant the sons of Gaytan[26] and will divide and threaten the city of Rome. He will be in sole possession of the spirit in Jerusalem; he will fall in thirty-two years, though he will live in his prosperity sixty-two years.[27]

He will be mildly treated twice in fifty years.[28] Rome he will look upon with a fierce eye, and his sons he will see rise up against him. In his time the sea will be reddened with holy blood,[29] and his common enemies will advance as far as Naples. When he has gathered a garrison from the north he will avenge the blood that has been spilled. Woe to those who cannot return to the vessels! After eighteen years he will be anointed and will hold the

monarchy in the sight of the envious.[30] At his death all who cursed him will
be frustrated.

Translated from O. Holder-Egger, "Italienische Prophetieen," *Neues Archiv* (1890),
15:175–177.

The Beginning of the Exposition of the Abbot Joachim
on the Sibyls and Merlin

Your Serenity[31] commands me to interpret Merlin, the British seer, and
the Erythraean prophetess of Babylon, as if when their prophecies were
gathered together the other prophetic figures had not said such things or ones
similar to them concerning your times and those of your heirs. If they sometimes so disagree that they conceal and dull the understanding of the reader,
even here I do not see how your rule could be brought to completion in more
adequate fashion, unless other advice is brought in to the contrary so that
you can make a stronger argument from it. You should prefer that the future
events understood by the announcements of Babylon[32] be denied, lest it
should at some time happen that you have to do public penance in your successors. Therefore we have combined the messages of each seer so that we
can expound their mind more correctly.[33]

A translation of the introductory letter of the unpublished pseudo-Joachite *Expositio Abbatis
Joachimi super Sibillis et Merlino* as found in Paris, Bibl. nat. ms. lat. 3319, ff. 9v–10r.

The Prophecies of Merlin

Chapter 86. "Now put in your writing that in the time of the champion
who will die in contumacy there will be a buzzard that will think himself a
young falcon.[34] In the time that he will think himself a young falcon he will
do great destruction on the son of a falcon in Modena and the surrounding
country. Before his father loses everything, the Romans of the City of B.
will capture him and will keep him in prison throughout almost all his
life."[35] "When will it be?" said Master Anthony. And Merlin said, "In the
time that the thing[36] which was once born near Jerusalem will be 1248 and a
half years old."

Chapters 174–175. . . . . Merlin was saying that it will come to pass
before the coming of the dragon of Babylon that a Champion will be
crowned with a crown of iron.[37] It will take place in a chapel of Monza, and
he shall not depart from there before burning a great number of men and
women. If you wish to know their number, I tell you that they shall be more
than four thousand, all heretics to the faith of Our Lord Jesus Christ, be-

cause they shall keep a faith which shall not be worthy of praise in the world.[38] I also want you to know that Merlin said that right there where they will be burnt a great rain will fall so that all the earth will be as wet as when it lies under water. . . .[39]

"I wish furthermore," Merlin was saying, "that you know that this champion will make a truce with the pagans in order to destroy the heretics who shall take example from Lombardy.[40] He will establish throughout his empire that anybody found not believing perfectly in the Holy Trinity and the sacraments of Holy Church will be taken and burnt to ashes. This shall be done everywhere, because he will command that at that time there shall be no more wars and everyone shall be obedient to this Champion of all men." "If you wish to know," said Merlin, "in what land he will be born, I tell you openly he will be from Wales. When he shall destroy all the heretics, the truce with the pagans will be over, and he will go by sea to the proximity of Jerusalem along with the Doge of the Good Sailors,[41] a great part of the Lombards, and the French who will go with him to avenge the death of their lineage.[42] Almost all the Christians will go with him, and the pagans of Babylon with them.[43] The pagans of all heathendom will go against them," said Merlin. "When they shall cross the sea in the ships of the Good Sailors, know for certain that because of the faith they will have in the Lord God the pagans from overseas, who will not have any confidence in the Lord God, will not last against them."

This text also stated that a little afterwards or before Merlin said there would be an army overseas near Jerusalem by whom the Holy Land should be taken away from the the hands of the pagans, as well as the great pagan land that is called T.[44] This shall be done by the Good Champion with the Doge of the Good Sailors, as you have heard here before. But the pagans will recover a great part of his towns. At that point Merlin said that almost all of great heathendom will be destroyed, and the pagans will never recover towns or castles. As he said, they will not recover what they have lost through the Champion of Wales, who will take almost the whole world for himself. He shall put under him Rome and all Italy; no part shall ever be recovered by the pagans.

Translated by Peter Dembowski for this volume from the edition of L. A. Paton, *Les Prophécies de Merlin*, 1:142, 219–21.

22. *The Angelic Pope*

The rise of the papacy to a position of universal religious authority and immense political prestige was the most striking institutional development of the late eleventh and early twelfth centuries. By the beginning of the thirteenth century, in the person of Innocent III, "Vicar of Christ," "Ordinary Judge of All Things," and holder of the "Fullness of Power," the papacy had reached its apogee. Later in the century, at least some of Innocent's successors, such as Innocent IV and Boniface VIII, appear to have gone beyond him in their claims, if not in the effectiveness of their rule.[1]

Not only the position but the occupants of the papal throne had changed. Since the time of Alexander III, the opponent of Barbarossa, the popes had increasingly come from a common mold; they were skilled lawyers, efficient administrators, subtle diplomats, but rarely men noted for personal sanctity.[2] As the popes took a more active role in the political questions of the day, as they became more embroiled in the administration and defense of the Papal States, they came to seem less and less different from the other princes of Europe. In an age when poverty of life was a supreme religious ideal, the financial necessities engendered by the papacy's position as a world power made it vulnerable to attacks for avarice, strictures that had already begun with such twelfth-century reformers as Bernard of Clairvaux and Gerhoh of Reichersberg.

The contrast between the compromised popes of the time and widespread hopes for more saintly popes to come was at the root of the formation of a new and potent apocalyptic myth during the course of the thirteenth century, the legend of the *pastor angelicus,* the Angelic Pope. Like the stories regarding the Last World Emperor, the hopes for the Angelic Pope that became a part of the apocalyptic scenario in the late Middle Ages were fundamentally an attempt to validate the meaning of the newly potent office in terms of the Christian understanding of history. If the papacy really was the central institution that the Great Reform had made it, it had to have a commensurate role in the final events which give history its full meaning, even though there was not the slightest hint of such a role in the canonical Scriptures. Unlike the myth of the Last Emperor, however, the peculiar position of the thirteenth-century papacy, where spiritual claims seemed to jar with political and financial realities, gave the apocalyptic understanding of the papacy a dialectical character. Apocalyptic themes could be used not only to strengthen hopes for a holy pope to come, but also as a weapon to attack a present pope whose lack of sanctity, opulence of life, or involvement in politics might be an occasion for scandal.[3] Since the Antichrist had long been portrayed as a false teacher sitting in the Temple (i.e., the Church), one might go a step further and identify some present or proximate occupant of the Chair of Peter with the Final Enemy. The identification of the pope with the Antichrist begins in the thirteenth not the sixteenth century.

The conception of a *pastor angelicus* who would rule over a better state of the Church to come is closely connected to Joachim's melioristic view of history. Although the Calabrian nowhere makes use of the term *pastor angelicus,* his speculations on the role of the papacy at the end of the second *status* and during the course of the third were vital to later developments. The early Joachite literature kept these hopes alive, as a passage from the *Commentary on Jeremiah* shows, but the first clear reference to an individual holy pope expected in the near future (though again the term *pastor angelicus* is not used) comes from the pen of Roger Bacon in the 1260s. The struggle between good and evil in the apocalyptic view of the papacy was highlighted in an important Joachite treatise probably written in the 1290s and known as the *Angelic Oracle of Cyril.* An angel appearing to the holy Carmelite Cyril during the sacrifice of the mass supposedly communicated these revelations to him on two silver tablets. Because of their excessive obscurity (that part at least of the story is true), Cyril sent them to Joachim, who composed a commentary upon them.[4] Among the most widely read of apocalyptic writings, especially in the fourteenth century, the *Oraculum* did much to popularize the conflict between a coming holy pope, or *orthopontifex,* and an evil *pseudopontifex.*

A number of late thirteenth-century popes, most notably Clement IV (1265–1268) and Gregory X (1271–1276), who were hailed by their contemporaries as reformers, contributed to the growth of the *pastor angelicus* figure. The most significant impetus for these notions, though, came from one of the strangest incidents in the long history of the papacy, the election of Pope Celestine V.

In making the College of Cardinals the sole body empowered to choose a new pope, the eleventh-century reformers eventually assured the end of the succession of imperial antipopes, but at the price of schisms or interminable conclaves when the Sacred College was deeply divided. One of the worst of these indecisive conclaves took place after the death of Nicholas IV in 1292 when, for over two years, pro- and anti-French groups among the cardinals failed to reach agreement on a successor. Eventually, either by desperation or by revelation, an aged Benedictine hermit of great sanctity, Peter Morrone, was unwillingly chosen pope in July of 1294, taking the name of Celestine V. Celestine reigned only until December of the same year, when he voluntarily abdicated. It is clear that he was totally unfitted for the task that the thirteenth-century papacy had become, but in his sanctity and poverty of life (the pope reportedly built himself a hut to live in in the papal palace at Naples), as well as in the favor he showed to the Franciscan Spirituals, Celestine was hailed by many as the long-awaited holy pope.[5] The unusual circumstances of his withdrawal and the fact that he was succeeded by one of the least spiritual men to hold the papal office, Boniface VIII (1294–1303), an avowed enemy of the Spirituals, who imprisoned Celestine for safekeeping, led to a rush of apocalyptic attacks on the contemporary papacy and many predictions of coming holy popes in the last decade of the thirteenth century and early years of the fourteenth.

The new circumstances produced a new genre. Among the most popular of the late medieval apocalyptic texts were the *Vaticinia de summis pontificibus,* or Papal Prophecies, frequently ascribed to Joachim of Fiore and known in more than fifty mss. and twenty printed versions.[6] The Prophecies were apparently composed during the summer of 1304 at Perugia during another crucial papal interregnum after the death of Boniface's brief successor, Benedict XI.[7] A group of Franciscan Spirituals under the leadership of Fra Angelo of Clareno had recently returned from the East where they may have come into contact with illustrated twelfth-century Byzantine prophecies of present and future emperors, the so-called Oracles of Leo the Wise.[8] The fusion of the Greek form with the Joachite content of hope for a coming holy pope or popes led to the composition of fifteen brief illustrated prophecies whose major intent was probably to seek to influence the crucial election of 1304. Using the *vaticinium ex eventu* technique, a series of easily identifiable descriptions and pictures extends from Nicholas III (1277–1280) to Benedict XI (1303–1304). Celestine V appears as a holy hermit; Boniface

VIII as the epitome of hypocrisy. Clement V, who was elected in June 1305, does not appear; in his stead there are figures judging Rome followed by five angelic popes.[9] As Reeves puts it: "The Joachites were able, through these symbols, to make a veiled but bitter commentary on the contemporary papacy and then to highlight the Joachimist expectation."[10] Another group of prophecies about the popes, though without illustrations, the *Book of Fiore,* may have been produced by the same circle and was also ascribed to Joachim.[11]

Predictions regarding future popes were to remain popular for many centuries. The original fifteen composed in 1304 were soon outdated by circumstances, so in the 1340s a second set of fifteen was produced by a group of Florentine Fraticelli (i.e., nonregular followers of St. Francis).[12] In later manuscripts and printed editions this series, ending with the Antichrist, was prefixed to the earlier group to produce a somewhat confusing compilation.[13] Many later writers made use of this material in a wide variety of ways. Enigmatic prophecies regarding coming popes down to the End of the world continued to be popular even into the sixteenth century, as the famous St. Malachy Prophecies probably composed in 1590 show. They end their series of one hundred and eleven popes with a *pastor angelicus.*[14]

COMMENTARY ON JEREMIAH[15]

The rest, O Prince, can take place among your heirs. Another High Priest, like Zedekiah, will fight against the empire,[16] because the popes were scarce able to bear the yoke of your fathers and your little finger is heavier than the loins of your father (1 Kings 12:10). This distress will last from the current year 1197 for sixty-four years that will be worse than the preceding ones. During these years there is no doubt that some popes will hazard something against the princes, others will be peaceful. Perhaps others, wishing to throw off every weight of slavery from the Church, will suffer more serious distress as their forces weaken. . . .[17] The future migration will indeed be worse than the former one because it will be arrogant, although not harder. Therefore Peter will be crucified, the pope will be killed, and according to the doctors, the conventual sheep and their subjects will be scattered at the death of the pastor.[18] I do not know if it will be after three days or three years that the Good Shepherd and Leader of the House of Israel will arise, because there is no passage concerning anyone being in charge during this space. Therefore, perhaps the Church will lack a ruler when Pilate rules as Antichrist with the support of the Jews, that is, grasping[19] traitors. The Christian people and even the pope will either actually be killed or will be afflicted in spirit.

Translated from *In Hieremiam* (Venice: Benalius, 1525), f. 53r.

ROGER BACON ON THE COMING HOLY POPE[20]

The Third Work[21]

O most holy Father and wisest Lord, may your glory deign to consider that you alone are able to bring the cure since there never has been, nor will be, I believe, a pope who knew the law as truly as you do. Even though some men know the law well, there is no hope that they will become pope. Forty years ago it was prophesied, and there have been many visions to the same effect, that there will be a pope in these times who will purify Canon Law and the Church of God from the sophistries and deceits of the jurists so that justice will reign over all without the rumbling of lawsuits. Because of the goodness, truth, and justice of this pope the Greeks will return to the obedience of the Roman Church, the greater part of the Tartars will be converted to the faith, and the Saracens will be destroyed. There will be one flock and one shepherd, as the prophet heard (John 10:16). One who saw these things through revelation has spoken of them,[22] and he said that he would see these marvels in his own time. Certainly, if God and the pope so wished, they could happen within the space of a single year, or even in less time. They could happen in your reign.

Translated from J. S. Brewer, *Fr. Rogeri Bacon Opera Quaedam Hactenus Inedita* (RS 15), p. 86.

The Compendium of Study.[23]

The proof of love is in action, as Gregory says,[24] and therefore since we see such great corruption of life everywhere, especially among the clergy, their education is also necessarily corrupt. Many wise men have thought about this. Reflecting upon divine wisdom, the knowledge of the saints, the truths of history, as well as prophecies both sacred and solid (like those of the Sibyls, of Merlin, of Aquila, of Festo, and of many other wise men),[25] they have thought that the days of the Antichrist would come in this period. Therefore it is necessary that evil be stamped out so that God's elect plainly appear. A very holy pope will first come who will remove all the corruptions in education and the Church and all the rest. Then the world will be renewed and the fullness of peoples will enter in; even the remnants of Israel will be converted to the faith.

Translated from J. S. Brewer in *RS* 15: 402.

SALIMBENE ON GREGORY X

In the year of Our Lord 1276, in the fourth indiction, Pope Gregory X died at Arezzo, a city in Tuscany, on the tenth of January, the feast of St. Paul the first hermit. This pope was most zealous in the things of God and proposed to do much that he was not able to bring to completion because he was prevented by death. . . .

These are the verses that were sent to some cardinals and also to a provincial chapter of the Dominicans many months before Gregory X was chosen pope, as a worthy Dominican priest who gave me the verses related. About three months before the election of Gregory X, I saw these verses in the original:[27]

> In the third year of Clement IV
> A holy pope will be given to the just people;
> By Christ's gift a more holy man will succeed Clement,
> A good and faithful servant from God's heaven. . . .

> God will adorn him and make him illustrious in a wondrous manner,
> He will make him holy, great, and glorious.
> He will give peace to the world and renew Jerusalem.[28]
> He will give fruits to the earth; God will give joy to the world. . . .
> About the year one thousand two hundred and seventy-four
> He, the Holy Pope, about forty years of age,
> Will appear. The man of angelic life
> Will hold to the decrees of Christ.
> You should fear, O you Giezites![29]
> O holy Christ, you will then restore your beautiful Sepulcher to us
> When the Saracens have been subject and rejected.[30]

Translated from Salimbene, *Chronica* (*MGH. SS.* XXXII), pp. 491–93.

THE ANGELIC ORACLE OF CYRIL AND
PSEUDO-JOACHIM'S COMMENTARY[31]

Chapter VI

. . . . Then you will behold the celibates and servants of the bed chamber weep with Rehoboam and the foolish mixed with the avaricious laugh with Jeroboam until the tears of Rehoboam water Jeroboam.[32] Aridity, grinding against the heavy altar of the prince, will preside, prophesying not in hatred of the cross, but of his saved ones. An unheard-of novelty will precede these things, because the moneychangers of the highest table will be gathered together at the leafy pear tree, high and thorny, watered by the Tiber. There the ancients of the diadem, the chiefs of poison, will place their treasure, lest it be snatched by the Romans. There they will play at dice, portraying themselves as men wholly expectant and ready to do great deeds. Drunken and asleep, they make little value[33] of the damage of the poor and the blood of the struggling slaves, until a wondrous bear, moved by the Spirit, comes forth from the rock and hastens to the Queen of Feathers and the New Seer.[34] He will smash the gaming table and scatter those sitting there. . . .

Commentary

"Then the celibates." This text alludes to the Elect One. We know that Rehoboam, the son of Solomon, was the true King of Israel, and Jeroboam a false king, though God tolerated him because of the people's sin, as we have it in 1 Kings 12–13. So it must soon happen that "the celibates and servants of the bed chamber," that is, the virtuous and true servants of the Roman Church, will follow Rehoboam, the true pope canonically elected. The "foolish and avaricious," that is, the lechers and gluttons, will follow Jeroboam, the evil and wicked false pope. May I not see such great confusion in the days of my life! . . .

"The money changers." By the name of moneychangers understand the cardinals and prelates who change spiritual things for temporal by committing the evil of simony. "The highest table" is the Church, or the altar where is eaten the true Lamb who gives life to the world. Hence he says of himself, "Who eats me, lives because of me" (John 6:52). "At the leafy pear tree." I do not clearly see what this pear tree is, unless we understand Perugia through it, because it is leafy (that is, well populated), has towers, and is watered by the Tiber which is beside it. . . .

"Until a wondrous bear comes." This bear is a Roman pope.[35] Just as a little bear is formed by the licking of its parents, the pope and any true prelate is appointed by the voice or tongue of the electors. It can also be said that before his election such a pope despised precious garments like a bear which among the beasts is covered with mean and contemptible wool. So he is said to be "wondrous" and moved by the "Feathered Spirit."[36]

Translated from the edition of P. Piur, "Oraculum Angelicum Cyrilli nebst dem Kommentar des Pseudojoachim," vol. 2, part 4, pp. 281–82, 289–92.

ROBERT OF UZÈS ON THE PAPAL CRISIS[37]

A Vision of Robert [38]

In the same place I saw in a dream that I was with my oldest brother and younger sister. While we were walking we came to a door and heard the words: "The pope is inside, if you wish to see him." We entered and kissed his feet as he stood on the ground. I was amazed that he would sit upon the ground and looked upon his short narrow bed with its very poor covering. I said: "Why is it, Father, that you have such a poor bed? The poorest of the poor bishops of the world would not have a meaner one." The pope said to me, "We must be humbled." Suddenly we were on our way down a mountain and I saw him in the habit of the Friars Minor.[39] I fell upon my face and kissed his naked foot; then I held him up on the right side. As we began to ascend the mountain, I held the pope up on the left side and a secular priest supported him on the right. While we ascended, the pope began to limp badly so that he would not have been able to go up had we not carried him. While we carried him, we entered a hospice at the top of the mountain; there were kettles and pots there, but the fire was out. We glanced all around and saw no one, but when we entered we looked in a small place as through a window and saw some women looking at the pope. He lifted up his hand and blessed them.

Translated from the edition of J. Bignami-Odier, "Les visions de Robert d'Uzès," p. 279.

Book of the Sermons of God [40]

On a Friday in the year and month mentioned above, while I was walking from Orange to Avignon on the bank of the Rhone on the imperial side, the word of the Lord came to me at sunrise saying: "My servant, speak to the pastors of my flock who are here about. Hide nothing from them of what I will say."

Say to the Angel of the Church:[41] " 'In your simplicity you nourish wolves who rend my flock' (Jer. 23:1). I will pay you a visit (Exod. 3:16), because you have been deceived and have not known the rending of my flock. I will bring a great plague unless you correct this sin.[42] I will demand the blood of my sheep at your hand. Remember your begging and resist proud thoughts (Rom. 12:16); as a humble man do not abandon the humble works you have begun. I will reward the humble. See what your subjects are doing and let not such things go unpunished. The day of your destruction upon which I shall take revenge is near."

You are to speak to the Idol of the Church, unless his heart be hardened.[43] Say this so that your word may be a witness: "Who has placed this Idol upon my throne to command my people? He has ears and does not hear (Ps. 113:6, etc.) the cries of those lamenting and of those who are going down to hell. Their wailing exceeds the sound of the trumpet, the loud voice of thunder. . . . He has a mouth and does not speak. He is always saying, "I have set men up over them to announce good things to them. It is enough that either through me or through others some good is done." Woe to the Idol! Woe to the one in possession! Who upon the earth is like this Idol? He has magnified his name upon the earth saying, "Who will put me down?"

Translated from J. Bignami-Odier, "Les visions de Robert d'Uzès," p. 290.

THE PAPAL PROPHECIES. FIRST SET

V. Title. The Raising of Poverty. Obedience. Chastity. Temperance. The Destroyer of Hypocrisy [44]

Again see the strange measure of one rising up. The large sickle and rose he bears (the third having been previously doubled) are divided in the first element. I write to you that four months[45] will be given to the sickle-bearer.[46] You consume every principality with the sword; you will bring the temples of the idols to life after a short time. You will live three years in the world as a very old man. At the end, through two tribulations, you will sink down to hell.[47]

VI. Title. The Harvest of Hypocrisy Will Be in Abomination

The fifth cow.[48] The end of the one feeding the bears.[49] The figure manifests his place and his duration. He will come alone from that place and will manifest his first friends to me. You have the virtues of the others. You give more to your friends, therefore you have found a most delicious end. You alone will be lifted on high by glory. Leaving dead powers behind in a powerful way, you will find powers like the rainfall.

XI. Title. A Good Mark of Respect

There will be revealed[50] an anointed one who has the first name of a monk. He will live on a rock.[51]

"The lamentations of the others have come to me. Having left the world, I have a peasant's diet of herbs. I live in the world like a dead man, one groaning. I gather together good things and scatter every reward of evil-doing."[52]

He will be totally justified when the Star appears black to you. You will then be naked and go into the depths of the earth.[53]

XIII. Title. Honor Anticipated. Concord Will Come[54]

This man will be of the first hidden kind.[55] After many years, he will enter in, at first as a single individual. Naked he will come from the dark rock that he may begin a second glorious life. He, the truest image of the second life, when he has been made so firm in double years, will die and enter the rock of the tomb.

XV. Title. Reverence and Devotion Will Increase[56]

You have found a good life far away from dishonor. You have received more from virtue than from fortune, but you have not gained virtuous grace. You have encountered judgments made harmful by envy. You will not be deprived by fate from above. Woe to the city of blood completely filled by the sundering of lies! Rapine will not depart from you, nor the sound of the whip, of the turning wheel, of the horse, of the howl!

These Prophecies are notoriously obscure and vary considerably in the numerous mss. and in the printed editions. These translations are based upon the texts found in *Profetie dell'Abbate Gioachino* (Padua: Stamparia Camerale, 1625), pp. 51, 54, 65, 70, 75, as corrected by comparison with two mss.: Vat. lat. 3822, f. 6r–v (one of the earliest known); and Vat. lat. 3816, ff. 15r–32r (dated 1448).

23. Bonaventure's Apocalyptic Theology of History

In 1257 when John of Parma was compelled to step down as head of the Franciscan order, he was succeeded by the young master of theology, John of Fidanza, better known as Bonaventure. The new general, who was to rule the order until his death in 1274, faced a difficult situation. There is no doubt that he had to act to suppress the lunatic fringe of Joachites within the Franciscans, and it was such activity that was the source of later stories of Bonaventure's vengeance on John of Parma and his opposition to the Spirituals.[1] Uncritical acceptance of these accounts has led some historians to see in Bonaventure an inveterate enemy of Joachim and of every form of apocalyptic thought.

Nothing could be farther from the truth. More recent research, especially that of Joseph Ratzinger in his work, *The Theology of History in St. Bonaventure,*[2] has shown that of the great Christian theologians of history, Bonaventure is among the most consistently apocalyptic in outlook. Deeply influenced by the Joachite tradition, he attempted to walk a delicate line between the extreme notions of Gerard of Borgo San Donnino and the complete rejection of Joachim expressed by Thomas Aquinas.[3] In spirit, if not in all particulars, Bonaventure was the ancestor of many of the later Spirituals, especially Peter Olivi.

From the early stages of his career as minister general, Bonaventure showed an interest in the apocalyptic interpretation of the person of St. Francis;[4] but it was not until the twilight of his rule as general that the full dimensions of his remarkable apocalyptic theory of history became evident. The Collations on the Hexaemeron were a series of sermons delivered to the Franciscan community at Paris in the Spring of 1273. Disturbed by the influence of Aristotelian philosophy on theological studies at Paris, concerned about the general state of the Church on the eve of the Second Council of Lyons, and troubled by the decline in fervor and the practice of poverty in the Franciscan Order, Bonaventure turned his efforts to expounding the meaning of history hidden in the *Hexaemeron,* the Genesis account of the six days of creation.

The intricate structure of the unfinished work is based upon the distinction of six visions, or ways of grasping truth, corresponding to the six days of creation. It is in the vision of the third day, that of Scripture, that the Franciscan presents both his theory of exegesis and the theology of history that grows out of it. While Bonaventure does not deny the traditional comparison of the Old Testament to the New in terms of the relation of letter to spirit, it is clear that he prefers the Abbot Joachim's historicizing concordances in which precise historical parallels can be worked out among the seven ages of each Testament. Bonaventure thought that his own time was witnessing the crisis of the sixth age prior to the time of peace before the End of the world. Both negative and positive apocalyptic signs announced the imminence of the great transition. The major evil sign of the times he found in the adulteration of the wine of revelation by the water of pagan philosophy;[5] the chief positive sign was the appearance of St. Francis, the Angel of the Sixth Seal and the harbinger of the "Seraphic order" of the coming seventh age of the Church,[6] a time when the full understanding of Scripture would be given and rational theology would be rendered superfluous. Although the Franciscan deliberately eschews any mention of a Joachite third *status* and rejects with horror the notion that the New Testament could ever be abrogated, his hopes for the dawning of the contemplative age bring him squarely within the complex of traditions initiated by Joachim. Where the Seraphic Doctor differs most markedly from the Abbot is in the profound Christocentric cast of his vision of history: "The Holy Spirit teaches the prudent man . . . that he must begin from the center which is Christ; for if this Medium is overlooked, no result is obtained."[7]

BONAVENTURE'S JOACHITE EXEGESIS

"The earth brought forth seedbearing vegetation according to its kind, and fruit trees each having fruit according to its kind" (Gen. 1:12). We said of this vision of the understanding taught by Scripture in the matter of spiritual intelligence that it was grasped through the gathering of the waters.[8] Again we said in the case of the sacramental symbol that it was understood through the germination of the earth. We have spoken of the "theories" understood through the seed and the fruit.[9] The "theories" multiply like seeds and nourish like food; therefore, they are understood partly through the seed and partly through the germination of fruit. In relation to the seed they consist in the correlations of the times in the way in which times succeed each other; in relation to the fruit of the tree they consist in the way in which the times mutually correspond to each other.[10] According to the comparison of the tree or of the seed to the seed, the times follow each other; according to the comparison of the bud to the branch, they correspond to each other, as is already clear.

The times are distinguished according to a threefold scheme, namely, according to three laws: that written within, that commanded from without, and that infused from on high, and according to a fivefold scheme: the morning, the third, sixth, ninth, and eleventh hours, the periods of vocation until the End of the world. According to this, you can also distinguish six ages, for all authors agree that the seventh age runs together with the sixth.[11] After the New Testament there will be no other Testament, nor can any sacrament of the New Law be withdrawn, because it is the Eternal Testament (Heb. 13:20).

These times follow one another and there is a great correspondence among them. They are like the germination of seed from seed; like that of tree from seed and of seed from tree. The times are so arranged that they correspond to one another, first in the order of unity, so that the one time of the Old Testament is compared to the one time of the New Testament as letter to spirit, promise to fulfillment, figure to truth, earthly to heavenly promise, fear to love. . . .

Collation 16:1–3. Translated from the edition of the Quaracchi Fathers, *S. Bonaventurae Opera omnia* (Quaracchi: College of St. Bonaventure, 1891), 5:403.

THE AGES OF THE CHURCH

According to this, the time of the founding of nature lasted from Adam to Noah, the time of the cleansing from sin from Noah to Abraham, the time of the chosen race from Abraham to Moses. God chose Abraham not Lot, Isaac not Ishmael, Jacob not Esau, and Judah from whom Christ was born. The time of the established Law lasted from Moses to Samuel, who anointed one king who was evil, one king who was chosen. The time of royal glory lasted from David to Hezekiah, when the migration of the ten tribes took place.

The time of the prophetic voice lasted from Hezekiah in the strict sense and from Uzziah the leper in the broad sense down to Zerubbabel. Under Hezekiah there was the great miracle of the thirty-two-hour day caused by the reversal of the sun. The time of peace and quiet lasted from Zerubbabel to Christ.

In the New Testament the time of the conferring of grace lasted from Christ and the Apostles to Pope Clement and included the death of John. The time of baptism in blood lasted from Clement to Silvester, because under Clement began the great persecution when the Jews were sold into slavery and expelled from Jerusalem, and Clement with his people was exiled to Chersonea in Greece. During the intervening time from Clement to Silvester there were ten great persecutions. The time of the general law lasted from Silvester to Pope Leo I; in this time the Creed was issued. The time of the law of justice lasted from Leo to Gregory, the Church Doctor; in this time the laws of Justinian were issued, as well as the canons and the monastic and canonical rules. In this time lived St. Benedict, who prophesied about St. Gregory and blessed his mother when she was pregnant with him.

The time of the lofty throne lasted from Gregory to Hadrian, under whom the empire passed to the Germans, and the rule of Constantinople was divided. Charlemagne was the emperor in the Western Church and Pepin was the first Frankish king of Italy, because when they were not able to bear the insult of foreign races they made him king of Italy and he fought the king of the Lombards and was victorious. The time of clear teaching extends from Hadrian, but who can say or has said how long it will last? It is certain that we are in it, and it is certain that it will last until the overthrow of the beast coming up from the abyss when Babylon will be confounded and destroyed and afterward peace will be given (Rev. 17:18). Nevertheless, it is first necessary that the tribulation come. The End is not to be placed there, because no one knows how long that time of great peace will last since "when they said 'Peace and security,' then suddenly destruction came upon them" (Matt. 24:21). The seventh time or age, that of quiet, begins with the shout of the angel who "swore through Him who lives forever and ever that there would be no more time; but in the days of the seventh angel the mystery of God will be completed" (Rev. 10:6–7).[12]

In the sixth age three things take place—excellence of victory, excellence of teaching, and excellence of the prophetic life. . . . In this age there ought to come a life through an order which will possess the prophetic life. This age is double. Just as in the Lord's Passion there was first light, then darkness, and then light, so it is necessary that first there be the light of teaching and that Josiah succeed Hezekiah, after which came the tribulation of the Jews through their captivity. It is necessary that one ruler, a defender of the Church, arise. He either is still to come or has already come. (He added: Would that he has not already come!)[13] After him will come the darkness of tribulations. In this age likewise Charlemagne exalted the Church and his successors attacked it. In the time of Henry IV there were two popes; the same was true under Frederick the Great. It is certain that some of them wished to destroy the Church, but "the angel ascending from the rising of the sun called out to the four angels, 'Do not harm the land and the sea until we have signed the servants of our God on their foreheads' " (Rev. 7:2–3). So the tribulation of the Church lasts even until now. It was said to the angel of Philadelphia, the sixth angel: "He who is holy and true, who has the key of David, who opens and no man closes, closes and no man opens, says this—'I know your works, and behold I have placed an open door before you' " (Rev. 3:7). (And he said that now for the first time the understanding of Scripture would be given and that the revelation, or key of David, would be given to a person or a large group, but I think rather to a large group.)[14]

In the seventh age we know that these things will take place—the rebuilding of the Temple, the restoration of the city, and the granting of peace. Likewise in the coming seventh age there will be a restoration of divine worship and a rebuilding of the city. Then the prophecy of Ezekiel will be fulfilled when the city comes down from heaven (Ezek. 40); not indeed that city which is above, but that city which is below, the Church Militant which will then be conformed to the Church Triumphant as far as possible in this life. Then will be the building and restoration of the city as it was in the beginning. Then there will be peace. God alone knows how long that peace will last.

Collation 16:17–19. Translated from *Opera omnia* 5:405–6, 408.

ST. FRANCIS AND THE CONTEMPLATIVE ORDERS

The day of human formation [the sixth day] is the age of the prophetic voice, the age of clear teaching when there will be a prophetic life. It was necessary that a single order come in this time, that is, a prophetic disposition like the order of Jesus Christ whose head would be "the angel ascending from the sun having the seal of the living God" (Rev. 7:2) and conformed to Christ. (And he said that he had already come.). . . .[15]

In the rank of the contemplatives whose task is to be concerned with divine matters there are three orders corresponding to the supreme hierarchy.[16] They consider divine things in three ways: some as supplicants, some as speculators, some as those elevated on high. In the first way are those who dedicate themselves totally to prayer, devotion, and divine praise except for the brief time when they engage in manual work or labor to support themselves and others. These are the monastic orders, whether white or black, such as the Cistercians, Premonstratensians, Carthusians, Grandmontines, and the Canons Regular. All these groups are given possessions so that they can pray for those who made the gifts. The Thrones correspond to this order.

The second order considers God through a speculative way in the manner of those who are concerned with the "speculation" of Scripture that can only be understood by those with purified minds. . . . The Cherubim correspond to this group. They are the Preachers and the Minorites. Some are principally concerned with the speculation from which they receive their name, and afterwards with piety; others principally with piety and afterwards with speculation. May that love and piety not depart from the Cherubim. (He added that St. Francis had said that he wished his brothers should study as long as they first practiced what they preached. Of what value is it to know much and to taste nothing?)

The third order is of those intent on God according to the mode of elevation, of ecstasy or of rapture. (And he said: Which is this one? It is the Seraphic order to which Francis seemed to belong. He said that even before Francis had taken the habit he had been in ecstasy when he was found near the hedge.)[17] The greatest difficulty is in the mode of elevation, because the whole body is weakened so that without some consolation from the Holy Spirit it would not be able to bear up. The Church will reach its consummation in these men. But what this future order will be, or now is, is not an easy thing to know.

The first order corresponds to the Thrones, the second to the Cherubim, the third to the Seraphim. These last are near Jerusalem and have nothing to do but fly. That order will not flourish unless Christ appears and suffers in his Mystical Body. (He said that the appearance of the Seraph to St. Francis, which was both expressive and impressed, showed that this order would correspond to him, but would nonetheless reach this through tribulations. In this vision there were great mysteries.) [18]

Collations 16:16 and 22:20–23. Translated from *Opera omnia,* 5:405, 440–41.

24. The Franciscan Spirituals

The early stages of the alliance between the radical wing of the Franciscans and apocalyptic expectations have already been portrayed, as has the modified Joachitism of Bonaventure. These encounters were followed by an equally important development in Franciscan apocalyptic—the prolonged conflict between the Spiritual and Conventual parties of the order from about 1280 to 1330.[1]

As the result of a series of papal bulls,[2] as well as Bonaventure's theology of poverty, it might have seemed that the order was on the way to a consensus regarding the issue of what constituted the theory and practice of poverty in the last quarter of the thirteenth century. Such was not to be the case. The sheer size and the key role of the Franciscans in the Church of the time made the practice of St. Francis' style of poverty difficult if not virtually impossible. The majority party, called the Conventuals, favored practical accommodations of the practice of poverty and were generally supported in this by the papacy. From the time of the death of Francis, however, a vocal minority had strenuously opposed any relaxation in poverty. Other orders had accommodated their original ideals to the service of the Church—why did this problem cause the Franciscans such particular anguish? The answer lies in the fact that the Franciscans based their uniqueness precisely upon the supposition that they and they alone practiced the "apostolic poverty" of Christ and his disciples, the poverty revived by Francis.[3] The Conventuals were generally content to have established the claim in law and have it recognized by the papacy; the opposed minority, called the Zealots, or Spirituals, continued to think that any relaxation was a betrayal of the essence of the order. To many in this group, apostolic poverty became the unique apocalyptic sign, the mark of their identification as the "spiritual men" who were to rule the Church in the age to come. For these men poverty was the outward sign of their inner devotion to the naked and crucified Christ, the very center of Francis' devotion.[4]

The opposed Conventual and Spiritual parties almost tore the order

apart. Their contention provoked continued papal interventions, and produced one of the most striking chapters in the history of medieval apocalypticism. This story can best be seen through a brief survey of the careers of
some of the most notable Spiritual leaders, specifically Peter Olivi, Angelo
of Clareno, Ubertino of Casale, and the poet Jacopone da Todi.

In the wake of rumors that the Second Council of Lyons (1274) was to
allow all orders to own possessions, and as a result of the increasingly
relaxed discipline regarding poverty in many of the houses,[5] definite centers
of resistance to any accommodation became increasingly evident about
1280. One important early center was among the Franciscan houses in Provence. It had as its spokesman the noted theologian, Peter Olivi
(c.1248–1298), a Provençal himself and student of Bonaventure, who was
certainly among the most remarkable of the sons of Francis.[6] As early as
1283, he and his followers were accused of various theological and philosophical errors. Although his opponents saw Olivi's views on apostolic poverty as dangerous to the order, he was willing to accept the papal distinction
between ownership and use. It was his continuing stress on the necessity for
the *usus pauper,* or "poor use," the strictest interpretation of poverty in
practice, that got him into trouble. Vindicated in 1287 and again in 1292, he
continued to teach at Florence, Montpellier, and Narbonne where he died. It
was during the last years of his life that he composed his major apocalyptic
work, the *Lectura,* or *Commentary on the Book of Revelation.*

No modern edition of this important text exists.[7] While Olivi cites both
authentic and pseudonymous works of Joachim, and refers to a three-*status*
theory of history, his use of Joachim is in many ways filtered through
Bonaventure's appropriation of the Calabrian's thought.[8] Central to Olivi's
view is the division of the history of the Church into seven periods. The fifth
period, that of laxity, and the sixth, the time of evangelical renewal and the
persecution of the Antichrist, overlap; the seventh period will see the age of
interior peace and spiritual understanding before the coming of Gog and the
Last Judgment. The concurrence of the fifth and the sixth periods in his own
time is visible in the conflict between the carnal Church, the body of evil-
doers within Christendom, and the spiritual Church, the true followers of
poverty. As he puts it: "Just as in the sixth age, when carnal Judaism and
the old age of the former era were rejected, the new man Christ came with a
new law, life, and cross, so the carnal Church and the old age of this era
will be rejected in the sixth *status,* for which reason Francis appeared at its

outset marked with the wounds of Christ, totally conformed to Christ and crucified with him.''[9]

The invective Olivi directs against the evidences of the carnal Church is concerned not only with the ecclesiastical abuses of the day, especially avarice and simony, but also, like Bonaventure before him, with the use of Aristotle in theology.[10] The Provençal Franciscan also expressed belief in a double Antichrist—the Mystical Antichrist, a coming false pope who would attack the Franciscan Rule,[11] and the Great, or Open Antichrist, whose defeat would usher in the final period of history. Characteristic of Franciscan apocalyptic is his emphasis on the role of Francis as the initiator of the period of renewal and his hope for the conversion of all peoples in the course of the final events.[12]

After his death, Olivi's followers, far less cautious than the master in their criticism of the contemporary Church, venerated him as almost the equal of Francis. As the campaign against the Spirituals and their sympathizers (also called Beguines in Provence)[13] grew warmer, so did the attacks on Olivi's memory. His books were burned at a Franciscan chapter in 1299, some propositions drawn from his writings were condemned by Clement V at the Council of Vienne in 1312, and after a series of investigations at Avignon his great work on Revelation was condemned by Pope John XXII in 1326.[14] Although influenced by the Joachite tradition and especially by Bonaventure, Olivi was an original thinker of great power. His writings deserve to be read on their own account, not through the haze occasioned by later controversy and misinterpretation.

The other two centers of the Spiritual party were found in Italy, specifically in Tuscany and in the Marches. A group of friars in the Marches of Ancona, under the leadership first of Conrad of Offida and later of Fra Liberato and Fra Angelo of Clareno (c.1255–1337),[15] had girded themselves for the defense of poverty from the late 1270s. After spending a number of years in Conventual prisons, Angelo and some of his followers were allowed to go to Armenia in 1289 to spread the Christian faith. They were fortunate to return in the time of Pope Celestine V, who decreed that the group was to be allowed to separate from the Franciscans and found their own order, the Poor Hermits of Celestine. After the Pope's resignation, Boniface VIII commanded them to return to the Franciscans, but they fled instead to the safety of an island in the Gulf of Corinth. Returning from exile after the death of the tyrant, they were present in Italy during the long papal interregnum of 1304–5 at which time some member of the group, whether Angelo or not, was possibly responsible for the earliest series of Joachite Papal Prophecies, as noted above. During the time of the destruction of the Spirituals under John XXII Angelo was imprisoned,[16] but he was eventually freed and remained a fugitive with other members of the proscribed order of Celestines down to his death in 1337.

Angelo's major apocalyptic work is his *History of the Seven Tribulations of the Order of Minors,* composed in the 1320s. In it the story of the true defenders of poverty from Francis on is portrayed by sketching the seven tribulations which they have had to undergo. The fourth of these was that of John of Parma attacked by Bonaventure, the fifth that of Olivi and the early Spirituals of the Marches, and the sixth (which was to last twenty-eight years) began with the abdication of Celestine and was then raging under John XXII. Angelo believed that the seventh and last persecution, the time of the Antichrist, was about to begin. After that would come an age of peace.

Tuscan Franciscans were also among the fervent proponents of ideal poverty who looked to apocalyptic ideas to defend their position. Ubertino of Casale (c.1259–c.1330) had met John of Parma and taught theology with Olivi at Florence.[17] During his career as a noted preacher, he supported Angelo's group and attacked the carnal Church until he was finally suspended in 1304. Retiring to Mount Alverna where Francis had received the stigmata, he wrote his most famous work, *The Tree of the Crucified Life of Jesus,* in 1305. This lengthy treatise mixes a wide variety of genera —scriptural commentary, scholastic *summa,* autobiography, and apocalyptic manifesto.[18] The fifth book of *The Tree of Life,* essentially a commentary on Revelation based on Olivi's work, centers on a concordance between the saving work of Jesus and the history of the Franciscan order—"a complete Franciscanizing of the Apocalypse," as G. Leff puts it.[19] In his emphasis on the laxity of the Church in the fifth age and its incipient renewal in the sixth,[20] Ubertino is an ideal representative of the apocalypticism of the Spirituals. Although he followed Olivi in most areas, unlike the Provençal he held that Celestine's abdication had been illegitimate. He was also more specific in his attacks on contemporaries, identifying Boniface VIII and Benedict XI with the two aspects of the Mystical Antichrist. For Ubertino the defeat of the Great Antichrist was to usher in the triumph of the New Jerusalem under the leadership of the Angelic Pope.

Among the other important personalities to be found in the Italian Spiritual groups was the noted poet Jacopone da Todi (c.1230–1306).[21] This wealthy Umbrian lawyer had a profound conversion experience about 1268 prompted by the death of his wife. From this time he began to compose a remarkable series of poems expressing his religious experiences, the so-called *Laudi,* mostly written in the Umbrian dialect.[22] For ten years he lived a private life of extreme asceticism and bizarre behavior, finally joining the Franciscan community at Todi about 1278. As his religious views matured and deepened, Jacopone became one of the spokesmen of the Spirituals. He spent time at the papal curia in the 1290s and supported the rebellion of the Colonna cardinals against Boniface. He suffered severely under Boniface's persecution, being imprisoned from 1298 to 1303. It was apparently from prison that the great Franciscan poet penned the *Laudi* that reflect the apocalyptic views of the Spiritual party.[23] Like Olivi, Jacopone was fortunate not to live to see the tragic conclusion to the story of the Spirituals.

Of the great leaders seen above, it was Ubertino who was most intimately involved in the dénouement. As the chaplain to Cardinal Orsini, he became the chief representative for the Spirituals at the time of Clement V's investigation of the Franciscan question prior to the Council of Vienne (1309–1312). Ubertino's defense of the "poor use" tended to cast doubts on the distinction between possession and use, the key to the Conventual position, as a mere legal fiction harmful to the true practice of poverty.[24] Clement's bull *Exivi de Paradiso* (1312) represented the last attempt at compromise—the Spirituals were not allowed to separate from the Conventuals, but some emphasis was given to the practice of poverty.

Still unsatisfied, the Spirituals in Provence and Tuscany continued their agitation. Clement's successor, the fierce old man who took the name John XXII (1316–1334), was scarcely the type to countenance such disorders. In cooperation with the new minister general, Michael of Cesena, he quickly moved against the Spirituals. The bull *Quorundam exigit* and the constitution *Gloriosam ecclesiam* damned the errors of the Beguines and Fraticelli, Olivi's Provençal followers, as well as the Tuscan Spirituals.[25] Many were arrested and imprisoned; four that refused to recant were burned as heretics at Marseilles in 1318. Although both Ubertino (who through his powerful friends received permission to transfer to the Benedictines) and Angelo survived this sixth persecution and continued to propagate their views, this action marked the end of the Spirituals as a real force in the Franciscan order. The numerous lay followers of Olivi were hounded by the Inquisition for more than a decade until they too were stamped out.[26]

The Spirituals were to have their revenge. For reasons still not perfectly clear, by about 1320 John XXII decided to reopen the whole question of Franciscan claims to apostolic poverty. In 1322 he issued a bull to this effect and heard numerous arguments on all sides, including presentations by Ubertino.[27] Despite the protests of the Conventuals and the problems created by a string of papal statements supporting the distinction between ownership and use and claiming that Christ and the apostles had owned nothing, John became convinced that the Franciscan claim to be living the absolute poverty of Christ was a sham. In 1323 he gave up the papal claim to the ownership of the consumable goods used by the order while retaining the immovables, like land and churches, and in the bull *Cum inter nonnullos* said that it was heretical to assert that Christ and the apostles had possessed nothing. A number of the Conventual leaders, among them Michael of Cesena, fled to the court of Lewis of Bavaria, the pope's enemy, from which position of safety they continued to issue broadsides against John, false pope, heretic, and tool of the Antichrist. In this at least, the Conventuals had rejoined the Beguines of the Spiritual movement for whom the condemnation of Pope John as the Antichrist was a cornerstone of belief.[28]

PETER OLIVI, *COMMENTARY ON REVELATION*

Francis as an Apocalyptic Figure

It must be understood that just as our own most holy Father Francis, after Christ and under Christ, is the first and chief founder, initiator, and exemplar of the sixth *status* and its evangelical rule, so after Christ he is designated first through this angel (Rev. 10:1–3). As a sign of this, he appears in the fiery chariot transfigured into the sun so that it might be evident that he has come in the spirit and image of Elijah and at the same time that he bore the perfect image of Christ, the true sun. He was singularly strong in every virtue and work of God. Through the deepest humility and recognition of the first source of every nature and every grace, coming down always from heaven, and through airy and subtle spiritual lightness free of every earthly weight, he was clothed with a cloud, that is, with the most profound poverty, and was filled with heavenly waters, that is, with the highest possession and draught of celestial riches. He was also clothed with a cloud, that is, the dark cloud of still contemplation which according to Dionysius in the book entitled *Mystical Theology* is signified by the cloud in which God appeared and spoke to Moses. . . .[29]

He has in his hand, that is, in fullness of work and full possession and power, the open book of the Gospel of Christ, as is evident from the Rule which he kept and wrote down, and also from the evangelical way of life that he founded. He placed his right foot upon the sea in that he went to convert the Saracens and labored with the highest energy and fervor to go to them three times to receive martyrdom, as is written in the ninth chapter of his *Life*.[30] In the sixth year from the time of his conversion he went as the Angel of the Sixth Seal and as a sign that through his order they would be converted to Christ in the sixth *status* of the Church. Again, he went in the thirteenth year from his conversion as a sign that beginning with the thirteenth century from the Passion and Resurrection of Christ, the Saracens and other infidels are to be converted through his order and its many martyrs.[31]

Translated from the partial text given in I. von Döllinger, *Beiträge zur Sektengeschichte,* 2:559–60, which I have compared with one of the better mss., Rome, Bibl. Angelica, ms. 382, ff. 72vb–73ra.

The Events of the Thirteenth Century

These generations begin from the incarnation of Christ and from the beginning parallel the generations of the Old Testament very clearly and with marvelous agreement. Joachim has a full calculation and noteworthy accuracy up to his time.[32] In the sixth year of the forty-first generation, the third *status* (that still runs along with the second) was fundamentally begun.[33] The opening of the sixth seal (still running along with the fifth) was also begun, because Francis, like the Angel of the Opening of the Sixth Seal (Rev. 7:2), was converted in that sixth year which was also the sixth year of the thirteenth centenary of the Incarnation of Christ. From that time on every persecution of his evangelical state looks forward to the persecutions of the Antichrist. Thus in Paris in the following forty-second generation there was the persecution by those masters who condemned evangelical mendicancy.[34] In the same generation, Frederick II and his accomplices persecuted the Church, for which he was deposed from the empire by Innocent IV at the General Council held at Lyons. Accordingly, just as there was a beginning from the time of the baptism of Christ, that is thirty years after the first beginning, so in the forty-first generation this evangelical order began to be famed throughout the whole Latin Church in teaching. The persecution or error of those who say the religious state of life is inferior to the secular state of the clergy having the care of souls began in the forty-second generation, as well as the error of those who say that because having something in common pertains to the evangelical perfection of Christ and the apostles, consequently to have nothing in common does not pertain to evangelical perfection.[35] Not a few others arose who erred against evangelical poverty. The declaration or decretal of Lord Nicholas III was issued against them in the same generation.[36]

In Paris in the same generation appeared those philosophical, or rather pagan, errors which the Doctors think are the major nursery of the party of the Great Antichrist, just as the preceding are the seedplots and sprouts of the errors of the Mystical Antichrist. Just as these things begin from the time of the death or of the Ascension of Christ, so in the beginning of the forty-first generation a great and wondrous comet appeared for about three months. Then, at a later time, Manfred, the son of Frederick, who held the Kingdom of Italy as a usurper against the Church, was defeated and killed by Charles.[37] A little after there was Conradin, the son of Conrad, the son of Frederick. And in the forty second generation, Peter, the king of Aragon, invaded Sicily, from which time followed many dissensions among kings and realms that seem to some learned men to be preparations for a great evil.[38] At the end of this forty-second generation there was the unusual election of Pope Celestine and his successor and certain other warnings.[39]

If these things take their beginning from the seventh year after the Passion of Christ, when Peter, after having had his seat at Jerusalem, was accepted as bishop in a gentile city,[40] just as he afterward had a third seat at Rome,[41] so at the end of this thirteenth century from the Incarnation, the forty-two generations of 1260 will be ended. Of this number there are now but three remaining.

Translated from von Döllinger, *Beiträge zur Sektengeschichte* 2:571–72, and compared with Bibl. Angel. ms. 382, ff. 83va–84ra.

The Two Antichrists

Know that anywhere in this book where it treats of the Great Antichrist in prophetic fashion, it also implies the time of the Mystical Antichrist preceding him. According to this, the beast ascending from the sea (Rev. 13:1

sqq.) signifies the bestial life and the race of carnal and worldly Christians which from the end of the fifth period also has many heads made up of worldly princes and prelates. . . .

The deeper and broader evangelical poverty and perfection is impressed and magnified in Christ's Church, the stronger the head of earthly cupidity and vile carnality beats against it. But already this head that was almost dead revives too much, so that all the carnal Christians are in awe of it and follow its earthly and carnal glory. When the apostate beast from the land of the religious rises on high (Rev. 13:11) with its two horns of false religious and false prophets, disguised like the two horns of the Lamb, then will be the strongest temptation of the Mystical Antichrist. "False Christs and false prophets will then arise" (Matt. 24:4, 11), who will cause all things to adore cupidity and carnality, or the earthly glory of the worldly beast. They will produce great signs to this effect. . . .

From the many things which Joachim wrote about Frederick II and his seed,[42] and from the things which St. Francis is thought to have revealed secretly to Brother Leo and some other of his companions, they think that Frederick with his seed is like the slain head in this age, and that he will revive at the time of the Mystical Antichrist in someone from his seed in such a manner that he not only will obtain the Roman empire, but will conquer the French and take their kingdom.[43] Five other Christian kings will be joined to him. He will set up as Pseudopope a certain false religious who will contrive something against the Evangelical Rule.[44] He will make an evil dispensation, promoting to bishops those professed in this Rule who consent to him and expelling clerics and earlier bishops who were opposed to the seed of Frederick and especially to that emperor himself, as well as to him and his state of life. He will persecute all who wish to observe and defend the Rule purely and fully. . . . But who these men will be or not be is to be left to divine direction, I think. The aforementioned scholars add that at that time the saying of the apostle in 2 Thess. 2:3, "unless the falling away comes," will be in part fulfilled. Then almost all will depart from the obedience of the true pope and will follow the false pope. He will indeed be false, because he will heretically err against the truth of evangelical poverty and perfection, and perhaps because beyond this, he will not be canonically elected, but be put in by schism.

Translated from I. von Döllinger, *Beiträge zur Sektengeschichte* 2:569–70, 572–73, and compared with Bibl. Angel. ms. 382, ff. 92vb–93rb.

UBERTINO OF CASALE, *THE TREE OF THE CRUCIFIED LIFE*

The Seven Ages

We have treated to some extent the acts of the life of the beloved Jesus and his most holy Mother, both taken up into the glory of majesty, and have finished the story of the blessed tree of the crucified life of Jesus and his revered Mother. The pen must now be turned to their varied offspring in the Church they planted, as to an abundant and desirable fruit of the remembered tree. The fifth book begins here so that we may arrive by ordered progression at the evangelical way of life with which we are principally concerned, the one renewed in the Church through Francis, the "Least of the Minorites," indeed, renewed through Jesus himself in Francis. For understanding this it should be noted that there are seven *status* forming and spreading the Church through the power of Jesus gleaming in her. . . . These seven are variously described under many figures and with much repetition by that most sublime eagle, John, in the Book of Revelation. . . .

As far as our first task is concerned, it should be known that the first *status* is the time of the primitive foundation, especially that performed by the apostles among the Jews. The second *status* is the time of strengthening proved through the martyrdoms done by the pagans throughout the world; the third, the time of teaching shining forth to make the faith clear and confound heresies. The fourth is the time of the anchoretic life austerely lived in solitude; the fifth is a time of decline under monks and clerics who possessed temporal goods. The sixth is the *status* of the renewal of the evangelical life and of the attack on the followers of the Antichrist under the leadership of poor men who voluntarily possess nothing in this life. The seventh *status,* insofar as it concerns this life, is a peaceful and wondrous participation of future glory . . . ; insofar as it concerns the other life, it is the *status* of the general resurrection of all.

Translated from Ubertinus de Casali, *Arbor Vitae Crucifixae Jesu* (Venice: Andrea de Bonettis, 1485; reprint, Turin: Bottega d'Erasmo, 1961), book 5, ch. 1, f. 204ab.

The Mystical Antichrist

The Mystical Antichrist will not be a true prelate, but a false Christ; he will condemn the Spirit of Christ in the evangelical life . . . and will therefore find his type in Annas and Caiaphas, who condemned Christ. The Open Antichrist will judge Babylon. (Note a doubt here—he may find it already judged.) Afterwards he will fight with the preachers of truth, Enoch and Elijah, who will then lie dead in the squares of the great city where the Lord was crucified (spiritually called Sodom and Egypt). Let the reader then behold the mystery concerning the spiritual men, the Enoch and Elijah of this time—they are Francis and Dominic sent to preach the Second Coming of Christ, just as Enoch and Elijah will be sent to preach the Third Coming to Judgment. They will fight, rather they have fought, against the Mystical Antichrist in the squares of the great city, that is, in the widespread relaxation of the Church. They lie dead in the corrupt state of their sons. . . .

From each state of life [i.e., that of the clerics and that of the religious] there is here described (Rev. 13:1) in different way and order an evil beast who becomes pope. We must now treat these. In the first case, he says that he saw the beast as a destroyer come from the sea, that is, from the turbulent life of the clergy, even as far as the highest position in the Church. . . . "And I saw one of his heads wounded unto death, and his deadly wound was cured. The whole earth wondered after the beast" (Rev. 13:3). . . .

Then he says that through these two cardinals he received a deadly blow when they publicly declared and solemnly proclaimed that he had not been canonically elected because Celestine was still alive.[45] Celestine's resignation was not valid, because it was procured with such malice and fraud by this seducer and his accomplices. Indeed, there was no way he could resign. . . .[46]

"And I saw another beast ascending from the earth, and it had two horns like the Lamb's" (Rev. 13:11). . . . This beast ascending from the earth is the horde of religious who for a long time have already hoped to ascend to high ecclesiastical positions. . . . The chief offices of the two orders can be signified by these two horns on the "religious" beast. They seem to imitate Jesus the pilgrim, poor man, and holy teacher in special fashion, but in this action they are like those according to their ranks who were the principal men caring for the beast. Since the cardinals, archbishops, bishops, lectors, and prelates of their orders, and the other masters and important men commonly preached such things, it is no wonder that a crowd of such men was able to fill the whole of the large wound and cure it. . . .

Jesus Christ showed the immovable authority of the Supreme Pontiff when he said: "You are Peter and upon this rock I will build my Church" (Matt. 16:18), that is, upon me the firm rock. . . . Thus many think that it is impossible that his vicar and universal spouse, the Supreme Pontiff, can be separated from the rule of the Church, and especially in a fraudulent and false manner, as was the case with Celestine. Therefore, the Open Antichrist will attempt to divide the divine union of Christ Jesus, something which the assertion of the possibility of dividing the Supreme Pontiff from the Church prepares for. Hence I would say that this error is an "Antichristian" one, and that its inventor is the Mystical Antichrist, the precursor of the Great Antichrist. . . .

"And his number is 666" (Rev. 13:18). . . . . I have heard from two true evangelical men of whom one knows Greek very well and the other a bit that while the former read Justin the Greek martyr and doctor's *Book on Revelation* at table, he came to the place where Justin computed the Greek letters and composed from letters in Greek having this numerical value the name *Benedictos,* the nominative singular of which in Latin is *Benedictus.*[47] He said that this was the future name of the beast who is to come. . . .[48]

Do not wonder then if this mystical name seems to refer literally to this second beast because he is more evil than the first, just as his reputation for holiness has given him far greater power to harm than his evil forebears. The famed cruelty, the reputation for every evil of the first beast, publicized of old throughout the world, enjoined almost all Christians to horror of his views and his acts; but the fame of this false prophet (for so John calls him) so pleases the world that no suspicion of him and his works seems to arise. Even now this blindness seems to craze many wise men who were not taken in by the works of the other. This is palpable darkness when according to every canon it clearly stands that neither the former nor the latter was a true pope. The latter is a worse beast, more harmful than the first, insofar as in the eyes of the simple he does not seem to have any stain. The first was such a horrid beast and intruded in so horrid a fashion that there was scarcely a person in the world on his side because of all the evils that had come together in him. . . . But the hypocritical appearance of this beast seems to give life to all his deeds so that many are already willing to hold it as confirmed. So it is said of the Antichrist that there will be two evil possibilities he will associate with himself—a fearful open evil, destructive beyond belief in all things, and an awesome hypocrisy and deceit. These roles will be verified in the Great Antichrist for their respective times so that the first will come at the end, the second will be fulfilled at the beginning. In the two figures who are the Mystical Antichrist they are fulfilled in reverse, because the first was the open destroyer, the second the shrewd and cowardly deceiver.

Translated from *Arbor Vitae,* book 5, ch. 8, ff. 230rb–233ra. Ubertino's digressive style makes it necessary to omit much.

The Angelic Pope

So the blessed Jesus will do to his elect in the splendor of his light as he reveals the mysteries of the new *status*. Hence the eighteenth chapter of Revelation, after the battle against both the Mystical and the Open Antichrists, says: "After these things I saw another Angel descending from heaven, having great power, and the earth was illuminated by his glory" (Rev. 18:1). The order of doctors who preach the fall that has already taken place can be understood through this figure;[49] they are different from those who will preach the future fall. Perhaps that Angel will be the same Supreme Pontiff spoken of above or another successor of his perfection. He is said to descend from heaven. This can be understood thus—that from the very high state in which God immovably fixed them, as if they were in heaven, they descend without interruption through profound humility reaching the lowest levels, especially in thinking of themselves as so unworthy of every degree of grace. The more they thus descend, the more they are elevated and wondrously strengthened. Hence it is said of that man that he will have great power, that is according to Joachim, in preaching God's word.

Translated from *Arbor Vitae*, book 5, ch. 11, f. 237vb.

ANGELO OF CLARENO, *HISTORY OF THE SEVEN TRIBULATIONS*

On Peter Olivi

Brother Peter John was meek and mild, humble, devoted to Christ, his Mother, and St. Francis. He was wise with a wisdom divinely infused and acquired. He was fluent and eloquent among all the men of his time, and above all his contemporaries and perhaps all men he was filled with spiritual wisdom. . . . He had the grace of seeing things to come, and foresaw many things and taught things very useful and necessary for avoiding spiritual dangers and for attaining the highest and truest good things of the last times. He was foreseen, prophesied, and shown forth from of old, like Dominic and Francis, by many trustworthy testimonies.

The Abbot of the Florensian Order prophesied of him and he was foreseen by the ancients and by others before him who had the spirit of prophecy. The whole first part of the prophecy of St. Cyril which Abbot Joachim exalted with great praise deals principally with Brother Peter John—the place of his birth, the order he was received into, and all the persecutions which he and his followers were to suffer from the envious. It determines and predicts the years, the ages, the signs, and the places, partly in enigmatic fashion, partly historically. . . .

What unbeliever will not easily acknowledge that a thousand years before Christ the Erythraean Sibyl predicted many future events in the Church, both good and bad, even those which seem unimportant to man? Among those she clearly set out were the simplicity of Peter Morrone, as well as his innocence, his papacy and its renunciation, his seduction and its place and its agents. . . . That prophecy which was given to St. Cyril by the angel calls Peter John the sun because of the glorious and perpetual incorruptibility of his virtues, because of the most splendid variety of the wisdom and knowledge divinely given to him, and because of the veracity of the burning and Christlike love he had toward God and neighbor. Those who envied him are like scorpions; they are born of scorpions and propagated as imitators of scorpions.

Translated from the edition of A. Ghinato, *Angelus a Clarino: Chronicon seu Historia septem tribulationum Ordinis Minorum* (Rome: Sussidi e Testi per la Gioventù Francescana, 1959), pp. 133–34.

On Ubertino of Casale

In that time when God sent those most illustrious and apostolic men, Dominic and Francis, into the world, Amaury was also sent by the devil.[50] Through him Satan overturned many and drew them to the unholy sect of the Antichristian "Spirit of Liberty." The famous King Philip of France[51] put it down and stamped it out with the help of the arguments and authorities of Master Ralph that confuted it.[52] But now it is reviving as the time of the reformed life of Christ draws near. At the command of the Supreme Pontiff or his legate it will be detected, confuted, and wiped out in a short time by Brother Ubertino, insofar as he is able. Before him no Inquisitor will presume to attack it. . . .

This Brother Ubertino dwelt on Mount Alverna in the Province of Tuscany and was devoted to Francis. He was a faithful witness of individual perfection, both first and last, and a sincere and fervent preacher of evangelical truth. By the example of his life and the power of his word he encouraged many in the religious life, especially in Tuscany, the Valley of Spoleto, and the March of Ancona. He enflamed them to the pure and faithful observance of the promised perfection. On the basis of the true charity and peace he enjoyed, he who rested in God and the saints and agreed with the acts of pardon and the counsels of holy men, knowingly gave himself up to many dangers and labors to be able to help the Spirituals in Tuscany and the Valley of Spoleto who suffered so much from their enemies.

Translated from A. Ghinato, *Angelus a Clarino,* pp. 186–90.

JACOPONE DA TODI, LAUDA 50 *THE GREAT BATTLE OF THE ANTICHRIST*

Now it will be clear who has faith!
I see the prophesied tribulation
Thundering on every side.[53]
The moon is black, the sun darkened;
I see the stars fall from heaven.
The ancient Dragon seems to be unleashed,
And I see the whole world follow him.
He has drunk up the waters on all sides;
He hopes to swallow the River Jordan,
To devour the people of Christ.[54]
The sun is Christ who now gives no sign
To strengthen his servants.
We see no miracle that supports
Faith in the people.
Evil folk make arguments about it;
I shame them with harsh speech:
By explaining the faith, we cannot draw them to it.
So the moon is the darkened Church
Which in the night shone upon the world,
Popes and cardinals and their court.
Light is turned into darkness;
The whole of the clergy
Has galloped off and taken the wrong way.
O Lord, who can escape?
The stars that are fallen from heaven
Are all the religious orders.[55]
Many have departed from the right path
And entered on the dangerous road.
The waters of the flood have risen up,
Covered the mountains, flooded everything.
Help, God, help us to swim!
I see the whole world upset
And cast in ruins,
Like a man in a frenzy

> To whom no one can give a cure,
> Whom the doctors have given up for lost,
> Because neither spell nor science can help.
> So we see the world in its last turmoil.
> I see all the people signed with the
> Mark of the ancient Dragon,
> And he has divided the signs into three parts:
> He who escapes from one, will be given pain by another.
> Avarice has entered their field,
> Discomfited them and killed many:
> There are few who wish to resist. . . .[56]
> Because no other has been as bad as this,
> Nor will there be another as strong.
> The saints had great fear of it
> (Of coming to take such a reward!);
> To feel secure is to appear foolish.

Translated from the edition of F. Ageno, *Laudi: Trattato e Detti* (Florence: Le Monnier, 1953), pp. 198–201. I wish to thank Paolo Cherchi for his assistance in correcting this translation.

BERNARD GUI, *INQUISITOR'S MANUAL*[57]

Chapter IV. Concerning the Sect of the Beguins

Concerning the Errors or Erroneous Opinions of the Beguins of Recent Times: Their Origin.—Now Beguins (for by this name are commonly called those who refer to themselves as the Poor Brethren of Penitence of the third order of St. Francis and who wear a garb of coarse brown or greyish brown woolen cloth, with or without a cape) of both sexes in recent times were discovered in the year of our Lord 1317, and year by year thereafter, in various places in the province of Narbonne and in some parts of the province of Toulouse, and they confessed before the court to having and clinging to many errors and wrong opinions. They set themselves up against the Roman Church and the Apostolic See, against the primacy of that see, and against the apostolic power of the lord pope and of the prelates of the Roman Church.

By lawful inquisition and through the depositions and confessions of a number of them, recorded before the court, as well as through declarations by many of them, in and for which they have chosen to die by burning rather than to recant as is canonically required, the source of their errors and pernicious opinions has been discovered. They have culled these, at least in part, from the books and pamphlets of Brother Peter John Olivi, who was born at Sérignan, near Béziers—that is to say, from his *Commentary on the Apocalypse,* which they have both in Latin and in vernacular translation, and also from some treatises which the Beguins say and believe that he wrote: one dealing with poverty, another with mendicancy, and a third with dispensations. . . .[58]

Also, they distinguish as it were two churches: the carnal Church, which is the Roman Church, with its reprobate multitude, and the spiritual Church, composed of people whom they call spiritual and evangelical, who follow the life of Christ and the apostles. The latter, they claim, is their Church. But some of them say there is only one, the one they call carnal— the great harlot in so far as it touches the reprobate, but spiritual and virginal, without stain or blemish, in respect of the elect, whom they call the evangelicals, meaning themselves, who claim to observe evangelical poverty, defend it, and suffer for it.

Also, they teach that the carnal Church, which is the Roman Church, will be destroyed before the preaching of the Antichrist, by wars waged against it by Frederick, the reigning king of Sicily, and his allies, called the ten kings, who are prefigured by the ten horns of the beast described in the Apocalypse. They put about some other tales on this subject, as false as they are foolish, having to do with the struggle between King Frederick and the king of France and King Robert of Naples.[59]

Also, they teach that at the end of the sixth era of the Church, the era in which they say we now are, which began with St. Francis, the carnal Church, Babylon, the great harlot, shall be rejected by Christ, just as the synagogue of the Jews was rejected for crucifying Christ. For the carnal Church crucifies and persecutes the life of Christ in those brethren whom they call the Poor and the Spirituals of the order of St. Francis. They are speaking here of both the first and the third order, with reference to their persecution as described above, which took place in the provinces of Provence and Narbonne.

Also, they teach that, just as Christ chose from the synagogue of the Jews, after it had been rejected, a few poor men through whom the primitive Church of Christ was founded in the first era of the Church, so, after the rejection and destruction of the carnal Church of Rome in the sixth or present era, there will remain a few chosen men, spiritual, poor, and evangelical. The majority of these, they say, will be drawn from both the orders of St. Francis, the first and the third, and through them will be founded the spiritual Church, which will be humble and good, in the seventh and last era of the Church, which begins with the death of Antichrist. . . .

Also, they teach that the Antichrist is dual; that is, there is one who is spiritual or mystical, and another, the real, greater Antichrist. The first prepares the way for the second. They say, too, that the first Antichrist is that pope under whom will occur and, in their opinion, is now occurring the persecution and condemnation of their sect.[60]

Also, they fix the time within which the greater Antichrist will come, begin to preach, and run his course. This Antichrist, they say, has already been born and will run his course, according to some of them, in the year of our Lord 1325. Others say it will be in the year 1330; while still others put it later, in the year 1335. . . .

Also, drawing further upon their imaginations, they teach that the destruction of the carnal Church will occur amid mighty wars and great destruction of Christian peoples. Large numbers of men will fall in the war they wage in defense of the carnal Church. Then, when almost all the men are dead, the surviving Christian women will embrace trees out of love and longing for men. On this subject they tell a number of other fabulous tales, which they read in the vernacular translation of the above-mentioned *Commentary*.

Also, they say that after the destruction of the carnal Church, Saracens will come to seize the Christians' land. They will invade this region of the kingdom of France, that is, Narbonne. They will abuse Christian women, taking many of them captive to misuse them. This, they claim, was revealed by God to Brother Peter John in Narbonne.

Also, they say that at the time of the persecutions, which are the work of Antichrist, and of the aforesaid wars, carnal Christians will be so afflicted that in despair they will cry that if Christ were God He would not permit Christians to suffer so many and such great evils. In their despair they will renounce their faith and die. But God will hide the aforesaid spiritual elect, lest they be found by Antichrist and his minions. Then the Church will be reduced to the same number of persons as founded the primitive Church; scarcely twelve shall survive. In them the Church will be established and upon them the Holy Spirit will be poured in equal or greater abundance than He came upon the apostles in the primitive Church, as is recounted above.

Also, they say that after the death of Antichrist, the said Spirituals will convert the whole world to the faith of Christ and the whole world will be good and merciful, so that there will be no malice or sin in the people of that era, with the possible exception of venial sin in some. Everything will be for use in common and there will be no one to offend another or tempt him to sin, for great love will there be among them. There will then be one flock and one shepherd. This state and condition of men will last, some of them think, for a hundred years. Then, as love wanes, malice will creep in little by little and gradually spread so far that Christ will be forced by the excesses of wickedness, as it were, to come to the universal judgment of all.

Translated by W. L. Wakefield and A. P. Evans, *Heresies of the High Middle Ages,* pp. 412, 424–26. The Latin text may be found in G. Mollat, *Bernard Gui: Manuel de l'Inquisiteur* (Paris: Les Belles Lettres, 1964) 1:108–10, 144–52.

25. *Arnald of Villanova*

In 1309 when Pope Clement V reopened the question of the Conventuals' treatment of the Spirituals it was in part due to the promptings of his personal physician, Arnald of Villanova. This Catalan layman was born about 1240, educated at Montpellier and possibly Naples, and had been physician to King Pedro III of Aragon from about 1280.[1] Although he had some acquaintance with Joachite speculation, Arnald's growing conviction of the imminence of the Antichrist appears to be the result primarily of his own study of the Bible and reflection on current events. The earliest version of his treatise, *The Time of the Coming of the Antichrist* (1297), was condemned by the theologians of Paris in 1300.[2] Arnald appealed to Boniface VIII against this ruling and was summoned to the papal curia for an investigation.

Having displayed his skill by curing the pope of the stone, he became the private physician to Boniface and later to Clement, despite his suspect views. From 1302 on he composed a series of apocalyptic works, defending his earlier treatise, announcing the perils to come, and pleading for the reform of the Church. His good personal relations with several popes did not lead to papal support for his program, so he turned his hopes to his friend and patron Frederick II, the Aragonese king of Sicily (1296–1337). As the holder of both the name and the realm of the Emperor Frederick II, as the enemy of the papacy which continued to support Angevin claims to Sicily against those of Aragon, and as a staunch supporter of the Spirituals, the pious Frederick had perhaps the best claims of any candidate for the role of a good Last Emperor. His long reign, however, was one of constant and ruinous conflict against an alliance of superior forces.

While in southern France, Arnald gained the acquaintance of some of the foremost Provençal Spirituals, especially Bernard Délicieux, one of the leaders who was to be imprisoned in 1317. This undoubtedly led to some development in his apocalyptic thinking and to his assumption of the role of curial defender of the Spirituals in the time of Clement V. His death in 1311 meant that he did not live to see the fate of his fellow apocalypticists.[3] Arnald's deep religious sentiments and his mastery of several fields of learning are indicative of a time when the educated laity were finally attaining an independent role in the intellectual life of the day. Salimbene records that doctors and other prominent laity had gathered in Hugh of Digne's cell in the 1240s to listen to the Joachite message. In the person of the versatile Arnald, doctor, astrologer, alchemist, and apocalypticist, we have a lay leader rather than a follower.

THE TIME OF THE COMING OF THE ANTICHRIST

Whoever reads this work should pay attention to three things—first, whether the assertions concerning the last times advanced in it are possibly true; second, whether they can be proved in Catholic fashion; third, whether they are apt for helping mortal hearts to despise earthly things and desire heavenly ones. This is the principal and proper intention of the Spouse of Christ, and if the three items are present in such a fashion, there is no doubt that the work was composed with God's permission.

By way of summary, there are nine chief claims of the work. First, there is an obligation on the visionaries of God's Church[4] to search the Sacred Scripture and expound the revelations concerning the last times that are found in it to the faithful, since Scripture is given to the faithful as a star to direct those heading towards Christ and as a column unceasingly guiding those passing through the desert of this life to the promised land, the Fatherland. . . . The second point is that it is important for the mass of Catholics to think about and have some prior knowledge of the last times and especially the time of the persecution of the Antichrist, so that forearmed by the weapons of the Christian religion, they may avoid the danger of deceit more cautiously, bear the attack of persecution more easily, and also avoid the taunt of mockery. For it would be ridiculous for the Church to spread the Gospel about the End and consummation of the world daily and not to attend to the approach of the event—nay more, by either attacking or neglecting the approach of the End to contradict silently the gospel message about it. Third, it is impossible to foreknow those times by human conjectures, whether they proceed from natural reason, or astronomical speculation, or from whatever other considerations of philosophers, magicians, or from the figments of diviners. We know this by the testimony of the Lord, who, when the apostles asked him about this from human curiosity, responded: "It is not for you to know the times or the moments which the Father has in his power" (Acts 1:7). . . . . Fourth, that God revealed those times to his Church through Daniel,[5] especially the time of the persecution of the Antichrist in the words: "From the time when the perpetual sacrifice was taken away and the Abomination of Desolation was set up there are twelve hundred and ninety days" (Dan. 12:11). Fifth, because nothing in Sacred Scripture is useless or vain, we should believe that through the number by which the time of the Antichrist is announced God wished the Church to know him before he actually is present. Otherwise, it would have been foretold in vain. Sixth, when the time from which the Angel began the computation is known, and the significance of what "day" means is also known, then the Church is able to foreknow that last time through its number. Seventh, it is taught that the time from which the computation begins is the time when the Jewish people totally lost the promised land and that through "days" is understood years—two points clear in the text. Eighth, because through days are to be understood lunar or solar years, the time of the persecution of the Antichrist will fall within the fourteenth century from the birth of Christ, about the seventy-eighth year of that century.[6] Ninth, that the prophecy of the Erythraean Sibyl of Babylon concerning the coming of Christ and the claim of Augustine in Book Twenty of *The City of God* agrees with this understanding and explanation.

Translated from the edition of H. Finke, *Aus den Tagen Bonifaz VIII,* pp. clvii–clix. This is the second version of the work, since Arnald at times responds to the Paris condemnations of 1300.

THE SWORD THAT SWALLOWS THE THOMATISTS[7]

The blindness of this Doctor [i.e., Thomas] is no less evident through the foundation upon which he rests. He says that it is not useful to know the final times. . . .[8] It is clear to you, dear brother, what sort of "star" that was which the Thomatists extoll so highly in our ears. When he dogmatized against the opinion of the holy Doctors and against the pure sense of the Scriptures in these questions, as mentioned above, it stands that he did not have the properties of the sun, because he spoke against the teaching of the true sun. Because he illumined many to the task of doing philosophy by the rays of his own philosophy, who can deny him the name and mode of a star? But because in this area he led an innumerable multitude of his followers away from sacred truth by the perversity of his teaching, he should not be designated by any other star than that which the Holy Spirit describes when through John he announces the future adversities of the Church. In the ninth chapter of Revelation John says that he saw a star fall from heaven (9:1), just as in this dogma Thomas fell from the height of divine truth to the earth, that is, into a dark, cloudy, and ignorant conception. "And the key of the abyss was given to him" (Rev. 9:2), that is, insight into the depth of inferior wisdom, worldly philosophy. "He opened the pit of the abyss" (9:2), that is, he manifested the depths of philosophical writings, "and the smoke ascended from the pit," because by means of his pen he made obscure and useless philosophical subtleties reach to the very heights of the Church. Then it follows, "And the sun was darkened," because the truth of Christ was darkened in two ways through the study of philosophy—first, because from that time his followers were less interested in the science of piety through which gleams the eternal sun; second, because after his teaching they devote less time to the study of the sacred text and the original holy teachers, since they suppose, as you have written, that this teacher has seen everything and has taught everything in his works. Therefore they are led astray by their self-confidence and are made strange by presumption. They are like a pestilent animal, adversaries of truth. Hence after those words there immediately follows: "Locusts went forth from the smoke of the pit into the earth" (9:3), because preachers pestilential and perverse from the curiosity of philosophy came into the Church.

Translated from the partial edition of F. Ehrle, "Arnaldo de Villanova ed i 'Thomatiste,' " pp. 499–500.

26. Fra Dolcino and the Apostolic Brethren

None of the apocalypticists that we have seen thus far could be described as revolutionary in the proper sense of the term. When apocalyptic ideology was invoked in favor of a particular political or military action, it was invariably used either in support of an established institution (e.g., the Christian empire against the Moslems) or against an evil *individual* (e.g., the papacy's identification of Frederick II with the Antichrist). When apocalyptic ideas were used as a critique of the whole *status quo,* their primary thrust was not towards active opposition, but in the direction of passive endurance, awaiting the action of God who alone had the power to defeat the forces of evil.

This picture begins to change at the end of the thirteenth century. In the severe criticisms of the Church that we have seen developing in the Franciscan Spirituals and in other groups, and in the failure of any figure, Last Emperor or other, to step forward to undertake the work of reform, the seeds for the use of apocalypticism as a revolutionary ideology were present. It is probably not until the time of the Taborite Brotherhood in the early fifteenth century that we can speak of a truly revolutionary apocalypticism in medieval Christianity, but about 1300 the forceful personality of Fra Dolcino was to make the fatal step from the mere preaching of apocalyptic ideas to armed resistance to the combined forces of Church and State.[1]

The Apostolic Brethren were one of the many movements of lay piety stressing poverty, preaching, and direct contact with God that sprang up in the later Middle Ages.[2] Founded about 1260 by an unlettered layman, Gerard Segarelli of Parma, they were condemned by Popes Honorius IV and Nicholas IV for not adhering to the Church's rules regarding the approbation of new religious orders.[3] Segarelli was imprisoned by the Inquisition and executed in 1300. The new leader of the group, Fra Dolcino, the son of a priest from Novara, was a far more formidable figure. Dolcino had received some education and had been influenced at some time by the themes of Joachite speculation. His two surviving letters (known through a summary made by the hostile Inquisitor, Bernard Gui) display considerable originality of thought in their attacks upon ecclesiastical authority. The sequence of events is partially obscure, but by about 1304 Dolcino and his faithful followers had retired to the Alpine valleys to await the coming of the Last Emperor, whom they expected to slaughter the representatives of the carnal Church and usher in the fourth age, the time of the triumph of the Apostolic Brethren. Dolcino apparently came to identify himself with the Angelic Pope. It is difficult to know whether Dolcino was forced into open rebellion as his radical program became known, or whether he decided to take up arms as the vanguard of the avenging forces of the Final Emperor. Although the former option seems more likely, the armed resistance that the Brethren put up against the forces sent against them and the support that they received from the peasants of the Valsesia made them a prototype of later peasant insurrections.[4] In March 1307 the Apostolic Brethren were decisively defeated in a pitched battle at Monte Rebello and many were slain. Dolcino, his consort Margarita, and about one hundred and forty followers were captured. The leader was executed in unusually cruel fashion, even for the times— a sign of the strong views that medieval society took toward violent apocalypticism in action. Had Dolcino been victorious he would undoubtedly have perpetrated like indignities upon his establishment foes.

BERNARD GUI, *THE SECT OF THE APOSTOLIC BRETHREN*

Dolcino wrote three letters which he addressed generally to all Christ's faithful and especially to his followers. In these letters he raged at length about the Holy Scriptures. At the beginning of them he pretended that he held the true faith of the Roman Church, though their course exposed his perfidy in a suitable manner. From the tenor of the two I possess, I have gathered together some excerpts in the summary which follows, for the sake of brevity leaving aside other things that seemed less relevant. One of these was given or written in August 1300. In it Dolcino first asserts that his congregation is a spiritual and proper one—proper in the truly apostolic way of life, and in a proper name with proper poverty.[5] Though without a bond of exterior obedience, it has an interior one. He claims that the congregation was specially chosen and sent by God in these last days for the salvation of souls. He who rules the congregation, that is, himself whom men call Brother Dolcino, was also specially chosen and sent by God, along with revelations made to him about present and future things which he asserts will soon fall upon both good and evil. These revelations were for the sake of opening up the prophets and for understanding the Old and New Testaments in these last times.[6]

Further, he holds that the secular clergy along with many of the populace and the rulers and tyrants are his enemies and the ministers of the devil. The same is true of all the religious, especially the Preachers and the Friars and others who persecuted him and the followers who held to the sect he calls a spiritual and apostolic congregation. For this reason Dolcino says that he flees and hides from the face of his persecutors, just as his predecessors in that sect had done, until the established time when his adversaries will be exterminated and he and his followers will appear in public and publicly preach to all. He says that all his persecutors along with the prelates of the Church will soon be slaughtered and destroyed. Those who are left will be converted to his sect and united to him. Then he and his sect will prevail over all. . . .[7]

He also says that from the time of Christ to the End of the world the Church is to undergo four changes. In the first it was to be as it had been— a Church upright, virginal, chaste, suffering persecutions. The Church was in this way until the time of Pope St. Silvester and the Emperor Constantine. In the second change it also was as it was supposed to be—rich, honored, steadfast in holiness and chastity. It was this way as long as the clerics, monks, and all religious persevered in their respective ways of life according to the examples of Saints Silvester, Benedict, Dominic, and Francis. In the third change it was supposed to be as it truly is—malicious, rich, and honored, as it is now when he writes these things, Dolcino says. It will remain so until the clergy, monks, and all religious are destroyed by a cruel destruction which later in the letter he asserts will happen within three years of the time he puts these things to paper. In the fourth change, it was supposed to be what it has already begun to be, viz., good, poor, and subject to persecutions in its reformed apostolic way of life. This fourth change was begun by Brother Gerard of Parma (whom he says was most beloved of God), and will persevere in perfect fashion, endure and bear fruit until the End of the world. . . .

All of the above [i.e., all religious and the leaders of the Church] will be destroyed by the divine sword through the emperor to be revealed and through the new kings he will create. They will be slaughtered and destroyed throughout the earth. He explains and asserts that the emperor to be revealed is Frederick, who was then king of Sicily, the son of Peter, the king of Aragon.[8] This Frederick is to be revealed as emperor, to create new kings, to fight against Pope Boniface and kill him along with the others marked for destruction. He adduces many texts from the Old and New Testaments to prove these things, expounding and interpreting them in his own evil way. He says that at that time all Christians will be at peace and there will be a single Holy Pope chosen and sent by God in a wonderful manner.[9] He will not be chosen by the cardinals; they will be slaughtered along with the others.

Those who belong to the apostolic state of life and the clerics and religious who will join them will be subject to that pope. By divine aid they will have been spared from the sword mentioned above . . . and they will bear fruit among others down to the End of the world. Frederick, the king of Sicily, son of Peter of Aragon (the emperor to be revealed), along with that Holy Pope who will come after Boniface who will be slain by the Emperor, as well as the new kings whom the revealed emperor will create, will all remain until the time of the Antichrist who will appear and reign in those days. . . .

Toward the end of the letter he explains the seven angels and their churches described in the Book of Revelation. He says that the Angel of Ephesus was St. Benedict and the congregation of monks was his church. The Angel of Pergamum was Pope St. Silvester and the clerics were his church. The Angel of Sardis was St. Francis and the Friars Minor; the Angel of Laodicea, St. Dominic and the order of Preachers. The Angel of Smyrna was Brother Gerard of Parma, whom they killed; the Angel of Thyatria was Brother Dolcino, himself of the Diocese of Novara. The Angel of Philadelphia is the coming Holy Pope.[10] These three final churches form the apostolic congregation sent forth in the last days.

Translated from the edition of A. Segarizzi found in *RIS*, vol. 9, part 5, pp. 19–22.

27. John of Rupescissa

Among the most prolific and best-known apocalyptic publicists of the period of the Avignon papacy (1308–1377) was the Franciscan John of Rupescissa (Jean de Roquetaillade).[1] Born about 1310, he studied at Toulouse, entered the Franciscan order, and later returned to the Minorite house at Aurillac near his birthplace. A series of visions he had beginning about 1340 brought him into conflict with his superiors. After a time in Franciscan prisons, he was called to the court of Pope Clement VI at Avignon in 1349 and imprisoned in the "Sultan's Jail" there. John spent most of his remaining years in the papal prison, though he continued to write and to retain good relations with some high ecclesiastical officials. With his irascible nature, his adherence to the condemned views of the Spirituals,[2] his violent opposition to the Dominicans,[3] and above all his ceaseless proclamation of a highly politicized and radical apocalyptic program, it is surprising that he was not more harshly treated. He appears to have died about 1365.

The bulk of John's voluminous writings, though still unedited, has been described by J. Bignami-Odier: His two most extensive productions are the long *Commentary on the Angelic Oracle of Cyril* and the *Liber Ostensor.* John is most accessible through the brief compendium of prophecy and apocalypticism which he called *Companion in Tribulation,* written in prison about 1356. Organized according to twenty instructions or points, it provides a good view of his historicizing and strongly pro-French apocalypticism. This Franciscan visionary believed that the great crisis of history was about to dawn in 1360 and was to last approximately ten years. The cardinals would soon leave Avignon, unheard-of catastrophes would plague mankind, and "popular justice" would overturn the corrupt social order. About 1365 the first of two Antichrists would appear and there would be a schism in the Church. The banner of good during the final events was to be carried by a reforming pope, a poor Franciscan,[4] whose protector would be that king of France who would become the Last World Emperor. Bignami-Odier has underscored the importance of the "caractère national" of John's prophecies.[5]

As incipient national consciousness grew stronger in the later fourteenth century and through the fifteenth, the political nature of apocalypticism moved in more overtly national directions. In this, as in so much else, John of Rupescissa, was a weathervane.

COMPANION IN TRIBULATION[6]

The Fifth Instruction[7]

The fifth instruction concerns the revelation of the horrible future events from 1360 to 1365, for from 1360 on there will be five continuous years of fearful novelties in the world. First, the earth's worms will have such strength and fierceness that they will most cruelly devour almost all the lions, bears, leopards, and wolves. The larks and the blackbirds and the owls will rend the birds of prey, the hawks and the falcons. This is required that the prophecy of the thirty-third chapter of Isaiah be fulfilled: "Woe to you who are predators, shall you not be preyed upon? And you who spurn, shall you not be spurned?" (Isa. 33:1) Within these five years will arise a popular justice. It will devour the treacherous and tyrannical nobles with a two-edged sword, and many princes, nobles, and powerful men will fall from their positions and from the glory of their wealth.[8] The affliction among the nobility will be beyond belief. The potentates, who by their betrayal despoiled an afflicted people, will be plundered.

Second, the Eastern Antichrist will publicly appear before we come to 1365, and his disciples will openly preach in the area of Jerusalem with false signs and portents and every form of error.[9] Third, within those five years from 1360 to 1365 there will be massacres terrible beyond human understanding, as well as storms in the heavens, floods never seen before (unheard of in many parts of the world, except for the Great Flood), unusually severe famines, pestilences and plagues, choking fits, and other incurable ailments. These plagues will kill the greater part of the present evil generation, so that the world may be renewed and led back to the unity of the Catholic faith when the hardened evil-doers have been wiped out. Fourth, during these five years there will be such great falsity, both against the great and among equals, that in those days he will be fortunate who can find a faithful servant or friend. Fifth, during those five years, the blind Jews will follow their false Messiah and inflict great injury on the Christian people.[10] Sixth, churches will be destroyed in many places and altars will be overturned. Seventh, there will be a horrible apostasy from the faith, so that scarcely one in ten will remain a true believer. Then will be fulfilled the saying of Christ: "Even the elect, if possible, will be led into error" (Matt. 24:24). From these seven points the understanding reader will be able to infer many other things that necessarily follow. I leave them unexplained for the sake of brevity.

Translated from the edition of E. Brown, *Appendix ad Fasciculum rerum expetendarum et fugiendarum* (London: R. Chiswell, 1690), p. 499.

The Twelfth Instruction

The twelfth instruction concerns the proximate restoration of the men of the Church and of the world through the celestial reformer who is at hand.[11] He is the Elijah who, according to the word of God, will restore all things. With this whip (literally made of little cords, that is, of humble Friars)[12] Christ will certainly expel all corrupt, lustful, and avaricious priests from the Temple lest they minister to him in sacrifice. He will depose simoniacs from their ministry, and will hand over those who offend against nature to the secular arm to be sacrificed by fire so that nature can be purged. He will restore the ancient liberty of choosing prelates to the episcopal sees. He will make the ravenous wolves flee the flock, will place holy men upon a candlestick and hide unworthy ones under a bushel basket, will castigate flesh and blood considerations, will restore collapsed justice, and will apply apt medicine against all evils. He will also replant all the gospel virtues in men who have collapsed and strengthen good men in their holy resolve. He will finish the book of the restoration of the world by the art of Christ whose power will endure forever.

The French king, who will come to see his angelic brightness at the time of his election, he will make Roman emperor, contrary to the custom of German elections.[13] God will generally subdue the whole world to him— West, East, and South. He will be of such sanctity that no emperor or king from the beginning of the world is his equal in sanctity, save the King of Kings and Lord of Lords, our Lord Jesus Christ. The emperor will refuse to be crowned with a golden crown in honor of the crown of thorns of Jesus Christ. As an emperor of the highest sanctity, he will execute all the commands of the Restoring Pope previously discussed. Through these two the whole world will be restored. They will destroy the entire law and tyrannical power of Mohammed;[14] both of them will pay personal visits to Greece and Asia, will end the schism, free the Greeks from the Turks, subjugate the

Tartars to the faith, and restore the kingdoms of Asia. The pope will command that as long as the world shall last the cardinals will be drawn from the Greek Church. . . . He will end the division of the Guelphs and Ghibellines in Italy, and will make arrangements for the lands of the Church in such a manner that the pope will never have to attack them.[15] He will stamp out all avarice and pride and wipe the clergy free of heresy. As I have already said,[16] it is soon to come to pass that infidels will invade Italy, Hungary, and many Christian provinces, and will afflict Christendom for forty-two months according to the literal sense of Scripture (Dan. 8:14). He will destroy them and free the Christian people from the hands of Mohammed. For the sake of brevity, this is enough—these things that I have briefly set forth about him. After nine years and six months (or possibly about nine months) the pope will die, and the emperor after about ten and a half years. In death, they will both shine forth with great miracles. . . .

Translated from Brown, *Appendix,* p. 502.

28. The Fraticelli

Papal persecution notwithstanding, groups of dissident Franciscans and their offshoots, generally called Fraticelli, or "Little Brothers," continued to survive in Italy.[1] The records of the papal inquisitors discriminate between the *Fraticelli de paupere vita*, the descendants of the Spirituals, and the *Fraticelli de opinione,* or Michaelists, who looked back to the Conventual leader Michael of Cesena as the true upholder of the Franciscan cause.[2] The groups were originally active in Tuscany, Umbria, and the Marches of Ancona, though they could soon be found in many other areas in Italy, especially in the Kingdom of Naples. Later they spread to Spain and even to Greece.

It is difficult to unravel the history of these shifting and frequently fugitive groups. Despite the differing origins of the two main strands, by the middle of the fourteenth century there appears to be a good deal of similarity of outlook among the various Fraticelli. Both traditions emphasized the role of the archheretic and Mystical Antichrist, John XXII, and the persecution that both underwent at the hands of papal inquisitors for their defense of their understanding of Francis' ideals undoubtedly enhanced a strong apocalypticism. The manifestoes and broadsides produced by the Fraticelli give us the best insight into this powerful underground religious force.[3]

The concentration of Fraticelli interest on the recent history of the papacy and the popularity of the earlier Papal Prophecies led one Fraticelli group, possibly in Florence, to create a second series of *vaticinia* about the popes. Reeves considers these fifteen brief oracles to be historical down to the tenth, which deals with the reign of Benedict XII (1334–1342), thus arguing for a date about 1340.[4] This second set was later prefixed to the earlier fifteen to form a series of thirty.[5] Other Fraticelli writings frequently took the form of public letters or of polemical treatises in Latin or in the vernacular. Hearkening back to the tradition of Jacopone da Todi, they also made use of vernacular poems to spread their views.[6]

Despite the activities of the Inquisiton and the opposition of such holy men as Giovanni delle Celle,[7] the Fraticelli survived, frequently with the support of the local nobility and episcopacy. The confusion attendant upon the outbreak of the Great Schism in 1378 provided them with a respite from persecution. L. Oliger, the foremost historian of the Fraticelli, has seen the period of the Schism as the highpoint of their activity and influence. The re-establishment of a strong papacy in Italy under Martin V in 1417 meant the resumption of activites against them. Their most determined enemies were the Observantine Franciscans, and in 1426 two Observantine leaders, John of Capestrano and James of the Marches, were appointed inquisitors for the specific task of stamping them out. A sad period of crusade and executions at the stake on one side, and determined resistance, including assassination, on the other, ensued. By 1466 when the last trial of a Fraticelli group was conducted at Rome the work was complete. One less dangerous group, the so-called Clarenists, were allowed to associate themselves with the Franciscans in 1473, but were finally suppressed by Pius V in 1568.

THE PAPAL PROPHECIES. SECOND SET.[8]

V. Title. By the fox's voice he will throw away the papacy.[9]

Blessed is he who comes in the name of the Lord of heaven, one who contemplates all heavenly things. A holy man, summoned from the dark earth, he ascends and descends.[10] A forked, fox-like voice will devour his dominion and he will die abroad in a thorny way. O how much will the Bride weep for the destruction of her legitimate Spouse handed over to be eaten by the lion! Why, O Holy One, have you left your Bride to be given to snarling savage dogs? Think upon your name and perform the first works that you may be received in the East.[11]

VIII. Title. He will be both movable and immovable and will lay waste many seas.[12]

See the Spouse of the Babylonian woman fleeing her as abominable to him and leaving her like a widow. His name is discordant;[13] he is cruel, unclean, unjust, lacking in virtue, immoderately seeks after vanity; he loosens the keys. Like a running slave and gladiator he gathers together and corrupts. The most brilliant star will lose its light in the face of the darkened sun.[14] Finally, the moon will prepare for battle and persecute him. He will fall to the depths and will darken lofty things. He will be both movable and immovable and will lay waste many seas.[15]

IX. Title. This most vile image of clerics will fight against the Dove.[16]

From a base stock will ascend a bloody beast who first and last will cruelly devour the harmless smallest son.[17] You are singular and you will not find a like in pouring out innocent blood. In your time will come the false prophet who will seduce many because your evils have found you out. You have wounded the Lamb most mild with your very cruel blows. You have spoken against Christ the Lord, obscuring the stars of heaven. By your evil you have made yourself a reproach; only in name are you glorious.

X. Title. He will illuminate six planets and finally surpass its sole splendor.[18]

From mountainy and solid districts, from a white land, a man will ascend and perform remarkable deeds.[19] He will partly light up the stars and partly darken them, but he will not take away the lofty things which the other beast had obscured.[20] The Lamb will remain gravely wounded. He will give away little, will gather in much. He will die a needy man and will lack a sepulcher of his own. The dove will persecute the crow, will reign alone, and as a total stranger will leave many spouses widowed.[21]

XIII. Title. This man alone will clearly open the book written by the finger of the living God.[22]

You are called to lofty things, O Prince of white hairs. Why are you in pain? Rise up and be strong. Slay Nero and you will be safe. Heal the wounded, take hold of the whip and destroy the flies. Throw the merchants out of the Temple. Adopt the illuminated teaching, announce the Just One, avoid the circumcised,[23] direct the Dove, repress the thirsty.[24]

XV. Title. You are dreadful. Who can resist you? (Ps. 75:8)[25]

This is the final wild beast, dreadful in aspect, that will drag down the stars. Then the birds will flee and only reptiles remain. Wild and cruel, it will consume everything. He will await you, after a time, times, and half a time.[26]

These translations are based upon *Profetie dell'Abbate Gioachino* (Padua: Stamparia Camerale, 1625), pp. 15, 23, 25, 27, 33, 37; and Vat. lat. 3816, ff. 15r–32r.

LETTER TO THE CITIZENS OF NARNI[27]

The Abomination of Desolation is the principal source from which have
come all the temporal and spiritual evils that have reigned, remained, and
grown wonderfully strong in the world for a long time now. Among them
are a manner of life that is bestial, voluptuous, brutal, vain, wanton, puffed-
up, unclean, polluted, stinking, and carnal, as well as innumerable wars
among Christians, earthquakes, accomplished slaughter, and the famines
and pestilences there have been. We are still in fear of many evils shortly to
come unless God provides a remedy. All the ills just mentioned and many
others have their origin, foundation, and root in the Abomination of Desolation which today rules in the holy place, that is, the Church. What is this
Abomination of Desolation which stands in the holy place, the Church? We
respond with a sorrowful soul that this Abomination of Desolation is the
condemnation of the life of Christ, of his poverty and that of his apostles
made by Pope John XXII thirty years ago and confirmed through his many
supporters in a variety of ways. . . .

This John drew up four decretals. . . . These evil heretical decretals
contain so many and such great heresies that we have never heard nor read
of any heretic, neither Arius, nor Sabellius, nor Pelagius, nor Nestorius, nor
Mani, nor Waldo, nor the Greeks who have discovered, defended, set up,
and spoken as many great heresies as this Pope John XXII accursed by God.
We can truly tell you, reverend Lords, that the accursed John preached and
set forth, taught, and defended more than two hundred errors and heresies.
We are ready to show these errors and heresies to anyone who does not
believe it or who says that our words are not true. . . .[28]

These errors and heresies listed above, along with others invented, set
forth, preached, and defended by Pope John XXII, and confirmed and approved by his successors,[29] are without doubt that Abomination of Desolation standing in the holy place (the Church) that Daniel prophesied and
Christ predicted and spread abroad so that faithful Christians might vigi-
lantly and diligently beware of it. Therefore Christ says in Matthew 24:15:
"Let him who reads understand," that is, let him read in such a way that he
understands lest he be led into error and eternal damnation by the Abomination. Do we not see what Christ said there about false Christs, that is, false
pontiffs and prelates, arising, and also about false prophets, that is, false
teachers and doctors, fulfilled almost to the letter? It will not be completely
fulfilled until the Great Antichrist comes. Without doubt we await him very

soon, because John and all his supporters without number are his messengers and chief disciples, just as the true prophets, Isaiah, Jeremiah, and the others were the messengers and precursors of our Lord Jesus Christ, the crucified man of poverty.

Translated from the edition of L. Oliger, "Documenta inedita ad historiam Fraticellorum spectantia," *Archivum Franciscanum Historicum* (1913), 6:288–89, 518.

29. Rome and Avignon during the Captivity

When Pope Clement V installed the papacy at Avignon in 1308 in the wake of the turmoil that had gripped the throne of Peter for over a decade, few thought that the exile from Rome would last for seventy years. The political instability of Italy and the notorious fickleness of the Romans were powerful factors in convincing Clement and his French successors to prolong their stay in the sumptuous palace successive popes built for themselves on the sunny banks of the Rhone.[1] Although recent scholarship has sought to give a more positive assessment of the achievements of the Avignon popes, stressing their administrative reforms, the severe criticism of contemporaries is hard to gainsay. While it may be true that the Avignon popes were not as subservient to the French monarchy as they have been painted, the luxury of their lives and their arbitrariness in dealing with the Church are still painfully evident. The Avignonese papacy only served to harden the structures against which late medieval reform movements were to protest in vain during the next century and a half; the years 1308–1378 were a momentous step on the road toward Luther.

It would be almost impossible to discern a writer concerned with apocalyptic themes during this time who was not touched by the "sign" of the papacy's withdrawal from its established home.[2] Perhaps John XXII was just that much more an Antichrist to the Franciscan Spirituals because he was no longer a truly *Roman* pope, and surely the prediction of John of Rupescissa that the pope and the curia would return to Rome before the outbreak of the final events was not a solitary hope. Some scholars have singled out the critiques of apocalyptically inclined authors as the source for the historical prejudice against the Avignon popes;[3] from the point of view of this study, their victory in the forum of both fourteenth-century and more recent public opinion is a good argument for the significance of the apocalyptic tradition.

The city of Rome itself was obviously thrown into a profound crisis by the withdrawal of the papal court. The traditional tensions between the

various noble families flared up, conflict between the city and the other communities in the Papal States grew apace, and local administration lan-
guished.[4] In this febrile atmosphere, hopes for a renewed glory for the Eternal City found easy root. As evidence for such expectations, we have the
remarkable careers of two very different personalities, Cola di Rienzo
(c.1314–1354) and St. Bridget of Sweden (c.1303–1373). Different in background, temperament, and fate, the two were joined by a common concern
for the reformation of the Church and for the renewed greatness of the city
that for one was birthplace, for the other adopted home. Though neither
could be described as primarily apocalyptic in outlook, both learned to make
use of apocalyptic themes to further their distinctive messages.

In the words of F. Gregorovius, the great historian of medieval Rome:
"The strange appearance of Cola has such distant perspectives both in the
past and the future, and presents such stern traits of tragic necessity, that it
offers more material for the contemplation of the philosopher than the long
and noisy reigns of a hundred kings."[5] Born of bourgeois Roman parents,
this young layman first made a name for himself as an envoy sent to convince Clement VI to return to Rome. He was appointed notary upon his return and in May 1347 staged a rebellion against the local government of
nobles to establish a new Roman republic with himself as tribune. Though
he initially professed himself to be working in alliance with the pope at
Avignon, Cola's bizarre ideas about the majesty of republican Rome soon
incurred papal displeasure. Renewed opposition from the Roman nobility
compelled him to abdicate in December of the same year. A wandering ex-
communicate, he took refuge with a group of Fraticelli in the Abruzzi. It
was here that he gained the profound knowledge of the prophetic literature,
most notably the Pseudo-Joachite *Angelic Oracle of Cyril,* that was to
buttress his new appeal for the renovation of the glory of Rome, as well as
provide ammunition for his attacks on the Avignon papacy and his defense
of the Fraticelli. Although imprisoned in Prague by Charles IV and in Avignon by Innocent VI, Cola was eventually to return to Rome as a papal sena-
tor in August 1354. His short period of renewed dictatorship was brought to
a tragic end when he was slaughtered by the Roman mob in October of the
same year. Renaissance hero, forerunner of Italian nationalism, charlatan,
opportunist—Cola was a mixture of many things.[6] What is clear for our purposes is that in his writings the Roman tribune adopted Joachite speculation
regarding the coming age to his own hopes for the city of Rome.[7] As he put
it in a famous letter to the Emperor Charles IV: "I have continued to hope

that in my coming you have sought a tribune for the New Jerusalem, that is, your Roman realm, and for the bountiful priestly and royal city which by the will of its donor, Our Lord Jesus Christ, is the capital of the world. . . . To heal the head is to heal all the members of the Christian people.''[8]

A similar obsession with the city of Rome is evident in the case of the Swedish visionary Bridget. Born in the highest circles of the nobility, the holy woman deserted the world after the death of her husband and founded a religious house at Vadstena. As her *Book of Revelations* tells us:

Christ spoke to his spouse in the monastery of Vadstena and said, "Go to Rome and stay there until you see the pope and the emperor. You will speak to them on my behalf the words I will say to you." The spouse of Christ came to Rome in her forty-second year and remained there fifteen years according to God's command, before Pope Urban V and the Emperor Charles of Bohemia came. She offered them revelations for the reformation of the Church.[9]

Bridget did not shirk her task; she continued to upbraid pope and emperor until her death in 1373. Like her successor, Catherine of Siena (1347–1380), Bridget's prime concerns were moral reform and the return of the papacy to Italy. In the name of Jesus, she was not afraid to issue the most direct and forceful appeals to the recalcitrant Avignon popes.[10] In the course of her voluminous prophecies, the influence of apocalyptic notions is evident.[11] The Swedish seer believed in a coming chastiser of the Church.[12] His career, and the return of the popes to Rome, appear to betoken a messianic age, though she is never explicit on this point. Bridget's speculations about the periods of Church history show that she saw in her own age a time of special crisis.[13] Bridget was not only consulted in her own time on questions of apocalyptic import,[14] but her reputation as a seer meant that a considerable number of prophecies were ascribed to her in subsequent centuries.[15]

COLA DI RIENZO

Letter 49[16]

I was not compelled by man, but inspired by God. In public parliament before the people I freely and solemnly laid down the tribune's crown and the scepter of justice. With the people in tears, I departed and "remained in solitude, awaiting him who would save me from faintheartedness and from the tempest" (Ps. 54:8–9). In the garb of poverty and in prayer I stayed with the hermits of the Apennines in the kingdom of Apulia. When I had led a strict life there for thirty months, a brother named Angelo of Monte Volcano arrived who said he was a hermit whom many hermits revered. . . .[17] He told me that a divine revelation had informed him I was staying there, adding that God was attending to the universal reform already foretold by many spiritual men, especially because of the prayers and insistence of the Glorious Virgin. He had sent great destruction[18] and earthquakes because of the multitude of sins, and he threatened another more serious affliction because of unholy pastors and their congregation. He had intended to punish the people and the Church and wound them terribly with these scourges before the coming of St. Francis, but at the insistence of Dominic and Francis, whom he claimed had held up the then collapsing Church of God by preaching in the spirit of Enoch and Elijah, the judgment of God was put off until the present time. . . .

He said that there would soon be great changes, especially for the reformation of the Church to the state of pristine sanctity. There would be great peace, not only among Christians, but between Christians and Saracens. Under a soon-to-come pastor the grace of the Holy Spirit would purify them. He asserted that the time was near when the age of the Holy Spirit would begin, when God would be known by men. He also said that God had chosen a holy man to execute this spiritual work.[19] He would be made known to all by divine revelation and together with the emperor-elect would reform the Church in many ways, separating the pastors of the Church from the unnecessary goods of failing earthly delights. When asked, he added that a man killed by a certain Church ruler or dead for four days would arise. At his voice great terror and flight would occur among the pastors of the Church in which even the Supreme Pontiff would be in personal danger. This same Angelic Pastor will assist the falling Church not less than Francis had done.[20] He will reform the entire state of the Church, and will build a great Temple of God from the Church's treasures, dedicated in honor of the Holy Spirit and called Jerusalem. Infidels, even from Egypt, will come there to pray.[21]

He counseled me that I should not utterly put off the work of advancing the Roman emperor, at present the hundredth in the succession of *Augusti*.[22] I should assist him as a precursor with advice and aid, nor should I doubt that the city of Rome would soon be decorated by the imperial and papal crowns, for forty years had already passed since the Ark of the Lord transferred from Jerusalem had remained outside its true place because of the sins of man.[23] He also said that it would have been acceptable to the Most High if, on the occasion of the fifty-year Jubilee recently celebrated, it had returned to its proper home according to the divine precept set out in Leviticus.[24] While I hesitated over these words and thought that my approach to the emperor would be thought to come from my old arrogance, he then showed me the prophecies of various spiritual men,[25] and explained to me how soon they were to be fulfilled. I knew that a large part of them were completed; in the case of the rest I hold what the Church of God does.[26] I received them and undertook the journey, fearing that if this task came from God I would appear a shirker because of my laziness. With a heart thus strengthened, I have come to the feet of Caesar and have shown him all this with real sincerity.

Translated from the edition of K. Burdach, *Vom Mittelalter zur Reformation*, (Berlin: Weidmann, 1912), vol. 2, part 3, pp. 192–96.

Letter 58 [27]

There was a man as simple as Tobias who appeared in their midst in our time—Merlin and Joachim had prophesied him very plainly.[28] By fraud and guile he was deceived into the renunciation of the papacy; he was finally imprisoned and killed. How much this sin displeased the King of Heaven, the prophets Merlin and Joachim clearly predicted before the time. Because of this sin the Church deserted its holy and proper place for a whorehouse under the leadership of the archbishop of Bordeaux, the first pope in France[29]—going to a bordello to do its whoredom so that the name might agree with the reality.

What can we believe is more detestable to God's nostrils than the stink of our filthy uncleanness as it ascends to him from our altar? How many unclean priests and clerics (not of the Lord but of Satan!) are there today who dare to enter church, to approach the altar in their stench, and—even worse—to dare to handle the Son of God and the Virgin with the same leprous hands which shortly before had handled a stinking whore? How many who dare to spit in the face of the Crucified from lips polluted with the saliva of an adulteress! What could be more annoying to God, who is complete peace, truth, justice, humility, patience, long-suffering, moderation, and the perfection of all virtues, than that all the factiousness, discrimination, slaughter and war, falsehood and guile, avaricious pomp, profit, and the vanity of worldly goods comes from his vicars? I would gladly be silent about them all, if God permitted me. I do not have to punish them, nor do I ask you, Caesar, to punish them. But because there is not one who does good (Ps. 13:3), I ask that you, as the Elect of God, become the good support of his people who labor under the stench of sins in God's anger. To you, as to Moses, it has been revealed on divine tablets.[30]

Translated from K. Burdach, *Vom Mittelalter zur Reformation,* vol. 2, part 3, pp. 304–5.

FRANCIS PETRARCH, SONNET 137[31]

Covetous Babylon has its sack full
Of the wrath of God and of impious and wicked vices
So much so that it bursts. It has made its gods
Not Jove and Pallas, but Venus and Bacchus.
While waiting for Reason,[32] I consume and weaken myself;
Yet I see a new Sultan for her,
Who will make (not when I would like it)
One See alone, and that in Baghdad.[33]
Its idols will be scattered on the ground
And its high towers, enemies of heaven,
And those who live in them will be burned inside and out.
Fair souls and friends of virtue
Will rule the world, and then we will see
The world becoming golden and full of ancient works.[34]

Translated from F. Neri et al., *Francesco Petrarca: Rime, Trionfi, e Poesie Latine* (Milan-Naples: Ricciardi, 1951), p. 202. I would like to thank Paolo Cherchi for his assistance in the translation and notes.

BRIDGET OF SWEDEN, *REVELATIONS* 6:67

The Son speaks: "The world is like a ship full of anxieties and disturbed by storms of temptations. No one can ever be safe until he has come to the peaceful haven. Just as a ship has three parts, the prow, the midship, and the poop, so there are three in the world, as I will describe to you.[35] The first was from Adam until my Incarnation and is figured in the prow which is high, wonderful, and strong—high in the piety of the Patriarchs, wonderful in the wisdom of the Prophets, and strong in the observance of the Law. . . . The middle of the ship, that is, the world, began to appear when I myself, the Son of the Living God, chose to take on flesh. Just as the midship is lower and more humble than any other part, so at my coming humility and total goodness began to be preached. Many followed them for a long time. But now, because impiety and pride grow strong, and because my Passion has been almost forgotten and neglected, the third part begins to arise. It will last until the Judgment. In this age I have sent my words to the world through you; whoever hears them and follows them, will be happy. . . . At the end of this age the Antichrist will be born. As the sons of God are born of a spiritual marriage, so Antichrist will be born of an accursed woman who pretends to appreciate spiritual things and from an accursed man. With my permission the devil will form his work from their seeds. The time of this Antichrist will not be as that brother whose book you have seen has described,[36] but rather in a time known to me, when iniquity will abound immeasurably and impiety grow to be immense. Know that before the Antichrist comes the gate of faith will be opened to some peoples. This will be a clear sign to those Christians who love heresy and to those evil men who tread the clergy and justice itself underfoot that the Antichrist will come quickly.''

Translated from the edition of C. Durante, *Revelationes Caelestes S. Birgittae Sueciae* (Munich: Rauch, 1680), pp. 540–41.

30. Political Prophecies: French versus German Imperial Legends

The political uses of apocalyptic literature have been a major theme of our story, but the kind of politics involved thus far is distant from most common twentieth-century understandings. Few today can have direct experience of universal political claims, like those of the papacy and the empire, based largely upon religious values. The abstraction of such systems from considerations of national identity, either territorially or linguistically conceived, is a further distancing factor. Despite the proto-nationalist aspects discerned in some earlier examples of the imperial legends, it was not until the later fourteenth century that we can detect imperial apocalyptic ideas serving nationalistic sentiments in direct fashion. The new prophecies produced then were developments of the millennium-old Last World Emperor myth tailored to serve the interests of the French monarchy or the German empire.[1]

The central figure in the late medieval round of imperial prophecies is the mysterious Telesphorus of Cosenza. Though the derivative character of the major work ascribed to Telesphorus, *The Great Tribulations and the State of the Church,* has led some to believe that he is a totally fictitious character, the best modern scholarship generally favors the view that there was a real Telesphorus, a Calabrian hermit active in the second half of the fourteenth century.[2] The Calabrian's description of himself as a *pauper heremita* indicates that he was probably associated with the Fraticelli, possibly the group stemming from Angelo of Clareno, a fact that would account for his knowledge of the prophetic and apocalyptic sources he wove together in his tract.[3] Although the Preface dates the completion of the work to 1386, E. Donckel has shown that this version is a reworking of an earlier compilation, either by Telesphorus himself or by his associate Eusebius, dating from c.1356–65. The revision, complete with a Letter of Dedication to the doge of Genoa and an Introduction, was designed to heighten the force of the message in the face of the Great Schism that had begun in 1378.

The Great Tribulations and the State of the Church is notable for its strongly pro-French version of the late medieval Joachite scenario of the End.[4] Telesphorus thought the Mystical Antichrist had been born in 1365 in the person of a coming Emperor Frederick III, who would be associated with a False Pope of German origin. Satan was to be released, and a period of great conflict between good and evil would last until 1409. The forces of good would be led by a French king, fittingly named Charles, who would help the True Pope, the *pastor angelicus,* to defeat Frederick and the False Pope. The Angelic Pope would then crown Charles emperor, ending German claims over the empire. The two messiah figures would also do battle against the Great Antichrist, who was set to appear in 1378 and who would lead the Church into schism. They would defeat him and end the schism by 1391 or 1393, and would then reform the Church before setting out on crusade to conquer the Holy Land. This messianic breathing space (which was to include four Angelic Popes in all) was to end in 1433 with the advent of the Final Antichrist, or Gog, at which time the Last Emperor Charles would lay down his crown at the Holy Sepulcher. Another earthly time of peace, however, the coming seventh age, would follow the defeat of the Final Antichrist.[5] This eclectic Francophile version of the last events was among the most popular late medieval apocalyptic works.[6] It survives in many mss., was translated into French and German, and was printed in Venice in 1516.[7]

Closely associated with the Telesphoran material in date, content, and even at times in manuscript tradition is the famous "Second Charlemagne Prophecy," the most influential of the late medieval French versions of the Last Emperor.[8] French Joachitism had been growing since the conflict between Charles of Anjou and the heirs of Frederick II—John of Rupescissa and Telesphorus were witnesses to its maturity in the fourteenth century. As M. Chaume has demonstrated,[9] in 1380 a French author pieced together aspects of the Last Emperor myths into a brief but potent political prophecy in favor of Charles VI (1380–1422) at the time of his accession. This text soon became known to the Italian Francophile imperialists, for by 1387 it had already been recast with the characteristic stamp of the Telesphoran program—the coronation of the emperor by the Angelic Pope.[10] Reeves has maintained that "it would seem that this Second Charlemagne text enjoyed the widest vogue of any political prophecy in the fifteenth and sixteenth centuries."[11] It is echoed in a wide variety of authors and appears in many versions, both in Latin and in the vernacular. Among these was the 1494 vernacular rendition of Guilloche of Bordeaux created for Charles VIII, who was crowned in 1484 in his fourteenth year.[12]

It is obvious that the Telesphorus tract was designed in part to be a pro-French answer to contemporary German versions of the Last Emperor stories centering upon the figure of the returning Third Frederick.[13] That these prophecies were rife in Germany we know from a number of sources, among them the lively account which the Franciscan John of Winterthur (c.1300–c.1349) gives under the year 1348 in his *Chronicle*. The spread of the opposing French version initiated a situation "in which we can speak of a true war of prophecies, growing sharper as we approach the time of the Great Western Schism."[14]

German polemicists soon took up cudgels against the Telesphoran view of the End. The noted theologian and conciliarist Henry of Langenstein, after a brief flirtation with apocalyptic ideas, rounded on Telesphorus, Joachim, Cyril, and all the other prophets in a treatise written in 1392.[15] The apocalyptic answer to Francophile Joachitism was given in the first half of the fifteenth century by a text ascribed to a fictitious Gamaleon and sometimes known as the "Anti-Telesphorus." Gamaleon was supposedly a holy relative of Pope Boniface IX (1389–1404) to whom a revelation about the future of the Church was made. Three Latin versions of the text exist, the earliest of which, that cited by Master John of Wünschelburg in a sermon given in 1439, appears to be the original.[16] The anti-French aspects are as strong as the anti-Roman ones in the Pseudo-Gamaleon. It is not surprising that the text was translated into the vernacular and was a favorite of the Reformers in the sixteenth century.

Many other forms of political prophecy based upon Last Emperor myths were to be found in fifteenth-century Europe. A number of them achieved a fair degree of notoriety by their ascription to the revered prophets of the past, such as the text beginning "Rex pudicus facie," "The King of chaste appearance," a product of the early years of the century that circulated under the name of Bridget.[17] Even a cursory glance indicates the strength of nationalistic political prophecy at this time; and, as the studies of Keith Thomas have shown,[18] political prophecy with a nationalist bent continued to be important in the sixteenth and seventeenth centuries.

TELESPHORUS OF COSENZA

Here begins the little book of Brother Telesphorus, priest and hermit, composed following the authoritative texts of the holy prophets and ancient chronicles. It treats of the causes, the condition, the recognition and the end of the present schism, and of the tribulations to come, especially in the time of the future king of the North calling himself the Emperor Frederick III down to the time of the future pope called the "Angelic Pope" and Charles the king of France, emperor after Frederick III. It also treats of the supreme pontiffs of the Roman Church and the condition of the Universal Church from the time of the Angelic Pope to the time of the Final Antichrist, and from his time and that of his death to God's Last Judgment and the End of the world.[19]

Humble Brother Telesphorus of Cosenza, a poor priest and hermit near Luzzi, sends greetings to each and every faithful Christian, both clergy and lay. Let us humble ourselves beneath the power of God's majesty (1 Pet. 5:6) for his grace and glory! When I was sad and sorrowful over the evils happening on the occasion of the present schism and those which probably will happen, I humbly and frequently entreated the most merciful Lord with a great flood of tears and fastings that he deign to show me, his servant, the causes of the threatening schism and which one of those who assert themselves to be pope in the schism is the true pontiff, which one the false. I also asked him what kind and how distant an end there would be to it, and how, when the schism was over, the Church of God would be ruled, especially with regard to worldly princes. In 1386, at about dawn on the day of the Lord's Resurrection, a vision arose in my sight as I was lightly sleeping and somewhat groggy. It was an angel of the Lord of virginal aspect and about two cubits high, adorned with two very gleaming wings and a broad robe and a tunic down to the ankles. He sweetly spoke these words to me: "The Lord has heard your prayer and says that through the Holy Spirit and an Angel he has already indicated and revealed to his beloved servants Cyril, priest and hermit of Mt. Carmel, and Abbot Joachim, and many other servants, all these things—the present and future schism,[20] its causes, who is the true, who the false pope, its end, and after the schism the coming government of the Church. Seek out the books and writings of these men and your desire will be satisfied. Write down what you find in their books and writings, and show and reveal it to others for your and their salvation!"

When he had said this, the angel immediately disappeared. I awoke fearfully from sleep and called my dearly beloved associate, Brother Eusebius of Vercelli, and revealed it all to him. With his assistance, we sought out with the greatest diligence the books of these men in Luzzi and Cosenza (where Joachim the holy prophet was born), as well as in many other places near these cities.

Translated from the edition of the Introduction given by E. Donckel, "Studien über die Prophezeiung des Fr. Telesphorus von Cosenza, O. F. M.," pp. 298–300.

THE SECOND CHARLEMAGNE PROPHECY

Charles, the son of Charles,[21] from the most illustrious nation of the Lily, will have a lofty forehead, high eyebrows, wide eyes, and an aquiline nose. He will be crowned at about thirteen years of age,[22] and in his fourteenth year he will gather a great army and destroy all the tyrants of his kingdom. Justice will accompany him as a bride with a bridegroom. He will make war until his twenty-fourth year, conquering the English, Spanish, Aragonese, Burgundians, Lombards, and Italians. He will destroy and burn with fire both Rome and Florence.[23] He will gain the double crown.[24] Afterwards, he will cross the sea with a large army and enter Greece. He will be called King of the Greeks. He will subdue the Syrians, Turks, Hispanos,[25] Barbarians, Palestinians, and Georgians. He will make an edict that whoever does not adore the Crucified One will die. None will be able to resist him because the arm of God will be always with him and he will possess dominion over almost all the earth. When these things are completed, he will be called the "Saint of Saints." He will come to Jerusalem, ascend the Mount of Olives, pray to the Father, and take the crown from his head. Giving thanks to God, in the midst of a great earthquake with signs and wonders he will give over his spirit in the thirty-first year of his reign. He will be crowned by the Angelic Pope and will be the first emperor after the Third Frederick—he will come after the present schism, tribulations, persecutions of false prophets, and the aforesaid Frederick.[26]

The text translated here is the Telesphoran version of the 1380 original as transcribed by M. Reeves from Vat. Reg. lat. ms. 580, f. 52r, and found in *Prophecy in the Later Middle Ages,* p. 328. The 1380 text may be found in M. Chaume, "Une prophétie relative à Charles VI," p. 29.

JOHN OF WINTERTHUR[27]

In these times many men of different kinds, indeed of all kinds, spread it very freely abroad that the Emperor Frederick II with whom I began the second part of this work would return in great strength to reform the totally corrupt state of the Church. Those who thought so added that even if he had been cut up into a thousand pieces or burned to ashes he must come, because it was divinely decreed that it must so happen and could not be changed. According to this claim, when he has been brought back to life and restored to the highest position of his empire, poor girls and women will be married to rich men and vice versa. Nuns and sisters living in the world will marry, and monks will take wives. He will give back to orphans, widows, and all who have been despoiled whatever was taken from them, and will give a full measure of justice to all men. He will persecute the clergy so harshly that they will spread cow dung over their crowns and tonsures if they have no other cover so that they do not seem to be tonsured.[28] He will drive the religious, especially the Franciscans, from the land, because by ordering the papal trial against him they threw him out of the empire. After he has governed the empire that he has resumed more justly and gloriously than before, he will cross the sea with a great army and on the Mount of Olives or at the dry tree will resign the Empire. . . .

Translated from *MGH*. SS. rer. Germ. n.s. 3, p. 280.

THE PROPHECY OF GAMALEON

In the year of our Lord 1439 on the Feast of St. Bartholomew, the famous and venerable Master John of Wünschelburg, professor of theology and distinguished preacher of the town of Amberg, spoke the following words in the pulpit of the Church of St. Martin.

"Gamaleon, a holy man of excellent piety and a relative of the saintly Pope Boniface, had a vision about the state of the Church, its condition in future times before the End of the world. It was like this. He saw an elegant and very beautiful youth of about three years with the body of an angel and crowned with a crown on which were depicted images of the seven planets and the seven liberal arts. On the crown was written: "You are terrible and who can resist you?" (Ps. 75:8). The youngster had four swords in his right hand, the first faced east, the second south, the third west, and the fourth he held in his hand and threatened the north. The young boy said to Gamaleon: "Hail! Good health! Farewell! Arise! Listen! Pay attention! Speak out! Seek! Write down!" Then Gamaleon said, "What is this young boy to me?" He answered: "I am the messenger of God most high, and I am sent to tell you wonderful and fearful events to come. . . . The seven images of the planets signify seven estates in which reign seven planets, each for a thousand years.[29] We are now in the last planet (also to last a thousand years) and have passed six hundred years, so the Judgment of God is in the future. . . . The image of the seven liberal arts signifies seven ages, and we are in the last age. Therefore, it is written of us: "We are the ones upon whom the final ages have come" (1 Cor. 10:11).

Of the four swords, three denote realms of the Church that are in great tribulation, namely, the kingdoms of the Greeks, the Romans, and the Germans. The fourth sword signifies a terrible king of the Romans, who will work the evil in the Church described in Jeremiah 6:22:"Lo, a people will come from the North, a great race will arise and snatch up arrow and shield. They will be cruel and have no mercy. . . ." After this, Gamaleon saw that the boy took the crown from his head and threw it on the ground. It was broken in pieces that were no longer seen. The boy said to Gamaleon: "Look to the South." An armed man came, clothed with red garments and having a red crown. On the crown was written: "All kingdoms are to be beneath my feet—I come from the field of the lily." The armed man bore an apple in his left hand,[30] in his right a bloody sword. The boy said, "The armed man is an emperor who will come from the South. He will begin the evil of the Church and will have an evil origin himself. He will be crowned by the pope, subdue most of Italy, and take power away from the Germans.[31] And the Germans will choose themselves an emperor from upper Germany, that is, from the Rhine. He will summon a secular council in Aachen and will set up a patriarch in Mainz who will be crowned pope.[32] This emperor-elect will attack the other Roman emperor and will slay him. Rome will not be attended to, the Apostolic See will be overwhelmed, and all spiritual authority[33] will rise up in Mainz. The Church will be stripped of possessions and the priests slain. Then will be fulfilled that saying of John's: "Everyone who slays you will think that he offers homage to God" (John 16:2).

Translated from the edition of Version A by E. Herrmann, "Veniet aquila . . . ," pp. 114–15.

31. Apocalypticism, the Great Schism, and the Conciliar Movement

> The Great Schism brought into the sharpest possible focus all the various elements of the prophetic tradition that we have been tracing: the forces of the Antichrist creating schism and persecution in the Church, the expectation of terrible tribulation and judgement, the prophetic summons of the Pope back to Rome to fulfill the full destiny of the *renovatio ecclesie*. Above all, it was the fact of the Great Schism itself which set the seal of truth on the prophets from Joachim and St. Francis to Jean de Roquetaillade.
>
> Marjorie Reeves, *Influence of Prophecy*, p. 422.

When Gregory XI finally returned to Rome from Avignon in 1377 it seemed that the Church's long ordeal was over. His premature death in 1378 was to usher in an even graver trial. Under pressure from the Roman populace, an Italian was elected as Urban VI; but the new pope's harsh and unbalanced behavior and the desires of the French faction of cardinals to quit Italy soon resulted in the election of another pope, Clement VII, who promptly returned to Avignon. The facts surrounding the double election were so complex that men of unimpeachable probity could be found in either camp, but the scandal of two popes competing for the leadership of Christendom could not but seem a confirmation of apocalyptic warnings concerning the approaching End. The countries of Europe rapidly lined up behind their respective candidates—France and her allies sided with Clement, the rest of Europe with Urban. Political implications were a decisive factor in the continuance of the Schism, as pope succeeded pope and the two "lines" of Rome and Avignon became more fully established.[1]

In the early years of the Schism theologians and publicists, especially those of the University of Paris, played an important role in attempts to end the split. In 1394, the Council of Paris outlined three possible solutions: the *via cessionis* whereby one pope would retire, the *via compromissi* in which the two popes would negotiate a settlement, and the *via concilii* which would leave the solution up to a general council. Unfortunately, the popes were only interested in what has been called the *via facti,* solution by military and political victory. Gradually, it became evident that only a council held hope of providing a settlement. The conciliar movement, based on the doctrine that a general church council possessed powers over the pope, had been growing since the early days of the Schism.[2] In 1409, the cardinals of the two lines, disgusted with the intransigence of their respective popes, met in council at Pisa, condemned both claimants, and elected a new pope, Alexander V. The fiasco of three popes rather than two, the pressing dangers to the Church from collapsing discipline and heresy in Bohemia, and the disturbed European situation, soon led to the summoning of another council by the Emperor Sigismund. The Council of Constance (1414–1418) deposed the Avignonese and Pisan popes, allowed the Roman pope to resign, and elected as universally accepted Pope Martin V (1417–1431). As a necessary basis for the reform of the Church, Constance declared its superiority to the pope and established a timetable for future reforming councils.[3] Martin V and his successor Eugene IV (1431–1447) saw to it that the conciliar movement and its claims did not win the day. The reforming Council of Basel (1431–1449) was consistently undercut by the papacy and ended in failure. With it died the hopes for reform of the medieval Church.

The Schism bulks large in almost every apocalyptic text of the period after 1380. From the wealth of material available, I have chosen two offerings as illustrative of the apocalyptic interpretation of the events of the Schism. The prophecy beginning "In illa die aquila veniens" has been ascribed to a number of authors, among them Joachim of Fiore, and the lawyer John of Legnano (1320–1383), a fervent defender of Urban VI much concerned with ending the Schism.[4] This text's stress on two popes, one legitimate and the other an intruder, certainly reflects the context of the Schism; but more precise dating is difficult. Elements of the scenario seem to suggest the events of the early years of the Schism (1380–1383), but the earliest surviving manuscripts are all of the fifteenth century.[5] In the 1440s a north Italian jurist named Tebaldus Civeri provided a glossed version of the text in an important anthology of apocalyptic materials that he compiled.[6]

St. Vincent Ferrer (c.1350–1419), a Spanish Dominican, was the most noted preacher of the early years of the fifteenth century. A close friend of Pedro de Luna, later Benedict XIII, he was a strong suppporter of the Avignonese line for many years before abandoning Benedict in 1415. Deeply affected by the Schism and by corruption in the Church, Vincent made the imminence of the Antichrist one of the major themes of his preaching. The saint's authentic writings (his reputation as a prophet led to a host of pseud-onymous texts being put under his name) [7] show him to be not so much a Joachite in inspiration as a moral reformer whose basic source was the text of Scripture, though he was not beyond making use of private revelations at times. [8]

Some of the most important figures in the conciliar movement dabbled in apocalypticism, among them Cardinal Pierre d'Ailly (1350–1420) and the noted Platonic theologian Cardinal Nicholas of Cusa (1401–1464). Among Cusa's voluminous theological, philosophical, and scientific works, his brief but original treatise on the last things, the *Conjecture regarding the Last Days* (written about 1440), shows that although the cardinal was no ardent apocalypticist in the manner of some of his contemporaries, his mind too was not untouched by hopes and fears for the age to come. [9]

IN THAT DAY THE EAGLE WILL COME

1. In that day the eagle will come from the North and will descend upon Liguria and almost no one will know it. [10] He will plant his nest with thicker feathers than the other eagles that have passed by. He will remain for a time and cross over into Tuscany; afterwards, he will go to the Elephant and remain there. [11] There will be two bridegrooms, the one legitimate, the other an adulterer. [12] This eagle will cross into Liguria and then tribulations and wars will begin, struggle on land and sea. The legitimate bridegroom will flee and will not be seized; [13] the adulterer will reign. "Peace! Peace!" will be the cry, but it will not be found. The name of the Lord will be blas-phemed and there will be no understanding in the land. Each man will act according to his strength.

The French lion will meet the eagle and will strike his head. There will be immense war and great slaughter. One will conquer, and the one who loses will flee into Tuscany and there regain his strength. [14] Behold, there will be battles and slaughters such as have not been from the beginning of the world nor will be until the End, because peoples from every nation of the earth will be gathered there. One of them will conquer in the end, and he who loses will flee. He who wins will go to the Elephant and will set up the ancient widowed See. [15] He will call the true bridegroom, will place him in his See, and will depose the illegitimate bridegroom. He will call the baron with whom he has estates, [16] make peace with him, and place him in his kingdom. He will call the fat bulls and barons and behead them because of the injustice they have done. He will lead the Church back to its pristine state and will restore each petitioner his rights. Then the earth will begin to give her fruits and there will be peace in the whole world.

2. Behold, in those days a new star of wondrous size will appear. In those times the Church and the Catholic Faith will prosper;[17] the Christian people will regain their powers and extend them. A very powerful lion full of faith and wisdom will arise from the tribe of the faithful; at his roar the whole earth will tremble. He will exterminate the yelping wolves, devouring some, wounding others. He will take to himself the wings of the eagle.[18] He will gather the Christian people and the faithful nations together with the Church and will cross the sea with them to overcome the barbarous nations of the Gentiles. He will stretch his tail to the ends of the earth, and under his right arm the whole world will take up once more the pattern of peace.[19]

This translation is based upon a preliminary collation of four mss.: Vat. lat. 3816, f. 62v; Vat. Ottobon. 1106, f. 24v; Venice, Bibl. Marc. ms. III, 177, f. 43r; and Turin, Bibl. Naz. Univ. K. IV.13, ff. 128r–129r. I wish to thank A. V. Brovarone of the staff of the Turin Library for assistance in reading the difficult glosses of the last ms.

ST. VINCENT FERRER

The Report on the Antichrist[20]

I am accustomed to declare in my sermons four conclusions about the time of the Antichrist and the End of the world. The first conclusion is that the time of the Antichrist and of the End of the world will coincide, the reason being the brevity of the duration of time after the death of the Antichrist. . . .[21] The second conclusion is that before the birth of the Antichrist that time will be generally hidden from all men. This conclusion is proved through two texts of Scripture, the first Matt. 24:3 ("Tell us when these things will be, etc."), the second in Acts 1:7 where to the apostles again asking about the same thing . . . Christ himself responds, "It is not for you to know the times or the moments."[22]

The third conclusion is that for about the past hundred years[23] the Antichrist ought to have come and this world truly have reached its End. This conclusion is held to be sufficiently manifested first from the revelation made to St. Dominic and St. Francis . . . about the three lances . . . ,[24] and second, through the revelation made to John the Evangelist when it says in the twentieth chapter of Revelation, "I saw an angel descending from heaven . . .'' The fourth conclusion is that the time of the Antichrist and of the End of the world will be soon and quite soon and very shortly. This conclusion, although it was present as an opinion in the First Homily of St. Gregory,[25] I demonstrate more strictly and more properly speaking in many ways.

First, the conclusion was made known to Saints Dominic and Francis. Second, it was made known in another revelation (irrefragable to me) given to a certain religious from the second of these orders. Third, the same conclusion is known through the revelation made to Daniel the Prophet in the eighth chapter concerning the ten horns of the fourth beast, for according to the *Ordinary Gloss* the fourth beast signifies the Roman empire which will have ten schisms . . . .[26] Fourth, the same conclusion is shown through another revelation related to me by a man who seemed both devout and holy. When I was preaching in Lombardy the first time (nine years ago now), this man came to me from Tuscany, sent, as he said, by some holy hermits who had lived there in great austerity of life for a long time.[27] He announced that manifest divine revelations had been made to these men that Antichrist was already born and that the fact should be announced to the world. . . . Fifth, the conclusion stands through another clear revelation which I heard in Piedmont by the report of a Venetian merchant very worthy of faith, I believe. He said that when he was overseas in a Franciscan monastery he heard Vespers on a feast day. At the end of the service, when they usually say ''Benedicamus Domino,'' two small novices of the monastery were immediately and visibly put in a trance before the eyes of all for a long space of time. Then they cried out together in a terrible voice: ''Today, in this hour, Antichrist, the destroyer of the world, is born.'' When I inquired and asked about the time of this vision, I found out that it was only nine years ago. . . .[28]

Most Holy Father, these points are what I preach throughout the world regarding the time of Antichrist and of the End of the world, subject to Your Holiness's correction and determination. May the Most High blessedly preserve you, as you desire. Amen.

Translated from the partial text given by S. Brettle, *San Vicente Ferrer*, pp. 170–71, with some additions from the version of the text found in T. Malvenda, *De Antichristo*, p. 55.

Second Sermon on the Antichrist [29]

According to divine disposition which is the cause of every operation and effect, as Sacred Scripture says, after Antichrist has reigned three years, then Christ will come and destroy him with the breath of his mouth. Then the world will last for only forty-five days. . . .[30] The Doctors say that after the death of Antichrist these forty-five days will be given to men for repentance out of God's great mercy, so that those who denied Christ, his Mother, all the saints, and angels, and the Catholic and ecclesiastical sacraments, will be able to repent. Nevertheless, only with difficulty will those who followed the Antichrist return to repentance. The reason is that those who received great treasures will not want to return them. The religious who received many beautiful diabolical wives and bore many children to increase their guilt will have become accustomed to their solace. They will never return to the true humble poverty of Francis and the other saints.[31] And the same in the case of nuns or laity of any state in life. After these days, there will immediately come a fire from East to West by the power of God and not by any natural motion. The whole earth and anything that is in it will burn, so that it will be like ashes in a furnace.

Translated from the text given in S. Brettle, *San Vicente Ferrer*, p. 182.

32. The Hussite Movement

The early fifteenth century witnessed the first use of the apocalyptic tradition in the service of political, social, and economic revolution—the Hussite movement in Bohemia. Though the movement must be seen in the light of the social struggles and revolts of the later fourteenth century, what distinguishes Bohemia is not only the remarkable completeness of its revolutionary ideology, but the deep religious feelings which were the source of its power. As H. Kaminsky has put it: "Hussitism is seen as beginning with a movement for reform, which then became a revolt; both then became wider and deeper, the reform passing into reformation, the revolt into revolution."[1] The complexity of the story and the vast literature that it has attracted prevent me from doing more here than sketching the broadest lines of the history of Hussitism, especially in the key years of 1412 to 1421.[2]

Bohemia, like so many other areas of Christendom, was strongly moved by currents of Church reform in the troubled latter half of the fourteenth century. The preachers who gathered at Prague, such as John Milíč (d. 1374) and his pupil Matthew of Janov (d. 1394), were not unlike other ardent reformers in their openness to apocalyptic language. Milíč once preached that the Emperor Charles IV was the Antichrist and Matthew thought that Antichrist had reigned in the Church since the time of Innocent III. The reform movement was considerably strengthened in the 1390s when the writings of the antipapal English thinker John Wycliff (d. 1384) became influential among the Czech masters of the University of Prague. The most important of these was John Hus (c. 1372–1415), a powerful preacher at the Bethlehem Chapel and a sincere moral reformer, who agreed with Wycliff that only by breaking the jurisdictional supremacy of Rome on the Church could true reform be achieved. Hus was summoned to the Council of Constance to be examined, and when he failed to make a full recantation of his errors he was burned as a heretic despite the guarantee of safety he had been given. His death was not an end but a beginning. The tragedy of Constance played right into the hands of the more radical antipapal reformers, like

Jakoubek of Stříbro and the German Nicholas of Dresden, who went beyond Hus in identifying the existing structure of the Church with the body of the Antichrist and were willing to make a dramatic break with it when the occasion arose. Hus the martyr became the figurehead for a movement more radical than he himself had been.

From the beginning, the divided character of the reform movement in Bohemia was evident. Among the few issues that both radicals and conservatives agreed upon was the sacramental theory known as Utraquism, i.e., the teaching that the laity should receive communion under the forms of both bread and wine. Orthodox Catholics, both inside and outside Bohemia, continued to oppose this view and many attempts at compromise broke down over the sacramental issue.[3] Utraquism, however, served as the basis for the working agreement among the reform groups that were increasingly dominant from the time of the formation of the Hussite League in late 1415. During the three years that followed, the radicals were active, both in Prague itself and in the provinces. The problem of the relation of the increasingly radical left wing of the movement to earlier forms of heterodoxy, especially Waldensianism and the so-called heresy of the Free Spirit, has never been adequately solved, nor has the question of the possible bonds between radical Hussitism and the Joachite tradition. The three-age pattern of history used by the radicals, as well as aspects of their exegesis, clearly betray affinities with Joachitism;[4] but it is important to stress, along with E. Werner, the true novelty of the Hussite program: "we see the medieval populace of town and country at a certain stage of development, building a new ideology out of traditions which as a rule had not dealt with them or with their interests at all."[5]

The crisis came in 1419 when King Wenceslaus IV, under the prodding of Pope Martin V, tried to crack down on the increasingly independent Bohemian Church. The result was open revolt. Under the leadership of John Želivský, another popular preacher, the radical elements in Prague rose up and overthrew the conservative city government—or rather literally threw them out the window of the town hall in the "Defenestration of Prague" of July 30, 1419. Wenceslaus died of apoplexy upon hearing the news, and the active revolutionary stage of Hussitism had begun. The activities in Prague, however, had been preceded in the spring of the same year by large rural gatherings of disaffected peasants who met to hear the word of God in their native tongue and celebrate the Utraquist liturgy. These groups, who frequently met on hilltops which they identified with Mt. Tabor, the place of the transfiguration of Jesus and therefore of the renewal of the Church, were to form the core of the revolutionary apocalypticists of the Hussite movement.[6]

Very soon the groups in attendance at Tabor and other centers took the decisive step of abandoning their ties with the feudal order of rural Bohemia, leaving behind farms and possessions, and constituting the embryo of a new society which stressed brotherhood and the common possession of goods.[7] Whether or not this action sprang solely from apocalyptic hopes for the coming Kingdom of God, by the latter part of 1419 apocalypticism had certainly become an important part of the Taborite movement. If we recall the uprooted character of the Apostolic Brethren who followed Fra Dolcino in the first years of the fourteenth century—the only previous movement in the Middle Ages that approached the Taborites in the use of armed resistance against the established order in the name of apocalyptic expectations[8]—we can appreciate the role that social and economic dislocation played in radicalizing Hussite apocalypticism.[9] Though the Taborites initially favored a pacifist position, by early 1420 their conviction that they alone were the saved remnant in the midst of a world under the control of Antichrist led them to believe that they had the duty to cleanse the world in the name of Christ. The militant phase of Hussite apocalypticism had been born.

The Taborite program, as known to us both from their own documents and from the accounts of their enemies, is a textbook case (the only one in the Middle Ages) of the radical millenarianism so dear to some historians and sociologists. It centered on belief that the new age of the Holy Spirit had dawned at Tabor. All other institutions, religious and secular, were marked for destruction; only the new model of society, ruled by the priests, dedicated to strict morality and marked by the common possession of goods, was to survive.

From their center at an abandoned castle in southern Bohemia rapidly built into the fortified city they named Tabor,[10] the apocalyptic and communistic left wing of Hussitism under the brilliant leadership of the blind general John Žižka became the center of resistance to the attempt of the Emperor Sigismund (1410–1437), the brother of Wenceslaus, to bring Bohemia back into obedience to the Roman communion. Although Prague was usually more dominated by conservative elements, all the Hussite factions combined against Sigismund's crusade. The basis for the agreement was the famous Four Articles of Prague (1420)—communion under both kinds, freedom of preaching, the end of clerical lordship and immorality, and severe punishment for public mortal sins.

It was Žižka's Taborites who were responsible for the emperor's defeat outside Prague in July 1420. The remarkable initial success of the Hussite movement, however, spelled the end of unity, even among the adherents of Tabor. Apparently some Taborite preachers had announced the End of the world for early 1420. When the event did not materialize, a rationalized interpretation concerning two adverts—a secret coming of Christ coincident with the founding of Tabor, and a still-awaited final coming—was put forward. Events were to show even more dramatically how difficult it was to keep the original solidarity and fervor of the Tabor community. The second half of 1420 saw the growth of the Pikart movement,[11] a more radical minority within Tabor which stressed antinomianism, denied Christ's presence in the Eucharist, and seemed to be willing to support a more vibrant apocalypticism than that of the bulk of the community. As Tabor moved toward organizing itself as a coherent, functioning, if unique, sub-society within medieval Christianity (it soon elected its own bishop), the Pikarts were cast out and ruthlessly suppressed. Their leader, Martin Húska, was burned at the stake.[12]

By 1421 the two successful groups in Bohemia, the moderate Utraquists centered in Prague and the new society of Tabor, had agreed, at least for the moment, to neutral coexistence. Tabor's adherence to its new model of society was continually tested in the years that followed. The military genius of Žižka (d. 1424) and later the priest Prokop the Great brought it many successes. The Taborite armies spread radical reform throughout Central Europe in their famous raids. The story of the savage Hussite Wars that raged until 1436 cannot be told here. Eventually, the negotiations between the Hussites and the leaders of Basel split a reform movement that had always included divisions into seriously opposed camps. The moderates decisively defeated the Taborites and their allies in 1434, and by the mid-fifteenth century the Hussite reform had clearly elected the model of a national Church tied to the social and economic order of the day rather than the Taborite new society. George Poděbrady, the heir of Hussitism's long Thermidor, destroyed Tabor in 1452.[13]

JOHN HUS[14]

Another error: that the pope is Antichrist. Response: I did not say this, but I did say that if the pope sells benefices, if he is proud, avaricious, or otherwise morally opposed to Christ, then he is the Antichrist.[15] But it should by no means follow that every pope is Antichrist; a good pope, like St. Gregory, is not the Antichrist, nor do I think he ever was.

Another error: that the Roman curia is the synagogue of Satan. I did not say this as my own firm conclusion, but as something I had heard from those who returned from the Roman curia. If there are ambitious, avaricious, and proud men there, as St. Bernard says in his book to Pope Eugene,[16] then it is true. It does not follow from this that everyone at the Roman curia is evil.

Translated from F. Palacký, *Documenta Magistri Joannis Hus* (Prague: F. Tempsky, 1869), p. 170.

THE BEGINNINGS OF TABOR

Account of Jakoubek of Stříbro [17]

In the year 1419 there took place a congregation of the laity on a certain mountain and in an open place near the village of Chrástán in the region of Písek and Bechyně, to which place people came from many other towns and regions of Bohemia and Moravia, to hear and obey the word of God and to take communion freely, with their children too, in the glorious sacrament of the body and blood of Lord Jesus. There they recognized, through the gift of the Holy Spirit and of the word of God, how far they had been led away and seduced by the foolish and deceitful clergy from the Christian faith and from their salvation; and they learned that the faithful priests could not preach the Scriptures and the Christian doctrine in the churches. And they did not wish to remain in that seduction.

This translation is that of H. Kaminsky, *Hussite Revolution,* pp. 279–80, reprinted here by the permission of the University of California Press. The Czech original may be found in F. M. Bartoš, "Sněm husitské revoluce v Betlémské kapli," *Jihočeský sborník historický* (1949), 18:99.

Manifesto of Bzí Hora (September 17, 1419)[18]

We declare in this letter, publicly and to all, that our meeting on the mountains and the fields is for no other purpose than for freely hearing the faithful and salutary message based on the Law of God, and for the necessary communion of the most worthy sacrament of the divine body and blood of our Lord and Savior Jesus Christ, in memory of his martyrdom and our redemption, and for fortification, preservation, and conformation in a salutary life. Accordingly, all of us with one will ask the dear Lord God that we may be of one Law, one faith, one heart, and one soul. First we ask God that we be purged of all that is evil and damaging to the soul, and developed in all that is good. We also ask God, now that we have recognized the cunning and damaging seduction of our souls by false and hypocritical prophets, guided by Antichrist against the Law of God, that we may beware of them and diligently be on our guard against them, so that they may no longer deceive and mislead us away from the old and true faith of the Lord Jesus and of the apostles. For we now clearly see the great abomination standing in the holy place, as prophesied by the prophet Daniel: the ridicule, blasphemy, suppression, and repudiation of all of God's truth, and the enormous glorification of all Antichristian hypocritical evil, under the name of holiness and benevolence. . . .[19]

Translation of H. Kaminsky, *Hussite Revolution,* pp. 299–300, reprinted with permission. The Czech text is in J. Macek, *Ktož jsú boží bojovníci* (Prague: Melantrich, 1951), pp. 43–45.

Lawrence of Březová, Chronicle[20]

At this time some of the priests of Tabor were preaching a new coming of Christ to the people. In this advent all the evil and those who envied truth would perish and be exterminated; at least the good would be preserved in the five cities. For this reason those cities that had freedom of the chalice, especially the city of Plzeň, would enter into no agreement with their adversaries. These priests of Tabor in the district of Bechyně and elsewhere, by falsely interpreting the writings of the prophets according to their own heads and by condemning the catholic positions of the holy doctors, were deceiving the people in their sermons in a wonderful way with many errors and things contrary to the Christian faith. To the extent that they desired to be saved from the wrath of Almighty God that they said was ready to come upon the whole world each and all should move from the cities, fortresses, villages, and towns to the five cities of refuge, as Lot left Sodom. These

were their names—Plzeň, which they called the city of the sun, Zatec,
Louny, Slany, and Klatovy. Almighty God wished to destroy the whole
world with the sole exception of those people who fled to the five cities.
They brought forward the writings of the prophets, falsely and erroneously
understood, as confirmation of this view, and they sent letters containing all
this throughout the kingdom of Bohemia. Many simple people who, as the
Apostle says, had zeal but not according to wisdom (Gal. 4:17), agreed that
their foolish opinions were true. They sold their goods, even at a low price,
and flocked to them from the different regions of the kingdom of Bohemia
and the margravate of Moravia along with their wives and children. They
cast the money at the feet of the priests.

Translated from the edition of J. Goll in *Fontes rerum Bohemicarum* (Prague: Palackého, 1893),
5:355–56.

John of Příbram, The Story of the Priests of Tabor [21]

The people, thus seduced, saw how they had evidently been deceived
and how they had been deprived of their property. And seeing that nothing
had come or was coming of the things that their prophets had prophesied, and
suffering hunger, misery, and want, they began to grumble and complain
greatly against the prophets.[22] At this point the false seducers thought up a
new lie somehow to console the people, and they said that the whole Christian Church was to be reformed in such a way that all the sinners and evil
people were to perish completely, and that only God's elect were to remain
on earth—those who had fled to the mountains. And they said that the elect
of God would rule in the world for a thousand years with Christ, visibly and
tangibly. And they preached that the elect of God who fled to the mountains
would themselves possess all the goods of the destroyed evil ones and rule
freely over all their estates and villages. And they said, "You will have such
abundance of everything that silver, gold, and money will only be a nui-
sance to you." They also said and preached to the people, "Now you will
not pay rents to your lords any more, nor be subject to them, but will freely
and undisturbedly possess their villages, fish-ponds, meadows, forests, and
all their domains."

Then the seducers, wanting to bring the people to that freedom and
somehow to substantiate their lies, began to preach enormous cruelty, unheard-of violence, and injustice to man. They said that now was the time of
vengeance, the time of destruction of all sinners and the time of God's wrath

. . . in which all the evil and sinful ones were to perish by sudden death, on one day. . . . And when this did not happen and God did not bring about what they had preached, then they themselves knew how to bring it about, and again thought up new and most evil cruelties, . . . that all the sinners were to be killed by the afflictions described in Ecclesiasticus (39:35–6). . . . And again those cruel beasts, the Taborite priests, wanting to excite and work up the people so that they would not shrink from these afflictions, preached that it was no longer the time of mercy but the time of vengeance, so that the people should strike and kill all sinners. . . . And they called us and others who admonished them to be merciful, damaging hypocrites.[23]

Translation of H. Kaminsky, *Hussite Revolution*, pp. 340–41, reprinted with permission. The Czech text is in J. Macek, *Ktož jsú boží bojovníci*, pp. 263–66.

TABORITE VIEWS

A Taborite Treatise [24]

When there is a very notable change in men, then the age will be ended. The change of the good for the better and the extermination of the evil is what I call the end of the age because it is written: "I will make an end in all the nations, but you I will not end" (Jer. 30:11). I call the day of the Lord the day of vengeance of which Isaiah says: "The day of vengeance is in my heart, the year of my retribution is coming" (Isa. 63:4), and the Holy Spirit sent me "to announce a year of expiation, a day of retribution" (Isa. 61:3), concerning which Luke also writes in his fourth chapter.

"The day will come like a thief in the night" (1 Thess. 5:2); "it will be revealed in fire" (1 Cor. 3:13). How the "falling away" will precede it, Paul predicts in 2 Thess. 2, and Zechariah describes in chapter fourteen. . . . What then now remains but that in the morning Christ slay the sinners and cast every evildoer out of the city of God (Ps. 100:8) so that they are discomfited at evening and vanish at daybreak?

Translated from Lawrence of Březová, *Chronicle*, in *Fontes rerum Bohemicarum*, 5:418–19.

The Articles against the Taborites [25]

First, that already in the present year, that is 1420, the End of the age, that is the extermination of all the evil, will be and indeed is. *This is an error.* . . .

Fourth, that in the present time of vengeance, the meekness, mildness, and mercy Christ showed to the adversaries of his Law are not to be imitated or followed, but rather only zeal, fury, cruelty, and just retribution. *This is pertinacious heresy.*

Fifth, that in this time of vengeance any one of the faithful is accursed who holds his sword back from the blood of the adversaries of Christ's Law, from personally pouring it out. Rather, each of the faithful ought to wash his hands in the blood of Christ's enemies, because blessed are all who return vengeance to the woeful daughter,[26] just as she has done to us. *This is heresy and tyrannical cruelty. . . .*

Eighth, that in this stage of Christianity while the Church Militant still lasts, only five earthly cities will remain during the predicted plague. The faithful must flee to them in the time of vengeance. Outside these five there is no salvation. *This is an error, a lie of false prophets. . . .*

Twelfth, that only those faithful who are gathered on the mountains are that body to which the eagles will gather, wherever it is.[27] They are the army sent by God into the whole world to execute all the plagues of the time of vengeance, to take revenge upon the nations, their cities, towns, and fortified places. They will judge every tongue that resists them. *This is an error and a lie. . . .*

Nineteenth, that for the restoration of the kingdom the elect will soon bodily rise up in the first resurrection which long precedes the second general resurrection. Christ will descend from heaven and live with them in the body. Every eye will see him. He will make a great banquet and supper in the real mountains and entering to see the guests will cast the evil into the darkness outside. All who were outside the mountains, like those who were once outside Noah's Ark in the Flood, will be consumed by fire in a moment. *This is an error. . . .*[28]

Twenty-seventh, that the written Law of God will cease in the Restored Kingdom of the Church Militant and written Bibles will be destroyed because the Law of Christ will be written in the hearts of all and there will be no need of a teacher.[29] *This is an error. . . .*

Twenty-ninth, that in the Restored Kingdom of the earthly Church women will bear sons and daughters without corporal disturbance and pain. *This is heresy. . . .*[30]

Forty-fourth, that in the sacrament of the bread and wine of the Eucharist true God and man is not there in terms of content, sacrament, and presence. *This is heresy.*[31]

Forty-fifth, that in the sacrament of the Eucharist true God and man is not to be adored with the homage of worship. *This is heresy.* . . .

Fiftieth, that as long as a man is in the state of grace he sacramentally receives the body and blood of Christ as much in any food as in the sacrament itself. *This is an error.*

Translated from Lawrence of Březová, *Chronicle*, in *Fontes rerum Bohemicarum*, 5:454–62.

A Chiliast Manifesto [32]

The grace of the almighty Father, our God in heaven——may it be granted to you and received by you faithfully, as befits saints! For the holy must fear God according to this prayer: "Oh boundless Grace who gives each enough, and does it from love and grace alone, not because of any merit!" And give him honor and praise, the homage of bowing down, prayer, and thanks for all time. Await the Lord in sobriety and holiness of life! Know that the Lord already stands at the gate, and the morning star has risen from the east and shines before him. Let us be very vigilant then, for we do not know what hour the third angel will blow his trumpet (Rev. 8:10–11), when the sun will blaze up, the clouds will vanish, darkness will go, blood will flow from wood, and he will reign who is not expected by those on earth. All, however, who hear his voice will tremble, and we must be ready for when he comes, to go with him to the wedding.

And who is ready? Only he who remains in Christ and Christ in him. And he is in Christ who eats him. But to eat Christ's body is livingly to believe in him, and to drink his blood is to shed it with him for his Father. He takes Christ's body who disseminates his gifts, and he eats his body who livingly listens to his word.[33] In this way we shall all be Christ's body, his very limbs as St. Paul says (Eph. 5:30).

Through this eating the just will shine like the sun in the kingdom of their Father, when he comes in clouds with his glory and great power, and sends his glorious angels before him to sweep out all scandals from his heritage. And then evil will be abashed, lies will perish, injustice will disappear, every sin will vanish; and faith will flower, justice will flourish, paradise will open to us, benevolence will be multiplied, and perfect love will abound.

But before this for a short time the living waters will cease to flow for three hours, the sun will darken, the moon will turn to blood, and the stars will fall from the heavens for the dragon will sweep them down with his tail

(Rev. 12:3–4). It will be a time when no one will be able to stand fast without stumbling and falling into error. The world will then return to the age of its ancient silence for seven days, so that no one will be left—just as in the first beginnings. A man will then be dear as gold; each will long to see some other and hear his voice, but he will not see or hear anyone. But happy he who stays alive for 1,000 days, and 300, and 35 days; for then the holy place will be cleansed as St. Daniel says (Dan. 12:12).

I write these things to you as adults able to digest all foods—not like those who live on milk and would choke on anything more. I write to you who are not stupid but wise and know how to rejoice ever in abundance with your Lord God. And we admonish you for the sake of the great Father— beware of idols! [34] Do not bow down to anything visible but only to the Father Himself, the infinite creator, who cannot be grasped by any human eye or heart or mind. That is why He is called infinite and immeasurable God. And I admonish you, beware of false and lying priests, for they are the dragon's tail that strikes the stars from the heavens, as the Prophet Isaiah says (possibly Isa. 14:13). And unless God shorten those days they would lead even God's elect into error (Matt. 24:22). May the Lord God strengthen you ever in all good, and greet each other in peace all you faithful! Amen. I admonish you in the name of God to make this letter known to the whole community.

My gratitude is owed to Howard Kaminsky for permission to include this previously unpublished full translation (part appears in *Hussite Revolution*, pp. 405–6). The Czech text is in F. M. Bartoš, *Do čtyř pražských artykulů* (Prague, 1925), pp. 96 sqq.

33. Germany on the Eve of the Reformation

During the seventy years before the Reformation, Germany served as a mirror in which was reflected both the worst and the best of the late medieval world.[1] Widespread corruption in the Church, political weakness in the empire, and social upheaval must be weighed against burgeoning urban development, the stirrings of humanism, and important movements of religious fervor to achieve a balanced picture of the times. Such a background provided an ideal milieu for apocalypticism, and late medieval Germany does not disappoint us here.[2]

German apocalyptic expectations were frequently tied to the careers of the emperors in whose hands many placed their hopes for the future, although the fifteenth-century emperors were not a promising lot for such high aspirations. Sigismund (1410–1437), the proponent of conciliarism and enemy of the Hussites, was sincerely interested in reform, but managed to achieve little. His reputation as a reformer is enshrined in the vernacular *Reformation of Kaiser Sigismund* of 1439, a treatise based on the reforming program of Basel with strong apocalyptic overtones.[3] Frederick III (1440–1493), the inheritor of the apocalyptic name and number, a weak ruler and amateur astrologer, was wise enough to eschew any apocalyptic role for himself.[4] His son, Maximilian I (1493–1519), under whose reign the consolidation of Hapsburg power began to be evident, was a more suitable candidate for the role of apocalyptic emperor, as we shall see below.

Equally important to the prophets and seers of the day was the problem of corruption in the Church. Feeling against Rome, and indeed against the entire structure of the late medieval Church, ran high; the desire for the elimination of abuses, especially financial abuses, was a burning issue. Finally, the conquest of Constantinople by the Turks in 1453 and their subsequent deep penetration into Europe raised the specter of Gog and Magog once again. All these concerns are evident in the apocalyptic writings of the period, as J. Rohr noted when he isolated three basic themes in fifteenth-century prophecy: antipathy to Rome, the confiscation of Church property, and the execution of judgment either by a northern emperor or the Turks.[5]

The groups and figures involved were varied. Among those that appear to have been influenced by the Hussites and to have provoked some popular following was the radical Joachite sect led by the brothers Janko and Livin of Wirsberg on the Czech–German border in the early 1460s.[6] Interesting as these brothers and their shadowy Franciscan adviser were, I have chosen to concentrate on three writers of the end of the century as a way of illustrating the most general themes of the period.[7]

John Lichtenberger, the court astrologer to Frederick III, reminds us of some earlier authors of the thirteenth century in the combination of astrology and apocalyptic found in his best-selling *Pronosticatio,* first published in 1488.[8] Lichtenberger was typical of the pedantry of the publicists of his age in his overwhelming accumulation of recondite sources and the lack of order that this introduced into his work. Nonetheless, the encyclopedic character of the *Pronosticatio* made it a useful tool, and it was immensely popular (over fifty full printings are known). The advent of the Turk convinced the German astrologer that the End was near, and although he confusingly made use of both German and French versions of the Last Emperor myth, he seemed to identify Philip, the son of Maximilian and Mary of Burgundy (and father of the future Charles V), as the coming emperor who would unite both streams of prophecy and usher in the new age which he expected to dawn between 1488 and 1499.

Wolfgang Aytinger, an Augsburg cleric (c.1460–after 1508), was also a typical figure. His two great concerns were the approaching End of the world, an event he judged to be near because of the ominous success of the Turks, and the reform of the Church, a cause for which he is one of the most eloquent spokesmen of the end of the century.[9] The Turkish threat had led to renewed interest in the Pseudo-Methodius (an edition was published as early as 1475 in Cologne). Aytinger's *Commentary on Methodius* was first published in 1496 by John Froschauer; in 1498 Sebastian Brant produced an illustrated version that proved very popular in the next century with seven later printings by 1576. For Aytinger the time of apocalyptic crisis began with the Fall of Constantinople and would end with the Last Emperor's victory over the Turks predicted for 1509. Aytinger has two possible candidates for the role—Philip of Burgundy, and Ladislaus, the King of Poland, Hungary, and Bohemia.

Both Lichtenberger and Aytinger are much like the learned apocalypticists we have seen before. Another figure, the so-called Revolutionary of the Upper Rhine, can perhaps be best described as a Taborite who fortunately never found a following, or alternatively as a leader of the Peasants' Revolt born before his time. All we know about the Revolutionary is contained in the massive, disorganized treatise he composed in German between about 1490 and 1508, known as *The Book of a Hundred Chapters,* or *The Statutes of Trier.*[10] This semi-educated layman was born in the Alsace about 1438 and accompanied a papal crusade to the Balkans in 1456 on which occasion he had a vision of St. Michael and a yellow cross, which was to be a key element in his bizarre apocalyptic program. The Revolutionary apparently attempted to interest Maximilian in his ideas about reform; his lack of success turned him against the emperor in a direction so violent that only among the most extreme Taborites can parallels be found. The nationalistic sentiment found in late medieval German prophecy reached its apogee in the Revolutionary. For him the original chosen people were the Germans not the Jews (Adam spoke German in Eden, Hebrew being introduced along with the other languages after the fall of the Tower of Babel). Teutonic greatness, in eclipse since the time of the German emperor, Alexander the Great (!), was soon to be restored by the coming of a "King from the Black Forest," a German Last Emperor, who would slaughter the clergy and establish a millenarian realm of distinctly communistic character on the basis of ancient German law, the supposed "Trier Statutes." The forerunners of the coming king, whose date of arrival was corrected as the work progressed (the last date given was 1515) were the "Brethren of the Yellow Cross," a group of anti-clerical laymen the Revolutionary had gathered around himself. Despite the revolutionary violence of his thought, there is no evidence that the group ever tried to put any of the ideas into practice.

JOHN LICHTENBERGER, *PRONOSTICATIO*

Book II, chapter 13

The Bishop of Trier and the bishop of Cologne ought to stand here having a crozier in their hands. A black bear and a gray wolf will come to snatch the crozier.[11] By this is understood that after the internal wars begun between the most reverend bishops of Trier and Cologne wild bears and murderous wolves will come. The secular state will afflict them under Maximilian, the French-born, and that tribulation will be like the tribulation in the time of the Maccabees when the office of the High Priest was occupied by Jason, Menelaus, Lysimachus, and Archimus (2 Macc. 4 sqq.). When these tribulations were over, Christ, the Prince of Peace, was born, and Octavian received world rule from the Roman people. Likewise, the High Priesthood was vacant through the death of the Maccabees. I believe that under Maximilian the See of Rome, alas, will be vacant for a year and a half, as is found in the sixth chapter of the *Angelic Oracle of Cyril*. At that time there will be great tribulation, a new order will arise and a renewal in the Church. There will be many false pontiffs and reformers in Italy and the Roman domains.[12]

Translated from *Pronosticatio in Latino* (Strasburg, 1488; reprinted 1890 at Manchester for The Holbein Society), unnumbered folios.

Book II, chapter 16. The Gauls and the Rulers of Gaul

I have gathered from the remarks of the ancients that Gaul took its name from the Greek "galla" which means milk in Latin, because the Gauls seem lighter in complexion than the Spaniards and others. It is also fittingly called Gaul because of the three-fold character of the cock [*gallus*]. . . .[13]

Note that from Priam to Faramund, and from Faramund to Childeric, all the kings and rulers of the Gauls were gentiles and pagans. Childeric had sex with so many wives and slaves that he was exiled to Thuringia and fled to King Basainus. He had illicit relations with the king's lonely wife and from this adultery of different peoples she bore Clovis, whom St. Remy baptized.[14] All the Christian kings of France descend from Clovis. The first Charles, called Martel, was born from an adultery between his father, Pepin, and his mother, Alpaida. He threw out Drogo and Ginnald, the legitimate sons of his father, and succeeded Pepin in the kingdom. He was a tyrant who made many attacks on the Church and clergy—a man from the bad cock. When he died, the pope finally ruled Rome because Charles Martel, the king of the Franks, had died in Trier and gone body and soul to hell. The pope sent messengers to the bishop of Trier, and when they opened the tomb they found a huge serpent but no body.

It says in *The Book of the Frankish Kings* that it will be from the Carolingians, that is from the race of King Charles of France, that an emperor named P. will arise in the last days. He will be a prince and a monarch and will reform the churches of all Europe. After him there will be no other emperor.

Translated from *Pronosticatio in Latino*, unnumbered folios.

Book II, chapters 36–37 [15]

Afterwards a hermit will arise known for his great sanctity, as Joachim says in his *Book of Concordance:* ''A man in great sanctity lifted up to the Roman throne like an apostle.'' God will do many miracles through him. Every man will reverence him; no one will disobey his laws. He will condemn plural benefices and incomes and will command that clerics live from tithes and offerings. He will forbid ostentatious clothing and all unseemly choruses and songs. He will command women to be without gold and jewels, and will bid the gospel be preached. He will be pope for only a brief time—when four years are up, this most holy man will happily go to God.

Immediately after this, God will raise up three other very holy men, one after the other. They will be alike in virtues and miracles and will confirm the decrees and deeds of their predecessor. Under their rule the condition of the Church will be renewed. They will be called ''Angelic Popes.''

Translated from *Pronosticatio in Latino,* unnumbered folios.

WOLFGANG AYTINGER, *COMMENTARY ON METHODIUS* [16]

Chapter Five. This treats of the principle of the fifty-six year calculation which is understood through the eight weeks of St. Methodius. The final period begins with the destruction of Constantinople and the empire of the Greeks.

''Woe, woe to the great city which was clothed with linen and purple and scarlet . . .'' (Rev. 18:16). John . . . says many things, especially in the sixteenth chapter, about the condition and the tribulations of the Church and about the seven angels who are said to be the seven scourges of the Church. . . .[17] The greatest tribulation in Christianity took place when the Turk conquered the eastern empire and Constantinople. Rightly, the calculations of the fifty-six years begin at last. . . .[18]

The root and origin of the Turks are illustrated by the seven branches and how the eighth branch, thought to be the most powerful, will be cut off by the king of the Romans. The fourth point is clear through John in the seventeenth chapter when he says: ''This is the meaning which gives understanding: the seven heads are seven mountains'' (17:9), that is, seven kingdoms. In my intention it signifies seven Turkish emperors who succeed each other in rule. The first is called Ottoman. . . . The sixth emperor, called

Mohammed, obtained the eastern empire and the rule of Constantinople and died in 1481.[19] Under his son who is now reigning the Turkish empire will end.[20] Hence John says at the end of chapter seventeen: "The beast which once was and now is not, is the eighth beast and yet one of the seven, and will be destroyed."

The destruction of the Great Whore Babylon, that is, Turkey. John shows the threefold path of Turkey, first its image, second its prosperity for a time, third its destruction. "One of the seven angels who had the seven vials came and spoke to me saying, etc." (Rev. 17:1). In the seventeenth chapter John does three things. In the first part he places an image of Turkey and the damnation and total destruction of the Saracen empire where it says, "Come and I will show you the damnation of the great Whore." In the second part he shows astonishment at its prosperity for a time where it says, "Why are you in awe? . . ." Third, he describes the way and manner of the destruction where it says, "The waters you have seen". . . .[21]

How a king of the Romans will prevail over the beast with seven heads and ten horns by divine protection. . . . "Why do you wonder, John? I will explain the mystery or meaning to you, first of the woman, second of the beast with seven heads and ten horns that carries the woman" (Rev. 17:7). First, through the woman John understood Turkey drunk with the blood of the saints and martyrs of Jesus. Second, I will expound the meaning of the beast. The beast that you saw is the person of Mohammed. . . .[22]

The third part of this chapter is that in which the human victory is treated. It will involve discord among the Turks and a rebellion of Christians. . . . "Then immediately a king of the Romans will rise up and come upon them in great fury." Note that according to the text of St. Methodius the king who will conquer the Turks will come from the western Roman empire and not from the eastern empire of Constantinople which the Turk occupies. . . .

The question concerns what province the king will come from who is now alive and who will triumph over the Turks, free the Christians, gain the promised land, and subdue all the cities, towns and fortresses of the Ishmaelites. . . . It seems from the words of St. Methodius that he will be a German king since the Roman empire now stands in Germany and her king is the head of the Romans. Second, it seems that it will be a French king because it says in the Legend of Charlemagne, King of France that from his stock there will arise in the last days one by the name of P. who will be prince and monarch of all Europe. . . .[23] Third, it seems that the present calamity of the Turks and the recovery of the Oriental Church will be the work of the king of Hungary. . . .[24] These things are hidden in God's judgment. But he who will do all this is already alive and will end the fifth scourge of the Church. . . .[25]

The king of the Romans of whom Methodius speaks will reform the Church, free the scattered clergy from their necessities, punish renegade Christians, conquer the infidels' land, choose new preachers of the Gospel, and make a new reformation of the Church. . . . Finally, he will make the greatest universal peace in the world so that through present peace we may merit to come to eternal peace. May Jesus Christ our Lord, the true lover of peace, deign to grant us this. Amen.

Translated from *De Revelatione facta ab Angelo Beato Methodio* (Basel: Furter, 1516), unpaged. This edition of the Pseudo-Methodius and Aytinger's Commentary is a reprint of the 1498 edition.

34. Savonarola and Late Medieval Italian Apocalypticism

Italy no less than Germany continued to provide fertile ground for apocalyptic hopes in the later fifteenth century. Wandering prophets preaching imminent destruction appeared in 1472, 1484, 1490, and 1492; mysterious new texts were spread abroad, such as the prophecy ascribed to St. Cataldus discovered at Taranto in 1492 and sent to King Ferdinand II of Sicily;[1] classic texts continued to be copied, revised, and began to be printed.[2] Many scholars have pointed out that it would be a mistake to view this strain of apocalypticism of the late *quattrocento* as a medieval anachronism grossly out of harmony with the prevailing spirit of Humanism.[3] "We are not dealing here with two opposed viewpoints or groups. . . . The Joachimist marriage of woe and exaltation exactly fitted the mood of late fifteenth-century Italy, where the concept of the humanist Age of Gold had to be brought into relation with the ingrained expectation of the Antichrist."[4]

The career of Girolamo Savonarola (1452–1498) is perhaps the best illustration of the point, for although this stern moralist, charismatic prophet, and wily politician was not a Humanist himself, his singular attraction for such key Humanists as Pico della Mirandola and the power that he came to wield over the city that was the undisputed Humanist capital show the strange combinations the age so frequently displays.[5]

Savonarola was born in Ferrara and entered the Dominican order at the age of twenty-three. At Florence in 1484 (a year of widespread apocalyptic expectations) he underwent a visionary experience that moved him to adopt the career of a prophet of approaching doom.[6] Although he began his apocalyptic preaching outside Florence, by 1490 he was back in the city and attracting large crowds to his sermons on the evils about to come upon the world. As D. Weinstein has demonstrated, the ills that befell Italy and Florence during the next four years came to convince Savonarola's hearers that his message was true. The most significant of the events that seemed to confirm the predictions of the passionate preacher was the advent of the Last Emperor to chastise the clergy and laity for their sins.

Charles VIII of France (1483–1498) was scarcely a more likely candidate than his older contemporary Frederick III for the role of Last Emperor; but unlike the German, the light-headed young French king eagerly sought the role. Numerous prophecies circulated about him, and Guilloche of Bordeaux produced a vernacular version of the Second Charlemagne Prophecy in verse that seemed to be particularly applicable to a young prince who had been crowned at the age predicted by the prophecy.[7] By 1492 Charles and his counselors were already planning an invasion of Italy to recover the kingdom of Naples for the French heirs of the Angevin; when the invasion was begun in the summer of 1494 it was announced as merely the first step in a campaign that would go on to conquer Jerusalem and restore the world to obedience to the Christian empire of the king of France.[8]

Charles's mighty army descended upon Florence in November, and since the destruction of Florence was a part of the job description of the Second Charlemagne (as well as an obvious conclusion from Savonarola's warnings), fear ran high. The Dominican visionary now came into his own. In the midst of this gloomy atmosphere, the populace cast out the Medici government and Savonarola soon became the chief spokesman for the city. He arranged for its peaceful submission to Charles, and partially as a result of this remarkable triumph, and partially due to the influence that the special Florentine sense of civic destiny had upon him, he evolved a fuller and more optimistic apocalyptic program in the months between late 1494 and mid-1495.[9] The Dominican now put all his energy behind the new republican government of the city and hailed Florence "as the chosen center of divine illumination and himself as the man sent by God, not only to warn Italy of the tribulations which had now come, but also to lead her out of the abomination of desolation."[10] As the leader of the city that was now the New Jerusalem and the New Rome, Savonarola replied to his critics in his *Compendium of Revelations* of mid-1495, a review of the remarkable success that his predictions had enjoyed and a defense of his prophetic mission.

Charles VIII's career as Last World Emperor was short-lived. After the conquest of Naples, he was compelled to withdraw in the face of overwhelming forces and died in France in 1498. His campaign may not have had lasting apocalyptic significance, but it did mark the beginning of the long French involvement in the welter of Italian politics.

The last three years of the Dominican prophet's life are among the most noteworthy examples of apocalypticism as an active political ideology. Insisting that political reform was the necessary prelude to moral renewal, Savonarola brought the full weight of his authority as prophet to bear in favor of the Florentine Republic.[11] His thought became increasingly dominated by an optimistic, millenarian view of the coming state that would prevail after the defeat of the Antichrist in the dawning Fifth Age of history. But all was not well in the proto-messianic republic of Florence under the rule of the divinely appointed prophet and his ascetic followers, the *Piagnoni*. Alexander VI, the corrupt Medici pope and member of the anti-French alliance, used Savonarola's apocalyptic criticism of Rome as the handle to summon him for investigation. The prophet refused, eventually appealing from an unholy pope to a general council and to the Angelic Pope to come. He was finally excommunicated in 1497. Opposition from Rome, the collapse of Charles VIII, and severe economic and political disturbances at home had eroded Savonarola's support among the volatile citizens of Florence. In 1498 he and some of his followers were arrested, put to the torture, and publicly executed on May 23. The prophet remained a sign of contradiction for ages to come. The *Piagnoni* revered his memory, while others execrated it. Shortly before Savonarola's execution, the noted Humanist philosopher Marsilio Ficino, once somewhat sympathetic to the prophet, reviled him as the Antichrist in a letter to the College of Cardinals. It was out of similar sentiments that the great Tuscan artist, Luca Signorelli, modeled his stupendous Antichrist fresco at Orvieto partly on the events of the prophet's life.[12]

RENOVATION SERMON[13]

Now let us begin with the reasons that for several years I have brought you as evidence to demonstrate and prove the renovation of the Church. Some reasons are probable and can be contradicted; others are demonstrative ones that cannot be contradicted because they are found in Sacred Scripture. The ones that I will tell you are all demonstrative, all founded in Sacred Scripture.

The first is because of the pollution of the prelates. . . .[14] The second is because of the lack of good and just men. . . . The third is because of the exclusion of the just. . . ; the fourth because of the desire of just men. . . ; the fifth because of the obstinacy of sinners. . . ; the sixth because of the multitude of sinners. . . ; and the seventh is because of the exclusion of the primary virtues, that is, charity and faith. . . . The eighth is because of the denial of articles of the faith. . . ; the ninth because divine worship has been lost. . . . The tenth is because of universal opinion. See, everyone seems to preach and expect the scourge and the tribulations, and it seems just to everyone that punishment of such great iniquity ought to come. The Abbot Joachim and many others preached and announced that the scourge was to come at this time.[15] These are the reasons through which I have preached the renovation of the Church to you. Now let us speak about the figures that demonstrate it. . . .[16]

I have said to you: "The sword of the Lord will come upon the earth swiftly and soon."[17] Believe me that the sword of God will come in a short time. Do not laugh at this "in a short time," and say that it is the "short time" of Revelation which needs hundreds of years to come. Believe me that it is soon. This belief will not harm you; on the contrary it will give you joy in that it makes you turn to penance and walk on the road of God. . . . Nevertheless, I have not told you a set time in order that you might always do penance and always be pleasing to God. If, for example, you were to say to the people: "The tribulation has ten years from now before it comes," everyone would say, "I can indulge myself a little more before being con- verted." This would be like giving them license to do evil in this way and would not be fitting. Therefore, God does not wish a set time to be preached. But I tell you this—that now is the time for repentance. Do not joke about this "in a short time," because I tell you that if you do not do what I tell you, woe to Florence, woe to the people, woe to the poor, woe to the rich!

Translated from the edition of V. Romano, *Prediche sopra i Salmi* (Rome: A. Belardetti, 1969), pp. 42–45, 60–61.

COMPENDIUM OF REVELATIONS[18]

The Early Stages of Savonarola's Prophetic Career

Therefore when Almighty God saw the sins of Italy multiply, especially among both ecclesiastical and secular princes, he was not able to bear it any longer and determined to purify his Church with a great scourge. Since, as Amos the prophet says: "The Lord God will not perform his word unless he first reveal his secret to his servants the prophets" (Amos 3:7), for the sake of the salvation of his elect he wished that scourge to be foretold in Italy, so that forewarned, his people might prepare themselves to endure it more firmly. Florence, located in the middle of Italy like the heart in a man, God deigned to choose to receive this message so that from there it might be widely spread through other parts of Italy as we now see fulfilled. He chose me, unworthy and useless among his other servants, to this task. At the bidding of my superiors, God saw to it that I came to Florence in 1489, and in that year on Sunday, August 1, I began to interpret publicly the Book of Revelation in our Church of San Marco.[19] Through the whole of the same year I preached to the people of Florence, continually stressing three things: first, the future renovation of the Church in these times; second, the great scourge that God would bring on all Italy before such a renovation; third, that these two things would come soon. . . .

Among other things, there was one that brought men of genius and learning to admiration, namely that from 1491 to 1494 I undertook continuous preaching upon Genesis through the whole of Advent and Lent, with the exception of one period spent in Bologna. . . . And with God willing and leading me on, I left off with the text, "Make a second and third floor in it" (Gen. 6:16), and began again the next September on the Feast of St. Matthew the Apostle with the following passage, that is, "Behold, I will bring flood waters upon the earth." Since everyone knew that the French king had invaded Italy with his forces, when I began my sermon with these words, that is, "Behold, I will bring flood waters upon the earth," suddenly many were astonished and thought that this passage of Genesis was furnished by God's hidden will for that moment in time. Among these was Count Giovanni della Mirandola, a man unique in our day for talent and learning; he later told me that he was struck with fear at these words and that his hair stood on end.

Translated from the edition of A. Crucitti, *Compendio di Rivelazioni*, pp. 134–37.

The Vision of the Two Crosses

In Lent of 1492, when I was preaching in the Church of San Lorenzo in Florence on Good Friday night, I saw two crosses in the sky. The first was black and in the midst of Rome, touching heaven with its top and stretching its arms through the whole world. It was inscribed with these words: "The Cross of God's Wrath." When I saw it, immediately I beheld a tempest darkening in the air with rushing clouds, winds, lightnings, thunderbolts, hail—all mixed together with fire and sword. An innumerable multitude of men was destroyed so that those that survived on earth were few. After this I saw a peaceful and bright time come and a golden cross in the midst of Jerusalem, the same height as the other, so gleaming that it illumined the whole world and filled it with new flowers and joy. Its inscription was: "The Cross of God's Mercy." Without delay all the nations of the earth, both men and women, came together from all sides to adore it and embrace it. For this purpose I received many other, even clearer, visions, as found in the other matters I have foretold, especially about the renewal and punishment of the Church. I have been strengthened by many visions and very clear showings at different times.

Furthermore, I predicted that the city of Florence would reform for the better and that this was the will of God—the citizens of Florence would have to do it. From that time, as I again predicted on God's part, the city would be more glorious, more powerful and more wealthy than it had previously been.[20] The event itself has proved that this was the purpose of God's will, because a reformation of the sort would have seemed the greatest contradiction, completely opposed to the manner and custom of that city as it seemed to everyone, had not the effect been produced that was thought impossible in human judgment.

Translated from A. Crucitti, *Compendio di Rivelazioni*, pp. 148–49.

MARSILIO FICINO ON SAVONAROLA AS ANTICHRIST[21]

I know, Venerable Prelates, that most of the Sacred College have been astonished that during almost the last five years one hypocrite from Ferrara has deceived so many Florentines, otherwise clever and learned men. They really ought to be astonished if they think that one man was able to outwit so many and such able men. But he is not a mortal man, but a demon of immense cleverness—not even one demon, but a crowd of them who attacked miserable mortals with hidden traps and outwitted them with marvelous artifices. No one ought to be in awe any longer. Without disagreement all will confess that our first parents, who like children of God were provided with divine wisdom and strength, established in Paradise, and taught by angels, were deceived by a single diabolical spirit. Why then should it seem marvelous that the Florentines, especially at a time like this, were so unfortunate that they were secretly possessed and seduced by a horde of demons in the guise of an angel?

Surely don't you believe that Antichrist will seduce in wondrous fashion many men famous for prudence and probity of life? There are many arguments that this Girolamo, the Prince of Seducers, acted more from a diabolical than a human spirit in seducing us as much by violence as by guile. The cunning in this Antichrist was altogether incomparable in its resolute ability to simulate virtue and to hide vice. He had profound intellect, wild daring, vain self-glorification, diabolical pride, shameless lying everywhere backed with curses and oaths, and an appearance, voice, and frequently enflamed oratorical style that affected the listeners not so much by voluntary persuasion as by violence. Frequently in the midst of a debate he would suddenly shout out, become enflamed, thunder, and altogether carry on like a person possessed by demons or the fury that the poets describe. Sometimes he did happen upon prophecy of a kind mixed with lies, so that he who fooled or compelled the people rather easily by some predictions of whatever kind might be finally convicted by his lies and evil works. Right now there is no time to discuss the reasons why astrologers and Platonists had foreseen that Savonarola would be led by many different and unfortunate astral influences. In summary, I can say that the astrologers and the Platonists, on the basis of various unlucky astral influences and conjunctions, or at least from certain signs, had guessed that Savonarola—or to speak more correctly, Sevonerola[22]—would be subject to various evil demons.

Translated from P. O. Kristeller, *Supplementum Ficinianum* (Florence: Olschki, 1937), 2:76–77.

35. Christopher Columbus

During the winter of 1501 to 1502, a fifty-year-old pensioner of the Spanish monarchs, Ferdinand and Isabella, was engaged in putting together what he called *The Book of Prophecies* with the help of a friendly friar, Gaspar Gorritio. To this book of excerpts from Scripture, the Fathers, and miscellaneous prophets, Christopher Columbus prefixed a letter to their royal highnesses in which he showed how his three earlier voyages of exploration under the inspiration of the Holy Spirit were intimately connected with the project that he now proposed, the recovery of the Holy Sepulcher. In the work itself the aging Admiral of the Ocean Seas reminded the rulers of the great things predicted of them: "Not unworthily nor without reason, Most Splendid Rulers, do I assert that even greater things are reserved for you, when we read that Joachim the Calabrian Abbot predicted that the future ruler who would recover Mt. Sion would come from Spain." [1]

To those accustomed to see the discovery of America as the work of a hard-headed practical seaman flouting the traditions of the past, the picture of Columbus as a religious visionary strongly influenced by centuries of apocalyptic hopes may seem strange, but the existence of this element in the great explorer's complex personality is undeniable, and its force became stronger as he neared the end of his adventurous life. The themes found in *The Book of Prophecies* are also evident in the account he wrote of his fourth and final voyage to the New World (1502–1504), the so-called *Lettera Rarissima*. Columbus thought that his own divinely inspired mission to open up a new path to Asia, coupled with a Spanish ruler's conquest of Jerusalem, would herald an age of universal conversion that would precede the End of the world. [2] He was the first, but by no means the last, to interpret the discovery of the New World in the light of an optimistic Joachite vision of the dawn of a more perfect age. The history of these interpretations lies outside the chronological limits of our story. Let us then if not end, at least rest at this moment in the history of apocalyptic traditions.

THE ACCOUNT OF THE FOURTH VOYAGE

The Genoese, Venetians, and all other nations that possess pearls, precious stones, and other articles of value, take them to the ends of the earth to exchange them for gold. Gold is the most precious of all commodities; gold constitutes treasure, and he who possesses it has all he needs in this world, as also the means for rescuing souls from purgatory, and restoring them to the enjoyment of paradise. . . . There were brought to Solomon at one journey six hundred and sixty-six quintals of gold, besides what the merchants and sailors brought, and that which was paid in Arabia. Of this gold he made two hundred lances and three hundred shields, and the entablature that was above them was also of gold, and ornamented with precious stones. . . . This is related by Josephus in his chronicle *On Antiquities;* [3] mention is also made of it in Chronicles and in the Book of Kings. [4] Josephus thinks that this gold was found in the Aurea; [5] if it were so, I contend that these mines of the Aurea are identical with those of Veragua, which, as I have said before, extends westward twenty days' journey, at an equal distance from the Pole and the Line. Solomon bought all of it—gold, precious stones, and silver—but your Majesties need only send to seek them to have them at your pleasure. David, in his will, left three thousand quintals of Indian gold to Solomon, to assist in building the Temple; and, according to Josephus, it came from these lands. [6]

Jerusalem and Mount Sion are to be rebuilt by the hands of the Christians, as God has declared by the mouth of his prophet in the fourteenth Psalm (vv. 7–8). The Abbot Joachim said that he who should do this was to come from Spain; [7] Saint Jerome showed the holy woman the way to accomplish it; and the emperor of China has, some time since, sent for wise men to instruct him in the faith of Christ. [8] Who will offer himself for this work? Should anyone do so, I pledge myself, in the name of God, to convey him safely hither, provided the Lord permits me to return to Spain.

Translated by R. H. Major, *Select Letters of Christopher Columbus* (London: Hakluyt Society, 1847), pp. 196–98. The Spanish text may be found in C. de Lollis, ed., *Raccolta di Documenti e Studi,* part 1, vol. 2 (Rome, 1894), p. 202.

Notes

Preface

1. There are, to be sure, various surveys in German and Italian, especially the important study of B. Töpfer, *Das kommende Reich des Friedens;* but even Töpfer does not cover the full span in equal detail. Two works in English do treat the later parts of the story, Norman Cohn's provocative but deeply flawed work, *The Pursuit of the Millennium,* and Marjorie Reeves's monumental *The Influence of Prophecy in the Later Middle Ages: A Study in Joachimism.* My debt to Reeves's work for the latter portion of this study will be evident. Other works, such as the compendious but eccentric four volumes of L. E. Froom, *The Prophetic Faith of Our Fathers,* and the totally inadequate popular work of E. R. Chamberlain, *Antichrist and the Millennium,* offer little to the serious student.

2. By way of preparation, I attempted a broad historiographical survey in my article "Apocalypticism in the Middle Ages: An Historiographical Sketch."

3. Two German compilations contain translations of a number of the texts included here. E. Staehelin's rich *Die Verkündigung des Reiches Gottes in der Kirche Jesu Christi,* of which the first three volumes deal with the period up to A.D. 1500; and A. Hübscher's rare work, *Die Grosse Weissagung,* which deals with prophecy from the biblical era to the present.

4. The most important and complete collection remains R. H. Charles et al., *The Apocrypha and Pseudepigrapha of the Old Testament in English.*

Introduction

1. Ernst Käsemann, "The Beginnings of Christian Theology," p. 40. The essay was originally published in German in 1960.

2. H. Schwartz in a recent review of studies on millenarianism has discerned a tendency among the "second generation" scholars to stress the theme of continuity. "The End of the Beginning: Millenarian Studies, 1969–75."

3. E.g., Gershom Scholem, *The Messianic Idea in Judaism,* and more recently his *Sabbatai Sevi: The Mystical Messiah.*

4. Such comparative studies would fulfill most of the general criteria (*mutatis mutandis*) suggested by M. Bloch in "A Contribution toward a Comparative History of European Societies," especially pp. 47–48.

5. These three differences are a refined version of criteria originally advanced in my article "St. Bernard and Eschatology," *Bernard of Clairvaux: Studies Presented to Dom Jean Leclercq,* p. 164. At that time I used them to support a distinction between general and special eschatology; I now find the distinction between eschatology and apocalyptic more satisfactory.

6. See G. Ahlström, "Prophecy," for the categories used here.

7. Gerhard von Rad, *Theologie des alten Testament*, p. 330.

8. Walter Schmithals, *The Apocalyptic Movement*, pp. 188–89.

9. For what follows I would like to express my thanks to John Collins for allowing me to use his paper, "The Jewish Apocalypses," SBL Seminar on Apocalypticism, forthcoming.

10. D. S. Russell, *The Method and Message of Jewish Apocalyptic*, p. 106. For another list of formal characteristics see K. Koch, *The Rediscovery of Apocalyptic*, pp. 24–28.

11. Collins thus distinguishes two main types in his "The Jewish Apocalypses."

12. Russell, p. 119.

13. A. Fletcher, *Allegory: The Theory of a Symbolic Mode*, especially the Introduction.

14. See N. Perrin, "Wisdom and Apocalyptic in the Message of Jesus"; in dependence on the categories of P. Wheelwright, *Metaphor and Reality*, pp. 93–94.

15. E.g., J. Collins, "The Symbolism of Transcendence in Jewish Apocalyptic," in direct response to Perrin.

16. E.g., various studies of A. N. Wilder, "The Rhetoric of Ancient and Modern Apocalyptic"; and the commentary on Revelation of A. Farrer, *A Rebirth of Images*.

17. J. Collins, "Pseudonymity, Historical Reviews and the Genre of the Revelation of John," pp. 330–33.

18. For a survey of interpretations, see Russell, *Method and Message of Jewish Apocalyptic*, pp. 127–39.

19. H. H. Rowley, *The Relevance of Apocalyptic*, pp. 40–42.

20. There is little of a general nature on the *vaticinium ex eventu*, but see E. Osswald, "Zum Problem der *vaticinia ex eventu*."

21. Russell, *Method and Message of Jewish Apocalyptic*, p. 380.

22. I cite from the English translation of the third edition, Gerhard von Rad, *Old Testament Theology*, 2:301–2.

23. *Ibid.*

24. Schmithals, *Apocalyptic Movement*, disagrees with von Rad's thesis on the origin of apocalyptic (pp. 128–35), but does not differ greatly in his list of essential characteristics.

25. See especially pp. 31–49, where he says: "This combination of unconditionally negative and absolutely positive aspects is made possible by the dualistic doctrine of the two ages." See also pp. 81–85 on the demonization of history, and pp. 94–110 for an interesting comparison of apocalypticism with Gnosticism.

26. The motifs Klaus Koch identifies are: 1) "an *urgent expectation* of the impending overthrow of all earthly conditions *in the immediate future*"; 2) "the end appears as a vast *cosmic catastrophe*"; 3)"the end-time is closely connected with the previous history of mankind and the cosmos," which leads to the division of ages and the appearance of determinism; 4) "in order to explain the course of historical events and the happening of the end-time, an army of *angels and demons* is mustered"; 5) "beyond the catastrophe a *new salvation* arises, paradisal in character," and also universalistically considered; 6) the transition to salvation is conceived of as an act issuing from the throne of God and making the Kingdom of God visible on earth (for Koch this is at the root of the more superficial "two aeons" doctrine); 7) "a *mediator with equal functions* is connected with this ascension of the throne"; and 8) the final state of affairs is seen as a total transformation of the world into a state of glory (*Rediscovery of Apocalyptic*, pp. 28–33).

27. Paul Hanson, *The Dawn of Apocalyptic*, pp. 11—12; see also his article "Jewish Apocalyptic against Its Near Eastern Environment," p. 35.

28. For an earlier statement of this position, see F. M. Cross, "New Directions in the Study of Apocalyptic." See Hanson's summary, pp. 402–13.

29. John Collins, "Apocalyptic Eschatology as the Transcendence of Death." Collins dis-

cusses three unsatisfactory formulations of the essence of apocalypticism: a) the idea of a definitive end (Wellhausen, Mowinckel, and van der Ploeg); b) the distinction of the two periods or aeons (Lindblom and von Radr; and c) apocalyptic as mythology (Cross, Hanson and, in an earlier period, the Gunkel and Bousset School). See also the same author's "The Symbolism of Transcendence in Jewish Apocalyptic."

30. Collins, "The Jewish Apocalypses," forthcoming.

31. O. Plöger, *Theocracy and Eschatology*. Translated from the German original of 1959.

32. Schmithals, *The Apocalyptic Movement*, pp. 135–50, especially p. 148: "But this also means that the apocalyptic understanding of existence is proposed as a basic experience of existence for every possible derivation from the existing situation. It is always more than a reaction to causal structures in existing reality."

33. D. Freedman, "The Flowering of Apocalyptic."

34. E.g., H.-D. Betz, "On the Problem of the Religio-Historical Understanding ot Apocalypticism"; and J. Z. Smith, "Wisdom and Apocalyptic"; and "A Pearl of Great Price and a Cargo of Yams." See also J. Collins, "Jewish Apocalyptic against Its Hellenistic Near Eastern Environment."

35. I do this in full consciousness that some Jewish formal apocalypses, especially of the "mystical journey" variety, and most early Christian apocalypses show little interest in the structure of history, though they do witness to my second and third characteristics.

36. Second Thessalonians, whose ascription to Paul is disputed by some, contains one of the earliest detailed accounts of the final apocalyptic enemy called Antichrist in the later Johannine texts. The best English introduction to the history of this most extraordinary of apocalyptic figures remains the work of W. Bousset, *The Antichrist Legend*. The fullest compilation of traditional material concerning the Antichrist is to be found in T. Malvenda, *De Antichristo Libri Undecim*.

37. Norman Perrin, *New Testament Introduction*, pp. 144–45, 162–65.

38. L. Hartman, *Prophecy Interpreted*, p. 172.

39. *Ibid.*, pp. 235–36 for summary.

40. *Ibid.*, p. 216.

41. *Ibid.*, pp. 247–48.

42. Käsemann states that: "while Jesus did take his start from the apocalyptically determined message of the Baptist, yet his own preaching was not constitutively stamped by apocalyptic but proclaimed the immediate nearness of God." "The Beginnings of Christian Theology," pp. 39–40. This approach has been seconded in recent American scholarship, especially in the works of N. Perrin. For a brief survey, see R. W. Funk, "Apocalyptic as an Historical and Theological Problem in Current New Testament Scholarship."

43. There are two classic modern commentaries on Revelation, penned by two of the premier students of apocalyptic literature of the past century: W. Bousset, *Die Offenbarung Johannis;* and R. H. Charles, *A Critical and Exegetical Commentary on the Revelation of St. John.*

44. A. Farrer, *The Revelation of St. John*, p. 52.

45. P. Vielhauer, "Apocalypses and Related Subjects. Introduction," pp. 606–7. See also N. Perrin, *New Testament Introduction*, pp. 46–47, 81–82.

46. A. Wikenhauser, *New Testament Introduction*, pp. 559–62.

47. As represented by A. Farrer, *A Rebirth of Images*; A. N. Wilder, "The Rhetoric of Ancient and Modern Apocalyptic."

48. The later Christian apocalypses are notoriously difficult to date and offer a host of problems regarding provenance, original language, and transmission. Perhaps for this reason little work of general character has been done on them. A useful article is H. Weinel, "Die

spätere christliche Apokalyptik.'' I have been much helped by the paper of A. Y. Collins, ''The Early Christian Apocalypses,'' prepared for the SBL Working Seminar on Apocalypticism, forthcoming.

49. A. Y. Collins.

50. For an introduction to the Latin texts, see C. Fritzsche, ''Die lateinischen Visionen des Mittelalters bis zur Mitte des 12. Jahrhunderts.'' For the vernacular literature, H. R. Patch, *The Other World,* has some value.

51. Martin Werner, *The Formation of Christian Dogma,* p. 22. Published in German in 1941.

52. Jaroslav Pelikan, *The Emergence of the Catholic Tradition (100–600),* p. 126. Pelikan's section on ''The Apocalyptic Vision and its Transformations'' (pp. 123–32) is a balanced account of the development.

53. For a discussion see Bousset, *The Antichrist Legend,* pp. 184–88.

54. The latest New Testament canonical text, 2 Peter (A.D. c.140) hints of this concern in 3:8.

55. Daniélou, *The Theology of Jewish Christianity,* pp. 377–404; and A. Luneau, *L'Histoire du salut chez les Pères de l'eglise. La doctrine des âges du monde.* Two articles of use are R. Schmidt, ''*Aetates mundi:* Die Weltalter als Gliederungsprinzip der Geschichte''; and H. Bietenhard, ''The Millennial Hope in the Early Church.''

56. Most authors use the terms *millenarianism* and *chiliasm* interchangeably. Among modern historians, anthropologists, and sociologists, *millenarianism* frequently assumes the wider sense of any hope for a coming more perfect age. I have preferred to retain *chiliasm* as a description of the specific Christian hope for the thousand-year reign of Christ on earth.

57. Daniélou, *Theology of Jewish Christianity,* p. 378.

58. *Ibid.,* p. 403.

59. *Ibid.*

60. On the connection with Genesis, see Daniélou, *Theology of Jewish Christianity,* p. 403, note 48. Speculation on the cosmic week was not a traditional Jewish feature, but must have come into Hellenistic Jewish circles of the Diaspora. Daniélou (pp. 397, 400) and Luneau, *L'Histoire* (pp. 41–45), suggest an Irano-Babylonian origin from a circle of Hellenized Magi.

61. An opposition that continues into the present, as the 1944 decree of the Holy Office of the Vatican condemning ''mitigated Millenarianism'' indicates.

62. Chs. 25–29 are concerned with the Antichrist; ch. 30 is a bridge section, and chs. 31–35 treat of the chiliastic kingdom.

63. Daniélou, *Theology of Jewish Christianity,* p. 386.

64. *Ibid.,* pp. 399, 403; and Luneau, *L'Histoire,* p. 103.

65. M. O'Rourke Boyle, ''Irenaeus' Millennial Hope: A Polemical Weapon.''

66. The most complete account of the Sibylline movement is A. Rzach, ''Sibyllen.'' A brief account in English is that of H. C. Lanchester, ''Sibylline Oracles.''

67. Fragment 92 in Plutarch, *The Pythian Oracle,* 396a.

68. Dionysius Halicarnassus, *Roman Antiquities,* 4:62.

69. On their function in Roman religion, see G. Dumézil, *Archaic Roman Religion,* 2: 604–5.

70. Dionysius Halicarnassus, *Roman Antiquities.*

71. Dio Cassius, *Histories,* 54:17; Tacitus, *Annals,* 6:12; and Suetonius, *Augustus,* 31.

72. Tacitus, *Annals,* 15:44.

73. Reported by Rutilius Namatianus, *On His Return* 2:51–52. Cf. E. Demougeot, ''Saint Jerome, les oracles sibyllins et Stilicon,'' pp. 91–92.

74. E.g., in *On Wonders* of Phlegon of Tralles (A.D. 2d cent.). See H. Diels, *Sibyllinische Blätter*, pp. 111–26.

75. Books I to VIII, edited in final form in the 6th cent., were completed by the discovery of Books XI to XIV in the nineteenth century. Book VIII is frequently counted as three books, hence the total number of fourteen.

76. Vielhauer in Hennecke and Schneemelcher, *New Testament Apocrypha*, p. 600. The relations between the literary genera of apocalypse and Sibylline oracle have been summarized by their most recent investigator as follows: "Despite the many resemblances between the sibyllina (in particular, Sib. v) and Jewish apocalyptic, neither Sib. III nor Sib. v ever become fully apocalyptic, because they never propose either a resurrection or a new creation." John J. Collins, *The Sibylline Oracles of Egyptian Judaism*, p. 118.

77. See C. C. McCown, "Hebrew and Egyptian Apocalyptic Literature"; and L. Koenen, "The Prophecies of a Potter."

78. B. Thompson, "Patristic Use of the Sibylline Oracles," p. 125.

79. Hennecke and Schneemelcher, *New Testament Apocrypha*, p. 581.

80. For an introduction, see A. Kurfess, "Christian Sibyllines"; and A. Collins, "Early Christian Apocalypses."

81. J. Geffcken, *Die Komposition und Entstehungszeit der Oracula Sibyllina*, pp. 47–53, preferred the third century; Kurfess opts for the second.

82. So Daniélou, *Theology of Jewish Christianity*, pp. 18–19, agreeing with Geffcken and Kurfess against Rzach.

83. Augustine, *City of God*, 18:23. The first letters of each line make up the words "Jesus Christ, Son of God, Savior, Cross" (Augustine's version lacks the "Cross" strophe). The text is also cited by Eusebius, *Oration of Constantine*, ch. 18.

84. See Thompson, "Patristic Use of the Sibylline Oracles," for a survey. For more complete treatment, K. Prümm, "Der Prophetenamt der Sibyllen in Kirchlichen Literatur."

85. As reported by Origen, *Against Celsus*, 5:61; 7:53,56.

86. Tertullian, *To the Nations*, 2:12; and *On the Cloak*, 2.

87. Besides the knowledge gained through the Fathers, there were also a number of partial Latin translations known in the Middle Ages. See B. Bischoff, "Die lateinischen Übersetzungen und Bearbeitungen aus den 'Oracula Sibyllina.' "

88. For an introduction to this complex movement, see R. M. Grant, *Augustus to Constantine*, pp. 131–44. On the dating of its outbreak, T. D. Barnes, "The Chronology of Montanism."

89. So W. Schneemelcher in Hennecke and Schneemelcher, *New Testament Apocrypha*, p. 688.

90. R. M. Grant, *From Augustus to Constantine*, pp. 138–40.

91. *Commentary*, 4:18–19, discusses two such manifestations. See the edition of G. Bardy, *Hippolyte: Commentaire sur Daniel*, pp. 11–18, for details.

92. In *Commentary*, 4:23–24, where we also find a detailed treatment of the ages of the world. Hippolytus shares this concern for chronological disproof of the imminence of the End with other late second- and early third-century authors, such as Theophilus of Antioch, Clement of Alexandria, and Julius Africanus.

93. Daniélou, *Theology of Jewish Christianity*, pp. 401–2.

94. For discussions of this work, cf. E. Fascher, "Testamentum Domini nostri Jesu Christi," p. 1019; H. Achelis in *Realencyclopädie für protestantische Theologie und Kirche*, 19: 557–59, and 24:560; and E. Amann in the *Dictionnaire de théologie catholique*, 15:194–200.

95. Testament 1:11, as translated by J. Cooper and A. J. MacLean from the Syriac version in *The Testament of the Lord*, pp. 57–58. There is a similar description in the Latin fragment edited by M. R. James in *Apocrypha Anecdota*, pp. 151–54; and in ch. 7 of the Apocalypse of St. John the Theologian, of uncertain date but most likely fifth century. Two pupils in one eye are a sign of evil in Pliny, *Natural History* 7:18.

96. J. Martin, *Commodiani Carmina*, pp. x–xii; and "Commodianus," p. 71.

97. Commodian, Song of the Two Peoples, lines 933, 935.

98. Eusebius, *Church History*, 7:25. Dionysius made his remarks to combat the chiliasm of Bishop Nepos of Arsinoe described in 7:24.

99. Eusebius, 3:24–25, and 28.

100. Eusebius, 7:25.

101. Daniélou, *Theology of Jewish Christianity*, p. 400.

102. There were subsequent additions to the Jerome revision, however, which were quite open to apocalyptic expectations, e.g., the comment on Rev. 13:18 which identified the Vandal leader Gaiseric with the number of the beast.

103. First noted by J. Bidez and F. Cumont in *Les Mages Hellénisés*, the text has recently been subjected to a thorough new investigation in J. R. Hinnells, "The Zoroastrian Doctrine of Salvation in the Roman World."

104. See the edition of A. D. Nock and A. J. Festugière, in *Corpus Hermeticum II*, pp. 326–31. On the Gnostic use, J. Doresse, *The Secret Books of the Egyptian Gnostics*, pp. 245–48.

105. See L. Koenen, "The Prophecies of a Potter."

106. Lactantius, *Epitome of the Divine Institutes*, 73.

107. Origen had condemned chiliasm in *On First Principles* 2:11, 2–4.

108. Luneau, *L'Histoire*, p. 128, with reference to Eusebius, *Church History*, 10:9.

109. A survey of Jerome's views may be found in J. P. O'Connell, *The Eschatology of St. Jerome*, especially ch. 4, "Millenarianism." Jerome's pedantry is partially explained by the fact that his commentary was designed to answer the perspicacious (but highly pedantic) attack on the traditional dating of Daniel by the pagan polemicist, Porphyry.

110. R. Lerner, "Refreshment of the Saints," pp. 101–3.

111. See R. A. Markus, *Saeculum*, pp. 41–44, 53–56.

112. *Sermon* 259:2. See the article of G. Folliet, "La typologie du sabbat chez saint Augustine."

113. Markus, *Saeculum*, ch. 3; and T. E. Mommsen, "St. Augustine and the Christian Idea of Progress."

114. Markus, *Saeculum*, pp. 133–35.

115. *Ibid.*, pp. 153–54.

116. Luneau, *L'Histoire*, pp. 12–14.

117. For a sketch of its influence, see W. Kamlah, *Apokalypse und Geschichtstheologie*. The classic work on Tyconius is T. Hahn, *Tyconius-Studien*. Of recent importance is H. D. Rauh, *Das Bild des Antichrist im Mittelalter*, pp. 102–21.

118. Especially from the Commentaries of Primasius (c. 540), Apringius (c. 550). Bede (d. 735), Beatus of Liébana (776), Ambrosius Autpertus (d. 784), Alcuin (d. 804), Pseudo-Haymo (9th cent.), Berengaudus (9th cent.), and Bruno of Segni (d. 1123). Important fragments have been recently edited by F. LoBue and G. G. Willis, *The Turin Fragments of Tyconius' Commentary on Revelation*.

119. Norman Cohn's *The Pursuit of the Millennium* was first published in 1957 with the subtitle "Revolutionary Messianism in Medieval and Reformation Europe and Its Bearing on

Modern Totalitarian Movements''; the revised and expanded edition of 1970 is subtitled "Revolutionary Millenarians and Mystical Anarchists of the Middle Ages."

120. The recent definition of R. Z. Werblowsky is a good example of the broad or "soft" variety: "Messianism . . . is used in a broad and at times very loose sense to refer to beliefs or theories regarding an eschatological . . . improvement of the state of man or the world, and a final consummation of history." *Encyclopaedia Britannica: Macropaedia*, vol. 11, p. 1017.

121. The most lucid analysis of the sociological understanding of millenarianism is to be found in Y. Talmon, "Pursuit of the Millennium: The Relation between Religious and Social Change." See also the papers in *Millennial Dreams in Action: Studies in Revolutionary Religious Movements*.

122. Cohn, *The Pursuit of the Millennium*, p. 15.

123. *Ibid.*, p. 16.

124. P. Worsley, *The Trumpet Shall Sound;* and K. Burridge, *New Heaven, New Earth.*

125. For Hobsbawm, the three main characteristics of the traditional European millenarian movement are: "First, a profound and total rejection of the present, evil world, and a passionate longing for another and better one; in a word, revolutionism. Second, a fairly standardized 'ideology' of the chiliastic type analyzed and described by Professor Cohn. . . . Third, millenarian movements share a fundamental vagueness about the actual way in which the new society will be brought about." E. Hobsbawm, *Primitive Rebels*, pp. 57–58.

126. Y. Talmon, "Pursuit of the Millennium," p. 127. On pp. 130–36, she summarizes the characteristics of millenarianism as "a forward-looking, future-oriented religious ideology," which nonetheless frequently establishes a connection between the meta-historical past and the meta-historical future and thus could incorporate traditional elements into its view of the future. Other characteristics include: 1) salvation viewed as a merger of the spiritual and terrestrial, 2) a collective orientation with a wide passivity-activity continuum, 3) a generally messianic orientation, and 4) a tone that is usually of high emotion. Talmon's analysis of characteristics is more valuable than her discussion of the conditions that give rise to the movements and her remarks concerning the social groups involved (pp. 136–40).

127. Frank Kermode, *The Sense of an Ending*, p. 4. The first essay in this volume, despite some historical errors, is among the most useful meditations on the significance of apocalypticism.

128. A. N. Wilder, "The Rhetoric of Ancient and Modern Apocalyptic," pp. 447–48. Wilder's positive evaluation of the function of the apocalyptic vision of history is well taken (pp. 442–44).

129. E.g., M. Barkun, *Disaster and the Millennium*, p. 1: "Men cleave to hopes of imminent worldly salvation *only* when the hammerblows of disaster destroy the world they have known and render them susceptible to ideas which they would earlier have cast aside."

130. Talmon recognizes this: "While bridging the gap between future and past, millenarianism also connects religion and politics." "Pursuit of the Millennium," p. 142; see also pp. 147–48.

131. E.g., J. G. A. Pocock: "The historian's first problem, then, is to identify the 'language' or 'vocabulary' with which and within which the author operated, and to show how it functioned paradigmatically to prescribe what he might say and how he might say it." *Politics, Language, and Time*, p. 25.

132. "Apocalypticism is Wisdom lacking a royal court and patron and therefore it surfaces during the period of Late Antiquity not as a response to religious persecution but as an expression of the trauma of the cessation of native kingship. Apocalypticism is a learned rather than a popular religious phenomenon." J. Z. Smith, "Wisdom and Apocalyptic," pp. 154–55.

133. A fact noted by Hobsbawm, *Primitive Rebels,* pp. 58–59.

134. For interpretations of the "Restraining Force," see Vielhauer in Hennecke and Schneemelcher, 2:614–15.

135. The point has been almost completely overlooked by the "millenarians," such as Cohn; but has been grasped by the political philosopher Pocock, who, in his investigations of early modern paradigms of political language discovered that "the apocalyptic mode was as often employed by ruling structures as by rebellions," *Politics, Language, and Time,* p. 25.

136. See B. McGinn, "Angel Pope and Papal Antichrist."

Part One: A.D. 400–1200

Introduction

1. For medieval commentaries on Revelation the central works are W. Bousset, *Die Offenbarung Johannis,* pp. 49–83; and W. Kamlah, *Apokalypse und Geschichtstheologie.*

2. Apocalyptic material may be found in some doctrinal summaries by Eastern writers, notably Theodoret of Cyrus (d. c. 466) and John of Damascus (d. c. 750).

3. Commodian was not widely known in the period and the metrical homilies of the Pseudo-Ephraem lost their form in translation.

4. As P. J. Alexander has put it: "One may, then, summarize the apocalyptic enterprise as follows: continually to reduce the scope of genuine eschatological prophecies by interpreting such prophecies as fulfilled by historical events as they happen, and continually to rewrite references to historical events in the language of eschatological prophecy and thereby to show that later historical events are in fact fulfillments of earlier prophecy. To put it differently, the apocalypticist is ever engaged in striking a new balance between fulfilled and unfulfilled prophecy, in paring down the scope of the latter in favor of the former in order to show that the interval between the present and the Second Coming is narrowing." See *The Oracle of Baalbek,* p. 127.

1. The Tiburtine Sibyl

1. E. Sackur, *Sibyllinische Texte und Forschungen;* S. Mercati, "E stato trovato il testo greco della Sibilla Tiburtina."

2. P. J. Alexander, *The Oracle of Baalbek.*

3. Edited by G. Steindorff, *Die Apokalypse des Elias.* There is an English translation by H. P. Houghton, "The Coptic Apocalypse." For studies, see Weinel, "Die spätere christliche Apokalyptik," pp. 162–67. and A.-M. Denis, *Introduction aux pseudépigraphes grecs d'ancien testament,* pp. 166–68.

4. Alexander, *Oracle of Baalbek,* p. 56, claims that the greater attention to the imperial role is a characteristic of the additions of the sixth century.

5. See on p. 295; reproduced from *Oracle of Baalbek,* p. 66.

6. Sackur, *Sibyllinische Texte,* p. 167 sqq.

7. P. J. Alexander, "Byzantium and the Migration of Literary Works and Motifs," pp. 52–60, especially note 35. It is evident that the version of the Tiburtine Sibyl edited by Sackur (W[1]) has been subject to the influence of the Pseudo-Methodius. The particular use of Psalm 67:32 and the presence of elements of the *Alexander Romance* are proof enough. This does not,

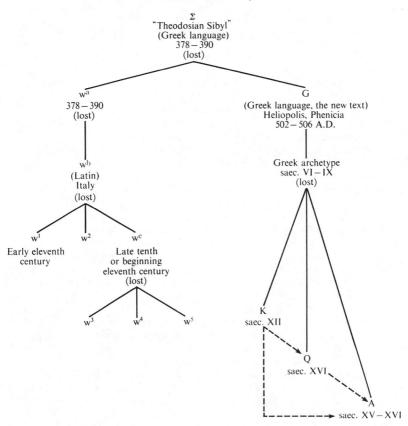

however, prove in conclusive fashion that the *entire* account of the Last Emperor is drawn from Methodius.

8. M. Rangheri, "La 'Epistola ad Gerbergam de ortu et tempore Antichristi' di Adsone di Montier-en-Der e le sue fonti," pp. 708–9, note 79; p. 710, note 85.

9. Among these might be mentioned the length of the reign, and the name Constans itself, as well as the description of fourth-century imperial regalia (*diadema*).

10. For comparisons of the versions of the Last World Emperor myth in the Sibyl, the Pseudo-Methodius, and Adso, see R. Konrad, *De Ortu et Tempore Antichristi*, pp. 43–52; Rangheri, "La 'Epistola ad Gerbergam,' " pp. 710–12; and Sackur, *Sibyllinische Texte*, pp. 102–3.

11. For a general introduction to the influence of the Alexander legends in medieval imperial ideology, see F. Kampers, *Alexander der Grosse und die Idee des Weltimperiums in Prophetie und Sage*, especially pp. 136–83.

12. Steindorff, *Die Apokalypse des Elias*, p. 158; and Houghton, "Coptic Apocalypse," pp. 188–90. W. Bousset, "Beiträge zur Geschichte der Eschatologie," pp. 277–78, thought this a reference to Constans I (337–50), the anti-Arian ruler of the West.

13. Translation of Houghton, "Coptic Apocalypse," p. 196.

14. Alexander, *Oracle of Baalbek*, pp. 57, 115, however, considers the King of Heliopolis to be a sixth-century interpolation.

15. G. von Zezschwitz, *Vom römischen Kaisertum deutscher Nation*, p. 58, argued that elements in the myth had to stem from the legends surrounding the visit of the Emperor Heraclius to Jerusalem in 630. Sackur, *Sibyllinische Texte*, pp. 165–68, showed that many of these elements are of earlier occurrence.

16. H.-I. Marrou, "L'Idée de Dieu et divinité du roi," pp. 479–80.

17. There are three Greek mss., and D. Verhelst has counted some 130 Latin mss., thirty before the thirteenth century. Translations into Arabic and Ethiopic are known.

18. According to Alexander, *Oracle of Baalbek* (p. 64), the sections given here (translating lines 1–103 and 173–227 of the Greek text) "provide a fairly accurate picture" of the original Theodosian Sibyl. Lines 104–72 are sixth-century additions.

19. The pagan Sibyllines were kept on the Capitol until 83 B.C. The mention of the nonexistent olive trees seems to be an attempt to bring the Sibyl's discourse into relation with the Synoptic Apocalypse delivered on the Mount of Olives (Alexander, pp. 68–69).

20. Sackur, *Sibyllinische Texte*, pp. 137–49, saw in the nine suns the influence of Chaldean astrology and from this postulated a basis in a Syriac text of the third century. No such document survives, though there is a parallel to the nine suns found in a late Armenian version of a Chronicle originally composed in Syriac. See also Alexander, pp. 69, 108–9.

21. An otherwise unknown *agraphon* or uncanonical saying of Jesus. The theme of the peoples of the seventy-two languages has been studied by A. Borst, *Der Turmbau zu Babel*, especially vols. 1 and 2.

22. The introduction of the Hebrew priests leads to an anti-Jewish polemic in which the Sibyl sets forth a Christology somewhat at variance with anti-Arian orthodoxy (Alexander, *Oracle of Baalbek*, pp. 69–74).

23. There is a break in the text at this point.

24. The original oracle most likely predicted a sixty-year duration for Constantinople (i.e., to 384). The tripling of this was the work of the sixth-century editor (Alexander, pp. 53–55).

25. The king who will be burned by fire is the Emperor Valens, who was burned to death by the Goths while fleeing the defeat at Adrianople (Ammianus Marcellinus, *Histories,* 31:13, 11–17). Valens was hostile toward the party of Athanasius and hence is viewed as a persecutor.

26. The beginning of the properly apocalyptic section. Parts are present in Sackur's Latin text, though in different order.

27. Olibos is conjectural. Alexander (pp. 111–12) thinks that this was an Antichrist figure in the Theodosian Sibyl and hence another witness to the popularity of the double Antichrist theme in the fourth century. In the Oracle of Baalbek, Olibos is a good figure.

28. According to Alexander (pp. 57–58, 111–17) the original sequence of apocalyptic rulers was: a) the Tetrarchy of two kings from the East and two from Syria; b) Olibos, the First Antichrist; c) the "King with Changed Shape," the Final Antichrist; and d) the Second Coming of Christ.

29. A poison also described in the Apocalypse of Elijah. Other details here are close to the Seventh Vision of Daniel, a Greek text of the late fifth century now known only through an Armenian translation.

30. The king from Heliopolis kills the king from the East a second time, indicating according to Alexander that we are dealing with a sixth-century interpolation; but, as mentioned above, a final good ruler who brings peace to the land is found in the Apocalypse of Elijah.

31. Constans was not a common name among Western rulers in the early Middle Ages.

32. Some texts give 122 years; 112 and 120 were well-known variants in Roman specula-

tion on the longest possible life span. Cf. Sackur, *Sibyllinische Texte,* pp. 146–49; and Bousset, "Beiträge," p. 279.

33. The extraordinary plenty of the Messianic age is a traditional *topos* in apocalyptic explanation. For a Marxist interpretation, see B. Töpfer, *Das kommende Reich des Friedens,* pp. 16–18.

34. This quotation from Ps. 67:32 (in a non-Vulgate text) is also found in the Pseudo-Methodius (Sackur, *Sibyllinische Texte,* p. 94).

35. Many mss. read 120 years or more. Obviously, the time is meant to be tied to the reign of the Last Emperor, but the traditions have become confused. The text from Isa. 11:10 concerning the Lord's sepulchre was to be given greater stress in the crusading context of Benzo of Alba's version of the Sibyl. See C. Erdmann, "Endkaiserglaube und Kreuzzugsgedanke," pp. 408–14.

36. This reference to the Alexander myth cannot have been found in the fourth-century original.

37. The description of the insignia of office (*diadema capitis, habitus regalis*) conforms to imperial Roman rather than Byzantine or early medieval uses. See Konrad, *De Ortu et Tempore Antichristi,* p. 46.

38. Reminiscent of 1 Cor. 15:24. Konrad, pp. 49–52, uses this text to argue that the picture of the Last Emperor is not solely a product of pagan imperial myths, as Sackur claimed, but is also modeled on Christian belief in Christ the eschatological ruler.

39. The Roman empire is conceived of as the *katechōn* of 2 Thess. 2:6.

40. Except for the slaying of the Antichrist by Michael, the scenario of the career of the final enemy follows a pattern standard since early patristic times.

2. Antichrist in the Fifth Century

1. On the details of the omission, see F. R. Hoare, *The Western Fathers,* p. 66.

2. For further information, see the introduction to the critical edition of R. Braun, *Quodvultdeus: Livre des promesses et des prédictions de Dieu,* pp. 101–2.

3. Based upon the apocalyptic *dimidium temporis* of Dan. 7:25; 12:7; and Rev. 12:14.

4. H. Weinel, "Die spätere christliche Apokalyptik," p. 149.

5. At an early date the *Dialogues* were erroneously split into three books rather than two. In older editions this text appears as 2:14.

6. This summary of the doctrine of the double Antichrist should be compared with the passages from Commodian and Lactantius discussed in the Introduction.

7. Like Lactantius, Martin believed that the Antichrist would be conceived by an evil spirit in blasphemous parallel to the conception of Christ. Jerome and other authors denied this. For discussion of this controversy, see T. Malvenda, *De Antichristo Libri Undecim,* pp. 73–76; and W. Bousset, *The Antichrist Legend,* pp. 138–43.

8. Hippolytus, *Commentarium in Danielem,* 4:23–24, held that Christ was born in the middle of the sixth millennium, hence there would be 470 years from his death until the End of the world.

9. The precise chronological indication enables us to date the work to 397.

10. The familiar identification of the Roman empire with the *katechōn* that will be brought to an end by the ten kings. It is interesting to note that at least one later commentator on Revelation, the ninth-century writer Berengaudus, identified the ten horns or kings of Rev. 17:12 with the barbarians who overran the Western empire in the fourth and fifth centuries (*PL* 17, 914 CD).

11. The text in *PL* 13 has "infidelium," but the sense demands "fidelium."

12. A rather neat way to fit the millennial kingdom into a six-thousand-year scheme of history.

13. Ch. 8 of this Book refers to the identification between Nero and the Antichrist.

14. Deeply imbued with the typological method of exegesis, the author has created a powerful concordance of the events of the Old Testament, those of the time of the primitive Church, and the coming drama of the End of time. This method of exegesis foreshadows that which Joachim of Fiore was to develop to a more systematic level.

15. A common theme in Augustine, e.g., *City of God*, 11:6(25); and 22:33(101).

16. The reference appears to be to the *Commentary* and not to the *Book of Rules*.

17. The identification of heretics as members of the Antichrist is an increasingly important theme from the fourth century on. The thought of Tyconius regarding the *corpus diaboli*, i.e., the historical opposition to the Church as the *corpus Christi*, was an important souce of this speculation. See H. Rauh, *Das Bild des Antichrist im Mittelalter*, pp. 98–121.

18. Augustine criticizes these views in *City of God*, 20:11. They are first witnessed to in Ambrose, *De fide ad Gratianum* 2:16, 138 (*PL* 16, c.611–12).

19. The book is based on that described in Rev. 5:1 sqq.

20. The description of miraculous productivity of the messianic age goes back to the *logion* mentioned by Papias in the second century. It should be noted that in this text the *logion* is not found in connection with a detailed account of a millenarian kingdom.

21. Compare this description of the Antichrist with that contained in the Testament of the Lord and in the fourth-century Apocalypse of Elijah where we read: "He is somewhat . . . young, thin-legged, while on the front of his head is a place (lock) of white hair. . . . His eyebrows reach even to his ears, while leprosy scabs are on his hands" (translation H. P. Houghton, "The Coptic Apocalypse," p. 198). For initial studies of the evolution of portraits of the Antichrist, cf. F. Nau, "Methodius, Clement, Andronicus," pp. 453–62; A.-M. Denis, *Introduction aux pseudépigraphes grecs d'ancien testament*, p. 165.

3. The Legend of Alexander

1. For a general introduction to the importance of these legends, see F. Kampers, *Alexander der Grosse und die Idee des Weltimperiums in Prophetie und Sage*. Also see F. P. Magoun, *The Gests of King Alexander of Macedon*.

2. A fundamental work is that of R. Merkelbach, *Die Quellen des griechischen Alexanderromans*.

3. A list may be found in W. Schmid and O. Stählin, *Geschichte der griechischen Literatur*, pp. 813–16.

4. English translation by A. M. Wolohojian, *The Romance of Alexander the Great by Pseudo-Callisthenes*.

5. G. Cary, *The Medieval Alexander*, p. 11.

6. The most complete study is that of A. Anderson, *Alexander's Gate*. See also Cary, *Medieval Alexander*, pp. 130–34, for a brief survey of Alexander's apocalyptic role.

7. Josephus, *Jewish Wars* 7:7,4; and *Antiquities* 1:6,1.

8. Anderson, *Alexander's Gate*, pp. 16–20.

9. Translated into English by E. A. Wallis Budge, *The History of Alexander the Great*, pp. 144–58. The account may reflect the devastations wrought by the Huns in East and West between 445 and 453.

10. Anderson, *Alexander's Gate*, pp. 26–28, for comments.

11. The building of the gate is described in lines 338–83. In this Christian version Alexander acts under the direct inspiration of God.

12. An extensive description of the depredations wrought by Gog and Magog follows.

13. The pagan king has become a source of revelation equated with key biblical figures.

14. The Antichrist who comes after Gog and Magog receives only a brief notice here. Compare with Western versions such as that of Quintus Julius Hilarianus.

4. Pseudo-Ephraem

1. An introduction can be found in "Ephrem," *Dictionnaire de spiritualité,* 4:788–822.

2. E. Beck, *Des heiligen Ephraem des Syrers: Sermones III,* 139:ix-x.

3. Beck, pp. 84–86.

4. For a discussion of these mss., see D. Verhelst, "La préhistoire des conceptions d'Adson concernant l'Antichrist," pp. 97–98.

5. W. Bousset, *The Antichrist Legend,* pp. 33–41. A. Anderson, *Alexander's Gate,* pp. 16–18, follows him in this.

6. C. Caspari, *Briefe, Abhandlungen und Predigten,* pp. 208–20 for the text, and pp. 429–72 for commentary. See also R. Konrad, *De Ortu et Tempore Antichristi,* p. 51.

7. Ephraem is thought to be under the particular inspiration of the Holy Spirit, perhaps a sign of the pseudonymous character of the work.

8. The strongly moral tone of the Sermon is true both to the spirit of the historical Ephraem and the use of apocalyptic themes in the contemporary writings of Gregory the Great.

9. More likely the campaigns of the late sixth and early seventh centuries than those of the time of Ephraem himself. See Caspari, *Briefe, Abhandlungen, und Predigten,* p. 443.

10. The two brothers have been thought to be Valentinian (364–375) and Valens (364–378), thus indicating a fourth-century base for some elements in the Sermon. See Caspari, pp. 438–440.

11. In the double Antichrist tradition, the final, Jewish, Antichrist defeats the earlier Roman one. Those who think that this text is largely fourth century would emend "Jewish" to "Gothic." However, we know that in the wars between the Persians and the Byzantines under the Emperors Phocas and Heraclius in the early seventh century the Jews rose in revolt against their Byzantine overlords, and this situation may well form the historical context for our work. See M. Avi-Yonah, *The Jews of Palestine,* pp. 257–65. I owe this suggestion to M. Hollerich.

12. The mixture of signs is taken from the Apocalyptic Discourse of the Synoptics and the older Sibyllines.

5. Gregory the Great

1. See the perceptive analysis of his career in E. Caspar, *Geschichte des Papsttums,* 2:306–514.

2. His biographer John the Deacon noted: "Therefore in all his sayings and works Gregory pondered upon the imminent final day of coming retribution, and the more he noted the End of the world to press more closely as its devastations mounted, the more carefully he considered the affairs of all." (*PL* 75, c. 214B).

3. On Gregory's apocalypticism, see R. Manselli, *La "Lectura super Apocalypsim,"* pp. 5–16; and D. Verhelst, "La préhistoire des conceptions d'Adson concernant l'Antichrist," pp. 77–80.

4. Gregory's well-known lament over Rome is a good example of his apocalyptic pessimism. Other passages in this vein are more generalized and sometimes invoke more directly the language of the Synoptic Apocalyptic Discourse, e.g., *Homilia in Evangelia*, I; and *Dialogi*, IV, 38.

5. In 593 Rome had been besieged by the Lombards.

6. Gregory is willing to make use of Old Testament prophecies fulfilled in an earlier time to interpret the events of his own day.

7. These two samples from Gregory's voluminous correspondence indicate the variety of ways in which he used apocalyptic motifs.

8. *Register*, VII, 30. In the early sixth century some bishops of Constantinople had begun to term themselves "ecumenical," or universal, patriarchs—an obvious challenge to the position of Rome as found in the Leonine-Gelasian tradition. Beginning in 595 Gregory reacted strongly against this claim, pitting the ideology implicit in his new title "Servant of the Servants of God" against the Eastern usurpations.

9. *Register*, XI, 37. In 596 Gregory took the unprecedented step of sending missionaries to convert the pagan Germanic tribes of England. Ethelbert of Kent, who had a Christian wife, received Augustine and his mission. The following letter, found in Bede's *History of the English Church and People* 1:32, shows the extent to which Gregory's motivation was influenced by his sense of the coming End.

10. Gregory, at least toward the end of his life, did not apparently think that he would live to see the End himself.

6. Byzantine Apocalyptic

1. Among older contributors to this important field should be mentioned various works of V. Istrin, *Otkrovenie Mefodiia Patarskago;* F. Nau, "Révélations et légendes,"; W. Bousset, *The Antichrist Legend;* A. Vasiliev, "Medieval Ideas of the End of the World"; and C. Diehl, "De quelques croyances byzantines sur la fin de Constantinople."

2. Especially in Alexander's "Medieval Apocalypses as Historical Sources."

3. B. Rubin, *Das Zeitalter Justinians,* 1:204. See especially the long note on pp. 441–54.

4. G. Podskalsky, *Byzantinische Reichseschatologie.*

5. P. Alexander, "Historiens byzantins et croyances eschatologiques"; and "Les débuts des conquetes arabes en Sicile et la tradition apocalyptique Byzantino-Slave." On the Pseudo-Daniel Visions in general, see Weinel, "Die spätere christliche Apokalyptik," pp. 160–61; and A.-M. Denis, *Introduction aux pseudépigraphes grecs d'Ancien Testament,* pp. 309–14.

6. The persecuting emperor Domitian was one of the favorite claimants for the role of Antichrist in the early Church. Rubin, *Das Zeitalter Justinians,* pp. 445, 447, 452, shows how Procopius consciously utilizes the tradition to denigrate Justinian.

7. Justinian and Theodora are described as superhuman spirits bent on the destruction of the human race.

8. As we have seen in the case of Sulpicius Severus, one of the stories about the Antichrist's birth is that he would be conceived by a human mother through the agency of the devil.

9. Pseudo-Daniel Visions are known in Greek, Old Church Slavonic, Armenian, Coptic, Arabic, Persian, Serbian, and Russian. See F. Macler, "Les apocalypses apocryphes de Daniel." Amidst this wealth of material, I have chosen a brief selection from a ninth-century old Slavonic text studied and translated by P. J. Alexander.

10. The Vision is structured around an account of the careers of the Byzantine emperors from 717 to about 829. The final ruler pictured here is Michael II (820–829).

11. Achradine, the land quarter of the city of Syracuse.

12. The text gives valuable and in places unique evidence about the beginnings of the Moslem invasion of Sicily. Briefly, Michael II, faced with rebellion at home, sent envoys to Sicily to demand increased taxes. This led to rebellion and fighting in Syracuse between pro- and anti-imperial forces. Euphemius, a Byzantine admiral (the rebel from the east), overcame the loyalists and proclaimed himself king (c.826), only to be soon defeated by his lieutenant Balata. Euphemius then went to Africa and received help from the Moslems who invaded western Sicily. Euphemius and the Moslems defeated Balata near Segeste, took Marianii, but were checked at Enna on their march to Syracuse. See Alexander, "Medieval Apocalypses as Historical Sources," pp. 1010–17; and "Les débuts . . . ," pp. 31–35.

7. Pseudo-Methodius

1. In a preliminary survey, D. Verhelst, "La préhistoire des conceptions d'Adson," p. 95, has counted 190 mss. of the Latin versions, 21 of these prior to the twelfth century.

2. Three mss. are presently known, one complete of the sixteenth century (Vat. Syr. 58, ff. 118–36), and two partial (Paris, Bibl. nat. ms. syr. 350, ff. 98–105; and Cambridge Univ. ms. add. 2054, ff. 1–2). On the basis of the latter two, F. Nau issued a partial Syriac text in "Révélations et légendes," pp. 425–34.

3. E. Sackur, *Sibyllinische Texte und Forschungen,* pp. 46–47, 56. He has been seconded by a number of scholars in this.

4. M. Kmosko, "Das Rätsel des Pseudomethodius," pp. 282–85.

5. P. J. Alexander, "Byzantium and the Migration of Literary Works and Motifs," pp. 57, 59.

6. Kmosko, "Das Rätsel des Pseudomethodius," pp. 286–91 and 293–95, where the possibility of the author's connection with Mt. Sinai is broached.

7. Alexander, "Byzantium and the Migration of Literary Works and Motifs," pp. 57–58.

8. Alexander, p. 59; cf. Kmosko, pp. 290–91 and 295, where the text is termed "eine politische Broschüre." The doubts expressed by some recent scholars on the overt political nature of the treatise (e.g., H. Rauh, *Das Bild des Antichrist im Mittelalter,* pp. 146, 150, note 23) are not convincing.

9. Alexander, "Byzantium and the Migration of Literary Works and Motifs," p. 56.

10. Explicit reference to the Pauline theme occurs in chapter 10 (Sackur, *Sibyllinische Texte,* pp. 78–80), where, after a quotation from 2 Thess. 2, the author asks: "Who then is in the middle if not the empire of the Romans?" For traditions of another type concerning the destruction of Constantinople before the End of the world, see C. Diehl, "De quelques croyances byzantines sur la fin de Constantinople."

11. Sackur, *Sibyllinische Texte,* pp. 77–78, 94. The presence of the Psalm text in the Syriac original is noted by Alexander, "Byzantium and the Migration of Literary Works and Motifs," p. 58. Kmosko, "Das Rätsel des Pseudomethodius," pp. 287–90, affirms that the emphasis on unbroken dynastic continuity upon which the argument depends is a Persian element not found in Byzantium. I. Shahid has recently suggested that the Pseudo-Methodius is responding to the legendary traditions at the basis of the *Kebra Nagast,* the national epic of Ethiopia which identifies the Ethiopian emperor with the apocalyptic ruler. See "The *Kebra Nagast* in Recent Scholarship," p. 175.

12. The figure of the Last Emperor is found in later Byzantine texts, such as the *Vita Sancti Andreae Sali* (J.-P. Migne, *Patrologia Graeca,* vol. 111, cc. 854–57) which has been seen as reflecting the reign of Basil I (867–886). See J. Wortley, "The Warrior-Emperor of the Andrew Salos Apocalypse."

13. Anderson, *Alexander's Gate*, p. 67.

14. Kmosko, "Das Rätsel des Pseudomethodius," pp. 273–74.

15. The Greek, Old Slavonic, and Russian texts were edited by V. Istrin in *Oktrovenie Mefodiia Patarskago*.

16. On these translations, cf. Sackur, *Sibyllinische Texte*, pp. 6–7; and A. M. Denis, *Introduction aux pseudépigraphes grecs*, p. 310.

17. Sackur's text of one version, edited from four eighth-century mss., appears in *Sibyllinische Texte*, pp. 59–96.

18. D. Verhelst, "La préhistoire des conceptions d'Adson concernant l'Antichrist," pp. 94–97.

19. Found complete in Paris, Bibl. nat. ms. lat. 13348 (8th cent.) and two later mss., as well as partially in one other. In a ninth-cent. ms. from Karlsruhe the preface introduces a different work (Verhelst, pp. 95–96). If Peter's preface can be taken as conveying the reasons for the first Latin translation, they indicate that belief in the fulfillment of the Methodian prophecies was viewed in the light of the Moslem successes in Western Europe: "I have endeavored to translate the doctrine of the blessed Methodius the martyr from Greek into Latin since these sayings are aptly prophesied for our times" (Sackur, p. 59).

20. See C. D'Evelyn, "The Middle English Metrical Version of the *Revelationes* of Methodius."

21. Ten editions between 1470/75 and 1677 are listed in A. J. Petty, *John Trevisa*, pp. liv–lv. The most important of these was the 1498 Basle edition of M. Furter with woodcuts by Sebastian Brant. See also Sackur, *Sibyllinische Texte*, pp. 3–7. It does appear, however, that the Pseudo-Methodius was always far more popular on the other side of the Alps than it was in Italy.

22. On these areas of influence, see Anderson, *Alexander's Gate*, pp. 58–104; and M. B. Ogle, "Petrus Comestor, Methodius, and the Saracens."

23. The reign of Alexander is placed in the fifth millennium of the six-thousand-year schema utilized by the Pseudo-Methodius. For the strongly Syriac character of this sketch of history, especially in the earlier parts, see Kmosko, "Das Rätsel des Pseudomethodius," pp. 277–82.

24. "Regio solis." In many versions of the Alexander Romance the hero travels to the great Ocean that surrounds the world.

25. As in the Syriac Alexander texts, the great king is seen as a worshiper of the true God.

26. The "Breasts of the North" are found in the earliest Christian version of the Alexander Romance, the fifth-century Syriac text. See Anderson, *Alexander's Gate*, pp. 24–25.

27. The Latin text of Sackur uses the word *asincitus*, related to the Greek *asynchytus*, or unmixed. Comparison with related accounts, particularly the mid-eighth century *Cosmography* of the Pseudo-Aethicus, indicate that unmixed bitumen is meant. See Anderson, pp. 25, 36, 40.

28. The *Cynocephali*, men with the heads of dogs, were among the fabulous races popular in late antiquity and in the Middle Ages. See R. Wittkower, "Marvels of the East. A Study in the History of Monsters."

29. On the various lists of the enclosed nations (usually either 22 or 24 in number), see Anderson, pp. 54–56, 70–86. From the twelfth century on the lost ten tribes of Israel were frequently included.

30. The identification of the sons of Ishmael with the Saracens or Agareni goes back to the *Chronicle* of Eusebius. See Ogle, "Petrus Comestor, Methodius, and the Saracens," p. 322.

31. The stress on male homosexuality as an apocalyptic sign results from a Syriac mistranslation of the *apostasia* mentioned in 2 Thess. 2:3. See Kmosko, "Das Rätsel des Pseudomethodius," pp. 281, 285–86.

32. The Saga of the Sleeping Hero is a very ancient one, and sleeping rulers were to play

an important part in later western imperial legends, especially the "Kyffhäuser Legend." See P. Munz, *Frederick Barbarossa,* ch. 1.

33. That is, Palestine, always the land of special apocalyptic activity.

34. The theme of the peace of the millennial kingdom of ancient Jewish and early Christian apocalyptic has now been transferred to the kingdom of the Last Emperor after his triumph over the Saracens.

35. Compare with Hippolytus, *In Danielem,* 4:50.

36. The cuisine of the invading nations was never highly recommended. The *topos* reflects late classical views of the Huns and is very close to the appearance of this theme in the sermon of the Pseudo-Ephraem (C. Caspari, *Briefe, Abhandlungen und Predigten,* p. 213).

37. A brief description of the career of the Antichrist follows.

8. Beatus of Liébana

1. Paulus Alvarus of Cordoba seems an exception. His *Indiculus luminosus* says of Mohammed: "Antichrist shows himself present in him in his entirety" (*PL* 121, c.554A). See P. Alphandéry, "Mahomet-Antichrist dans le moyen âge latin," *Mélanges Hartwig Derenbourg,* pp. 261–62.

2. Bede's most important treatise in this area was his *De ratione temporum.* For a summary of his doctrine, see Manselli, *La "Lectura super Apocalypsim,"* pp. 17–21. An important version of the Tiburtine Sibyl was later ascribed to Bede and is found among his works in *PL* 90, cc.1181–86.

3. The *Commentary* has been unsatisfactorily edited by Henry A. Sanders, *Beati in Apocalipsin Libri Duodecim.*

4. See the lengthy reply in *Heterii et S. Beati ad Elipandum Epistola* II (*PL* 96, cc.977–1050).

5. Among the significant Tyconian themes that are evident two can be mentioned as primary: the corporate moralizing interpretation of apocalyptic symbols and the stress on the intermingling of good and evil in the visible Church. In the latter connection, see the remarks on Rev. 16:19 (Sanders, p. 552). Like Tyconius, Beatus tends to see past, present and future coalescing in the unique moral message of the sacred text. As the Preface puts it: "For he [John] never separates the present time from the last time in which the Antichrist will be revealed, because what will then take place visibly is now invisibly happening in the Church." Sanders, p. 17; cf. also pp. 567, 619.

6. There is an extensive literature. The most complete study is W. Neuss, *Die Apokalypse des hl. Johannes in der Altspanischen und Altchristlichen Bibel-Illustrationen.*

7. This review of the doctrine of the six ages is based upon Isidore of Seville's *Chronicle.*

8. Beatus is making use of the so-called Era of Spain which dates events from the conquest of Spain in 38 B.C.

9. The former chronological precisions are muted by the appeal to those scripture texts traditionally opposed to any fervent apocalypticism.

10. Cerinthus was a Gnostic heretic of c. A.D. 100, later accused of harboring chiliastic ideas.

9. Muspilli

1. For a general introduction, see J. K. Bostock, *A Handbook on Old High German Literature,* pp. 120–34.

2. W. E. Peuckert, "Germanische Eschatologien," has argued for a dependence on Iranian, and specifically Manichaean, themes.

3. A. R. Bell, *"Muspilli:* Apocalypse as Political Threat," especially pp. 94–95.

4. The wise men, or *weroltrehwison,* unknown elsewhere in Old High German, have been variously interpreted, sometimes as learned secular lawyers importing their own conceptions of trial by combat into Christian apocalyptic teachings, or alternatively as proponents of pagan apocalyptic ideas.

5. The struggle of the Antichrist with Elijah has, of course, perfectly legitimate Christian origins, not only in the two witnesses of Rev. 11, but also in the Gospel of Nicodemus, the most popular of all the apocryphal gospels in the Middle Ages. According to chapter 25 of this work (seventh/eighth century in origin): ". . . we [Enoch and Elijah] have not tasted death, but we are received unto the coming of the Antichrist to fight against him with signs and wonders of God." James, *The Apocryphal New Testament,* p. 140.

6. There has been considerable controversy over the meaning of what are apparently two opposed views of the fate of Elijah in the poem, that of the "wise men in the law" who see him as victorious, and that of the "many men of God" *(vilo gotmanno)* who in more orthodox fashion expect him to be killed by the Antichrist. For an introduction to the issues, see Bostock, *Handbook on Old High German Literature,* pp. 128–32.

7. Later Russian and Macedonian texts contain the same motif of Elijah's blood igniting the world. See Peuckert, "Germanische Eschatologien," pp. 17–18.

10. Adso's Letter on the Antichrist

1. As pointed out by H. D. Rauh, *Das Bild des Antichrist,* p. 149.

2. E.g., as in the Fourth Council of Toledo (633), canon 66 *(PL* 84, c. 381D). For a summary of uses of the Antichrist figure during this time see R. Konrad, *De Ortu et Tempore Antichristi,* ch. 3, "Eschatologische Anschauungen und Erwartungen im Frankreich," pp. 54–70.

3. Agobard, *Epistola de iudaicis superstitionibus* 27 *(PL* 104, c. 100).

4. The most complete biographical study is in Konrad, pp. 16–24.

5. D. Verhelst, *Adso Dervensis.*

6. The works of Konrad, Rangheri, Verhelst, and Rauh all contribute to this area of investigation.

7. Adso bequethed his personal library of twenty-three volumes to his monastery.

8. See especially Verhelst, "La préhistoire des conceptions d'Adson concernant l'Antichrist," *passim.*

9. Konrad's outline of sources may be found in *De Ortu et Tempore Antichristi,* pp. 28–53; Rangheri's discussion occupies pp. 713–32, with his critique of Konrad most directly expressed on pp. 701–3 and 716–17.

10. See Konrad, pp. 26, 114–15, 144.

11. Konrad, pp. 42–43; Verhelst, "La préhistoire," p. 100; and Rangheri, p. 712.

12. Verhelst, p. 101; Rangheri, pp. 711–12.

13. Konrad, pp. 33, 37–42, 49, 52; and P. J. Alexander, "Byzantium and the Migration of Literary Works and Motifs," pp. 53, 61.

14. See Konrad, *De Ortu et Tempore Antichristi,* p. 37.

15. Verhelst, "La préhistoire," pp. 100–1 (who cites some implicit appearances); Rangheri, pp. 711–12. Adso himself says that the teaching is not his, but stems from "Doctores nostri."

16. On the importance of these notions in Adso, see Konrad, pp. 90–91.

17. This first option could lead to two possible reactions: a belief that the empire had

collapsed and that the present age was a brief reprieve before the End; or the assertion that now the process was free to begin all over again—a cyclical revision of the Danielic theme. The latter option was put forward by Notker the Stammerer in his *Life of Charlemagne* I:1 (c.885): "He who ordains the fate of kingdoms and the march of centuries, the all-powerful disposer of events, having destroyed one extraordinary image, that of the Romans, which had, it was true, feet of iron, or even feet of clay, then raised up among the Franks the golden head of a second image, equally remarkable, in the person of the illustrious Charlemagne." (Trans. of L. Thorpe in Penguin Classics.)

18. For a brief introduction to the theme of *translatio imperii,* see Konrad, *De Ortu et Tempore Antichristi* pp. 97–103. A basic work on the subject is W. Goez, *Translatio imperii.*

19. Konrad, pp. 89–113.

20. See *ibid.,* pp. 104–13, 134, 144–45.

21. These are: 1) *Descriptio cuiusdam sapientis de Antichristo* from the beginning of the eleventh century; 2) Albuinus, *De Antichristo quomodo nasci debeat,* also early eleventh century; 3) Pseudo-Augustine, *Sermo de Antichristo,* later attributed to Rabanus Maurus (based on Alboin and also eleventh century); 4) Pseudo-Alcuin, *Vita Antichristi ad Carolum Magnum edita,* based on (1) and done at the end of the eleventh century; 5) *De Tempore Antichristi,* perhaps of the twelfth century; 6) *Epistola Methodii de Antichristo,* early twelfth century in Flanders; and 7) Pseudo-Anselm of Canterbury, *Liber de Antichristo,* twelfth century.

22. This piece of etymological lore was a commonplace found in Isidore of Seville, *Etymologiae* 8:9 (*PL* 82, c. 316B), and in Haymo's *Expositio in Epistolam II ad Thessalonicenses* (*PL* 117, c. 779D).

23. The three are mentioned in Jerome's *Commentarium in Dan.* (*CSEL* 75A, p. 920) and in Paulus Alvarus, *Indiculus luminosus* (*PL* 121, c. 535B).

24. This collective element in Adso's picture of the Antichrist shows the influence of the Tyconian tradition. See Konrad, *De Ortu et Tempore Antichristi,* pp. 74–76; and Rauh, *Das Bild des Antichrist im Mittelalter,* p. 161.

25. Gen. 49:17. The association of the tribe of Dan with the Antichrist is a very ancient theme. It appears to have its origin in Judaism, since in the Testaments of the Twelve Patriarchs (Tes. Dan, 5–6) Dan is already becoming associated with Beliar. Irenaeus, writing about A.D. 190, says that Antichrist will come from Dan (*Adversus Haereses* V, 30, 2), and the *topos* is repeated by many of the Fathers. Frequent scripture texts used were Gen. 49:17, Deut. 33:22, and Jer. 8:16. For a brief discussion, see Bousset, *The Antichrist Legend,* pp. 170–74, and the literature cited there. Among Adso's more immediate sources were probably Gregory the Great, *Moralia in Job 31:24* (*PL* 76, c. 596CD), and Alcuin, *Interrogationes et responsiones in Genesim* (*PL* 100, c. 564D).

26. The tradition that the Antichrist would be born from a virgin was at least as old as the time of Sulpicius Severus. Adso's position, which allows for a human father, still stresses diabolical activity to a strong degree. The final sentence here is taken from Haymo's *Expositio* (*PL* 117, c. 779D).

27. Alcuin, *De fide Trinitatis* 3:19 (*PL* 101, c. 51C), and Haymo, *Expositio in Apocalypsim* (*PL* 117, c. 1073AB) have similar threefold divisions.

28. Adso's immediate source here is Haymo, *Expositio in II Thessalonicenses* (c. 779D).

29. There has been a good deal of controversy over whether the *reges Francorum* were meant to include only West Frankish kings or any Frankish king of East or West. Nineteenth-century authors generally held the former view; beginning with G. Zeller in 1934 many recent students have opted for the latter. Konrad, *De Ortu et Tempore Antichristi,* pp. 104–8, agrees that the exclusivistic, "French," sense is the correct one. His views have been criticized by H. Grundmann in a review published in the *Deutsches Archiv* (1965), 21:636–37.

30. Who are the *doctores nostri* to whom Adso refers? Konrad, pp. 36–38, asserts that the phrase must refer to patristic sources, especially the Pseudo-Methodius. Others (Rangheri, 711–12; Rauh, 159; Verhelst, "La préhistoire des cenceptions d'Adson," p. 101; and Grundmann, Review of Konrad, pp. 636–37) more correctly hold that it probably refers to Adso's Carolingian predecessors.

31. Konrad notes, pp. 92–94, that in Adso's work Rome plays no part; everything is centered on Jerusalem.

32. A reminiscence of Col. 2:3, a verse applied in a positive sense to Christ.

33. The second half of the paragraph is from Haymo, *Expositio in II Thessalonicenses* (c. 781BC).

34. This important *topos* has been exhaustively surveyed by R. Lerner, "Refreshment of the Saints." Adso's immediate source is Haymo's *Expositio in II Thessalonicenses* (c. 781D) which allows for a forty-five day period. For a discussion of the texts, see Lerner, pp. 106–8, and Rauh, p. 162.

35. The uncertainty of the final coming is not to be gainsaid by the chronological discussions already given. Adso stresses this theme more than many of his sources.

11. Apocalyptic and Non-Apocalyptic Themes of the Eleventh Century

1. The sixteenth-century Church historian Cardinal Baronius appears to have been the originator of the myth which Jules Michelet did much to spread, see E. Gebhardt, "L'état d'âme d'un moine de l'an mil." The legend has been revived, if in more nuanced fashion, by H. Focillon in *The Year 1000*. For a detailed attack, see J. Roy, *L'an mil*.

2. See also N. Cohn, *The Pursuit of the Millennium*, pp. 61–70, who follows Alphandéry.

3. C. Erdmann, "Endkaiserglaube und Kreuzzugsgedanke im 11. Jahrhundert."

4. For an introduction to the various images of Jerusalem in medieval thought, see A. Bredero, "Jerusalem dans l'Occident médiévale."

5. For accounts of the speech, D. C. Munro, "The Speech of Pope Urban II at Clermont, 1095," pp. 231–42. Other contemporary witnesses, e.g., the *Sibylla Cumana* (c. 1090), rejected the identification of Henry IV with the Last Emperor (Erdmann, "Endkaiserglaube und Kreuzzugsgedanke," pp. 395–402).

6. L. Sumberg, "The Tafurs and the First Crusade," is far too sanguine in his claims for the veracity of the picture of the Tafurs presented in the *Chanson d'Antioche*.

7. For an expansion on these points, see my paper *"Iter sancti Sepulchri:* The Piety of the First Crusaders." See also G. Miccoli, "Dal Pellegrinaggio alla Conquista," and P. Classen, "Eschatologische Ideen und Armutsbewegungen im 11. und 12. Jahrhundert."

8. For this explanation of the genesis of the crusading movement, see B. McGinn, *The Crusades*.

9. Abbo (c.945–1004) was a monastic reformer and abbot of Fleury. His *Apologeticus* dates from about 995 and is a defense of monastic rights.

10. Abbo was an adherent of the Tyconian–Augustinian tradition of opposition to the literal interpretation of scriptural apocalyptic texts.

11. This was a long-lived expectation. The twelfth-century *Vita Altmanni* (*MGH. SS.* XII, 230), recounting the events of the great German pilgrimage to Jerusalem in 1065, says that many believed the End of the world would come on an Easter Sunday following a Good Friday that fell on the Feast of the Annunciation (March 25).

12. Ralph, a monk of Cluny, died about 1050. His *Historiae,* while quite credulous, is an important source for the period 900–1050.

13. A reference to a major French pilgrimage of 1033. See E. Pognan, *L'an mil,* p. 123. For other comments of Ralph on the evil times c.1000, cf. II, 6 and 12 of his *Historiae.*

14. Benzo (died c. 1090) was a northern Italian adherent to the imperial side in the investiture controversy. The *Panegyrikus* was written in 1086.

15. The author was doubtless familiar with the later editons of the Tiburtine Sibyl.

16. Bizas is the legendary founder of Byzantium. Benzo is predicting that when Henry has subdued the Normans in southern Italy, he will receive the imperial crown at Constantinople.

17. Following Erdmann in rendering *Calliopea* as "song" rather than as a personal name.

18. 2 Sam. 20:18, where Abel is one of the repositories of Israelite tradition in the time of the Judges. Benzo seems to be suggesting that the Sibylline texts play a similar role in the Christian religion.

19. For more on Benzo's apocalyptic views, see *Panegyrikus* 1:17 and 19, and 3:2 (*MGH.* SS. XI, 606–7, 623).

20. Guibert (c.1064–c.1125) was a northern French abbot and prolific writer, perhaps best known for his autobiographical *Memoirs.* His account of Urban's speech of November 27, 1095, comes from a work written about 1110.

21. On the etymology, see note 22, Selection 10.

22. Jerome, *Commentarium in Danielem* (*CSEL* 75A, pp. 933–35).

23. The identification of the three kings the Antichrist will defeat at the outset of his career with rulers of Egypt, Africa, and Ethiopia results from a collation of Dan. 11:43 and 7:8. It is found as early as Irenaeus, *Adversus Haereses,* V, 26, 1, and Hippolytus, *De Antichristo,* 51. Guibert shows himself well informed about the main lines of the Antichrist legend.

24. .Ekkehard (d. 1125) wrote his account of the crusade about 1115.

25. Sigebert of Gembloux mentions the comet under the year 1097 and the star under 1098.

26. The heavenly Jerusalem appearing in the air as a portent is found in a number of ancient authors, among them Tertullian, *Adversus Marcionem,* 3:24.

27. Another ancient apocalyptic portent found in a number of texts, e.g., Testament of the Lord, 1:7.

12. Apocalypticism and the Great Reform

1. N. F. Cantor, *Church, State, and Lay Investiture in England,* pp. 6–9. Cantor sees the Great Reform as a "world revolution" in the sense that what began from complaints about particular evils in society broadened out to embrace a program for a new ideal order, called forth intense opposition from the representatives of the old order, and after much conflict resulted in a compromise in which neither side triumphed.

2. *Gregorii VII Registrum* (*MGH.* Epist. Sel. II), Book 8:5.

3. E.g., *Registrum,* 1:11,13; 4:1,2,24; and *Epistolae collectae,* 42.

4. Other Gregorians explicitly denied it. Thus in 1106 Pope Paschal II (1099–1118) condemned the teaching of Bishop Rainer of Florence that the Antichrist was already born (see Erdmann, "Endkaiserglaube und Kreuzzugsgedanke," pp. 386–94).

5. *Epistolae collectae,* 46.

6. E. Kantorowicz, *Selected Studies,* p. 78.

7. Besides the work of N. F. Cantor, see the classic study of G. Tellenbach, *Church, State, and Christian Society at the Time of the Investiture Contest.*

8. There is a tradition in twentieth-century German scholarship, represented by A. Dempf, J. Spörl, and most recently by H. Rauh (*Das Bild des Antichrist*, pp. 165–78), which would restrict such interest to German writers. As M. D. Chenu has pointed out in *Nature, Man, and Society in the Twelfth Century*, p. 192, such a limitation is unwarranted.

9. J. Leclercq, *The Love of Learning and the Desire for God*, p. 219, says of him: "He is the source par excellence for traditional monastic theology."

10. The basic books on Rupert include W. Kahles, *Geschichte als Liturgie;* M. Magrassi, *Teologia e Storia nel Pensiero di Ruperto di Deutz;* Rauh, pp. 178–235. For the *Commentary*, see Kamlah, *Apokalypse und Geschichtstheologie*, pp. 75–104.

11. Opinions are still divided regarding the authenticity of the work, but the weight of authority supports its ascription to Rupert. See Magrassi, pp. 30–31.

12. The most detailed study may be found in Rauh, pp. 179–96.

13. "Rupert ist kein Chiliast," Rauh, p. 193.

14. Otto's great work has produced a substantial modern literature. Among the most significant works are: J. Schmidlin, "Die Eschatologie Ottos von Freising," pp. 445–81; and *Die geschichtsphilosophische und kirchenpolitische Weltanschauung Ottos von Freising;* P. Brezzi, "Ottone di Frisinga"; J. Koch, "Die Grundlagen der Geschichtsphilosophie Ottos von Freising"; and Rauh, *Das Bild des Antichrist*, pp. 302–65.

15. Originally, the *translatio* theme was worked out to explain the gradual passage of the authority of imperial rule from East to West, see W. Goez, *Translatio imperii*. Otto also makes use of a *translatio studii* (book 5 Prologue) and a *translatio religionis*, (book 7, p. 39). See also Chenu, *Nature, Man, and Society*, pp. 185–90.

16. For Gerhoh's life and works, see P. Classen, *Gerhoch von Reichersberg;* D. van den Eynde, *L'oeuvre littéraire de Gerhoch de Reichersberg*. Fundamental treatments of his views on history are, E. Meuthen, *Kirche und Heilsgeschichte bei Gerhoh von Reichersberg;* and Rauh, pp. 416–74.

17. van den Eynde, pp. 121–24, 131–39, for the two redactions.

18. R. Manselli, *La "Lectura super Apocalypsim,"* pp. 63–64.

19. Of the extensive literature on Hildegard the following should be mentioned: H. Liebeschütz, *Das allegorische Weltbild der heiligen Hildegard von Bingen;* and B. Widmer, *Heilsordnung und Zeitgeschehen in der Mystik Hildegards von Bingen*. For her apocalyptic views, see B. Töpfer, *Das kommende Reich des Friedens*, pp. 33–44; and Rauh, *Das Bild des Antichrist*, pp. 474–527.

20. E.g., Epist. 48 (*PL* 197, cc.248D–49C); and the *Liber divinorum operum* 3:10 (*PL* 197, c.1005C) for Henry as the precursor of the Antichrist. On the *tempus muliebre*, see Rauh, pp. 489–93.

21. As in the other verse translations, no attempt is made to preserve the meter.

22. Rev. 12:3. The tail of the dragon (Satan) is Henry IV, the Antichrist, whom many prelates (stars) have followed.

23. A reference to the first beast of Rev. 13:1 and following, here identified with Henry.

24. Henry and his Antipope Clement III were in control of Rome.

25. The Antipope is identified with the second beast of Rev. 13:11, and with Simon Magus.

26. A reference to the death of Gregory VII at Salerno in 1085.

27. The noted Hermann (bishop of Metz, 1073–90), a strong Gregorian to whom Gregory directed two of the most noted defenses of his position (Reg. 4:2; 8:21).

28. In 1078 Henry (Attila) led an expedition against Metz and some other French cities. See Sigebert of Gembloux, *Chronicon* (*MGH*. SS. VI, 364–66) for these events.

29. A reference to Halley's comet.

30. That is, Henry IV (1056–1106).

31. The incidents referred to are Gregory VII's attack on Philip I of France in 1074 (Reg. 2:5) and the well-known denial of the sacrament to Theodosius by Ambrose in 390.

32. The central role of the Church as the stone that smote the last of the empires suggests the imminence of the End.

33. That is, from the creation of Guibert of Ravenna as Antipope Clement III in 1080.

34. The traditional source of evil in Scripture, e.g., Isa. 14:13.

35. Hildegard goes on to exegete her vision in cc.710C–724D. The five beasts are evil kingdoms of the last days. The prophetess does not become more explicit.

36. The mountain with the five peaks signified the cumulative power of evil connected with the five kingdoms.

37. The youth is the Son of Man, seen in earlier visions, whom Eph. 2:11–22 describes as the cornerstone uniting Jew and Gentile.

38. The gleaming from the navel to the groin represents the good works performed by the elect until the time of the appearance of the Antichrist; the lyre is the joyful song of those who will suffer persecution at the time of the Enemy. The shadiness down to the two-finger measure from the heel (two fingers for the two witnesses, Enoch and Elijah) is the shaking of the faith of the Church at that time. The feet brighter than milk signify the triumph of faith when the Antichrist is overcome.

39. The woman is the Church, the scaly spots the evils the Church will suffer in the time immediately preceding the Antichrist, especially the attacks from those who ought to love her. The monstrous head, of course, is the Antichrist. For a summary of Hildegard on the Final Enemy, see Rauh, *Das Bild des Antichrist*, pp. 513–25.

40. White because the Antichrist will first act mildly, red because he later persecutes, causing the bloody appearance of the lower legs down to two tranverse zones indicating the two witnesses.

41. The Antichrist separates himself from the Church, gathers the congregation of the evil to himself, and attempts to scale heaven to show that he is God (cc. 721B–22A).

42. God then strikes down the Antichrist. The fetid cloud left behind by the Antichrist convinces those who had been led astray that they should do penance and return to God.

43. Hildegard's vision ends on an optimistic note, the white feet of the triumphant Church.

13. Gerhoh of Reichersberg

1. On the various schemes of history in Gerhoh, see E. Meuthen, "Der Geschichtssymbolismus Gerhohs von Reichersberg."

2. Meuthen, *Kirche und Heilsgeschichte*, pp. 134–35; Rauh, *Das Bild des Antichrist*, pp. 428–32, 448–51, who says: "Gerhoch interessiert sich weniger für den Endfeind als für sein Corpus . . ." (p. 429).

3. Rauh, pp. 446, 463, 471–72, emphasizes the new note of imminence present in *De investigatione Antichristi* 1:66–67, and in *De quarta vigilia noctis*.

4. For Augustine's attack on such notions, see my Introduction, pp. 26–27. The significance of Gerhoh's concordances has been noted by many investigators, e.g., Meuthen, "Der Geschichtssymbolismus," pp. 240–44; Rauh, p. 470; and Manselli, *La "Lectura super Apocalypsim,"* p. 67.

5. B. Töpfer, *Das kommende Reich des Friedens*, pp. 30–31.

6. In the first watch of the Church the martyrs triumph over persecution, in the second the

holy confessors over the heretics. The third watch is characterized by the struggle of the holy preachers of morality, especially Gregory the Great, against moral evils.

7. Gerhoh is referring to the excommunications which Gregory VII issued against Henry IV in 1076 and 1080. Guibert is the antipope Clement III (1080–1100) put up by Henry.

8. For Gerhoh, as for many of his contemporaries, avarice was the special sign of the last dark age of the Church, cf. *De investigatione Antichristi*, 1:19, 49.

9. The author of these lines has not been identified.

10. The Jezites (Jesaaritae or Isaaritae) of Num. 3:27 and 1 Chron. 26:23–29 were a Levitical family in charge of the Temple treasures, here used as a type of clerical involvement in financial transactions.

11. *De Consideratione*, 3:4.

12. On Antiochus as an Old Testament concordance for the Antichrist, see especially *De investigatione Antichristi*, 1:15–16 (*Libelli de lite*, 3:321–23).

13. For another passage in which Gerhoh speaks of the imminence of the End, see *De investigatione Antichristi* 1:67 (*Libelli de lite*, 3:383).

14. The events described took place in the summer of 1167 when malaria killed many of Frederick Barbarossa's army and compelled a retreat from Rome.

15. Octavian was Barbarossa's first Antipope, taking the name Victor IV (1159—1164). He was succeeded by Guido, who called himself Paschal III (1164–1168).

16. Beatrice, the wife of Frederick.

14. The Ages of the Church

1. For a brief introduction, see the literature cited in the Introduction, note 55.

2. For Rupert's theology of history see the works listed in Section 12, note 10.

3. The *translatio* theme is found in Otto, *De duabus civitatibus,* prologus, and 4:5, as well as 5, prologus and ch. 31. For Hugh's theology of history, see W. A. Schneider, *Geschichte und Geschichtstheologie bei Hugo von St. Viktor*; and R. A. Southern, "Aspects of the European Tradition of Historical Writing: 2. Hugh of St. Victor."

4. See Bernard of Clairvaux, *Epistolae*. Nos. 124–27.

5. *Ibid.*, Epist. 336, 338. On these texts and Bernard's views in general, see my article "St. Bernard and Eschatology."

6. Bernard, Epist. 56 (dated either 1124 or 1128). "When I asked him [Norbert] what he thought about the Antichrist, he declared himself quite certain that it would be during this present generation that he would be revealed. But upon my asking, when he wished to explain to me the source of this same certainty, I did not think, hearing his response, that I ought to take it for certain." (J. Leclercq, *S. Bernardi Opera*, 7:148).

7. *Super Cantica* 33:7 (written about 1138; *Opera,* 1:243–45); and *Sermones super "Qui habitat"* 6 (written in 1139; *Opera,* 4:404–9).

8. "Sententia Quatuor sunt Tentationes," edited by J. Leclercq in *Études sur Saint Bernard et le texte de ses écrits* in *Analecta Sacri Ordinis Cisterciensis* (1953), 9:134.

9. See especially *Vita S. Malachiae* (*Opera,* 3:307), and the discussion in McGinn, "St. Bernard and Eschatology," pp. 170–71, 182–84.

10. There have been a number of studies devoted to Anselm. The two most recent introductions may be found in Rauh, *Das Bild des Antichrist,* pp. 268–302; and W. Edyvean, *Anselm of Havelberg and the Theology of History.*

11. It was found in the commentaries of Primasius, Bede, and Haymo, and summarized in the *Glossa ordinaria.* For the use of this schema in Anselm, cf. Rauh, pp. 276–82; Edyvean, pp. 20–34; and W. Kamlah, *Apokalypse und Geschichtstheologie,* pp. 64–70.

12. Joachim of Fiore will also have a notion of works and states (*status*) of history proper to each Person.

13. That is, it concerns the *Hexaemeron* itself down to the Fall of man.

14. The thirty books of the second part deal with the work of the Son in sacred history, especially during the Old Testament.

15. The nine books of the third part, more a summary of doctrine than a survey of historical themes, concern the work of the Holy Spirit in the life of the Church.

16. The division of the works of creation from the works of restoration forms the basis for Hugh's major doctrinal synthesis, the *De sacramentis* (c.1135).

17. The Atlantic seaboard is meant.

18. The parable of the laborers in the vineyard was used in connection with a five-age theory of history as early as Origen's *Commentary on Matthew*. See Schmidt, "*Aetates mundi,*" pp. 301–4.

19. The last temptation, that of the Antichrist, symbolized by the attack of the "noonday devil" of Ps. 90:6 is not treated in this text, but is described in a related sermon, *In "Psalmum Qui Inhabitat,"* 6:7 (*Opera*, 4:410–11).

20. Gerard of Poehlde writes to Evermord, the prior of the important Norbertine house of Our Blessed Lady at Magdeburg on the German frontier, in 1147 at the time of the beginning of the Crusade against the Wends. His opposition to the crusade is based upon an apocalyptic reading of the recent troubled state of the Church. In the letter he asks Evermord to persuade the Margrave Albert the Bear, the ruler of Brandenburg, to preserve the peace.

21. The letter continues to expand on the divisive tendencies present in Christian society.

22. A list of recent opponents and defenders of ecclesiastical interests follows. Gerard's suggestions here smack of the continuing presence of some Tyconian themes.

23. Augustine was the first to state that the Chuch began with Abel, though the formula used by Anselm here comes from Gregory the Great. See Y. Congar, "Ecclesia ab Abel."

24. There follows a review of the progress of the religious life in the fourth state, beginning with Augustine and stressing the careers of Norbert, the founder of the Premonstratensians, Bernard, and other monastic reformers.

25. Anselm makes no explicit predictions about the states still to come, but keeps close to the text of Revelation.

15. Imperial Apocalyptic

1. A shorter version is found in the *Annales Corbienses* (*MGH*. SS. XVI, 14), and there is a notice in the *Annales S.Jacobi Leodienses* (*MGH*. SS. XVI, 641).

2. The most complete survey of these dramas is in K. Aichele, *Das Antichristdramas des Mittelalters der Reformation und Gegenreformation*.

3. Rauh, *Das Bild des Antichrist*, p. 374, speaks of it as "klassische Theologie des Imperiums," and emphasizes the antireform stance.

4. Rauh notes that "The handing over of the empire is the pivot of the whole drama; the play enters the properly eschatological sphere from the political one" (p. 387).

5. Rauh, pp. 393–94.

6. Otto is referring to the time of the preaching of the Second Crusade (1146–47), the pilgrimage (*peregrinatio*) *par excellence*.

7. These obscure remarks may refer to the city of Jerusalem described in Rev. 21:9–27 as a perfect square with twelve gates.

8. The *Annales Corbeienses* text has the "son of your mother" here, but the phrase is obscure in all versions.

9. This completely obscure sentence is missing in the *Annales Corbienses* version.

10. The bridegroom (Christ) whose bark (the Church) bears a sail symbolizing the Trinity has set up the Last Emperor as a mainsail.

11. The C refers to Cyrus, who according to Herodotus (*Histories* 1:191) diverted the waters of the Euphrates to conquer Babylon. Victory over the king of Babylon (i.e., the Moslem enemy) by a king whose name begins with C may well recall the Constans of the Tiburtine Sibyl.

12. The appearance of the angel indicates that the emperor is God's elect.

13. According to a suggestion of K. Young, *The Drama of the Medieval Church*, 2:376, a fuller Responsory was sung at this point.

14. The surrender of the *regalia* before the altar in the Temple is a peculiar feature of the play. The Tiburtine Sibyl does not specify a location for this act; the Pseudo-Methodius places it on Golgotha after the advent of the Antichrist. Adso has it take place on the Mount of Olives.

15. Another novelty. No earlier accounts speak of the survival of the Last Emperor, and the Pseudo-Methodius specifically mentions his death.

16. In the transition to the second part of the drama, *Ecclesia, Gentilitas,* and *Synagoga* repeat the identifying themes sung at the outset of part one.

17. The appearance of the Antichrist is emphasized by a change in the meter.

18. The Hypocrites attack worldly priests (*saeculares prelati*), just as did the Gregorian reformers—an indication of the author's sympathies. The present Church, filled with hypocrisy, is the ally of the Antichrist.

19. A blasphemous parody of the reaction of Mary to the Annunciation; see Luke 1:34.

20. Antichrist born within the Church is a Tyconian theme.

21. This remark reflects the author's opposition to the abdication of the German Emperor, as Rauh notes, *Das Bild des Antichrist,* pp. 388–90.

16. The Erythraean Sibyl

1. O. Holder-Egger edited two verions of the text from seven mss. in his "Italienische Prophetieen des 13. Jahrhunderts" (1890), 15:155–73; and (1905), 30:323–35. Other mss. are described by E. Jamison in *The Admiral Eugenius of Sicily,* p. 21, note 3.

2. Jamison, *Admiral Eugenius,* pp. 21–32, 303–04.

3. C. H. Haskins, *Studies in the History of Mediaeval Science,* p. 174.

4. Jamison (p. xx) suggests that it might have been brought by the translator and diplomat Henricus Aristippus upon his return from Constantinople in 1158.

5. A ms. gloss identifies the lion with Charlemagne, but this is certainly mistaken, as noted by F. Kampers, *Kaiserprophetieen und Kaisersagen im Mittelalter,* p. 254.

6. In its present form it obviously includes several interpolations, see Jamison, pp. 29–30.

7. There are many variants on the name in the ms. tradition. Holder-Egger's text reads *Vedoxa.*

8. With Jamison (*Admiral Eugenius,* p. 22) I read *regis Sicilie* rather than the *regni Sicilie* of Holder-Egger.

9. Highly poetic language is used throughout, e.g., Danaans for Greeks, Teucrians for Trojans, etc.

10. Helen.

11. The Greeks.

12. According to legend, Achilles (the son of Peleus, hence the "Pellidean") and Calchas, the son of Nestor, were sent to consult the shrine of Apollo at Delphi before the Greeks set sail.

13. The preceding lines enshrine a number of Sibylline themes, particularly the condemnation of polytheism, and the ecstatic character of Sibylline prophecy (see, e.g., Aen. 6:41–53, 77–80). There follows an account of Greek and Roman history stressing the succession of mighty rulers. Animal symbolism is strong throughout.

14. After an account of the spread of Christianity, the text turns to the rise of Mohammed.

15. Like the beast in Rev. 13:1, though he differs in other particulars.

16. The number of feet of symbolic animals generally indicates the length of a reign. Holder-Egger suggests that the compiler erroneously thought that Mohammed had died in 663. Could the number be an attempt to date the duration of Mohammed's religion before the appearance of the Last Emperor?

17. A gloss suggests that these are the two orders of *viri spirituales* of the Joachite tradition. If such be the case, we are dealing with an interpolation.

18. As Kampers and Jamison have suggested, this is an account of the Last Emperor. It is important to note that it differs from the tradition in a number of particulars, notably in the lack of any abdication in Jerusalem and in the failure to inflict complete defeat on the enemies of Christianity.

19. A succession of material and moral woes follows in true Sibylline fashion.

20. *Subsideo apellineo* in the text. The term *apella,* originally meaning a Jew, could be used to indicate anyone without faith. *Apellineus,* used several times in this text, is unknown to medieval lexicons.

21. Holder-Egger thought that these signs referred to a famous landslide in the area of Chambéry in 1248. Jamison, *Admiral Eugenius,* pp. 31–32, more plausibly connects them with the earthquake, eruption of Mt. Etna, and tidal wave in the Straits of Messina that took place on Feb. 4, 1169.

22. Later glosses identify the Spouse as the Roman Church and the cock as the pope, but such a strong papal apocalyptic, if intended, would make this a thirteenth-century addition.

23. The Antichrist is a false Messiah who will renew the Old Testament and deny the New. A fairly conventional picture of the three-and-a-half year reign of the Antichrist follows.

24. The final section of part 3 marks a return to apocalyptic signs, an obvious repetition that indicates varying editorial strata in the text. Jamison, p. 32, note 1, sees this as part of the original Sibyl.

25. Jamison prefers the reading "idols of Egypt."

26. A return to the events of 1169.

27. Originally an island near Alexandria, where the famous lighthouse was built. Here the term is used for the Straits of Messina which witnessed the severe tidal wave of 1169.

28. Further lists of Sibylline woes follow.

17. Joachim of Fiore

1. A fact recognized by Johann von Herder in the eighteenth century and reaffirmed more recently by such diverse scholars as K. Löwith (*Meaning in History*), F. Manuel (*Shapes of Philosophical History*), E. Bloch (*Man On His Own*), and E. Voegelin (*The New Science of Politics*).

2. Joachim's three major works were printed in the early sixteenth century in Venice: the *Concordia novi ac veteris Testamenti* (also called *Liber Concordiae*) in 1519, and the *Expositio in Apocalypsim* and the *Psalterium decem chordarum* in 1527. They are available in photographic reprint (Frankfort: Minerva G.M.B.H., 1964).

3. F. Russo complied an extensive but uncritical *Bibliografia Gioachimita.* The review of literature and issues by M. Bloomfield, "Joachim of Flora," *Traditio,* remains a valuable in-

troduction. A reprinting of classic essays on Joachim and his influence together with a bibliography of recent items can be found in D. C. West, *Joachim of Fiore in Christian Thought*. For a brief popular introduction to Joachim and his influence, see M. Reeves, *Joachim of Fiore and the Prophetic Future*.

4. I have argued more fully for the positions taken here in three articles: "The Abbot and the Doctors: Scholastic Reactions to the Radical Eschatology of Joachim of Fiore"; "Joachim and the Sibyl"; and "Symbolism in the Thought of Joachim of Fiore," to be published in a festschrift for Marjorie Reeves.

5. The most important study of Joachim's life also contains an edition of the early lives: H. Grundmann, "Zur Biographie Joachims von Fiore und Rainers von Ponza."

6. Both Joachim himself and his early biographers witness to this, see McGinn, "Joachim and the Sibyl," pp. 104–6. The most complete account of the visions is in M. Reeves, *Influence of Prophecy*, pp. 21–25.

7. Luke of Cosenza, *Vita* (Grundmann, ed., "Zur Biographie Joachim," p. 540). Joachim continued to revise the three works throughout his lifetime.

8. As first suggested by H. Grundmann, "Kirchenfreiheit und Kaisermacht um 1190 in der Sicht Joachims von Fiore"; and developed in McGinn, "Joachim and the Sibyl," especially pp. 108–16, 124–25.

9. After a brief period of expansion, the order fell rapidly into decay. The best account is in F. Russo, *Gioacchino da Fiore e le Fondazioni Florensi in Calabria*.

10. For a survey of these encounters, see Reeves, *Influence of Prophecy*, pp. 3–15.

11. The best account of Joachim's exegesis is now H. Mottu, *La manifestation de l'Esprit selon Joachim de Fiore*. See also H. Grundmann, *Studien über Joachim von Fiore*, pp. 18–55; H. de Lubac, *Exégèse médiévale*, 1:437–558; and M. Reeves, "History and Prophecy in Medieval Thought," pp. 55–60.

12. Joachim's treatise attacking Peter Lombard has not survived, but see A. Maier, "Zu einigen Handschriften der Biblioteca Alessandrina," p. 6. For a list of Joachim's attacks on Scholasticism, see McGinn, "The Abbot and the Doctors," pp. 32–33.

13. Key passages which outline the seven *species* of the "typical" sense are found in *Concordia*, f. 61r–v; and *Psalterium*, ff. 265r–266r.

14. McGinn, "The Abbot and the Doctors," *ibid*.

15. M. Reeves and B. Hirsch-Reich, *The Figurae of Joachim of Fiore*, p. x. Discovered in 1937 by L. Tondelli, the definitive edition of the text appeared at Turin in 1953.

16. The most important disagreement concerns the relation of the two-age theory of history (indicating little break with traditional themes) to the three-*status* pattern from which flows the radical features of the Joachite tradition. Reeves has shown the continuity of both patterns in the Abbot's thought, but her own solution stressing the "historical" character of the first pattern and the "mystical" character of the second is not convincing. More recent work of Reeves ("History and Prophecy," pp. 59–60, 67) shows a new appreciation of the radical aspects of Joachim's influence.

17. On trees in Joachim, see Reeves and Hirsch-Reich, *The Figurae*, especially pp. 24–38.

18. The earliest stage of Joachim's fame after his death saw him primarily as a prophet of the imminence of the Antichrist. While Joachim never affixed a precise date to the appearance of the Last Enemy, there seems to be no reason to doubt the accounts which report that in 1191 he told Richard the Lionhearted that the Antichrist had already been born in Rome. On the authenticity of this report, see Reeves, *Influence of Prophecy*, pp. 6–10.

19. Mentioned as early as the *De prophetia ignota* of 1184, the figure is also present in later works, especially in the *Concordia*. For further discussions, see McGinn, "Angel Pope

and Papal Antichrist,'' pp. 158–59; Reeves, *Influence of Prophecy,* pp. 395–400. Also consult F. Baethgen, *Der Engelpapst.* A text in the *Expositio* (f. 168ra) suggests that Joachim feared a coming papal Antichrist too.

20. The most important study on the *viri spirituales* in Joachim and the later tradition is to be found in Reeves, *Influence of Prophecy,* pp. 133–292.

21. Joachim believed that each of the first two *status* flourished for forty-two generations and that his own time in the second *status* marked the end of the fortieth generation. The exact length of the last two generations could not be calculated; they might actually be quite short.

22. Particularly involved were the role of the papacy, the dominance of the clergy, and the necessity of the sacraments.

23. McGinn, ''The Abbot and the Doctors,'' pp. 34–35. On Joachim's radicalism, see H. Mottu, *La manifestation,* pp. 308–28.

24. E. Bloch, *Man on His Own,* p. 137.

25. E. Voegelin, *The New Science of Politics,* p. 184. Like N. Cohn in his *The Pursuit of the Millennium,* Voegelin, p. 113, also ties the Joachite tradition to the millennial aspects of the Nazi movement.

26. Joachim's own account of the vision or revelation he had while at Casamari that opened the meaning of the Book of Revelation to him. The Abbot mentions another vision, this time at Pentecost, revealing the mystery of the Trinity (*Psalterium,* f. 227r–v). Later tradition, though not Joachim himself, spoke of a vision of God the Father on Mt. Tabor, thus giving a Trinitarian structure to the manifestations.

27. Probably a reference to his negotiations to have Corazzo fully incorporated in the Cistercian order.

28. The vision gave Joachim the incentive for his two most extensive works, the *Concordia* and the *Expositio,* just as the Pentecost vision led to the writing of the *Psalterium.*

29. Joachim's earliest surviving work is both a witness to the popularity of new Sibylline productions in the twelfth century and a valuable source for the earliest stages of his prophetic career. The text on which this translation is based is my edition of Padua, Bibl. Antoniana, ms. 322, ff. 149v–151v. Since that edition, several other mss. have come to my attention that have enabled me to improve the text.

30. St. Augustine, whose use of the Sibyl in the *City of God* Joachim cited at the outset of the work.

31. Sometimes called the *Sibilla Samia,* this obscure text was edited by O. Holder-Egger from two of the eight known mss. in *Neues Archiv* (1890), 15:177–78. He assigned it to the thirteenth century, but it seems to be of the twelfth, as I have argued in ''Joachim and the Sibyl,'' pp. 118–22, especially since the first verse can easily be applied to the quarrels between the popes and the Roman commune that marked the latter part of that century.

32. A recently deceased cardinal known as a reformer.

33. The concordance of the seven persecutions of the Jews with seven trials of the Church is a hallmark of Joachim's thought. The list given here is closest to that in the *Liber figurarum,* plates IX and X. The double-seven schema of history is frequently connected with the seven seals of Revelation; see M. Reeves and B. Hirsch-Reich, ''The Seven Seals in the Writings of Joachim of Fiore,'' pp. 216–23. Note the lack of any reference to a third *status* here.

34. Joachim surpasses other twelfth-century authors in the degree to which he historicizes Scripture, i.e., is willing to identify biblical texts with precise historical events in the life of the Church.

35. Alexander III was compelled to flee Rome in July 1179. Lucius III, his successor, who seems to be ''the Roman who was put in place of the Roman,'' also fled the city in 1182 and in alliance with imperial forces put military pressure on the rebellious Roman commune.

36. Later references in the text make it clear that the "king of Babylon" is the emperor who will persecute the Church.

37. On the importance of the theme of *libertas* in Joachim, see Grundmann, *Studien,* pp. 135–42.

38. A reference to the *viri spirituales* and their role in the third *status*.

39. According to Joachim's scheme, the three *status* are organically interconnected. Each of the earlier *status* consists *in toto* of sixty-three generations, but the second *status* has its germination in the figure of King Uzziah in the forty-second generation of the first *status* and reaches its fructification in Christ. The third *status* germinates in the figure of St. Benedict and will fructify at the end of the forty-second generation from Christ.

40. A text based on John 5:17, but revised by Joachim to stress the activity of the Spirit in the third *status*.

41. Joachim sees no conflict among the different ways of dividing the ages of salvation history.

42. The Psalm text reminds Joachim of the forty-two generations during which each of the first two *status* flourishes, this despite the fact that the number mentioned is forty. Six weeks (i.e., ages) of seven days yields the number exactly.

43. The forty-first generation was to begin in 1201 (*Concordia,* f. 55v). Joachim always asserted that the precise time of the last two generations could not be calculated. An earlier text from the *Concordia* makes this clear: "I say openly that the time when these things will happen is near, but God alone knows the day and the hour. Insofar as I can estimate according to the harmony of the concordance, if peace from these evils is granted up to the year 1200, thereafter I will observe the times and the moments in every way so that these things do not happen unexpectedly" (f. 41v).

44. Babylon equals Rome. The *novus dux* appears to be different from the pope of the time of the Antichrist referred to in *Concordia,* v, 92 (f. 121r), and elsewhere, as the orders of the "new people of God" in the time of the Holy Spirit differ from the two orders of the time of crisis.

45. Joachim is the first to identify this figure with a leader of the last days. For the later application of the text to St. Francis, see Part II, Sections 23–24 *passim,* and the literature cited there.

46. By the persecution of the Antichrist.

47. This account from Joachim's last work (left unfinished at his death) is based on the concordance of Solomon's succession to David in the Old Testament, the Presentation of Christ in the Temple in Luke 2:22–38, and the succession of the new order in the third *status*. For a study of this text, see H. Mottu, *La manifestation,* pp. 129–46.

48. Simeon represents the papacy; the Christ child the coming contemplative order.

49. Passages such as this have led many to claim that the Abbot looked forward to the abolition of the papacy in the third *status*. Such is surely not the case, but there are still many ambiguities in Joachim's writings on the future role of the popes. Joachim himself may not have been totally clear on the issue. One thing seems certain—contemplative charisma and not hierarchical authority was to be the controlling force in the coming time.

50. This very possibly enshrines Joachim's reflections upon his own departure from the Cistercians.

51. The most perfect institution in the third *status* will be the *ordo monachorum* and not the papacy as such, but see the selection "The New People of God," and especially note 61.

52. The two orders are definitely seen as future. Joachim did not identify his own order with either to the best of our knowledge, nor did he cast the Cistercians in this role, despite the respect that he kept for them (cf. *Liber figurarum,* plate xxiii). On his views on the history of

monasticism, see especially the early work, *De vita S. Benedicti et de officio divino,* C. Baraut, ed., *Analecta sacra Tarraconensia* (1951), 24:42–118. The two orders of the end of the second *status* prefigure the *ordo monachorum* of the third *status,* but are not to be identified with it.

53. The seven heads of this commentary accompanying the dragon figure are identified with the seven chief persecutors of the seven ages of the Church: Herod, Nero, Constantius, Mohammed, Mesemoth (unidentifiable, but clearly a Mohammedan leader, real or imaginary), and Saladin. The final head is labeled: "This is the seventh king, who is properly called Antichrist, although there is another like him, not less in evil, signified in the tail." The tail itself is marked: "Gog. He is the last Antichrist." The Abbot of Fiore then, like many of the Fathers, held to a double Antichrist tradition, though this seems to come more from the inner necessity of his system than from direct contacts with patristic sources. The passages translated here deal with the sixth and seventh heads.

54. A reference to Rev. 13:3, and the beast arising from the sea. Joachim appears to be conflating the two beasts here, since they will combine their powers.

55. For the role of Islam and of Saladin in particular in the apocalypticism of the Abbot, see E. R. Daniel, "Apocalyptic Conversion," pp. 132–35; and M. Reeves, "History and Prophecy," pp. 60–61.

56. Other texts of the Abbot express a fear about the alliance of Western and Eastern enemies of the Church. Notable is *Expositio,* f. 134r–v where Joachim says that he met a man in Messina in 1195 who told him of a projected alliance between the Moslems and the Patarene heretics.

57. Joachim is probably referring to patristic traditions concerning the space of time between the judgment of the Antichrist and the time of the End. See R. Lerner, "The Refreshment of the Saints," pp. 115–19.

58. The conversion of the Jews played an important role in Joachim's thought from the earliest writings. On this see B. Hirsch-Reich, "Joachim von Fiore und das Judentum."

59. For discussions of this, perhaps the most unusual of the *figurae,* see H. Grundmann, *Neue Forschungen über Joachim von Fiore,* pp. 85–121; and M. Reeves and B. Hirsch-Reich, *The Figurae,* pp. 232–48. The sections excerpted here deal with the various oratories containing the "orders" of the third *status.* The suggestion of translating the general term *novus ordo* as the "New People of God," I take from J. Ratzinger, *The Theology of History in St. Bonaventure,* p. 39.

60. Each of the oratories is distinguished by a patron saint, an identifying animal (the tetramorph in the case of the four circling the central oratory), one of the gifts of the Holy Spirit, and by a part of the body.

61. Is the "Spiritual Father" to be identified with the *novus dux,* or pope of the third *status?* Such a solution would remove much of the ambiguity in Joachim's views of the future of the papacy; and, although to my knowledge he nowhere says this explicitly, it seems very likely. It is important to point out, however, that even if such be the case, the source of the future pope's authority is charismatic and not hierarchical.

62. The precise indications of distance between the oratories, as well as the fairly minute regulations, indicate that Joachim had a real and not a mystical community in mind. Such factors form a strong argument for the historicity of the third *status.*

63. Joachim's utopian vision has clear "communistic" elements.

64. Although doubts have been raised about the authenticity of this letter prefaced to the *Expositio,* most authorities accept it. For a survey of opinions, see Bloomfield, "Joachim of Flora," pp. 253–54. The Latin is obscure in places.

65. Clement III (1187–1191), one of Joachim's supporters.

66. Lucius III (1181–1185) and Urban III (1185–1187). On Joachim's papal supporters, see McGinn, "Joachim and the Sibyl," pp. 108–16.

67. Both these works (the latter also known as the *De articulus fidei*) have been edited in modern times in the *Fonti per la Storia d'Italia.*

Part Two: A.D. 1200–1500

Introduction

1. E.g., as in the Hussite tract known as *The Old Color and the New.* See H. Kaminsky et al., *Master Nicholas of Dresden.*

2. M. Reeves, *Influence of Prophecy,* part 2, provides the fullest evidence for this aspect of the tradition.

3. The most noteworthy exception to the "antichristian" aspect of many late medieval popes in the eyes of the apocalypticists was Celestine V, whose career is described in Section 22.

18. Moslems, Mongols, and the Last Days

1. It was well known to some fourteenth-century authors, though earlier witnesses to the Latin version are lacking. For the text see J. Bignami-Odier and G. Levi della Vida, "Une version latine de l'apocalypse syro-arabe de Serge-Bahira."

2. Three authorities cite it under 1184. See B. McGinn, "Joachim and the Sibyl," pp. 120–21.

3. Caesarius, *Dialogus miraculorum,* dist. 4, cap. xv. Caesarius' source identified the Otto with Otto IV who died in 1212.

4. The discovery of the text is noted under the year 1221 in the *Annales de Dunstaplia* (*RS* 36, 3:62). This text is not to be confused with the more ancient *Liber Clementis* which Jacques de Vitry noted was also present in the crusader camp at this time.

5. Translated from Matthew of Paris, *Chronica major* (*RS* 57, 3:538) with the correction "secundus deus *abiit,*" rather than *adiit.* A more obscure version is found in the *Annales de Dunstaplia* (p. 151), and the text is also present in the thirteenth-century apocalyptic commonplace book, Vat. lat. ms. 3822, f. 6v.

6. See, e.g., *Annal. Ratis.* (*MGH.* SS. xvii, 605). For a preliminary review, see R. Lerner, "Medieval Prophecy and Religious Dissent," pp. 11–15.

7. For the context, see S. Runciman, *A History of the Crusades,* 3:338 sqq.

8. Prester John was a legendary Christian king of Asia (or sometimes Africa) of whom we hear reports from the twelfth century on.

9. D. Bigalli, *I Tartari e l'Apocalisse,* p. 11. Also see G. A. Bezzola, *Die Mongolen in abendländischer Sicht.*

10. The most famous embassy was that of William of Rubruck, a Dominican sent by Louis IX of France, who visited the court of Karakorum in 1254.

11. Composed in 1237, Julian's *Descriptio de bello Mongolorum* is discussed in Bigalli, pp. 13–18.

12. See Bigalli, pp. 31–33, 64–69; and A. Anderson, *Alexander's Gate,* pp. 58–86.

13. Some of these signs did take place, as pointed out in various accounts.

14. Possibly a reference to the Last Emperor.

15. The title as found in the single surviving Latin ms. Some of the Old French versions ascribe the text to Hannan, the son of Isaac, obviously Hunein ben Isaac, the famous doctor and philosopher who died in 873. For my interpretation I am dependent on the notes of J. Röhricht in his edition in *Quinti Belli Sacri Scriptores Minores*.

16. In several of the vernacular versions the comet seems to refer to Charlemagne (Röhricht, p. xli); in the Latin it is more obscure and appears to be considered as only a heavenly sign.

17. There follows a brief account of Islamic history to about 1180.

18. A description of the events of the Third Crusade (1189–1192). The first king is Philip of France, the king who aids him is Richard the Lionhearted, and the king with the golden standard is Saladin.

19. The Fifth Crusade landed in Egypt in May 1218.

20. The glowing description applies to Cardinal Pelagius, the papal legate who arrived in September 1218, and took charge over the protests of John of Brienne, the king of Jerusalem. The cardinal's party obviously had a hand in the production of this text.

21. A series of woes follows, first on Damietta (captured in November 1219), then on Cairo and Egypt in general.

22. According to other accounts, rumors of outside help circulated in the crusading host, many connected with Prester John who was frequently associated with the rising power of the Mongols (Röhricht, p. xliv, note 3). E.g., see the letter of Pope Honorius III in June 1221 (*Registrum Honorii III*, #1478).

23. Pelagius had brought news of the intention of Emperor Frederick II, the ruler of Southern Italy, to take the cross. The text reads "de Alberi"; Röhricht interprets "de Calabria."

24. Röhricht (p. xlv) suggests possible Arabic roots for this mysterious name.

25. William's account of the rise and progress of Islam is more accurate than that of most Westerners. Heraclius (610–641) and the conquest of Palestine by the Arabs were discussed in ch. 10.

26. Hulagu (Hulaon in the text) actually conquered Baghdad in 1258.

27. The *Opus Majus*, written between 1266 and 1267, was Bacon's attempt to compose an encyclopedia of all the sciences in order to convince the new Pope Clement IV of the necessity of revising the educational system. The apocalyptic materials translated here are contained in the long section devoted to mathematics, for Bacon the key to the natural sciences.

28. Albumazar (Abu Mashr) was a noted ninth-century Moslem astrologer; his *Liber conjunctionum* was of great influence on Latin thought in the twelfth and thirteenth centuries.

29. Like William of Tripoli, Roger was greatly impressed with the Mongol conquest of Baghdad. The twelve years that he gives may result from his dating of the destruction from the beginning of Hulagu's campaign.

30. The *Cosmographia* of Aethicus Ister, supposedly a translation by St. Jerome of a fourth-century Greek work, was actually produced in the eighth century in the circle of Virgil, the Irish bishop of Salzburg.

31. From this and other passages it might seem that Bacon identified the Mongols with Gog and Magog, but the identity is never explicitly affirmed. He later notes that other races have migrated from the far reaches of Asia to Palestine, and "Therefore the invasion of the Tartars is not sufficient to fix the time of the coming of the Antichrist, but other facts are required . . ."

32. A reference to the journey of William of Rubruck in 1253–1255. Bacon came to know William after his return.

33. The friar's list of prophetic authorities is a varied one, some of the figures not easily identifiable. Aquila may be the second-century translator of the Hebrew Bible who enjoyed the reputation of a magician. Seston (Sestion in Latin) is more obscure. Could it be *Sextus* Julius Africanus, the third-century author of the earliest Christian world history?

34. This passage is taken almost word-for-word from Friar William's account of his journey, available in English in C. Dawson, *The Mongol Mission*, pp. 213–14. The prophet Akaton is otherwise unknown to me.

35. Bacon's stress on the necessity of a good knowledge of geography for the proper view of the End has been discussed by D. Bigalli, *I Tartari e l'Apocalisse*, pp. 173–76.

36. Orosius' *Seven Books against the Pagans*, 3:18–20, discusses the oriental exploits of Alexander, but without the legendary accounts of the enclosed nations.

19. The Joachite Movement before 1260

1. Some twenty-five works long and short have been falsely ascribed to him. For an introduction to this literature, see Reeves, *Influence of Prophecy*, especially pp. 518–33.

2. Besides Reeves, *Influence of Prophecy*, see also M. Reeves and M. Bloomfield, "The Penetration of Joachism into Northern Europe."

3. Reeves, *Influence of Prophecy*, pp. 39–43; and H. Grundmann, "Dante und Joachim von Fiore."

4. "We therefore condemn and reprove the pamphlet or treatise which the Abbot Joachim put out concerning the unity or essence of the Trinity against Master Peter Lombard, calling him a heretic and insane for what he wrote in his *Sentences*." This decree "Damnamus," which specifically refrained from attacking Joachim's person and also mentions his Testament, is most readily available in H. Denzinger, *Enchiridion Symbolorum*, #431–33.

5. E.g., C. Ottaviano, "Un nuovo documento intorno alla condanna di Gioacchino da Fiore nel 1215."

6. The *Liber contra Lombardum* ascribed to Joachim was probably written in the later 1230s.

7. The Tübingen theologian Karl Friderich's disproof of the authenticity of this and the *Commentary on Isaiah* marked the beginning of modern critical studies of medieval apocalypticism. See McGinn, "Apocalypticism in the Middle Ages," pp. 255–57.

8. M. Reeves, "The Abbot Joachim's Disciples in the Cistercian Order"; and *Influence of Prophecy*, pp. 145–60.

9. See B. Töpfer, *Das kommende Reich des Friedens*, pp. 108–15; and the reply by Reeves in *Influence of Prophecy*, pp. 156–58, note 2. More recently the Franciscan origin has also been defended by F. Simoni, "Il *Super Hieremiam* e il Gioachimismo Francescano."

10. *Interpretatio preclara Abbatis Ioachim in Hieremiam Prophetam*, f. 62r, though Reeves claims that this passage may be an interpolation.

11. E. R. Daniel, "A Re-examination of the Origins of Franciscan Joachitism."

12. For an introduction to this important theme, see S. Bihel, "S. Franciscus fuitne Angelus Sexti Sigilli?"

13. The *Introductorius* seems to have perished, though B. Töpfer claims that portions survive in a Dresden ms., see "Eine Handschrift des *Evangelium aeternum* des Gerardino von Borgo San Donnino." On Gerardo, see also Reeves, *Influence of Prophecy*, pp. 60–62, 187–90.

14. The most remarkable of these was William's own *De periculis novissimi temporis* which uses the misdeeds of the mendicants as a sign of the advent of the Antichrist. Of the

large literature on this dispute, I mention only the classic article of Y. Congar, "Aspects ecclésiologiques de la querelle entre mendiants et séculiers."

15. The outbreak of the Flagellent movement in Italy in 1260 does not appear to have been directly connected with Joachite expectations, contrary to the views of N. Cohn, *The Pursuit of the Millennium,* pp. 128–29. See R. Manselli, "L'Anno 1260 fu Anno Gioachimitico?"

16. The seminal study for recent sociological discussions of the phenomenon of "cognitive dissonance" is L. Festinger, H. Riecken, and S. Schachter, *When Prophecy Fails.*

17. This commentary on a *figura* apparently very similar to that now known as "The Tree of the Two Advents" (*Il Libro delle Figure,* plate 2) appears to come from Joachim's earliest disciples.

18. The famous verses predicting the coming of Antichrist in 1260 were widespread during the early Joachite period. Reeves, *Influence of Prophecy,* p. 49, holds that they originated before 1250, but are a later interpolation in this text. See also O. Holder-Egger, "Italienische Prophetieen," (1890) 15:175.

19. The *Commentary* survives in more than twenty mss. and has been printed three times (Venice, 1516 and 1525; Cologne, 1577).

20. This concordance of scriptural examples of the younger rising up against the older with the conflict between the *viri spirituales* and the established clerical order is typical of the argument of the work.

21. Caleb and Joshua (Num. 14:30,38) alone among the Jews who left Egypt with Moses were found worthy to enter the promised land.

22. A number of other scriptural duos are omitted here.

23. The concordance with the Genesis account of the two birds sent out by Noah is fundamental to the rest of the passage. The crows are clearly the Dominicans.

24. The use of the terms "order of preachers" and "order of minors" for the two groups of spiritual men could not be more explicit. It is so clear that Reeves has suggested that it might be a gloss that has crept into the text.

25. The passage is based on a concordance of three events: 1) the persecution of Jeremiah by King Zedechiah (Jer. 37:1–15), 2) the plot of Caiaphas against Jesus (John 11:49 sqq), and 3) the condemnation of Joachim's views on the Trinity under Innocent III at the Fourth Lateran Council. For further remarks, see Reeves, *Influence of Prophecy,* pp. 34–36, 115–18, 149–50, 397–98.

26. The text in John has *homo* rather than *doctor*.

27. In Jer. 36:23 King Jehoiakim, the father of Zedechiah, cut off parts of the prophet's scroll as they were read and cast them into the fire.

28. The author sees the tribulations of the Church under Frederick II as a punishment for the condemnation of Joachim. Babylon is Rome as the persecuting empire; the "new republic" is Frederick's attempt at imperial revival.

29. An obscure phrase for which I hazard this translation.

30. Celestine III (1191–1198) was one of Joachim's patrons. Herod, of course, is Innocent III (1198–1216).

31. The star signifies Joachim himself.

32. The Fourth Lateran Council of 1215.

33. As Reeves has said, we find in the *Super Hieremiam* "a peculiar attitude towards the Cistercian order which, on the one hand, is denounced for the machinations of its conspiring Pharisees, and, on the other, is viewed as the repository of true spiritual religion." "The Abbot Joachim's Disciples in the Cistercian Order," p. 365.

34. Issued at Milan in the midst of the crisis over the "Eternal Gospel," this letter shows that both the Franciscans and the Dominicans made use of the ideology of the spiritual men.

One of the last acts of the Generalate of John of Parma, the letter was reissued under Bonaventure in 1257.

35. Humbert of Romans was Master of the Dominicans from 1254 to 1263.

36. A reminiscence of Gen. 1:16 begins the list of scriptural images (dependent on Joachite sources such as the Jeremiah *Commentary*) ascribed to the two orders.

37. See the Erythraean Sibyl (Holder-Egger, "Italienische Prophetieen" (1905), 30:162–63). The remainder of the letter is an appeal for mutual cooperation in the spirit of the first fervor of the two orders.

38. The three cardinals were Odo of Châteauroux, Stephen of Vancsa, and the well-known theologian Hugh of St. Cher.

39. Other lists of errors cited by chapters of the *Introductorius* follow.

40. These are the minutes of the second session of the Commission. Master Florence was an inveterate foe of Joachim and his followers. Not satisfied with the verdict of Anagni, when he became Bishop of Arles he presided over a local synod that condemned Joachim's views of history in explicit fashion in 1263. Cf J. D. Mansi, *Sacrorum Conciliorum Nova et Amplissima Collectio,* vol. 23, c.1004.

41. *Liber Concordie* II, Tr. 1, ch. 4. (Venice ed., f. 8r). Quotations from the *Liber* follow, showing the importance that the investigating prelates attached to this aspect of Joachim's thought.

42. There follows a quotation and summary of the passage partially translated on pp. 135–36.

43. Salimbene (1221–1288), a Franciscan since 1238, wrote his *Chronicle* in the last years of his life. It is one of our most important sources for the thirteenth-century Joachite movement. The standard edition is that of O. Holder-Egger in *MGH*. SS. XXXII (Hannover-Berlin, 1905–13). Sections of the *Chronicle* have been translated by G. G. Coulton in *From St. Francis to Dante*.

44. Hyerès on the Mediterranean coast not far from Marseilles. The date of the incidents recounted is 1248.

45. 1243–1247.

46. Salimbene was at Ravenna in 1264.

20. *Frederick II versus the Papacy*

1. For an introduction to the relations of Joachim and the Joachite tradition to Frederick, see H. Grundmann, "Frederico II e Gioacchino da Fiore," pp. 293–99.

2. E. Kantorowicz, *Frederick the Second,* p. 608.

3. The best general study of this literature is that of F. Graefe, *Die Publizistik in der letzten Epoche Kaiser Friedrichs II.* See also H. M. Schaller, "Endzeit-Erwartung und Antichrist-Vorstellungen in der Politik des 13. Jahrhunderts"; and "Das letzte Rundschreiben Gregors IX." See also Töpfer, *Das kommende Reich des Friedens,* pp. 108–41, and 155–82.

4. On this circle, see P. Herde, "Ein Pamphlet der päpstlichen Kurie gegen Kaiser Friedrich II."

5. From the Letter "Convenerunt in unum" edited and studied by H. M. Schaller, "Die Antwort Gregors IX auf Petrus de Vinea I, 1 'Collegerunt pontifices,' " pp. 151–52.

6. On this Letter, see Schaller, "Das letzte Rundschreiben."

7. On Rainer, see Kantorowicz, *Frederick the Second,* pp. 591–95; T. C. Van Cleve, *The*

Emperor Frederick II of Hohenstaufen, pp. 481–83; and especially E. von Westenholz, *Kardinal Rainer von Viterbo.*

8. There were three basic documents: 1) the treatise in letter form beginning "Iuxta vaticinium Isaiae," which was apparently sent to Emperor Baldwin of Constantinople in June 1245, along with 2) a covering letter "Confusa est mater," and finally, 3) the pamphlet "Aspidis ova ruperant." These texts have been edited by E. Winkelmann, *Acta imperii inedita*, pp. 568–69, 709–21. See Graefe, *Die Publizistik*, pp. 119–27, on this material.

9. Winkelmann, p. 711.

10. E. Winkelmann, ed., *Fratris Arnoldi De Correctione Ecclesiae et Anonymi de Innocentio IV P.M. Antichristo.* Graefe, pp. 240–63, and Töpfer, *Das kommende Reich*, p. 156, note 10, hold that the two works are from the same pen. H. Grundmann, *Ketzergeschichte des Mittelalters*, p. 47, thinks that they may have originated in the Schwäbisch Hall heretical group active c.1248.

11. See the editions and discussion in Holder-Egger, "Italienischen Prophetieen" (1905), 30:335–49. The version translated here is the "English" variant found in Matthew Paris and elsewhere.

12. Schaller, "Das letzte Rundschreiben," pp. 313–14.

13. In the second half of the fifteenth century the verses were used during the conflict between Mohammed II and Pope Sixtus IV.

14. German scholars (e.g., Westenholz, *Kardinal Rainer von Viterbo*, pp. 108–32; Herde, "Ein Pamphlet," p. 501; and Schaller, "Endzeit-Erwartung," pp. 936–39) have claimed that Rainer and his circle were under Joachite influence. More work needs to be done on this important question in order to distinguish unmistakable Joachite themes from ones that can be explained through common biblical background. Nevertheless, there are significant parallels, as note 37 indicates. The fact that Rainer himself was a Cistercian and that the *Commentary on Jeremiah* may have been written in Florensian-Cistercian circles is suggestive.

15. Among other reports, Salimbene even recounts a prophecy that Joachim himself was supposed to have made to Henry VI regarding his son: "Your boy will be perverse, O Prince, your son and heir will be evil. O God! He will disturb the earth and crush the saints." *Chronica (MGH. SS.* XXXII, p. 31).

16. This is the version of the prophetic verses found in the shorter edition of the *Sibilla Erithraea* (Holder-Egger, *Neues Archiv*, 30:333–34). Slightly different versions are found in the longer text of the Sibyl, in Salimbene, in the pseudo-Joachite *De oneribus*, and in Albert Milioli's *Liber de temporibus*. See Reeves, *Influence of Prophecy*, p. 525.

17. The best introductions to these texts are in Töpfer, *Das kommende Reich*, and Reeves.

18. Printed in Venice in 1517, f. 30v of this edition contains a passage delaying the coming of the third *status* to 1290 (or 1390 in the printed text). If this is not an interpolation, it would seem to suggest that the original was composed after the year 1260 had passed.

19. For introductions, Reeves, *Influence of Prophecy*, pp. 332–46; and N. Cohn, *Pursuit of the Millennium*, pp. 113–26.

20. See K. Hampe, "Eine frühe Verknüpfung der Weissagung vom Endkaiser mit Friedrich II und Konrad IV."

21. L. Tondelli, "Profezia Gioachimita del Sec. XIII delle Regioni Venete." The Celestine mentioned would be Celestine IV who reigned briefly in 1241. Innocent IV, the enemy of Frederick, would be the proud pope; Alexander IV (1254–1261), the French pope who called in Charles of Anjou, the heretic.

22. For these texts, see Reeves, *Influence of Prophecy*, pp. 311–12; Töpfer, *Das kommende Reich des Friedens*, pp. 169–70, 172–73; and R. Lerner, "Medieval Prophecy and Religious Dissent," p. 15, note 38; p. 21, note 53.

23. The sermon was preached in the emperor's presence at Bitonto, most probably in 1229, shortly after he had been crowned king of Jerusalem and subdued a rebellion in Apulia.

24. Gen. 49:10, Jacob's prophecy to Judah, universally regarded as a prediction of the permanence of the Davidic line and of the first coming of Christ, is here applied to Frederick's house and the second coming. The suggestion has been made that the curious relief on the pulpit of the Bitonto cathedral is to be understood as an iconographic presentation of the same theme. Four figures in ascending order, Barbarossa, Henry VI, Frederick with the imperial globe, and his son Conrad, form a secularized version of the Tree of Jesse. See H. M. Schaller, "Das Relief an der Kanzel der Kathedrale von Bitonto."

25. The Emperor as "Vicar of Christ" was another of the themes of Frederick's imperial ideology.

26. Ps. 71:7–9, somewhat altered to make it more easily applicable to Frederick.

27. Frederick was born on St. Stephen's Day, 1194.

28. The text is dated to June 21, 1239; contemporary notices declare that Cardinal Rainer drafted the letter.

29. Accusations of heresy were one of the constants in the papal polemic against Frederick.

30. A long account of Frederick's misdeeds follows, especially his attacks on the Christian religion.

31. Written in July 1239, this letter shows that Frederick's chancery was fully capable of adopting the apocalyptic mode.

32. Standard medieval dualistic political theory is here turned against the papacy. Frederick's claim is that Gregory, in attempting to destroy this dualism, has proved that he is not a true pope, but actually the Antichrist.

33. The letter includes a lengthy defense of the emperor's orthodoxy.

34. There is no reference to which bull of Innocent's the author had in mind, but an obvious guess would be the bull of deposition of July 1245. The numerical values for the Roman letters are taken from the *Glossa ordinaria* (*PL* 114:734 BC).

35. Töpfer, *Das kommende Reich des Friedens,* pp. 118–21, and Reeves, *Influence of Prophecy,* p. 306, point out that the *Super Hieremiam* holds that there will be three persecutions marking the transition from the second to the third *status:* that of the New Babylon, or empire, described here; that of the heretics; and that of the Saracens and heathen.

36. Ezek. 26–28 predicts the destruction of Tyre.

37. This passage identifying Frederick with the basilisk of Isa. 14:29 provides a point of contact with the apocalyptic themes of Cardinal Rainer's curial circle. As early as August 1241, in the Letter "Vox in Rama" (Schaller, "Das letzte Rundschreiben," p. 320), Frederick was identified with the basilisk of Isa. 59:5. The same identification is found in two of Rainer's polemic writings of 1245, the "Iuxta vaticinium Isaiae" (Winkelmann, *Acta imperii inedita,* 2:709), and the "Aspidis ova ruperant," where it forms the introductory theme: "Henry and Philip of the seed of Frederick the schismatic have broken the serpent's eggs according to the prophet. He who was cherished by the Church, the young Frederick, has grown up a basilisk and by the deadly breath of his command has destroyed many birds flying to heaven" (Winkelmann, 2:717).

38. Possibly a reference to the capture of the Cardinals in 1241. I read *principes* rather than the *principem* of the text.

39. Frederick was frequently condemned for making use of Moslem troops.

40. The bird that the basilisk will seek to absorb is the Church. As Töpfer, *Das kommende Reich des Friedens,* points out (pp. 118–20), there is some ambiguity about whether Frederick

or his seed is the true and final Antichrist, but such ambiguity is characteristic of many apocalyptic texts.

41. That is, God will destroy the Antichrist.

42. The first head is the Kingdom of Sicily whose crown Frederick received in 1198; the sixty feet are a mistake, for Frederick was in his fifty-sixth year when he died.

43. Based on Rev. 13:2, thus possibly suggesting a knowledge of Gregory IX's "Ascendit de mari bestia."

44. Frederick, who was a ward of the Church during his infancy, was crowned emperor in 1220 (the second head) and king of Jerusalem in 1229 (the third head).

45. A reference to the emperor's marriages and progeny. His first wife was Constance of Aragon, his second Isabella of Jerusalem. The two sons referred to are Henry VII, king of Germany, later deposed for treason and imprisoned; and Conrad IV, king of Germany from 1250 to 1254.

46. Isabella of England married Frederick in 1235 and bore at least two sons.

47. The bastard Enzio, Frederick's favorite and king of Sardinia, was born to a German concubine. The French wife who outlives the emperor has no known historical counterpart. There follows a lengthy passage on Frederick's wars.

48. The passages that follow describe the struggle of Conrad IV to claim Frederick's heritage in Italy and argue for a date in the early 1250s for this Joachite version of the Sibyl.

49. This passage suggests that at least the latter portions of the work date to after 1266 when Charles of Anjou had defeated the most serious Hohenstaufen threat in the person of Manfred.

50. Apparently a prediction of a coming defeat of the papal and Angevin forces at the hands of the heirs of Frederick.

51. A reference to the Saracen troops used by the Hohenstaufen.

52. An obscure passage. The chick from the third nest may refer to a son from Frederick's third marriage, but we are not sure how this author reckoned the number of the emperor's wives.

53. The preceding sentences make it difficult to determine whether the author is speaking of Frederick or of one of his sons. A plausible reading is that Frederick is the seventh beast, one of his sons (possibly Manfred) is the eighth beast, who is yet one of the seven because of his descent. Manfred, though defeated in the Sixth Age, will be revived as a future Antichrist. It should be noted that the final part of the Isaiah *Commentary* (ff. 49–59) is based upon an analysis of the seven seals of Revelation as a prophecy of the seven ages of the Church.

54. H. Grauert, "Meister Johann von Toledo," pp. 147–57, has seen this poem as reflecting the hopes of the English Cardinal John of Toledo for the imperial candidature of Richard of Cornwall in the period after 1254. Töpfer, *Das kommende Reich des Friedens,* pp. 182–84, on the other hand, associates it with the similar claims of Edmund Crouchback. While these identifications cannot be ruled out, certain lines of the poem, such as those concerning the victory over the evil tribe of Frederick, seem to speak the language of *vaticinium ex eventu,* reflecting the victories of Charles of Anjou in the 1260s. Similarly, the explicit invocation of the Last Emperor is far more understandable in the case of a French ruler than an English one, especially a French ruler who was plotting an attack on the East.

55. If my interpretation is correct, here the text passes from an invocation of Charles's victories over the Hohenstaufen to a prophecy of his coming role as Last Emperor. This would suggest a date after 1268 but before the Sicilian Vespers of 1282 when the Angevin hopes for the conquest of Constantinople and the Holy Land were dashed.

21. Merlin, the British Seer

1. See R. W. Hanning, *The Vision of History in Early Britain*, ch. 5.

2. The story is based upon Nennius' *Historia Brittonum*, chs. 40–42, dating from the early ninth century.

3. The Celtic "Wild Man of the Woods" is present in the "Lailoken" texts from Scotland and in the Irish tale of "The Frenzy of Suibne." For the background of this complicated development, see B. Clarke, *The Life of Merlin*, Introduction; and also H. M. and N. K. Chadwick, *The Growth of Literature*, 1:123–32. The two Merlins were also well known to Gerald of Wales (1147–1223), who made considerable use of the prophecies ascribed to them.

4. The role of Merlin in political prophecy has been surveyed by R. Taylor, *The Political Prophecy in England*.

5. The best guide is P. Zumthor, *Merlin le Prophète*. Among the older works, see San-Marte (A. Schulz), *Die Sagen von Merlin;* and I. Sanesi, *La Storia di Merlino*. See also A. Hübscher, *Die Grosse Weissagung*, pp. 102–6.

6. E.g., Robert de Boron's lost *Merlin* and the works derived from it. See R. S. Loomis et al., *Arthurian Literature in the Middle Ages*.

7. Five commentaries were devoted to the obscure political prophecies of the seventh book of the *History of the Kings of Britain* between 1150 and 1250, including one falsely ascribed to the famous Scholastic Alan of Lille (P. Zumthor, *Merlin le Prophète*, pp. 78–80). This pseudo-Alan text, printed at Frankfurt in 1603, was composed between 1156–1183. It appears to be the work of a monk of continental origin, but resident in England, and shows a strong astrological as well as apocalyptic interest. I am indebted to John Trout for particulars regarding this text.

8. Zumthor, p. 114.

9. Zumthor, pp. 97–113, for an introduction.

10. This text is translated from H. Grundmann's fragment of the unpublished treatise in his review of L. A. Paton, *Les Prophécies de Merlin*, p. 570.

11. See *ibid.*, pp. 568–77. Not all of Grundmann's arguments are valid, however, e.g., his guess (p. 572) that the late fourteenth-century Second Charlemagne Prophecy belonged to the earliest version of the *Book of Kings*.

12. Matthew of Paris, *Chronica Major* (*RS* 57, 4:130) under 1241; and Salimbene, *Chronica* (*MGH.* SS. XXXII, 359–60) under 1250.

13. See Holder-Egger, "Italienische Prophetieen," (1890) 15:144–51; and Reeves, *Influence of Prophecy*, pp. 57, 520. Holder-Egger thinks that the original *Dicta* must have been composed after the death of Frederick in 1250, which would date the *Exposition* to the 1250s at the earliest.

14. Such prophecies were common in the thirteenth century, as the Pseudo-Joachim *Liber de oneribus* and the *Vaticinia* attributed to Michael Scot, the court astrologer of Frederick II, show. These verses may be found in Salimbene (*MGH.* SS. XXXII, 539–41).

15. L. A. Paton, *Les Prophécies de Merlin*, 2:1–33. Grundmann's hypothesis that they depend upon the lost *Liber regum* needs more investigation.

16. After introducing the boy wizard, Merlin Ambrosius, in Book 6, Geoffrey turns to his prophecies in Book 7. The letter of dedication to Bishop Alexander highlights the originally independent character of this section, portions of which also appear in Ordericus Vitalis, *Historia Ecclesiastica*, 12:57.

17. There is no evidence that Geoffrey actually knew Welsh, but he could have had Welsh material translated for him.

18. At the end of Book 6 Merlin had shown the evil King Vortigern that his tower could not be built until the pool beneath it was drained.

19. The remainder of the text of Book 7 consists of highly obscure political prophecy with heavy use of animal symbolism. The style is reminiscent of the slightly later Erythraean Sibyl, though scarcely as well organized.

20. References to Frederick Barbarossa and his death on crusade. Holder-Egger suggests that the two crows may refer to place names.

21. Henry VI, the son of Barbarossa, grew ill near Milazzo on the northern coast of Sicily and died at Messina in 1197.

22. Frederick II's mother Constance was of an advanced age when he was born.

23. Holder-Egger thinks this is a reference to the children born to Frederick by his first wife, Constance of Aragon.

24. Frederick's second wife, Isabella of Jerusalem, was a distant blood relation.

25. Apparently the author thought of Henry, the son of Isabella of England, Frederick's third wife, as the heir to Frederick's realm. This would indicate that the text was written before Henry's death in 1253.

26. Possibly a reference to Frederick's planting of colonies of Saracen troops in his domains.

27. Frederick crowned himself king of Jerusalem in 1229, but died in 1250 in his fifty-sixth year. For the thirty-two years given here, Holder-Egger suggests the period between Frederick's coronation as king of Rome in 1212 and his deposition in 1245. If, however, we add thirty-two years to the date of Frederick's Jerusalem coronation, as the context suggests, we have a date close to 1260, when Frederick the Antichrist was to be destroyed.

28. Perhaps a reference to the emperor's two excommunications considered as "medicinal" punishments less serious than the later deposition.

29. The famous sea battle in 1241 where Frederick's navy captured the prelates on the way to the proposed Council at Rome.

30. Frederick was crowned king of Rome at the age of eighteen. The sense of the text seems to demand *crismatus* rather than the printed *crismatis*.

31. The letter purports to have been written to Henry VI, to whom many of the earlier pseudo-Joachite works were dedicated. The real Joachim had not been unaware of his fellow prophet Merlin; he cites him in ch. 29 of his *De vita sancti Benedicti* (C. Baraut, ed., *Analecta sacra Tarraconensia* (1951), 24:63).

32. This is the reading of the version in Vat. lat. ms. 5732, f. 51r. The Paris ms. reads ". . . understood in the vices of the other Babylon . . ."

33. The text proper begins with the citation of a variant version of the *Dicta Merlini*.

34. This chapter provides the clue for Paton's dating of the work to the mid-1270s (see 2:5–10 for her discussion). The champion who will die in contumacy (of the papacy) is Frederick II; the buzzard who will think himself a falcon is the bastard Enzio who was captured by the Guelphs of Bologna in 1249 in the battle of Fossalta.

35. Enzio died in captivity in 1272.

36. *Chose,* literally "thing," but it can also mean "affair," "creature," "person." The prophetic polyvalence is deliberate.

37. Paton held that the prophecy concerning the Champion of Wales (chs. 174–76) made reference to the career of Charlemagne, both real and legendary (2:72–82). Grundmann, review of Paton (pp. 578–81), with far more reason felt that it was a "Merlinite" version of the Last Emperor myth.

38. The suppression of heresy as a special task of the Last Emperor is a reflection of the

northern Italian context in which the text was produced. This role was to be highlighted by fourteenth-century authors such as John of Rupescissa and Telesphorus.

39. An obscure passage follows which seems to argue that this punishment is the beginning, or prototype, of the pains the evil will undergo at the End of time.

40. The truce with the pagans mentioned here in ch. 175 is unusual and may well reflect a current political event.

41. The "Good Sailors," or Venetians, play a large role in the text and help to indicate the probable background and sympathies of the author.

42. That is, those killed in earlier crusades.

43. Babylon in this period means Cairo. Hence it seems that it was the Egyptians who the author felt would become the temporary allies of the Last Emperor.

44. Louis IX's second crusade of 1270 was aimed at Tunisia.

22. The Angelic Pope

1. On papal theory in the thirteenth century, see J. A. Watt, *The Theory of Papal Monarchy in the Thirteenth Century.*

2. Between Gregory VII (d. 1085) and Celestine V (abdicated 1294) no pope was canonized.

3. Reeves, *Influence of Prophecy,* pp. 397–98, notes this double character.

4. The *Oraculum angelicum* has been given a modern edition by P. Piur in K. Burdach, *Vom Mittelalter zur Reformation,* vol. 2, part 4, pp. 223–343. For the account of the angel's appearance, see pp. 244–45. B. Zimmerman in his *Monumenta historica Carmelitana,* fasc. 1, 296–311, dates the text to c.1287. B. Töpfer, *Das kommende Reich des Friedens,* pp. 239–40, with better reason, suggests a date in the late 1290s.

5. Among the important studies on the pontificate of Celestine are F. X. Seppelt, *Studien zum Pontifikat Papst Coelestins V;* F. Baethgen, *Der Engelpapst;* and A. Frugoni, *Celestiniana.*

6. See F. Russo, *Bibliografia Giochimita,* pp. 41–48, for a partial listing.

7. The important studies are those of H. Grundmann, "Die Papstprophetien des Mittelalters"; and M. Reeves, "Some Popular Prophecies from the Fourteenth to the Seventeenth Centuries."

8. Leo VI (886–912) was noted for his learning and numerous writings; many pseudonymous works were issued under his name. An imperfect edition of the Oracles with accompanying illustrations may be found in *Patrologia Graeca,* 107:1121–68. Grundmann, "Die Papstprophetien," pp. 82–84, reminds us that prophetic lists of emperors were well known in the Byzantine tradition.

9. The complex arrangement of the judgment figures and the succeeding holy popes clearly betrays the influence of the Leo Oracles, as well as of Joachite expectations of a coming age of peace. See the chart in Reeves, "Some Popular Prophecies," pp. 132–33.

10. *Ibid.,* p. 115.

11. The work was studied and partially edited by H. Grundmann, "Die *Liber de Flore.*"

12. These were sometimes applied to Joachim, sometimes to the fictional Anselm of Marsico.

13. Reeves has suggested that the combined form was first put together in the time of the Great Schism and owed its popularity to the fact that the Antichrist figure now came in the

middle of the series and could be interpreted as indicating the outbreak of the Schism, thus keeping alive hopes for the *pastores angelici* who were still to come. "Some Popular Prophecies," p. 119.

14. For a more detailed consideration of the origin and significance of the apocalyptic role of the papacy, see my article, "Angel Pope and Papal Antichrist."

15. For comments on this text, see Reeves, *Influence of Prophecy*, p. 398; Töpfer, *Das kommende Reich des Friedens*, p. 118; and Baethgen, *Der Engelpapst*, p. 94.

16. A reference either to Innocent III or to one of the popes in the struggle against Frederick II.

17. A passage follows in which Nebuchadnezzer and the Babylonian exile are used as a concordance for the coming imperial persecution of the Church.

18. That is, the Franciscans will flee at the death of the pope.

19. *Carpinalis,* a play on words suggesting *Cardinalis.*

20. For Bacon's view of the coming holy pope, see E. R. Daniel, "Roger Bacon and the *De seminibus scripturarum,*" pp. 465–66.

21. *The Third Work* of Bacon (so called because it comes after his *Opus Majus,* or *Longer Work,* and *Opus Minus,* or *Shorter Work*) was the last of the books that he sent to his friend Pope Clement IV in 1267.

22. There is no certainty regarding the work or works that forty years earlier gave a report of the coming pope.

23. The *Compendium* was written for Gregory X in 1272.

24. Gregory the Great, *Homiliae in Evangelia,* 2:30 (*PL* 76: c.1220 C).

25. Compare this with the list found in the *Longer Work,* and translated above on p. 156.

26. Among the claimants for the title of the reforming holy pope to come was Gregory X (1271–1276) who summoned the Second Council of Lyons in 1274.

27. It is highly unlikely that Salimbene actually saw these verses before Gregory's election, because they display a knowledge of the Second Council of Lyons.

28. Gregory died in the midst of plans for a new crusade.

29. These evil priests are mentioned in 2 Kings 5:20–27 and became a medieval *topos* for avaricious ecclesiastics.

30. There is another version of these verses that makes no mention of Gregory; see L. Delisle, *Notices et extraits des manuscrits de la Bibliothèque Nationale,* 38:739–40.

31. The text is written in a highly obscure Latin that may be based on a Greek original or may be deliberately Hellenizing for effect.

32. The good Rehoboam has been interpreted as Celestine V, the evil Jeroboam as Boniface VIII; see Töpfer, *Das kommende Reich des Friedens,* pp. 239–41.

33. A conjectural translation of *floccipendent* which I find in no Latin dictionary.

34. Also conjectural. I read *vatemque* for the *vastimque* of the text.

35. The bear was the symbol of the Orsini family, one of the most important Roman aristocratic families, and one that gave a number of popes to the Church.

36. That is, the Holy Spirit.

37. Robert was a French Dominican who died in 1296. His writings, edited and studied by J. Bignami-Odier, "Les visions de Robert d'Uzès," show that apocalypticism was by no means confined to Franciscans at the time. The *Visiones* and *Liber sermonum Dei,* composed 1291–1296, were occasioned by the papal crisis in these years.

38. This, the thirteenth vision, that "On the Future State of the Church," took place in the city of Orange and immediately followed a vision in which the ship of the Church lost its rudder and was in serious danger.

39. Nicholas IV (1288–1292) was the first Franciscan Pope, and Robert may have had him in mind; but the mountain locale is also reminiscent of Celestine V, called from his mountain hermitage to be pope. See Bignami-Odier, p. 279, note 26.

40. The *Liber* recounts the second part of Robert's showings. According to his account: "After these I saw many visions and dreamed many dreams which are written elsewhere. They are fearful to the reader, but these are more fearful still."

41. That is, to Celestine V.

42. That is, the abdication.

43. The Idol of the Church is Boniface. Robert holds out hope for his conversion.

44. The titles vary greatly and it is difficult to determine their original form. This title is discussed by Reeves, "Some Popular Prophecies," p. 115. The pope depicted here is Celestine V.

45. Reading *mensium* with Vat. lat. 3822, as more in harmony with the short career of Celestine who was pope from August 29 to December 13, 1294.

46. The accompanying illustration pictures a monk holding a rose and a sickle.

47. Possibly a reference to Celestine's survival after his abdication and to the hardships he suffered in prison.

48. The illustration is of a pope with a cow and two disembodied heads.

49. Boniface VIII, the subject of this prophecy, was allied with the Orsini family whose symbol was the bear. The positive content of the text, which contrasts with the negative title, may be a holdover from the Leo Oracles.

50. The reading of Vat. lat. 3816, f. 27v.

51. The accompanying picture is of a semi-naked monk sitting on a rock.

52. These are apparently the words of the holy monk who will become the *pastor angelicus*.

53. Vat. lat. 3816, f. 27v closes with the gloss: "This is the Angelic Pope according to Joachim."

54. The picture shows a pope being crowned by an angel.

55. That is, of the same kind as the Angelic Pope described in XI.

56. The image accompanying this text does not depend on the *Leo Oracles*. It shows a pope holding a tiara over a horned animal which might signify papal domination over the empire (Reeves, *Influence of Prophecy,* p. 403), or perhaps over the Antichrist.

23. *Bonaventure's Apocalyptic Theology of History*

1. The only account of the supposed trial of John is given by the avowed Spiritual, Angelo of Clareno.

2. See also McGinn, "The Abbot and the Doctors"; and "The Significance of Bonaventure's Theology of History."

3. McGinn, "The Abbot and Doctors," pp. 37–41.

4. Cf. the *Legenda maior* and the *Legenda minor,* his two lives of Francis dating from about 1261 (*Opera omnia,* 8:504, 545, 577, 579).

5. Since about 1267 Bonaventure had begun to attack the misuse of Aristotle. Ratzinger, ch. 4, "Aristotelianism and the Theology of History," is the best introduction.

6. The Doctor distinguishes the Franciscans and Dominicans of the present age from this order to come.

7. Collation, 1:1.

8. The "vision of understanding taught by Scripture" is the third of the visions around which Bonaventure organized his unfinished Collations.

9. On the basis of Gen. 1:9–11, Collation 13:2 lists three types of understanding of scriptural texts—the "spiritual intelligences" imaged in the gathering of the waters; the "sacramental symbols" figured in the multiplication of beings; and the "manifold theories" whose figure are the seeds of the fruit-bearing trees. The third type, discussed here, is the properly Joachite one.

10. Bonaventure's "correspondence of times" is Joachim's notion of concordance.

11. The Franciscan saw the seventh age as beginning with St. Francis, and therefore as running concurrently with the sixth. This idea may have been influential on Peter Olivi, for whom the fifth and the sixth ages were concurrent.

12. The concordance of the seven ages of the Old Testament with the seven of the New is the basis for Bonaventure's periodization of history and recalls Joachim's pattern of double sevens figured by the seven seals of Revelation.

13. The Collations survive in the form of *reportationes,* that is, notes taken down by hearers and later edited. Hence Bonaventure is sometimes referred to in the third person as in this restrained reference to the Last Emperor myth. I have placed such asides in parentheses.

14. The *viri spirituales* of the coming order would possess the full understanding of Scripture.

15. Bonaventure's identification of Francis with the angel of the sixth seal is one of the cornerstones of Franciscan apocalypticism. Apparently John of Parma was the first to make this identification.

16. Collation 22 studies the various orders within the Church Militant. When the orders are considered according to practice, i.e., their involvement in action, contemplation, or a mixture of both, the contemplatives rank highest. This is the ranking within the contemplative orders.

17. Francis belonged to the Seraphic order to come; his less perfect followers of the Franciscan order are on a lower level.

18. The appearance of the Seraph both expressed the inner meaning (love and perfect understanding) of the coming order, and was also impressed on Francis's own body as the sign of his membership in it.

24. The Franciscan Spirituals

1. The literature on the Spiritual movement is large. Among the most important works are F. Ehrle, "Die Spiritualen, ihr Verhältnis zum Franciscanerorden und zu den Fraticellen"; D. Douie, *The Nature and Effect of the Heresy of the Fraticelli;* E. Benz, *Ecclesia Spiritualis;* L. Oliger, "Spirituels"; G. Leff, *Heresy in the Later Middle Ages,* vol. 1, part 1, "Poverty and Prophecy"; and *Franciscains d'Oc: Les Spirituels c. 1280–1324.*

2. The most important of these are *Quo elongati* of 1230, *Ordinem vestrem* of 1245, and *Exiit qui seminat* of 1279.

3. The juridical conception of apostolic poverty as worked out in the papal bulls and by Bonaventure involved the total denial of ownership (*dominium*) and also the "right of use" (*ius utendi*). All the order retained was what was called "simple use" (*simplex usus facti*) of the lands, buildings, and goods owned by the papacy. For a survey of the development of this complex legal fiction, see M. D. Lambert, *Franciscan Poverty.*

4. This has been well brought out by E. R. Daniel, "Spirituality and Poverty."

5. See Lambert, ch. 7, for the context.

6. There is also an extensive literature relating to Olivi. Among the important studies I single out F. Ehrle, "Petrus Johannis Olivi"; R. Manselli, La "Lectura super Apocalypsim" di Pietro di Giovanni Olivi; C. Partee, "P. J. Olivi: Historical and Doctrinal Study"; David Flood, Peter Olivi's Rule Commentary; the articles of David Burr mentioned below (see note 10); and the papers of R. Manselli and E. Pásztor in the Bullettino dell'Istituto Storico Italiano per il Medio Evo (1970), vol. 82.

7. R. Manselli promised one many years ago, and more recently another was announced by W. Lewis. Two useful discussions of the text may be found in Manselli, La "Lectura super Apocalypsim," ch. 5; and G. Leff, Heresy, 1:122–39.

8. On Olivi and Bonaventure, see Leff, pp. 101–2, 113–17.

9. Among the important sources for the Lectura, besides the few surviving mss., are the excerpts made from the work for the various commissions of investigation. Two of these have been published, one by S. Baluze in his Miscellanea, 2:258–76; the other by I. von Döllinger, Beiträge zur Sektengeschichte des Mittelalters, 2:527–85. This passage is from von Döllinger, p. 532.

10. On this aspect of his thought, see D. Burr, "The Apocalyptic Element in Olivi's Critique of Aristotle"; and "Petrus Ioannis Olivi and the Philosophers."

11. Olivi did not identify the Mystical Antichrist with any current pope nor did he say that the carnal Church was the institutional Roman Church of his time, cf. Manselli, La "Lectura super Apocalypsim," p. 219; Leff, Heresy, pp. 126, 129.

12. See E. R. Daniel, The Franciscan Concept of Mission in the High Middle Ages, pp. 84–86.

13. For the history of this struggle, see R. Manselli, Spirituali e Beguini in Provenza.

14. For the complicated history of the various condemnations of Olivi, see J. Koch, "Der Prozess gegen di Postille Olivis zur Apokalypse"; E. Pásztor, "Le polemiche sulla 'Lectura super Apocalypsim' di Pietro di Giovanni Olivi"; and D. Burr, The Persecution of Peter Olivi.

15. On Angelo, see Leff, Heresy, 1:172–75, 233–34; and Douie, Heresy of the Fraticelli, ch. 3.

16. Angelo tells the story of the group up to 1317 in his noted Epistola excusatoria, edited and studied by F. Ehrle in the Archiv für-Literature- und Kirchengeschichte (1885), 1:515–33.

17. Among the works on Ubertino, besides Douie and Leff, see F. Callaey, L'Idéalisme franciscain spirituel au XIVe siècle; P. Godefroy, "Ubertin de Casale"; and C. T. Davis, "Le Pape Jean XXII et les spirituels: Ubertin de Casale."

18. Douie, Heresy of the Fraticelli, p. 133, has described it as "a prose epic of the life and passion of Christ, to which has been added a commentary on the Apocalypse bearing the unmistakable traces of Joachite influence."

19. Leff, Heresy, 1:152

20. Like Bonaventure and Olivi, Ubertino coordinated a three-age schema of world history with a theory of seven stages in the history of the Church.

21. The best account in English is E. Underhill, Jacopone da Todi, Poet and Mystic.

22. These have been edited numerous times, most recently by F. Ageno, Laudi: Trattato e Detti.

23. E.g., Nos. 50–53. No. 56 is a sharp attack on Boniface VIII.

24. Cf. Leff, Heresy, 1:147–49; and Davis, "Le Pape Jean XXII."

25. "The first error which issues from the murky workshop of these men is to fashion two Churches, one carnal, weighed down by riches . . . which they assert the bishop of Rome and the other prelates rule, the other spiritual, girt with poverty, in which they alone and their ac-

complices are contained . . . They also dream many things about the course of the ages and the End of the world. With lamentable vanity they publish much about the coming of the Antichrist whom they assert is now threatening.'' From *Gloriosam ecclesiam* as found in Denzinger, *Enchiridion symbolorum*, Nos. 485, 490.

26. Manselli's *Spirituali e Beguini* is a full account; see also Leff, *Heresy*, 1:212–30.

27. Davis, ''Le Pape Jean,'' pp. 276–81.

28. The effect of this controversy on the growth of notions of papal infallibility has been studied by B. Tierney, *Origins of Papal Infallibility 1150–1350*.

29. The text goes on to specify details in an allegorical comparison between Francis and the Angel.

30. See the ninth chapter of Bonaventure's *Legenda major* (*Opera omnia*, 8:531). Francis was converted in 1206. In 1212 he attempted to go on mission for the first time. In 1214–15 he journeyed through France and Spain hoping to reach Africa, and finally in 1219 did succeed in getting to Egypt.

31. The relation between the Franciscan movement and conversion theology in the thirteenth century has been recently investigated by E. R. Daniel, *The Franciscan Concept of Mission*.

32. In the *Liber Concordie* and other works.

33. This shows that Olivi made use of both the schema of the double sevens and that of the three *status*.

34. Reference to William of St. Amour and the group associated with him.

35. This objection reflects the view of those religious orders who owned goods in common, as opposed to that of the Franciscans, who claimed to own nothing.

36. The bull *Exiit qui seminat* of Nicholas III (the ms. erroneously has Nicholas IV) was issued in 1279.

37. The argument is that just as the comet announced the victories of Charles of Anjou in 1266–1268, the various persecutions and troubles that began about 1233 announced the coming of the two Antichrists.

38. Peter's invasion of Sicily took place in 1282. Olivi follows the early Joachite tradition in viewing the career of Frederick and the fate of Sicily as having important apocalyptic significance.

39. Unlike other Spirituals, Olivi defended the validity of Celestine's abdication and the legitimacy of his successor, though he did give their careers apocalyptic significance. The vague ''warnings'' may refer to the position of the Spirituals.

40. Following von Döllinger, *Beiträge zur Sektengeschichte*, p. 572.

41. Olivi is attempting to defend the Joachite tale of forty-two generations for the duration of the second *status*, but still explain why the third *status* has not been fully established. The answer is that the generations must be computed from the year A.D. 40, and this suggests a unique importance for the coming year 1300.

42. A reference to the *In Hieremiam* and other treatises.

43. This reference to the Third Frederick legend is similar to that already seen in the *Super Esaiam* text in Section 20.

44. The Franciscan Rule is meant.

45. Referring to the attack of the Colonna Cardinals on Boniface in 1297.

46. This is a constant theme of the last chapters of Book V. Ubertino refutes all arguments concerning historical precedents for papal abdication of f. 234 r–v.

47. The text later makes it clear that the two friars were members of Angelo's group. Justin on the Book of Revelation is unknown; the reference is possibly to Irenaeus who in *Adversus haereses*, 5:30, speculates on the names of the Antichrist.

48. Benedict XI (1303–04).

49. That is, the Spirituals, who preached against the Mystical Antichrist.

50. Amaury of Bène (d. c.1206), a teacher at Paris, was condemned for teaching pantheistic doctrines and his followers severely persecuted.

51. Philip II (1180–1223).

52. Most likely Radulphus Ardens, a disciple of Peter Lombard, active in Paris in the late twelfth and early thirteenth centuries.

53. Reference to Matt. 24:29, whose imagery appears in the next few lines.

54. The picture of the Dragon is from Rev. 12. The waters he drinks up are the baptized.

55. The equation of the religious orders with stars was a commonplace of Joachite imagery.

56. The lines omitted (46–59) mention other evils afflicting those living at the End, specifically doctrinal errors and false prophecies.

57. Bernard Gui (1261–1331) was a Dominican Inquisitor in Southern France. His important *Inquisitor's Manual* was finished about 1324.

58. Omitted is a lengthy section outlining the history of the sect. In Bernard's long discussion of the errors of the Beguines, I concentrate on the specifically apocalyptic ones.

59. Frederick of Sicily (1296–1337) was the great object of hope for the Spirituals.

60. This, of course, is John XXII.

25. *Arnald of Villanova*

1. The best account of Arnald is by R. Manselli, "La religiosità di Arnaldo da Villanova." Also important is H. Finke, *Aus den Tagen Bonifaz VIII.* For accounts in English, cf. Leff, *Heresy*, 1:176–91; and H. Lee, *"Scrutamini Scripturas:* Joachimist Themes and *Figurae* in the Early Religious Writing of Arnald of Villanova."

2. For an account of this controversy, see also *Influence of Prophecy,* pp. 314–17. Later Henry of Harclay, Chancellor of Oxford, also entered the fray with a *Quaestio* on the Second Coming of Christ that has been edited by F. Pelster, "Die Quaestio Heinrichs von Harclay über die zweite Ankunft Christi."

3. He himself was posthumously condemned in 1316.

4. Visionaries or *speculatores* (a term found as early as Gregory the Great in apocalyptic literature) play an important part in Arnald's views about the End, e.g., pp. cxxix–cxxx in this treatise.

5. A constant theme is the reliance, not upon human conjecture, but upon the revealed word of God. At other times, however, Arnald did claim special revelation about the End.

6. It was the setting of a precise date that most upset the Augustinian-minded theologians of Paris and Oxford. Later, Arnald thought that the Great Antichrist had already been born and was three years old. The 1378 date was to be taken up by Telesphorus of Cosenza, see below p. 247. Some mss. have 1376.

7. As a friend of the Spirituals, Arnald was heir to the tradition of Bonaventure and Olivi which saw in rampant Aristotelianism one of the clearest signs of the imminence of the Antichrist. In this 1304 reply to the attacks of Dominican theologians, Arnald goes a step further by identifying Thomas Aquinas and his followers as a distinct apocalyptic evil.

8. For Aquinas' attacks on radical apocalypticism, see my "The Abbot and the Doctors," pp. 37–41.

26. Fra Dolcino and the Apostolic Brethren

1. For the Marxist historian B. Töpfer, the only true revolutionaries among the medieval apocalypticists were the Taborites (*Das kommende Reich,* pp. 308–9). See also E. Werner, "Popular Ideologies in Late Medieval Europe."

2. The best modern accounts of the movement are Töpfer, *Das kommende Reich des Friedens,* pp. 289–324; and E. Anagnine, *Dolcino e il Movimento ereticale all'Inizio del Trecento.*

3. Our main sources are Salimbene's *Chronica,* the anonymous *Historia Fratris Dulcini,* various papal bulls, and Bernard Gui's treatise *De secta illorum.* The texts have been edited by A. Segarizzi in RIS vol. 9, part 5 (1907).

4. Töpfer, *Das kommende Reich des Friedens,* pp. 318–19. Other scholars deny that the Apostolic Brethren's military activity shared any aspects of a peasant revolt, e.g., C. Violante, "Eresie urbane e eresie rurale in Italia dall'XI al XIII secolo," pp. 179, 182–83. For a study of the influence of apocalyptic and millenarian ideas on modern peasant insurrections, see E. Hobsbawm, *Primitive Rebels.*

5. The stress on poverty and the apostolic life mark Dolcino as belonging to a widespread religious movement of the high Middle Ages, albeit on the extreme left wing.

6. The Joachite theme that the full understanding of the Scriptures will be given only in the last days.

7. A long account of Dolcino's theory of the four *status* of world history follows. Briefly put, the theory involves: *1st State*—the time of the Old Testament Patriarchs until the coming of Christ, the age of the married life; *2d State*—from the coming of Christ to the time of Silvester and Constantine, the age of virginity and poverty; *3d State*—from Silvester and Constantine to Gerard Segarelli, the age of religious founders, such as Benedict, Francis, and Dominic; *4th State*—from Segarelli until the End. Each state undergoes a decline at the end, but is then reformed by the initiator of the following period. The similarities and differences of this scheme of world history to the standard Joachite one are apparent.

8. Dolcino's hopes for Frederick of Sicily also seem to display Joachite influence.

9. Dolcino gives more information on the coming *pastor angelicus* in the second letter summarized by Gui, pp. 22–23.

10. Olivi also associates the Angel of Philadelphia with the coming Holy Pope. Other reports indicate that Dolcino may later have come to identify himself with the Holy Pope. See Töpfer, *Das kommende Reich des Friedens,* p. 304.

27. John of Rupescissa

1. The fundamental work is J. Bignami-Odier, *Études sur Jean de Roquetaillade.* For an English introduction, see E. F. Jacob, "John of Roquetaillade."

2. John was a strong defender of apostolic poverty, though paradoxically he also believed that the bull *Exiit* of Nicholas III and the *Cum inter nonnullos* of John XXII were not in conflict.

3. Bignami-Odier, p. 120.

4. Some of his works, making use of the Joachite Papal Prophecies, predict a series of Angelic Popes.

5. See Bignami-Odier, pp. 203–9.

6. The only work of John ever printed, the *Vade mecum in tribulatione* has been described

by Bignami-Odier, *Études sur Jean de Roquetaillade,* pp. 164–73; and Jacob, "John of Roque-taillade," pp. 191–94.

7. The work is arranged according to twenty instructions (*intentiones*), not necessarily in chronological order. The first four deal with the conversion of all men to Christianity, the reform of the clergy, the persecution of ecclesiastics, and the abandonment of Avignon by the curia that was supposed to take place in 1362.

8. The protest against wealth and power (here to be replaced with "popular justice") may be described as the polemical side, increasingly evident in the later Middle Ages, of one of the ancient themes of the apocalyptic tradition, the hope for a coming just order to be found in the equality and bounteous wealth of the Messianic Kingdom.

9. Like almost all late medieval thinkers, John held to a double Antichrist tradition. In his division, the Eastern Antichrist is the false Messiah of the Jews; the Western Antichrist, de-scribed as Nero, is discussed in the eighth instruction. In earlier works John kept closer to the teaching of the Franciscan Spirituals, sometimes identifying the Mystical Antichrist with the Emperor Lewis of Bavaria (r. 1314–1347), and sometimes with Louis of Sicily (r. 1342–1355).

10. The identification of a specific Antichrist for the Jews often involves a strong dose of antisemitism, e.g., the case of Commodian in the Patristic period.

11. In the ninth instruction mention was made that "through the ministry of a holy angel Christ would cause a Supreme Pontiff, the restorer of the world, to be elected canonically dur-ing a papal interregnum" (Brown, *Appendix,* p. 500).

12. The tenth instruction (Brown, p. 501) identified the two prophets of Rev. 11 with two poor Franciscans who about 1365 would arise to fight the beasts. One would be the Restoring Pontiff, the other a cardinal who would accompany him.

13. John is one of the most important witnesses to the Francophile version of the Last Em-peror myth as it developed in the later Middle Ages; see Reeves, *Influence of Prophecy,* pp. 320–25.

14. The apocalyptic significance of conflict with Islam is a frequent theme in John's works.

15. Papal military involvement in central Italy was an important problem for the Avignon popes.

16. A reference to the sixth intention (Brown, *Appendix,* p. 500).

28. The Fraticelli

1. The term was used in papal documents as early as 1317 by John XXII. It was applied not only to groups associated with the Franciscans, but also to associations of pious men who had no such connection.

2. The classic early study of the Fraticelli movement is F. Ehrle, "Die Spiritualen, ihr Verhältnis zum Franciscanerorden und zu den Fraticellen." Later important treatments are D. Douie, *The Nature and Effect of the Heresy of the Fraticelli,* especially ch. 7, pp. 209–47; and L. Oliger, "Spirituels." See also Reeves, *Influence of Prophecy,* pp. 212–20.

3. Important literature of the Fraticelli has been edited by a number of scholars. The most significant collection of sources is L. Oliger, "Documenta inedita ad historiam Fraticellorum spectantia," *Archivum Franciscanum Historicum* (1910–1913), vols. 3–6.

4. H. Grundmann, "Die Papstprophetien," pp. 117–24, first determined the origin, but his dating (c.1380) was too late. John of Rupescissa already cited them in 1356. Reeves's suggestion may be found in "Some Popular Prophecies," p. 118.

5. Reeves thinks that the combination became popular at the time of the Great Schism; see "Some Popular Prophecies," p. 119.

6. A. Messini, "Profetismo e profezie ritmiche italiane d'ispirazione Gioachimito-Francescana nei secoli XIII, XIV, e XV," *Miscellanea Francescana* (1937) and (1939).

7. A friend of Bridget of Sweden and Catherine of Siena, this hermit and reformer was active against the Florentine Fraticelli about 1380. See Douie, *Heresy of the Fraticelli,* pp. 232–40.

8. Like the earlier series, these prophecies appear to begin with Nicholas III (1277–1280), the Orsini pope characterized by bears.

9. The 1625 ed. reverses the order of numbers 4 and 5. I follow Vat. lat. 3816, f. 17r which identifies number 5 with Celestine V. The figure shows a praying pope being attacked by a fox.

10. A reference to Celestine's abdication.

11. In number 6, Boniface VIII is portrayed as an evil pope (*neronice regnans*) behind whom sits a sorrowing monk. Benedict XI is number 7.

12. In this prophecy Clement V (1305–1314) is severely blamed for deserting Rome. The illustration shows a pope leaving Rome on horseback with a personification of the grieving city behind.

13. I.e., Clement is not really clement.

14. Probably a reference to the troubles of the Spirituals.

15. The repetition of the title is lacking in the printed edition.

16. A savage portrait of John XXII, pictured as wounding the Lamb of God with a sword.

17. *Filium minimum* obviously equals the Friars Minor.

18. The illustration shows a pope with a dove, a tiara, and six stars.

19. Benedict XII was born in the French Pyrenees and had been a Cistercian, or white monk, before his election.

20. Vat. lat. 3816, f. 19v reads *construxerat* ("built up") rather than *obfuscavit* ("obscured"). This might suggest that the lofty things (*excelsa*) referred to in several places have to do with the Papal Palace at Avignon.

21. Numbers 11 and 12 following seem to be coming Angelic Popes.

22. The illustration shows a seated pope being handed the keys by an angel. With his other hand the pope holds a fan or whip over a peacock.

23. The ms. and printed edition both read *vita circumcisos*. Since one of the accomplishments of the Angelic Pope would be to convert the Jews and infidels, we might perhaps read *vivifica circumcisos,* "convert the Jews."

24. In number 14 a pope is attacked by a soldier, possibly a reference to the persecution of the ten kings at the time of the Antichrist.

25. This rendition of the Antichrist, pictured like a basilisk with a human head, is appended after number 30 in Vat. lat. 3816. In the printed edition it appears as number 15.

26. Daniel's apocalyptic number is found in Vat. lat. 3816, f. 31r, but not in the printed edition.

27. The text was written in Campania about 1354 to the chief citizens of Narni in Umbria to ask them to help some Fraticelli imprisoned by the Conventuals. Its violent tone (see Douie, *Heresy of the Fraticelli,* pp. 221–23) makes it one of the more distinctive Fraticelli tracts.

28. There follows a refutation, based on Scripture, the Fathers, and earlier papal statements, of twelve errors drawn from John's decretals. Such lists are a standard feature of Fraticelli polemics, the most widespread example being the *Apellatio* incorrectly ascribed to William of Ockham (ed. S. Baluze, *Miscellanea,* 3:341–55).

29. A later passage expressly mentions Benedict XII, Clement VI, and Innocent VI as falling under the same condemnation of open heresy as John.

29. Rome and Avignon during the Captivity

1. The Avignon Line included John XXII (1316–1334), Benedict XII (1334–1342), Clement VI (1342–1352), Innocent VI (1352–1362), Urban V (1362–1370), and Gregory XI (1370–1378).

2. For an introduction, E. Duprè Theseider, "L'attesa escatologica durante il periodo avignonese."

3. E.g., W. Ullmann, "Avignon Papacy," p. 1135.

4. For an introduction to the history of the Papal States, P. Partner, *The Lands of St. Peter*.

5. F. Gregorovius, *Rome in the Middle Ages*, 6:376.

6. Aside from the letters, the primary source for the fascinating career of the tribune is the *Vita*, recently translated by J. Wright, *The Life of Cola di Rienzo*.

7. See Gregorovius, *Rome in the Middle Ages*, 6:345–46; and Reeves, *Influence of Prophecy*, pp. 318–19.

8. Letter 58, written in 1350. Cola's letters have been edited in K. Burdach, *Vom Mittelalter zur Reformation*, vol. 2, part 3. This passage is on p. 326.

9. L. Hollman, ed., *Sancta Birgitta. Revelationes Extravagantes*, ch. 8, p. 120.

10. E.g., *Revelationes*, 4:142. Only a portion of Bridget's *Revelations* have appeared in modern editions. For the texts translated herein I have made use of the 1690 Munich edition.

11. Duprè Theseider, "L'attesa escatologica," pp. 114–18.

12. *Revelationes*, 4:22: "Therefore a plowman will come from the Most High, one sharpened by Highest Wisdom. He will not seek lands and the beauty of bodies; he will not fear the strong nor the threats of princes."

13. E.g., *Revelationes*, 3:27; 6:67.

14. In *Revelations*, 6:110, an unnamed *Magister* asks her to explain the significance of the seven trumpets of the Book of Revelation.

15. See Reeves, *Influence of Prophecy*, "Bridget, St., of Sweden," under General Index.

16. This is the first letter addressed to Charles IV. It was written from prison in Prague about July 1350.

17. This Angelo, the head of the hermits of Monte Maiella where Cola stayed, is perhaps the same as the Frater Angelus mentioned as the head of one of the three groups of Fraticelli in a document of 1362. See Burdach, *Vom Mittelalter*, vol. 2, part 5, p. 301.

18. Possibly a reference to the Black Death of 1348–49.

19. The association of the *pastor angelicus* with the coming age of the Holy Spirit is a sure sign of the Joachite cast of Angelo's thought. Cola made these ideas his own in the lengthy Letter 58 (Burdach, pp. 313–15, 322–23).

20. Burdach, vol. 2, part 4, p. 194, in his note to these lines claims that Cola identified himself with the *pastor angelicus* prophesied by Angelo, since in other places he speaks of his own "resurrection" from prison and disgrace. Nevertheless, the claim is not directly made.

21. Rome is spoken of as Jerusalem in Letters 57 and 58.

22. Charles IV (1347–1378) was actually the one hundred and fourteenth in the imperial succession.

23. The Avignon Captivity had begun forty years before.

24. Lev. 25:10–11 commanded all Israelites to return to their original homes to celebrate the fifty-year jubilee. Rome celebrated its second Papal Jubilee in 1350 during the Avignon Captivity.

25. Especially the *Oraculum Cirilli* and various other Pseudo-Joachite works, as Letters 57 and 58 make clear.

26. When challenged by the Archbishop of Prague concerning his dependence on such prophecies (Letter 61, p. 338), Cola somewhat disingenuously emphasized the secondary influence of these productions on his program (Letters 62–64). In 1352 when in prison at Avignon, he directly rejected some of his earlier prophetic interpretations (Letter 73, pp. 415–16).

27. Among the lengthiest of the tribune's apocalyptic missives, Letter 58 contains this passage showing how far Cola had accepted the anticlerical themes of the Fraticelli.

28. The reference is to Pope Celestine V appearing in the midst of the worldly clergy.

29. Clement V had been the Archbishop of Bordeaux.

30. The *Oraculum Cirilli* was enscribed on silver tablets.

31. The great Italian poet and man of letters (1304–1374), who spent much of his life at Avignon, had hailed the advent of Cola and addressed a number of laudatory letters to him in the early days of his career. Later, Petrarch expressed strong disapproval of the tribune's tyrannical actions. From the period shortly before 1350, we possess a number of products of Petrarch's pen which witness to his intense dissatisfaction with the Avignonese papacy. This sonnet, dated to 1347 by E. H. Wilkins, *The Life of Petrarch*, pp. 61–62, shows the poet's acquaintance with apocalyptic themes.

32. Reason here is perhaps best understood in the sense of God's Reason, or Judgment.

33. The poet looks forward to the purification of the Church by a coming Ruler (Sultan). Babylon (Avignon) will be destroyed, and Baghdad (presumably Rome) will once again be the center of Christendom.

34. Spiritual men will triumph and the Golden Age will return. Petrarch makes use of the classical rather than the Joachite myth in his description of the coming age.

35. Hugh of St. Victor had compared the six ages of the Church's history to Noah's ark in his *De Arca Noe mystica* (*PL* 176: c. 685D).

36. We are not sure to whom the saint refers here, although among contemporaries John of Rupescissa would certainly fill the bill. It is obvious that Bridget was opposed to radical apocalypticism.

30. Political Prophecies: French versus German Imperial Legends

1. For an introduction to the relations of apocalypticism and nationalism in the late Middle Ages, see D. Kurze, "Nationale Regungen in der spätmittelalterliche Prophetie," especially p. 23 on the paradox of the use of universalistic apocalyptic myths in the service of nationalistic particularism.

2. The fundamental study is that of E. Donckel, "Studien über die Prophezeiung des Fr. Telesphorus von Cosenza, O.F.M."; see also Reeves, *Influence of Prophecy*, pp. 325–31, 342–45, 423–24.

3. On the sources, see section 3 of Donckel's study, pp. 50–74.

4. For the development of this scenario from the time of John of Rupescissa, see M. Reeves, "History and Prophecy in Medieval Thought," pp. 68–70.

5. For surveys of the program, cf. Reeves, *Influence of Prophecy*, pp. 326–27, and Donckel, pp. 77–78, 81–83. The dates given obviously stem from the revision of 1386.

6. See Reeves, *Influence of Prophecy, passim*, for the spread and influence.

7. Donckel, p. 45, points out the political context here. Telesphorus saw England and Venice as allies of the French Charles in his struggle against Frederick, a prophecy which would fit some of the circumstances of the Holy League (1511–13) of the papacy, France, England, and Venice against the empire.

8. Reeves, *Influence of Prophecy*, pp. 320–21.

9. M. Chaume, "Une prophétie relative à Charles VI."

10. Reeves, *Influence of Prophecy*, pp. 329–30.

11. *Ibid.*

12. Chaume, "Une prophétie," pp. 31–35.

13. The best introduction in English to this material is in Reeves, *Influence of Prophecy*, pp. 332–46.

14. Donckel, "Telesphorus von Cosenza," p. 31.

15. Reeves, *Influence of Prophecy*, pp. 425–27.

16. E. Herrmann, " 'Veniet aquila, de cuius volatu delebitur leo.' "

17. Dan. 8:23 had spoken of a "rex impudicus facie," a text taken by many to refer to a coming persecutor of the Church. The fifteenth-century text reverses this to announce a good German "rex pudicus facie" who will reform the Church and usher in the Golden Age.

18. Keith Thomas, *Religion and the Decline of Magic*, pp. 128–46, 389–432.

19. This title appears to be a later addition.

20. The confusing habit of referring to the Schism at some times as present (*instans*), at other times as future (*futurum*) appears to reflect the two stages of the text. See Donckel, "Fr. Telesphorus von Cosenza," pp. 82–83.

21. Charles V who died in 1380.

22. Charles VI was crowned before his fourteenth year, thus indicating the date of 1380 for the original composition (Chaume, "Une prophétie relative à Charles VI," p. 30). The physical description is based upon twelfth-century versions of the Tiburtine Sibyl.

23. Chaume's version adds: "He will be able to sow salt and sand abundantly on that land. He will slay the evil clerics who have invaded the Apostolic See of Peter and Paul."

24. That is, he will be elected Emperor.

25. *Yspanos* here; *ypsicos* in Chaume. *Hispani* was used for Moslems in some crusading narratives.

26. This final sentence is missing in Chaume's version. As Reeves suggests, *Influence of Prophecy*, pp. 329–30, it seems to have been added by the followers of Telesphorus to place the traditional French version of the Last Emperor myth within an optimistic Joachite context.

27. On John of Winterthur, see P. Hosp, "Ketzertum und deutsche Kaisersage beim Minoriten Johann von Winterthur."

28. This unusual image is said to have been first used in the *Oraculum Cirilli*.

29. The seven-thousand-year scheme of history with astrological overtones is typical of the fifteenth century.

30. The imperial globe.

31. The conquering French Emperor of Telesphorus.

32. This might be seen as the *translatio imperii* theme applied to the papacy; see Herrmann, " 'Veniet aquila, de cuius volatu delebitur leo,' " p. 112.

33. I read *spiritualitas* rather than *spiritualitos* of Herrmann's text.

31. Apocalypticism, the Great Schism,
and the Conciliar Movement

1. The Roman line included Urban VI (1378–1389), Boniface IX (1389–1404), Innocent VII (1404–1406), and Gregory XII (1406–1415). The Avignon line included Clement VII (1378–1394) and Benedict XIII (1394–1423).

2. The most important study in the active field of Conciliar history has stressed the deep roots of Conciliarism in earlier medieval ecclesiology. See B. Tierney, *Foundations of the Conciliar Theory*.

3. By the decrees *Haec sancta* (April 6, 1415) and *Frequens* (October 9, 1417). For the debate on the significance of these decrees, see R. McNally, "Conciliarism and the Papacy."

4. The most recent discussion of John's *corpus*, J. McCall, "The Writings of John of Legnano with a List of Manuscripts," p. 431, rightly considers the attribution doubtful.

5. There are at least eight surviving fifteenth-century mss. in two versions; a shorter, and apparently original version in two parts; and a longer version in three parts, known as the "Mestre Prophecy" and printed in the 1516 Venice edition of the *Expositio Joachim in librum beati Cirilli* . . . , ff. 51v–52r.

6. Turin, Bibl. Naz. Univ. ms. K². IV.13, ff. 128r–129r. This important ms. has been partially studied by G. Vinay, "Riflessi culturali sconosciuti del minoritismo subalpino." Vinay does not discuss Tebaldus' other prophetic anthology in ms. K². V.8.

7. For a list of his authentic prophetic writings, see S. Brettle, *San Vicente Ferrer und sein literarischen Nachlass*, pp. 157–95.

8. On Vincent's apocalyptic ideas, see Reeves, *Influence of Prophecy, passim;* E. Delaruelle, "L'Antéchrist chez S. Vincent Ferrer, S. Bernardin de Sienne et autour Jeanne d'Arc," pp. 40–46; and J. Rohr, "Die Prophetie im letzten Jahrhundert vor der Reformation," pp. 32–36.

9. For a brief discussion of Cusa's work, Rohr, pp. 37–38. The future cardinal divided the history of the Church into thirty-three periods of fifty years each ("Jubilee Years") that paralleled the life of Christ. Antichrist was to come in the thirty-fourth Jubilee Year, i.e., after 1700 (see 4:93–97 of the *Opera omnia* in the Leipzig edition).

10. The two Vatican mss. begin with a pseudonymous ascription to Joachim omitted here. Tebaldus' glosses interpret the eagle as an emperor and Liguria as Lombardy.

11. Tebaldus interprets the Elephant as Rome.

12. The two bridegrooms are clearly two rival popes, possibly Urban VI and Clement VII if the text reflects the events of the beginning of the Schism.

13. The Venice and Turin mss. have "will not be found."

14. Tebaldus interprets the *leo gallicus* as "The Duke of Burgundy carrying lions on his shield," though he also seems to admit the interpretation as the king of France in a subsequent gloss. The conflict between the German Eagle and the French Lion may be totally prophetic, but it might also reflect the struggle between Charles of Durazzo and Louis of Anjou in the period 1380–1383. Charles claimed the throne of Naples in the name of Louis of Hungary, invaded Italy in 1380, and was crowned by Urban VI in 1381. In 1382, Louis of Anjou, the French claimant to Naples who had been crowned at Avignon by Clement VII, invaded Italy with such force that Charles was compelled to avoid battle. At this juncture Charles was given financial aid by his Florentine allies. For the history of this struggle, see N. Valois, *La France et le grand schisme d'Occident*, vol. 2.

15. Reading *viduatam* with the Turin ms. The author expects the victor in the struggle to restore the true pope to a Rome long abandoned through the Avignon captivity. If the text

belongs to the early years of the Schism, it would have to date before 1384, the year of the death of Louis of Anjou.

16. *Mensam* in three mss.; *rixum* in the Venice ms.

17. Reading *prosperabit* with the Venice ms.

18. The *leo potentissimus* is undoubtedly a French king who becomes the Last Emperor, i.e., takes the wings of the Eagle to himself. The author of this text is generally in the Telesphoran camp.

19. The Venice ms. continues with a prophecy regarding a "royal griffin born in France" that appears to be a later addition.

20. *The Report* was sent to the Avignon Pope Benedict XIII in July of 1412.

21. This excludes any Joachite third *status*.

22. The text continues with a rebuttal of two false opinions: first, that the time from Christ until the End of the world will be equal to the time from Creation to Christ; and second, that there remain as many years until the End as there are verses in the Psalms.

23. That is, since the time of the Avignon Captivity.

24. According to a story found in the life of Dominic in the *Legenda aurea* Christ was about to destroy the world with three lances when he was forestalled by the Blessed Virgin along with Dominic and Francis.

25. Gregory the Great, *Prima Homilia in Evangelia* (*PL* 76, c. 1089).

26. Vincent then enumerates the schisms down to "The tenth under our Lord Pope Benedict XIII, true Vicar of Jesus Christ . . ."

27. Apparently a group of Tuscan Fraticelli.

28. The Dominican goes on to list other reasons—further private revelations, confessions of demons during exorcisms, and the appearance of precursors of the Antichrist, especially false religious.

29. From a collection of sermons preached at Freiburg, Switzerland, in March of 1404.

30. There follows a discussion based on Dan. 12:6–11. On this text, see R. Lerner, "Refreshment of the Saints," pp. 132–33.

31. The first sermon of this series (Brettle, *San Vicente Ferrer*, p. 178) said that the Antichrist: "will allow men to marry four, six, or as many wives as they want, and the same for women. Demons will take human form becoming *incubi* and *succubi*."

32. The Hussite Movement

1. H. Kaminsky, *A History of the Hussite Revolution*, p. 3.

2. My chief guide has been the detailed and excellent work of Kaminsky. See also his earlier articles, especially "Chiliasm and the Hussite Revolution." I have also made use of the brief work of the Czech Marxist historian J. Macek, *The Hussite Movement in Bohemia*, and the East German E. Werner, "Popular Ideologies in Late Medieval Europe."

3. As Kaminsky points out (*Hussite Revolution*, ch. 3), what was at issue in the Utraquist controversy was really a fundamental split in ways of viewing the nature of the Church.

4. Cf. Kaminsky, pp. 351–58; and R. Kestenberg-Gladstein, "The Third Reich: A Fifteenth-Century Polemic against Joachimism and its Background."

5. E. Werner, "Popular Ideologies," p. 361.

6. The most complete account is in Czech, J. Macek, *Tabór v husitském revolucním hnuti*. In English, besides Kaminsky, see N. Cohn, *The Pursuit of the Millennium*, pp. 205–22.

7. Kaminsky's emphasis on the importance of severing ties as a motif to radical action is well taken. *Hussite Revolution*, pp. 317–26, 341–42.

8. On the comparison, Werner, "Popular Ideologies," pp. 357–61.

9. Marxist historians, such as Macek, Werner, and Töpfer, have tended to view the Taborites as essentially an expression of class struggle. Kaminsky, while recognizing the importance of the economic and social elements, rightly takes issue with this, e.g., p. 285, note 74; pp. 287–89, 341–42.

10. In the words of Macek (*The Hussite Movement*, p. 37): "It was the first time in world history that a rebellious people, dreaming of a classless society, set to work and built a new town in which from the beginning decisive power lay in the hands of the common people."

11. There are still doubts about the origin of the term. Most would connect it with "Beghardi," a generic name applied to many heretical groups.

12. The wandering Pikarts were called "Adamites" by their persecutors because of their use of ritual nudity and promiscuous sex practices. See T. Büttner and E. Werner, *Circumcellionen und Adamiten*, pp. 73–141.

13. Tabor seemed to maintain an interest in apocalypticism down to the end. Its first and only bishop, Nicholas Biskupec (1420–1452) wrote a lengthy commentary on Revelation.

14. Hus's response to the articles drawn up against him in 1412 by Michael de Causis.

15. Hus's words were not all that radical for the time. As a matter of fact, they are less severe than those of Wycliff in his *De Christo et suo adversario Antichristo*.

16. Bernard's *De consideratione* was a popular text among the Hussites.

17. A passage from a Czech speech opening the Hussite Diet of January 12, 1426, and ascribed by F. M. Bartoš to Jakoubek.

18. A circular letter in Czech issued from one of the hilltop centers of early Taboritism.

19. Kaminsky argues that the "great abomination" refers to the agreements between the moderate Hussites and the Catholics that in the Taborite view threatened the apocalyptic work of reform.

20. Lawrence was a Hussite Master in Prague who belonged to the moderate party. He wrote his valuable *Hussite History* or *Chronicle* in the 1420s.

21. This hostile account in Czech comes from the pen of a Master originally quite forward in the Prague reform, but later violently opposed.

22. Probably a reference to the failure of the predicted End of the world in February 1420.

23. The Taborite call for holy war provoked a considerable debate in the Hussite movement.

24. Kaminsky has argued that the use of Scripture in this text shows definite Joachite tendencies, especially in the concordances of the Old and New Testaments (see *Hussite Revolution*, p. 351, note 119).

25. Among the best sources for the views of the Taborites, especially the Pikarts, are the lists of articles drawn up against them by the Masters of Prague in 1420. A number of versions of these exist, both in Czech and in Latin. The extracts are drawn from the full list of seventy-two with which the moderates confronted the Taborites at a meeting in Prague on December 10. The list combines both main-line Taborite positions and some specifically Pikart ones.

26. That is, the Roman Church.

27. This text from Matt. 24:28 served as a touchstone for Taborite claims for the necessity of extreme violence.

28. A series of articles follows (numbers 20 to 33) describing the characteristics of the millennial kingdom, among them the end of all suffering as well as material exactions of one man from another.

29. The Taborites were not Joachite in their vocabulary—*regnum reparatum*, "Restored Kingdom," is their favorite term for the millennium; but the content, as here, is frequently that of extreme Joachitism.

30. Articles 29 to 33 deal with marriage, allowing marriage to close relatives, refusal of the marriage debt, and freedom of separation from family members who refuse to flee at the time of vengeance. Women are allowed equal rights with men.

31. In the later articles, especially numbers 44 to 50, a number of errors concerning the Eucharist are advanced that are characteristic of the Pikarts and not of the majority of Tabor.

32. This text, probably by Martin Húska, was written in either 1420 or 1421. For the context of the document, see Kaminsky, *Hussite Revolution*, pp. 405–7.

33. This totally spiritual interpretation of eating and drinking Christ's body and blood was the root of the Pikart rejection of the Eucharist.

34. That is, the Eucharist.

33. Germany on the Eve of the Reformation

1. See the essays edited by G. Strauss, *Pre-Reformation Germany*.

2. Only a handful of studies have surveyed this rich field. Among older works, see J. Rohr, "Die Prophetie im letzten Jahrhundert vor der Reformation als Geschichtsquelle und Geschichtsfaktor"; and H. Preuss, *Die Vorstellungen vom Antichrist im späteren Mittelalter*. More recently, see W.-E. Peuckert, *Die Grosse Wende;* and D. Kurze, "Nationale Regungen in der spätmittelalterlichen Prophetie."

3. Edited by H. Koller, *MGH. Staatsschriften des Späteren Mittelalters*, VI. For apocalyptic sections, see especially the description of the coming Priest-King Frederick of Lantnaw, pp. 332–44.

4. He was the last emperor crowned at Rome (1453). One chronicler recounts that Pope Nicholas V asked him what he thought of the prophecies made about him and he hastened to assure the pope of his good intentions toward the Church.

5. Rohr, "Die Prophetie," p. 461.

6. For this group, cf. O. Schiff, "Die Wirsberger"; Cohn, *The Pursuit of the Millennium*, pp. 223–25; Kestenberg-Gladstein, "The Third Reich," pp. 271–74; and Reeves, *Influence of Prophecy*, pp. 476–79.

7. Kurze, "Nationale Regungen," pp. 14–16, notes the revival of German prophecy after the death of Frederick III.

8. Reeves, *Influence of Prophecy*, pp. 347–51, contains a useful introduction. The study of D. Kurze, *Johannis Lichtenberger*, has not been available to me, but I have been able to make use of the same author's "Prophecy and History." The *Pronosticatio* was translated into German, French, Dutch, Italian, and English. Luther published an edition with his own preface in 1527, and Paracelsus an extensive commentary.

9. F. Zoepl, "Wolfgang Aytinger—Ein Deutscher Zeit-und Gesinnungsgenosse Savonarolas."

10. The work, known in only one ms., consists of two parts, a lengthy historical and prophetic introduction (the Hundred Chapters) and a list of laws to govern the new empire (the Statutes). See H. Haupt, "Ein Oberrheinischer Revolutionär aus dem Zeitalter Kaiser Maximilians I," pp. 77–228; and in English, Cohn, *Pursuit of the Millennium*, pp. 119–26. The fundamental work is now the edition and study of A. Franke and G. Zschäbitz, *Das Buch der hundert Kapitel und der vierzig Statuten des sogenannten oberrheinischen Revolutionärs*.

11. The caption for the accompanying illustration. Most chapters are given a suitable woodcut illustration.

12. Lichtenberger has constructed a fairly authentic Joachite concordance.

13. There follows a division of cocks into three categories—bad, good, best.

14. The source of this legendary history is apparently *The Book of the Frankish Kings* mentioned below.

15. The account of the four Angelic Popes given here is standard Joachite fare.

16. I have tried to give the sense of the whole of the fifth and last chapter of the *Commentary*. This has made necessary many omissions. Section captions are given in italics.

17. There follows a passage linking the seven angels to seven persecutions of the Church, five of which have already passed.

18. In what follows the prophet Norseus, the pseudo-Joachite *In Hieremiam,* and the Cumaean Sibyl are all cited in support of the calculations drawn from Methodius.

19. Aytinger counts eight emperors in all down to Mohammed II (1451–1481), but he says that the first was not counted by John since he did not conquer any Christian territory.

20. Bayazit II (1481–1512).

21. The rest of the chapter keeps the same exegetical structure.

22. Aytinger here repeats earlier material about the seven Turkish emperors. One interesting note is that he expects mass conversions of Christians to Mohammedanism during the time of its supremacy.

23. Philip of Burgundy, the same prince in whom Lichtenberger put his hopes.

24. A prophecy concerning a "triangular rock" is then cited and applied to Ladislaus II, king of Poland, Hungary and Bohemia (1471–1516).

25. The two final scourges will be those of Gog and Magog and of the Antichrist, but Aytinger is not concerned with them here.

34. Savonarola and Late Medieval Italian Apocalypticism

1. The Cataldus prophecy has been studied by G. Tognetti, "Le fortune della pretesa profezia di San Cataldo." The same author has also provided a valuable study of the prophetic literature of the period in his "Note sul Profetismo nel Rinascimento e la Letteratura Relativa," pp. 129–57.

2. Ubertino's *Arbor vitae* was printed at Venice in 1488. In the early sixteenth century a Venetian group led by the Augustinian Hermit Silvestro Meuccio began the publication of the works of Joachim, both authentic and spurious (Reeves, *Influence of Prophecy,* pp. 262–68).

3. Cf. E. Garin, "L'attesa dell età nuova e la 'Renovatio' "; A. Chastel, "L'Antéchrist à la Renaissance," pp. 177–86; and D. Weinstein, *Savonarola and Florence,* ch. 4.

4. Reeves, *Influence of Prophecy,* pp. 430–31.

5. The best account of Savonarola the prophet is found in D. Weinstein cited above, a book on which I am heavily dependent. Also important is the classic R. Ridolfi, *The Life of Girolamo Savonarola.*

6. Weinstein, *Savonarola,* pp. 88–91.

7. Charles VIII was crowned at fourteen; there was actually some disagreement among the extant Latin and vernacular versions of the Second Charlemagne whether the coronation was to take place in his thirteenth or fourteenth year. See Reeves, *Influence of Prophecy,* pp. 354–58; and Chaume, "Une prophétie relative à Charles VI," pp. 31–35.

8. For the prophetic dimensions of Charles's invasion, see H. Delaborde, *L'Expédition de Charles VIII en Italie,* pp. 313–20.

9. Weinstein, *Savonarola,* pp. 67, 77, 132, 178–79, 309, 374–77.

10. Weinstein, p. 116.

11. For a summary of his views during this period, see Weinstein, pp. 161–82, who points out that for the Dominican preacher it was always the necessity for reform and not the coherence of his apocalyptic views that was essential.

12. See A. Chastel, "L'Apocalypse en 1500."

13. Among the most famous of Savonarola's sermons, this piece was preached on January 13, 1495, after the departure of Charles VIII. For the context, see Ridolfi, *Life of Savonarola*, pp. 106–12.

14. Later in the sermon, especially in the parable of the fig tree, Savonarola attacks the corruption of the clergy with vigor.

15. The Dominican mentions Joachim with approbation several times, but in the *Compendium revelationis* he denies any serious influence, see A. Crucitti, ed., *Compendio di Rivelazione*, p. 169. Savonarola may not have had extensive knowledge of Joachite texts and toward the end of his career was naturally anxious to assert his own independence as a prophet. However, as M. Reeves has said: "when he goes on to the message of *renovatio* it is difficult to see where his hope had been fed except at some Joachimist spring." *Influence of Prophecy*, p. 435.

16. The "figures" are the various symbolic portrayals of the coming tribulation found in Scripture (e.g., the four horsemen of Revelation). Savonarola also makes use of parables of his own construction and of his foreknowledge of future events through exterior signs and inward visions.

17. Non-scriptural words of God (given in Latin) addressed to Florence through the prophet.

18. The *Compendium* was published in the Summer and Fall of 1495 in both Italian and Latin versions. Weinstein, *Savonarola,* pp. 68–77, has shown that the prophet gives a somewhat "doctored" version of his career that presents greater continuity than was actually the case.

19. Savonarola had not made the unique role of Florence an element in his early apocalyptic preaching, as this passage suggests, nor was the minatory preaching begun in the city, but rather at San Gimignano.

20. The optimistic, millenarian element of Savonarola's later thought becomes evident here.

21. Ficino (1433–1499) was one of the most famous of the Florentine Humanists and Platonists. Under the influence of his friend Giovanni Pico della Mirandola, he had been sympathetic to Savonarola in late 1494, but this letter of spring 1498 shows the unremitting hatred he later had toward the prophet.

22. Ficino's own word play—*saevus Nero* (savage Nero).

35. Christopher Columbus

1. *Libro de las Profécias*, C. de Lollis, ed., in *Raccolta di Documenti e Studi*, p. 148. Columbus says that the prediction was found in a letter from the Genoese legates to the monarchs in 1492, but surviving copies contain no such reference. The editor suggests that Columbus was using an *Oraculum Turcicum* of uncertain date which is frequently printed with the Pseudo-Joachite *Vaticinia de summis pontificibus*.

2. The best study of this side of Columbus is to be found in J. Phelan, *The Millennial Kingdom of the Franciscans in the New World*, pp. 19–23.

3. *Antiquities*, 8:7.

4. 2 Chron. 9:13–14, and 1 Kings 10:14–15.

5. The Aurea was the gold-producing region of the Malay peninsula.

6. See the account in I Chron. 22.

7. A reference to the same pseudo-Joachite prophecy mentioned in *The Book of Prophecies*.

8. Columbus apparently had knowledge of accounts of the Mendicant missionaries.

Bibliography

The primary and secondary sources for the history of medieval apocalypticism are immense. The texts from which the translations for this volume have been made are briefly listed at the end of each selection. More complete references, as well as a list of the major studies used in the course of this work, are given here.

Achelis, H. "Testamentum domini nostri Jesu Christi." In *Realencyclopädie für protestantische Theologie und Kirche,* 19:557–59, 24:560. Leipzig: Hinrichs, 1896–1913.

Ahlström, G. W. "Prophecy." In *Encyclopaedia Britannica: Macropaedia,* 15:62–68. Chicago: Encyclopaedia Britannica, 1976.

Aichele, Klaus. *Das Antichristdrama des Mittelalters der Reformation und Gegenreformation.* The Hague: M. Nijhoff, 1974.

Alexander, Paul J. "Byzantium and the Migration of Literary Works and Motifs: The Legend of the Last Roman Emperor." *Mediaevalia et Humanistica* (1971), n.s. 2:47–82.

—— "Les débuts des conquêtes arabes en Sicile et la tradition apocalyptique Byzantino-Slave." *Bollettino del Centro di Studi filologici e linguistici siciliani* (1973), 12:5–35.

—— "Historiens byzantins et croyances eschatologiques." In *Actes du XIIe congrès international d'études byzantines,* 2:1–8. Belgrade: Naučno Delo, 1964.

—— "Medieval Apocalypses as Historical Sources." *American Historical Review* (1968), 73:1997–2018.

—— *The Oracle of Baalbek: The Tiburtine Sibyl in Greek Dress.* Washington, D.C.: Dumbarton Oaks, 1967.

Alphandéry, Paul. "Mahomet-Antichrist dans le moyen âge latin." In *Mélanges Hartwig Derenbourg,* pp. 261–77. Paris: Leroux, 1909.

Alphandéry, Paul and Alphonse Dupront. *La Chrétienté et l'idée de la croisade.* 2 vols. Paris: Albin Michel, 1954–59.

Amann, E. "Testament de Notre-Seigneur Jésus-Christ." In *Dictionnaire de théologie catholique,* 15:194–200. Paris: Letouzey and Ané, 1923–50.

Anagnine, Eugenio. *Dolcino e il movimento ereticale all'inizio del Trecento.* Biblioteca di cultura, vol. 69. Florence: La nuova Italia, 1964.

Anderson, Andrew R. *Alexander's Gate: Gog and Magog and the Enclosed Nations.* Monographs of the Mediaeval Academy of America, no. 5. Cambridge, Mass.: Mediaeval Academy of America, 1932.

Avi-Yonah, Michael. *The Jews of Palestine: A Political History from the Bar Kokhba War to the Arab Conquest.* New York: Schocken, 1976.

Baethgen, Friedrich. *Der Engelpapst: Idee und Erscheinung.* Leipzig: Koehler and Amelang, 1943.

Baluze, Étienne. *Miscellanea.* 7 vols. Paris: F. Muguet, 1678–1715.

Baraut, Cipriano. "Un Tratado Inédito de Joaquin de Fiore." *Analecta Sacra Tarraconensia* (1951), 24:33–122.

Barkun, Michael. *Disaster and the Millennium.* New Haven: Yale University Press, 1974.

Barnes, Timothy D. "The Chronology of Montanism." *Journal of Theological Studies* (1970), n.s., 21:403–8.

Beck, Edmund, ed. *Des heiligen Ephraem des Syrers Sermones III.* Corpus Scriptorum Christianorum Orientalium, vols. 320–321: Scriptores Syri, vols. 138–139. Louvain: Secretariat du Corpus SCO, 1972.

Bell, A. Robert. *"Muspilli:* Apocalypse as Political Threat." *Studies in the Literary Imagination* (1975), 8:75–104.

Benz, E. *Ecclesia Spiritualis.* Stuttgart: Kohlhammer, 1934.

Betz, Hans Dieter. "On the Problem of the Religio-Historical Understanding of Apocalypticism." In *Journal for Theology and the Church:* vol. 6, R. W. Funk, ed., *Apocalypticism,* pp. 134–56. New York: Herder and Herder, 1969.

Bezzola, Gian Andri. *Die Mongolen in abendländischer Sicht, 1220–1270.* Bern and Munich: Francke, 1974.

Bidez, Joseph and Franz Cumont. *Les mages héllenisées.* 2 vols. Paris: Les Belles Lettres, 1938.

Bietenhard, Hans. "The Millennial Hope in the Early Church." *Scottish Journal of Theology* (1953), 6:12–30.

Bigalli, Davide. *I Tartari e l'Apocalisse: Ricerche sull'escatologia in Adamo Marsh e Ruggero Bacone.* Florence: La nuova Italia, 1971.

Bignami-Odier, Jeanne. *Études sur Jean de Roquetaillade.* Paris: Vrin, 1952.

—— "Les visions de Robert d'Uzès." *Archivum Fratrum Praedicatorum* (1955), 25:258–310.

Bignami-Odier, Jeanne and G. Levi della Vida. "Une version latine de l'apocalypse syro-arabe de Serge-Bahira." *Mélanges d'archéologie et d'histoire* (1950), 62:125–48.

Bihel, S. "S. Franciscus fuitne Angelus Sexti Sigilli?" *Antonianum* (1927), 2:59–90.

Bischoff, Bernhard. "Die lateinischen Übersetzungen und Bearbeitungen aus den 'Oracula Sibyllina.' " In *Mittelalterliche Studien,* 1:150–71. Stuttgart: Hiersemann, 1966.

Bloch, Ernst. *Man On His Own.* New York: Herder and Herder, 1970.

Bloch, Marc. "A Contribution toward a Comparative History of European Societies." In *Land and Work in Mediaeval Europe,* pp. 44–81. Berkeley and Los Angeles: University of California Press, 1967.

Bloomfield, Morton W. "Joachim of Flora: A Critical Survey of his Canon, Teachings, Sources, Biography, and Influence." *Traditio* (1957), 13:249–311.

Bloomfield, Morton W. and Marjorie Reeves. "The Penetration of Joachism into Northern Europe." *Speculum* (1954), 29:772–93.

Borst, Arno. *Der Turmbau zu Babel.* 4 vols. Stuttgart: Hiersemann, 1957–63.

Bostock, John Knight. *A Handbook on Old High German Literature.* Oxford: Clarendon Press, 1955.

Bousset, Wilhelm. *The Antichrist Legend*. London: Hutchinson, 1896; translated from the original German of 1895.

—— "Beiträge zur Geschichte der Eschatologie." *Zeitschrift für Kirchengeschichte* (1899–1900), 20:103–31, 261–90.

—— *Die Offenbarung Johannis*. 1906; reprint, Göttingen: Vandenhoeck and Ruprecht, 1966.

Boyle, M. O'Rourke. "Irenaeus' Millennial Hope: A Polemical Weapon." *Recherches de théologie ancienne et médiévale* (1969), 36:5–16.

Braun, René. *Quodvultdeus: Livre des promesses et des prédictions de Dieu*. SC, vols. 101–102. Paris: Cerf, 1964.

Bredero, Adriaan, H. "Jerusalem dans l'Occident Médiévale." In *Mélanges offerts à René Crozet*, 1:259–71. Poitiers: Société d'Études Médiévales, 1966.

Brettle, Sigismund. *San Vicente Ferrer und sein literarischer Nachlass*. Vorreformationsgeschichtliche Forschungen, vol. 10. Münster: Aschendorff, 1924.

Brezzi, P. "Ottone di Frisinga." *Bollettino dell'Istituto storico italiano per il Medio Evo* (1939), 54:129–328.

Budge, E. A. Wallis. *The History of Alexander the Great*. Cambridge: At the University Press, 1889.

Büttner, Theodora and Ernst Werner. *Circumcellionen und Adamiten: Zwei Formen mittelalterlicher Haeresie*. Berlin: Akademie, 1959.

Burr, David. "The Apocalyptic Element in Olivi's Critique of Aristotle." *Church History* (1971), 40:15–29.

—— *The Persecution of Peter Olivi*. Transactions of the American Philosophical Society, vol. 66, part 5. Philadelphia: American Philosophical Society, 1976.

—— "Petrus Ioannis Olivi and the Philosophers." *Franciscan Studies* (1971), 31:41–71.

Burridge, Kenelm. *New Heaven, New Earth: A Study of Millenarian Activities*. New York: Schocken, 1969.

Callaey, Frédégand. *L'Idéalisme franciscain spirituel au XIVe siècle: Étude sur Ubertin de Casale*. Louvain: Bureau du Recueil, 1911.

Cantor, Norman F. *Church, Kingship, and Lay Investiture in England, 1089–1135*. Princeton, N.J.: Princeton University Press, 1958.

Cary, George. *The Medieval Alexander*. Cambridge: At the University Press, 1967.

Caspar, Erich. *Geschichte des Papsttums*. 2 vols. Tübingen: Mohr, 1930–33.

Caspari, C. P. *Briefe, Abhandlungen, und Predigten aus den zwei letzten Jahrhunderten des kirchlicher Alterthums und dem Anfang des Mittelalters*. 1890; reprint, Brussels: Culture et Civilisation, 1964.

Chadwick, H. Munro and N. Kershaw Chadwick. *The Growth of Literature*. 3 vols. Cambridge: At the University Press, 1932.

Chamberlin, E. R. *Antichrist and the Millennium*. New York: Dutton, 1975.

Charles, Robert Henry. *A Critical and Exegetical Commentary on the Revelation of St. John*. The International Critical Commentary, vol. 44. Edinburgh: T. & T. Clark, 1920.

Charles, Robert Henry et al., ed. *The Apocrypha and Pseudepigrapha of the Old Testament in English*. Oxford: Clarendon Press, 1913.

Chastel, André. "L'Antéchrist à la Renaissance." In E. Castelli, ed., *L'Umanesimo e il Demoniaco nell'Arte*, pp. 177–86. Rome: Fratelli Bocca, 1953.

—— "L'Apocalypse en 1500: La fresque de l'Antéchrist à la chapelle Saint-Brice d'Orvieto." *Bibliothèque d'humanisme et renaissance* (1952), 14:124–40.

Bibliography of Secondary Sources

Chaume, Maurice. "Une prophétie relative à Charles VI." *Revue du moyen âge latin* (1947), 3:27–42.
Chenu, M. D. *Nature, Man, and Society in the Twelfth Century.* Chicago: University of Chicago Press, 1968.
Clarke, Basil, ed. *The Life of Merlin.* Cardiff: University of Wales Press, 1973.
Classen, Peter. "Eschatologische Ideen und Armutsbewegungen im 11. und 12. Jahrhunderten." In *Povertà e Richezza nella Spiritualità dei Secoli XI e XII,* pp. 128–62. Convegni del Centro di Studi sulla Spiritualità Medievale, vol. 8. Todi: Accademia Tudertina, 1969.
—— *Gerhoch von Reichersberg.* Wiesbaden: Steiner, 1960.
Cohn, Norman. *The Pursuit of the Millennium.* Rev. ed. New York: Oxford University Press, 1970.
Collins, Adela Y. "The Early Christian Apocalypses." For the Society of Biblical Literature. Working Seminar on Apocalypticism, forthcoming.
Collins, John. "Apocalyptic Eschatology as the Transcendence of Death." *Catholic Biblical Quarterly* (1974), 36:21–43.
—— "The Jewish Apocalypses." For the Society of Biblical Literature. Working Seminar on Apocalypticism, forthcoming.
—— "Jewish Apocalyptic against Its Hellenistic Near Eastern Environment." *Bulletin of the American Schools of Oriental Research* (1975), 220:27–36.
—— "Pseudonymity, Historical Reviews, and the Genre of the Revelation of John." *Catholic Biblical Quarterly* (1977), 39:330–43.
—— *The Sibylline Oracles of Egyptian Judaism.* The Society of Biblical Literature Dissertation Series no. 13. Missoula, Mont.: Scholars' Press, 1974.
—— "The Symbolism of Transcendence in Jewish Apocalyptic." *Biblical Research* (1974), 19:5–22.
Congar, Yves. "Aspects ecclésiologiques de la querelle entre mendiants et séculiers." *Archives d'histoire doctrinale et littéraire du moyen âge* (1961), 28:35–151.
—— "Ecclesia ab Abel." In Marcel Reding, ed., *Abhandlungen über Theologie und Kirche: Festschrift für Karl Adam,* pp. 79–108. Düsseldorf: Patmos, 1952.
Cooper, James and Arthur J. Maclean, trans. *The Testament of the Lord.* Edinburgh: T. & T. Clark, 1902.
Coulton, George Gordon. *From St. Francis to Dante.* 2d ed., rev. Philadelphia: University of Pennsylvania Press, 1972.
Cross, Frank M. "New Directions in the Study of Apocalyptic." In *Journal for Theology and the Church:* vol. 6, R. W. Funk, ed., *Apocalypticism,* pp. 157–65. New York: Herder and Herder, 1969.
Crucitti, Angela, ed. *Compendio di Rivelazione: testo volgare e latino e dialogus De veritate prophetica: Girolamo Savonarola.* Rome: A. Belardetti, 1974.
Daniel, E. Randolph. *The Franciscan Concept of Mission in the High Middle Ages.* Lexington: University Press of Kentucky, 1975.
—— "A Re-examination of the Origins of Franciscan Joachitism." *Speculum* (1968), 43:671–76.
—— "Apocalyptic Conversion: The Joachite Alternative to the Crusades." *Traditio* (1969), 25:127–54.
—— "Roger Bacon and the *De seminibus scripturarum.*" *Mediaeval Studies* (1972), 34:462–67.
—— "Spirituality and Poverty: Angelo da Clareno und Ubertino da Casale." *Mediaevalia et Humanistica* (1973), 4:89–98.

Daniélou, Jean. *The Theology of Jewish Christianity*. Chicago: Regnery, 1964.

Davis, Charles T. "Le Pape Jean XXII et les spirituels: Ubertin de Casale." In *Franciscains d'Oc,* pp. 263–83. Cahiers de Fanjeaux, vol. 10. Toulouse: Privat, 1975.

Dawson, Christopher H. *The Mongol Mission*. New York: Sheed and Ward, 1955.

Delaborde, Henri François. *L'Expédition de Charles VIII en Italie*. Paris: Firmin Didot, 1888.

Delaruelle, Etienne. "L'Antéchrist chez S. Vincent Ferrer, S. Bernardin de Sienne, et autour de Jeanne d'Arc." In *L'Attesa dell'Età Nuova nella Spiritualità della Fine del Medioevo,* pp. 39–64. Convegni del Centro di Studi sulla Spiritualità Medievale III. Todi: Accademia Tudertina, 1962.

Demougeot, Émilienne. "Saint Jérôme, les oracles sibyllins et Stilicon." *Revue des études anciennes* (1952), 54:83–92.

Denifle, Heinrich. "Das *Evangelium aeternum* und die Commission zu Anagni." *Archiv für Literatur- und Kirchengeschichte des Mittelalters* (1885), 1:49–98.

Denis, Albert Marie. *Introduction aux pseudépigraphes grecs d'Ancien Testament.* Leiden: Brill, 1970.

Denzinger, Heinrich. *Enchiridion Symbolorum*. Rome: Herder, 1957.

D'Evelyn, Charlotte. "The Middle English Metrical Version of the *Revelationes* of Methodius." *Publications of the Modern Language Society of America* (1918), 33:135–203.

Diehl, C. "De quelques croyances byzantines sur la fin de Constantinople." *Byzantinische Zeitschrift* (1930), 30:192–96.

Diels, Hermann. *Sibyllinische Blätter*. Berlin: G. Reimer, 1890.

Döllinger, J. J. Ignaz von. *Beiträge zur Sektengeschichte des Mittelalters*. 2 vols. Munich: Beck, 1890; reprint, New York: Burt Franklin, 1960.

Donckel, Emil. "Studien über die Prophezeiung des Fr. Telesphorus von Cosenza, O.F.M." *Archivum Franciscanum Historicum* (1933), 26:29–104, 282–314.

Doresse, Jean. *The Secret Books of the Egyptian Gnostics*. New York: Viking, 1960.

Douie, Decima L. *The Nature and Effect of the Heresy of the Fraticelli*. Manchester: Manchester University Press, 1932.

Dumézil, Georges. *Archaic Roman Religion*. 2 vols. Chicago: University of Chicago Press, 1970.

Edyvean, Walter. *Anselm of Havelberg and the Theology of History*. Rome: Pontificia Universitas Gregoriana, 1972.

Ehrle, Franz. "Arnaldo de Villanova ed i *Thomatiste*," *Gregorianum* (1920), 1:475–501.

—— "Petrus Johannis Olivi, sein Leben und seine Schriften." *Archiv für Literatur- und Kirchengeschichte des Mittelalters* (1887), 3:409–552.

—— "Die Spiritualen, ihr Verhältnis zum Franciscanerorden und zu den Fraticellen." *Archiv für Literatur- und Kirchengeschichte des Mittelalters* (1885), 1:509–69; (1886), 2:106–64, 249–336; (1887), 3:553–623; (1888), 4:1–190.

Erdmann, Carl. "Endkaiserglaube und Kreuzzugsgedanke im 11. Jahrhundert." *Zeitschrift für Kirchengeschichte* (1932), 51:384–414.

Eynde, Damien van den. *L'Oeuvre littéraire de Géroch de Reichersberg*. Rome: Athenaeum Antonianum, 1957.

Farrer, Austin M. *A Rebirth of Images: The Making of St. John's Apocalypse*. London: Dacre Press, 1949.

——— *The Revelation of St. John the Divine.* Oxford: Clarendon Press, 1964.

Fascher, Erich. "Testamentum Domini nostri Jesu Christi." In A. F. von Pauly and G. Wissowa, eds., *Realencyclopädie der classichen Altertumswissenschaft,* ser. 2, 5A:1016–1020. Stuttgart: Metzler, 1894–1952.

Festinger, Leon, Henry W. Riecken, and Stanley Schachter. *When Prophecy Fails.* Minneapolis: University of Minnesota Press, 1956; reprint, New York: Harper and Row, 1964.

Finke, Heinrich. *Aus den Tagen Bonifaz VIII.* Vorreformationsgeschichtliche Forschungen, vol. 2. Münster: Aschendorff, 1902.

Fletcher, Angus. *Allegory: The Theory of a Symbolic Mode.* Ithaca, N.Y.: Cornell University Press, 1964.

Flood, David. *Peter Olivi's Rule Commentary.* Wiesbaden: Steiner, 1972.

Focillon, Henri. *The Year 1000.* New York: Harper and Row, 1971.

Folliet, G. "La typologie du *sabbat* chez saint Augustin: Son interprétation millénariste entre 388 et 400." *Revue des études augustiniennes* (1956), 2:371–90.

Freedman, David N. "The Flowering of Apocalyptic." In *Journal for Theology and the Church:* vol. 6, R. W. Funk, ed., *Apocalypticism,* pp. 166–74. New York: Herder and Herder, 1969.

Fritzsche, C. "Die lateinischen Visionen des Mittelalters bis zur Mitte des 12. Jahrhunderts." *Romanische Forschungen* (1886), 2:247–79.

Froom, Le Roy Edwin. *The Prophetic Faith of Our Fathers.* 4 vols. Washington, D.C.: Review and Herald, 1946–54.

Frugoni, Arsenio. *Celestiniana.* Istituto Storico Italiano per il Medio Evo, Studi Storici, nos. 6–7. Rome: Sede dell'Istituto, 1953.

Funk, Robert W. "Apocalyptic as an Historical and Theological Problem in Current New Testament Scholarship." In *Journal for Theology and the Church:* vol. 6, R. W. Funk, ed., *Apocalypticism,* pp. 175–91. New York: Herder and Herder, 1969.

Garin, Eugenio. "L'Attesa dell'età nuova e la *renovatio.*" In *L'Attesa dell'Età Nuova nella Spiritualità della Fine del Medioevo,* pp. 11–35. Convegni del Centro di Studi sulla Spiritualità Medievale, III. Todi: Accademia Tudertina, 1962.

Gebhart, Émile. "L'État d'âme d'un moine de l'an mil." *Revue des deux mondes* (1891), ser. 9, 107:600–28.

Geffcken, Johannes. *Die Komposition und Entstehungszeit der Oracula Sibyllina.* Leipzig: Hinrichs, 1902.

Godefroy, P. "Ubertin de Casale." In *Dictionnaire de théologie catholique,* 15: 2021–34. Paris: Letouzey and Ané, 1923–50.

Goez, Werner. *Translatio imperii: Ein Beitrag zur Geschichte des Geschichtsdenkens und der politischen Theorien im Mittelalter und in der frühen Neuzeit.* Tübingen: Mohr, 1958.

Graefe, Friedrich. *Die Publizistik in der letzten Epoche Kaiser Friedrichs II.* Heidelberger Abhandlungen zur mittleren und neueren Geschichte, no. 24. Heidelberg: C. Winter, 1909.

Grant, Robert M. *Augustus to Constantine.* New York: Harper and Row, 1970.

Grauert, Hermann. "Meister Johann von Toledo." *Sitzungsberichte der philosophisch- philologischen und der historischen Classe der Akademie der Wissenschaften zu Münich* (1901), pp. 111–325.

Gregorovius, Ferdinand. *History of the City of Rome in the Middle Ages.* 6 vols. London, 1898; reprint, New York: AMS Press, 1967.

Grundmann, Herbert. "Dante und Joachim von Fiore, zu Paradiso X-XII." *Deutsches Dante-Jahrbuch* (1932), 14:210–56.

—— "Frederico II e Gioacchino da Fiore." In D. C. West, ed., *Joachim of Fiore in Christian Thought*, 2:293–99. New York: Burt Franklin, 1975.

—— *Ketzergeschichte des Mittelalters.* Göttingen: Vandenhoeck and Ruprecht, 1963.

—— "Kirchenfreiheit und Kaisermacht um 1190 in der Sicht Joachims von Fiore." *Deutsches Archiv für Erforschung des Mittelalters* (1963), 19:353–96.

—— "*Liber de Flore:* Eine Schrift der Franziskaner-Spiritualen aus dem Anfang des 14. Jahrhunderts." *Historisches Jahrbuch* (1929), 49:33–91.

—— *Neue Forschungen über Joachim von Fiore.* Marburg: Simons, 1950.

—— "Die Papstprophetien des Mittelalters." *Archiv für Kulturgeschichte* (1929), 19:77–138.

—— Review of *Les Prophécies de Merlin,* by L. A. Paton. *Göttingische gelehrte Anzeigen* (1928), 190:562–83.

—— Review of '*De ortu et tempore Antichristi,*' by Robert Konrad. *Deutsches Archiv für Erforschung des Mittelalters* (1965), 21:636–37.

—— *Studien über Joachim von Fiore.* 1927; reprint, Darmstadt: W. B., 1966.

—— "Zur Biographie Joachims von Fiore und Rainers von Ponza." *Deutsches Archiv für Erforschung des Mittelalters* (1960), 16:437–546.

Hahn, Traugott. *Tyconius-Studien: Ein Beitrag zur Kirchen- und Dogmengeschichte des vierten Jahrhunderts.* Leipzig: Dieterich, 1900.

Hampe, K. "Eine frühe Verknüpfung der Weissagung vom Endkaiser mit Friedrich II und Konrad IV." *Sitzungsberichte der Heidelberger Akademie der Wissenschaften, phil.-hist. Klasse* (1917), vol. 8, part 6.

Hanning, Robert W. *The Vision of History in Early Britain.* New York: Columbia University Press, 1966.

Hanson, Paul D. *The Dawn of Apocalyptic.* Philadelphia: Fortress Press, 1975.

—— "Jewish Apocalyptic against Its Near Eastern Environment." *Revue Biblique* (1971), 78:31–58.

Hartman, Lars. *Prophecy Interpreted.* Coniectanea Biblica, New Testament, ser. 1, vol. 1. Lund, Sweden: Gleerup, 1966.

Haskins, Charles Homer. *Studies in the History of Mediaeval Science.* Cambridge, Mass.: Harvard University Press, 1927.

Haupt, H. "Ein Oberrheinischer Revolutionär aus dem Zeitalter Kaiser Maximilians I." *Westdeutsche Zeitschrift für Geschichte und Kunst,* Ergänzungsheft (1893), 8:77–228.

Herde, Peter. "Ein Pamphlet der päpstlichen Kurie gegen Kaiser Friedrich II. von 1245–46, *Eger cui lenia.*" *Deutsches Archiv für Erforschung des Mittelalters* (1967), 23:468–538.

Herrmann, Erwin. " 'Veniet aquila, de cuius volatu delebitur leo': Zur Gamaleon-Predigt des Johann von Wünschelburg." In K. Schnith, ed., *Festiva Lanx: Studien zum mittelalterlichen Geistesleben,* pp. 95–117. Munich: Salesianische Offizin, 1966.

Hertel, Gustav. *Urkundenbuch des Klosters Unser Lieben Frauen zu Magdeburg.* Halle: O. Hendel, 1878.

Hinnells, J. R. "The Zoroastrian Doctrine of Salvation in the Roman World: A

Study of the Oracle of Hystaspes." In E. J. Sharpe and J. R. Hinnells, eds., *Man and his Salvation: Studies in Memory of S. G. F. Brandon,* pp. 125–48. Manchester: Manchester University Press, 1973.

Hirsch-Reich, Beatrice. "Joachim von Fiore und das Judentum." In Paul Wilpert, ed., *Judentum im Mittelalter,* pp. 228–63. Miscellanea Mediaevalia, vol. 4. Berlin: de Gruyter, 1966.

Hoare, Frederick Russell. *The Western Fathers.* New York: Harper and Row, 1965.

Hobsbawm, Eric J. *Primitive Rebels: Studies in Archaic Forms of Social Movement in the 19th and 20th Centuries.* Manchester: Manchester University Press, 1959.

Holder-Egger, O. "Italienische Prophetieen des 13. Jahrhunderts." *Neues Archiv der Gesellschaft für ältere Deutsche Geschichtskunde* (1890), 15:143–78; (1905), 30:322–86; (1908), 33:96–187.

Hollman, Lennart, ed. *Den Heliga Birgittas "Revelationes Extravagantes."* Uppsala: Almquist and Wiksell, 1956.

Hosp, P. "Ketzertum und deutsche Kaisersage beim Minoriten Johann von Winterthur." *Franziskanische Studien* (1916), 3:161–68.

Houghton, H. P. "The Coptic Apocalypse." *Aegyptus* (1959), 39:40–91, 179–210.

Hübscher, Arthur. *Die Grosse Weissagung.* Utrecht: Heimeran, 1952.

Istrin, Vasilii Mikhailovich. *Otkrovenie Mefodiia Patarskago.* Moscow: n.p., 1897.

Jacob, E. F. "John of Roquetaillade." In *Essays in Later Medieval History,* pp. 175–94. Manchester: Manchester University Press; New York: Barnes and Noble, 1968.

James, M. R., ed. *Apocrypha Anecdota: A Collection of Thirteen Apocryphal Books and Fragments.* Texts and Studies: Contributions to Biblical and Patristic Literature, vol. 2, part 3. Cambridge: At the University Press, 1893.

James, M. R., trans. *The Apocryphal New Testament.* 2d. rev. ed. Oxford: Clarendon Press, 1953.

Jamison, Evelyn. *Admiral Eugenius of Sicily.* London: Oxford University Press, 1957.

Käsemann, Ernst. "The Beginnings of Christian Theology." In *Journal for Theology and the Church:* vol. 6, R. W. Funk, ed., *Apocalypticism,* pp. 17–46. New York: Herder and Herder, 1969.

Kahles, Wilhelm. *Geschichte als Liturgie: Die Geschichtstheologie des Rupertus von Deutz.* Münster: Aschendorff, 1960.

Kaminsky, Howard. "Chiliasm and the Hussite Revolution." *Church History* (1957), 26:43–71.

—— *A History of the Hussite Revolution.* Berkeley and Los Angeles: University of California Press, 1967.

Kaminsky, Howard et al., eds. *Master Nicholas of Dresden: The Old Color and the New.* Transactions of the American Philosophical Society, vol. 55, part. 1. Philadelphia: American Philosophical Society, 1965.

Kamlah, Wilhelm. *Apokalypse und Geschichtstheologie: Die mittelalterliche Auslegung der Apokalypse vor Joachim von Fiore.* Historische Studien, vol. 285. Berlin: Ebering, 1935; reprint, Vaduz: Kraus Reprints, 1965.

Kampers, Franz. *Kaiserprophetieen und Kaisersagen im Mittelalter.* Munich: H. Lüneburg, 1895.

—— *Alexander der Grosse und die Idee des Weltimperiums in Prophetie und Sage.* Frieburg-im-Breisgau: Herder, 1901.

Kantorowicz, Ernst. *Frederick the Second, 1194–1250.* London: Constable, 1931.
—— *Selected Studies.* Locust Valley, N.Y.: Augustin, 1965.
Kermode, Frank. *The Sense of an Ending: Studies in the Theory of Fiction.* London: Oxford University Press, 1966.
Kestenberg-Gladstein, Ruth. "The Third Reich: A Fifteenth-Century Polemic against Joachimism and Its Background." *Journal of the Warburg and Courtauld Institutes* (1955), 18:245–95.
Kirchmeyer, Jean. "Ephrem." In *Dictionnaire de spiritualité,* 4:788–822. Paris: Beauchesne, 1932– .
Kmosko, Michael. "Das Rätsel des Pseudomethodius." *Byzantion* (1931), 6:273–96.
Koch, J. "Die Grundlagen der Geschichtsphilosophie Ottos von Freising." In Walter Dürig and Bernhard Panzram, eds., *Studien zur Historischen Theologie: Festgabe Franz Xavier Seppelt,* pp. 79 ff. Munich: Zink, 1953.
Koch, Klaus. *The Rediscovery of Apocalyptic.* Studies in Biblical Theology, 2d ser., vol. 22. Napierville, Ill.: Allenson, 1970.
Koenen, L. "The Prophecies of a Potter: A Prophecy of World Renewal Becomes an Apocalypse." In D. H. Samuel, ed., *Proceedings of the Twelfth International Congress of Papyrology,* pp. 249–54. Toronto: A. M. Hakkert, 1970.
Konrad, Robert. *De ortu et tempore Antichristi: Antichristvorstellung und Geschichtsbild des Abtes Adso von Montier-en-Der.* Münchener historische Studien, Abteilung Mittelalterliche Geschichte, vol. 1. Munich: Kallmünz, 1964.
Kurfess, Alfons. "Christian Sibyllines." In E. Hennecke and W. Schneemelcher, eds., *New Testament Apocrypha,* 2:703–45. Philadelphia: Westminster, 1964.
Kurze, Dietrich. *Johannis Lichtenberger: Eine Studie zur Geschichte der Prophetie und Astrologie.* Historische Studien, no. 379. Lübeck: Matthiesen, 1960.
—— "Nationale Regungen in der spätmittelalterlichen Prophetie." *Historische Zeitschrift* (1966), 202:1–23.
—— "Prophecy and History." *Journal of the Warburg and Courtauld Institutes* (1958), 21:63–85.
Lambert, Malcolm D. *Franciscan Poverty.* London: S. P. C. K., 1961.
Lanchester, H. C. "Sibylline Oracles." In *Encyclopedia of Religion and Ethics,* 11:496–500. New York: Scribners, 1908.
Leclercq, Jean. *The Love of Learning and the Desire for God.* New York: Mentor, 1960.
Lee, Harold. "*Scrutamini Scripturas:* Joachimist Themes and *Figurae* in the Early Religious Writing of Arnold of Villanova." *Journal of the Warburg and Courtauld Institutes* (1974), 37:33–56.
Leff, Gordon. *Heresy in the Later Middle Ages.* 2 vols. New York: Barnes and Noble, 1967.
Lerner, Robert E. "Medieval Prophecy and Religious Dissent." *Past and Present* (1976), 72:3–24.
—— "Refreshment of the Saints: The Time After Antichrist as a Station for Earthly Progress in Medieval Thought." *Traditio* (1976), 32:97–144.
Liebeschütz, H. *Das allegorische Weltbild der heiligen Hildegard von Bingen.* Leipzig-Berlin: Teubner, 1930.
LoBue, Francesco and G. G. Willis, eds. *The Turin Fragments of Tyconius' Commentary on Revelation.* Texts and Studies: Contributions to Biblical and Patristic Literature, new ser., no. 7. Cambridge: At the University Press, 1963.

Löwith, Karl. *Meaning in History*. Chicago: University of Chicago Press, 1949.
Lollis, Cesare de, ed. *Libro de las Profécias*. In *Scritti di Cristoforo Colombo*. Raccolta di documenti e studi pubblicati dalla R. Commissione colombiana, part 1, vol. 2. Rome: Forzani, 1894.
Loomis, Roger S. *Arthurian Literature in the Middle Ages*. Oxford: Clarendon Press, 1959.
Lubac, Henri de. *Exégèse médiévale: Les quatres sens de l'Écriture*. 4 vols. Paris: Aubier, 1959–64.
Luneau, Auguste. *L'Histoire du salut chez les Pères de l'Église: La doctrine des âges du monde*. Théologie Historique, vol. 2. Paris: Beauchesne, 1964.
McCall, John. "The Writings of John of Legnano with a List of Manuscripts." *Traditio* (1967), 23:415–37.
McCown, C. C. "Hebrew and Egyptian Apocalyptic Literature." *Harvard Theological Review* (1925), 18:357–411.
Macek, Josef. *The Hussite Movement in Bohemia*. Prague: Orbis, 1958.
—— *Tàbor v Husitském revolučním hnutí*. 2 vols. Prague: Nakl. Československé akademie věd, 1952–55.
McGinn, Bernard. "The Abbot and the Doctors: Scholastic Reactions to the Radical Eschatology of Joachim of Fiore." *Church History* (1971), 40:30–47.
—— "Angel Pope and Papal Antichrist." *Church History* (1978), 47:155–73.
—— "Apocalypticism in the Middle Ages: An Historiographical Sketch." *Mediaeval Studies* (1975), 37:252–86.
—— *The Crusades*. Morristown, N.J.: General Learning Press, 1973.
—— "Iter sancti Sepulchri: The Piety of the First Crusaders." In *Essays in Medieval Culture: The Twelfth Annual Walter Prescott Webb Memorial Lectures*, pp. 33–71. Austin: University of Texas Press, 1978.
—— "Joachim and the Sibyl." *Cîteaux* (1973), 34:97–138.
—— "St. Bernard and Eschatology." In *Bernard of Clairvaux: Studies Presented to Dom Jean Leclercq*, pp. 161–85. Washington, D.C.: Cistercian Publications, 1973.
—— "The Significance of Bonaventure's Theology of History." In David Tracy, ed., *Celebrating the Medieval Heritage*. *Journal of Religion*. Supplement (1978), 58:s64–s81.
—— "Symbolism in the Thought of Joachim of Fiore." In a forthcoming festschrift for Marjorie Reeves.
Macler, Frédéric. "Les apocalypses apocryphes de Daniel." *Revue de l'histoire des religions* (1896), 33:37–53, 163–76, 288–319.
McNally, Robert E. "Conciliarism and the Papacy." *Proceedings of the Catholic Theological Society of America* (1970), 25:13–30.
Magoun, Francis P. *The Gests of King Alexander of Macedon*. Cambridge, Mass.: Harvard University Press, 1929.
Magrassi, Mariano. *Teologia e storia nel pensiero di Ruperto di Deutz*. Studia Urbaniana, vol. 2. Rome: Pontificia Universitas de Propaganda Fide, 1959.
Maier, Anneliese. "Zu einigen Handschriften der Biblioteca Alessandrina in Rom und ihrer Geschichte." *Rivista di Storia della Chiesa in Italia* (1964), 18:1–12.
Malvenda, Tomás. *De Antichristo libri undecim*. Rome: Carlo Vulietti, 1604.
Manselli, Raoul. "L'anno 1260 fu anno gioachimitico?" *Il movimento dei disciplinati nel settimo centenario dal suo inizio (Perugia 1260: Convegno inter-*

nazionale, Perugia, 25–28 settembre 1960, pp. 99–108. Perugia: Deputazione di storia patria per l'Umbria, 1962.

—— *La "Lectura super Apocalypsim" di Pietro di Giovanni Olivi: Richerche sull'escatologismo medioevale*. Istituto Storico Italiano per il Medio Evo, Studi Storici, nos. 19–21. Rome: Sede dell'Istituto, 1955.

—— "La religiosità d'Arnaldo da Villanova." *Bollettino dell'Istituto Storico Italiano per il Medio Evo* (1951), 63:1–100.

—— *Spirituali e Beguini in Provenza*. Istituto Storico Italiano per il Medio Evo, Studi Storici, nos. 31–34. Rome: Sede dell' Istituto, 1959.

—— "La Terza Età, Babylon e l'Anticristo Mistico." *Bollettino dell' Istituto Storico Italiano per il Medio Evo* (1970), 82:47–79.

Manuel, Frank E. *Shapes of Philosophical History*. Stanford, Calif.: Stanford University Press, 1965.

Markus, Robert A. *Saeculum: History and Society in the Theology of St. Augustine*. Cambridge: At the University Press, 1970.

Marrou, Henri Irenée. "L'Idée et la divinité du Roi." In *The Sacral Kingship*, pp. 478–80. Studies in the History of Religions, vol. 4. Leiden: Brill, 1959.

Martin, Josef. "Commodianus." *Traditio* (1957), 13:1–71.

Mercati, S. "E stato trovato il testo greco della Sibilla Tiburtina." In Jacques Moreau, ed., Παγκαρπεια: *Mélanges Henri Grégoire*, pp. 473–81. Brussels: Éditions de l'Institut de Philologie et d'Histoire orientales et slaves, 1949.

Merkelbach, Reinhold. *Die Quellen des griechischen Alexander-Romans*. Zetemata: Monographien zur klassischen Altertumswissenschaft, vol. 9. Munich: Beck, 1954.

Messini, A. "Profetismo e profezie ritmiche italiane d'ispirazione Gioachimito-Francescana nei secoli XIII, XIV, e XV." *Miscellanea Francescana* (1937), 37:39–54; (1939), 39:109–30.

Meuthen, Erich. "Der Geschichtssymbolismus Gerhohs von Reichersberg." In W. Lammers, ed., *Geschichtsdenken und Geschichtsbild im Mittelalter*, pp. 200–46. Darmstadt: Wissenschaftliche Buchhandlung, 1965.

—— *Kirche und Heilsgeschichte bei Gerhoh von Reichersberg*. Leiden: Brill, 1959.

Miccoli, G. "Dal Pellegrinaggio alla Conquista: Povertà e Richezza nelle Prime Crociate." In *Povertà e Richezza nella Spiritualità dei Secoli XI e XII*, pp. 43–80. Convegni del Centro di Studi sulla Spiritualità Medievale, vol. 8. Todi: Accademia Tudertina, 1969.

Mommsen, Theodor E. "St. Augustine and the Christian Idea of Progress." *Journal of the History of Ideas* (1951), 12:346–74.

Mottu, Henri. *La manifestation de l'Esprit selon Joachim de Fiore*. Neuchatal and Paris: Delachaux and Niestlé, 1977.

Munro, Dana C. "The Speech of Pope Urban II at Clermont, 1095." *American Historical Review* (1906), 11:231–42.

Munz, Peter. *Frederick Barbarossa: A Study in Medieval Politics*. Ithaca, N.Y.: Cornell University Press, 1969.

Nau, F. "Révélations et légendes: Méthodius, Clément, Andronicus." *Journal asiatique* (1917), 2d ser., 9:425–62.

Neuss, Wilhelm. *Die Apokalypse des hl. Johannes in der altspanischen und altchristlichen Bibel-Illustrationen*. 2 vols. Spanische Forschungen der Görresgesellschaft, vols. 2–3. Münster: Aschendorff, 1931.

Nock, A. D. and A. J. Festugière. "Asclépius." In *Corpus Hermeticum*, 2:259–355. Paris: Les Belles Lettres, 1945.

O'Connell, John P. *The Eschatology of St. Jerome*. Mundelein, Ill.: St. Mary's of the Lake Seminary, 1948.

Ogle, Marbury B. "Petrus Comestor, Methodius, and the Saracens." *Speculum* (1946), 21:318–24.

Oliger, Livarius. "Documenta inedita ad historiam Fraticellorum spectantia." *Archivum Franciscanum Historicum* (1910), 3:253–79, 505–29, 680–99; (1911), 4:688–712; (1912), 5:74–84; (1913), 6:267–90, 515–30, 710–47.

—— "Spirituels." In *Dictionnaire de théologie catholique*, 14:2522–49. Paris: Letouzey and Ané, 1923–50.

Osswald, Eva. "Zum Problem der *vaticinia ex eventu*." *Zeitschrift für die Alttestamentliche Wissenschaft* (1963), 75:27–44.

Ottaviano, Carmelo. "Un nuovo documento intorno alla condonna di Gioacchino da Fiore nel 1215." *Sophia* (1935), 3:476–86.

Partee, Carter. "Peter John Olivi: Historical and Doctrinal Study." *Franciscan Studies* (1960), 20:215–60.

Partner, Peter. *The Lands of St. Peter*. Berkeley and Los Angeles: University of California Press, 1972.

Pásztor, Edith. "Giovanni XXII e il Gioachimismo di Pietro di Giovanni Olivi." *Bollettino dell'Istituto Storico Italiano per il Medio Evo* (1970), 82:81–111.

—— "Le polemiche sulla *Lectura super Apocalipsim* di Pietro di Giovanni Olivi fino alla sua condanna." *Bollettino dell'Istituto Storico Italiano per il Medio Evo* (1958), 70:365–424.

Patch, Howard R. *The Other World, According to Descriptions in Medieval Literature*. Cambridge, Mass.: Harvard University Press, 1950.

Paton, Lucy Allen, ed. *Les Prophécies de Merlin*, 2 vols. New York: Heath; London: Oxford University Press, 1926–27.

Pelikan, Jaroslav. *The Emergence of the Catholic Tradition, 100–600*. Chicago: University of Chicago Press, 1971.

Pelster, Franz. "Die Quaestio Heinrichs von Harclay über die zweite Ankunft Christi und die Erwartung des baldigen Weltendes zu Anfang des XIV. Jahrhunderts." *Archivio Italiano per la Storia della Pietà* (1951), 1:51–82.

Perrin, Norman. *The New Testament, an Introduction*. New York: Harcourt, Brace, Jovanovich, 1974.

—— "Wisdom and Apocalyptic in the Message of Jesus." *Proceedings of the Society of Biblical Literature* (1972), 2:543–72.

Perry, Aaron J. *John Trevisa: "Dialogus inter militem et clericum,"* etc. Early English Text Society, vol. 167. London: Oxford University Press, 1925.

Peuckert, Will-Erich. "Germanische Eschatologien." *Archiv für Religionswissenschaft* (1935), 32:1–37.

—— *Die Grosse Wende: Das apokalyptische Saeculum und Luther*. 2 vols. Hamburg, 1948; reprint, Darmstadt: Wissenschaftliche Buchgesellschaft, 1966.

Phelan, John L. *The Millennial Kingdom of the Franciscans in the New World*. 2d. rev. ed. Berkeley and Los Angeles: University of California Press, 1970.

Piur, Paul. "Oraculum Angelicum Cyrilli nebst dem Kommentar des Pseudojoachim." In Konrad Burdach, ed., *Vorm Mittelalter zur Reformation*, vol. 2, part 4, pp. 233–343. Berlin: Weidmann, 1912.

Plöger, Otto. *Theocracy and Eschatology*. Richmond, Va.: John Knox, 1968.

Pocock, J. G. A. *Politics, Language, and Time.* New York: Atheneum, 1971.

Podskalsky, Gerhard. *Byzantinische Reichseschatologie: Die Periodisierung der Weltgeschichte in den vier Grossreichen (Daniel 2 und 7) und dem tausenjährigen Friedensreiche (Apok. 20).* Munich: Fink, 1972.

Pognon, Edmond. *L'An mille.* Paris: Gallimard, 1947.

Preuss, Hans. *Die Vorstellungen vom Antichrist im späteren Mittelalter, bei Luther, und in der konfessionellen Polemik.* Leipzig: Hinrichs, 1906.

Prümm, Karl. "Der Prophetenamt der Sibyllen in kirchlicher Literatur." *Scholastik* (1929), 4:54–77, 221–46, 498–533.

Prutz, Hans. *Kulturgeschichte der Kreuzzüge.* Berlin: E. S. Mittler, 1883.

Rad, Gerhard von. *Theologie des alten Testament.* 4th ed. Munich: Kaiser, 1965.

Rangheri, Maurizio. "La *Epistola ad Gerbergam reginam de ortu et tempore Antichristi* di Adsone di Montier-en-Der e le sue fonti." *Studi Medievali* (1973), 3d ser., 14:677–732.

Ratzinger, Joseph. *The Theology of History in St. Bonaventure.* Z. Hayes, trans. Chicago: Franciscan Herald Press, 1971. Originally published in German in 1959.

Rauh, Horst D. *Das Bild des Antichrist im Mittelalter: Von Tyconius zum Deutschen Symbolismus.* Beiträge zur Geschichte der Philosophie und Theologie des Mittelalters, n.s., vol. 9. Münster, Aschendorff, 1973.

Reeves, Marjorie. "The Abbot Joachim's Disciples and the Cistercian Order." *Sophia* (1951), 19:355–71.

—— "History and Prophecy in Medieval Thought." *Mediaevalia et Humanistica* (1974), n.s., 5:51–75.

—— *The Influence of Prophecy in the Later Middle Ages: A Study in Joachimism.* Oxford: Clarendon Press, 1969.

—— *Joachim of Fiore and the Prophetic Future.* London: S. P. C. K., 1976.

—— "Some Popular Prophecies from the Fourteenth to the Seventeenth Centuries." In *Studies in Church History:* vol. 8, G. J. Cuming and D. Baker, eds., *Popular Belief and Practice,* pp. 107–34. Cambridge: At the University Press, 1972.

Reeves, Marjorie and Beatrice Hirsch-Reich. *The Figurae of Joachim of Fiore.* Oxford: Clarendon Press, 1972.

—— "The Seven Seals in the Writings of Joachim of Fiore." *Recherches de théologie ancienne et médiévale* (1954), 21:211–47.

Ridolfi, Roberto. *The Life of Girolamo Savonarola.* London: Routledge and Kegan Paul; New York: Knopf, 1959.

Röhricht, Reinhold. *Quinti Belli Sacri Scriptores Minores.* Publications de la Société de l'Orient Latin, séries historique, vol. 2. Geneva: J. G. Fick, 1879.

Rohr, J. "Die Prophetie im letzten Jahrhundert vor der Reformation." *Historisches Jahrbuch* (1898), 19:29–56, 447–66.

Rowley, Harold. *The Relevance of Apocalyptic.* New York: Association, 1964.

Roy, Jules. *L'An mille: Formation de la légende de l'an mille.* Paris: Hachette, 1885.

Rubin, Berthold. *Das Zeitalter Justinians,* vol. 1. Berlin: de Gruyter, 1960.

Runciman, Steven. *A History of the Crusades.* 3 vols. Cambridge: At the University Press, 1955.

Russell, David S. *The Method and Message of Jewish Apocalyptic: 200 BC–AD 100.* Philadelphia: Westminster, 1964.

Russo, Francesco. *Bibliografia Gioachimita.* Florence: Olschki, 1954.

—— *Gioacchino da Fiore e le Fondazioni Florensi in Calabria.* Naples: Fiorentino, 1959.

Rzach, A. "Sibyllen." In A. F. von Pauly and G. Wissowa, eds., *Realencyclopädie der classischen Altertumswissenschaft,* ser. 2, 2:2073–2183. Stuttgart: Metzler, 1894–1952.

Sackur, Ernst. *Sibyllinische Texte und Forschungen.* Halle: Niemeyer, 1898.

Salet, Gaston, ed. *Anselme de Havelberg: Dialogues I. SC,* vol. 118. Paris: Cerf, 1966.

Sanders, Henry A., ed. *Beati in Apocalipsin libri duodecim.* Rome: American Academy in Rome, 1930.

Sanesi, Ireneo, ed. *La Storia di Merlino di Paolino Pieri.* Biblioteca storica della letteratura italiana, vol. 3. Bergamo: Istituto Italiano d'arti grafiche, 1898.

Schaller, Hans Martin. "Die Antwort Gregors IX. auf Petrus de Vinea I, 1, *Collegerunt pontifices.*" *Deutsches Archiv für Erforschung des Mittelalters* (1954–55), 11:140–65.

—— "Endzeit-Erwartung und Antichrist-Vorstellung in der Politik des 13. Jahrhunderts." In *Festschrift für Hermann Heimpel,* 2:924–47. Göttingen: Vandenhoeck & Ruprecht, 1972.

—— "Das letzte Rundschreiben Gregors IX." In P. Classen and P. Scheibert, eds., *Festschrift für Percy Ernst Schramm,* 1:309–21. Wiesbaden: F. Steiner, 1964.

—— "Das Relief an der Kanzel der Kathedrale von Bitonto: Ein Denkmal der Kaiseridee Friederichs II." In *Stupor Mundi: Zur Geschichte Friederichs II. von Hohenstaufen,* pp. 591–616. Darmstadt: Wissenschaftliche Buchgesellschaft, 1966.

Schiff, O. "Die Wirsberger." *Historische Vierteljahrschrift* (1931), 26:776–86.

Schmid, Wilhelm and Otto Stählin. *Geschichte der griechischen Literatur,* vol. 2. Handbuch der Altertumswissenschaft, vol. 7. Munich: Beck, 1924–48.

Schmidlin, Josef. "Die Eschatologie Ottos von Freising." *Zeitschrift für katholische Theologie* (1905), 29:445–81.

—— *Die geschichtsphilosophische und kirchenpolitische Weltanschauung Ottos von Freising.* Freiburg-im-Breisgau: Herder, 1906.

Schmidt, Roderich. "*Aetates mundi:* Die Weltalter als Gliederungsprinzip der Geschichte." *Zeitschrift für Kirchengeschichte* (1955–56), 67:287–317.

Schmithals, Walter. *The Apocalyptic Movement: Introduction and Interpretation.* Nashville, Tenn.: Abingdon, 1975.

Schneemelcher, Wilhelm. "Apocalyptic Prophecy of the Early Church: Introduction." In E. Hennecke and W. Schneemelcher, eds., *New Testament Apocrypha,* 2:684–89. Philadelphia: Westminster, 1964.

Schneider, Wilhelm A. *Geschichte und Geschichtsphilosophie bei Hugo von St. Viktor.* Münsterische Beiträge zur Geschichtsforschung, 3d ser., vol. 2. Münster: Coppenrath, 1933.

Scholem, Gershom. *The Messianic Idea in Judaism.* New York: Schocken, 1971.

—— *Sabbatai Sevi: The Mystical Messiah, 1626–1676.* Princeton, N.J.: Princeton University Press, 1973.

Schulz, Albert. [San-Marte], ed. *Die Sagen von Merlin.* Halle: Buchhandlung des Waisenhauses, 1853.

Schwartz, Hillel. "The End of the Beginning: Millenarian Studies, 1969–1975." *Religious Studies Review* (1976), 2:1–15.

Seppelt, Franz Xavier. *Studien zum Pontifikat Papst Coelestins V.* Abhandlungen zur Mittleren und Neuren Geschichte, no. 27. Berlin and Leipzig: Rothschild, 1911.

Shahid, Irfan. "The *Kebra Nagast* in the Light of Recent Scholarship," *Le Muséon* (1976), 89:133–78.

Simoni, Fiorella. "Il *Super Hieremiam* e il Gioachimismo Francescano." *Bollettino dell'Istituto Storico Italiano per il Medio Evo* (1970) 82:13–46.

Smith, Jonathan Z. "A Pearl of Great Price and a Cargo of Yams: A Study in Situational Incongruity." *History of Religions* (1976), 16:1–18.

—— "Wisdom and Apocalyptic." In B. A. Pearson, ed., *Religious Syncretism in Antiquity*, pp. 131–56. Missoula, Mont.: Scholars' Press, 1975.

Southern, Richard, W. "Aspects of the European Tradition of Historical Writing: 2. Hugh of St. Victor and the Idea of Historical Development." *Royal Historical Association, Transactions* (1971), 5th ser., 21:159–79.

—— "Aspects of the European Tradition of Historical Writing: 3. History as Prophecy." *Royal Historical Association, Transactions* (1972), 5th ser., 22:159–80.

Staehelin, E. *Die Verkündigung des Reiches Gottes in der Kirche Jesu Christi.* 7 vols. Basel: Reinhardt, 1951–64.

Steindorff, G., ed. *Die Apokalypse des Elias.* Texte und Untersuchungen, n.s. 2, no. 3a. Leipzig: Hinrichs, 1899.

Strauss, Gerald, ed. *Pre-Reformation Germany.* London: Macmillan 1972.

Sumberg, Lewis. "The *Tafurs* and the First Crusade." *Mediaeval Studies* (1959), 21:224–46.

Talmon, Yonina. "Pursuit of the Millennium: The Relation between Religious and Social Change." *Archives européennes de sociologie* (1962), 3:125–48.

Taylor, Rupert. *The Political Prophecy in England.* New York: Columbia University Press, 1911.

Tellenbach, Gerd. *Church, State, and Christian Society at the Time of the Investiture Contest.* Oxford: Blackwell, 1940.

Theseider, Eugenio Duprè. "L'Attesa escatologica durante il periodo avignonese." In *L'Attesa dell'Età Nuova nella Spiritualità della Fine del Medioevo*, pp. 65–126. Convegni del Centro di Studi sulla Spiritualità Medievale, III. Todi: Accademia Tudertina, 1962.

Thomas, Keith. *Religion and the Decline of Magic.* New York: Scribners, 1971.

Thompson, B. "Patristic Use of the Sibylline Oracles." *Review of Religion* (1952), 16:115–36.

Thrupp, Sylvia L., ed. *Millennial Dreams in Action: Studies in Revolutionary Religious Movements.* New York: Schocken, 1970.

Tierney, Brian. *Foundations of the Conciliar Theory.* 2d ed. Cambridge: At the University Press, 1968.

—— *Origins of Papal Infallibility, 1150–1350.* Leiden: Brill, 1972.

Töpfer, Bernhard. "Eine Handschrift des *Evangelium aeternum* des Gerardino von Borgo San Donnino." *Zeitschrift für Geschichtswissenschaft* (1960), 8:156–63.

—— *Das kommende Reich des Friedens.* Berlin: Akademie, 1964.

Tognetti, Giampaolo. "Le fortune della pretesa profezia di San Cataldo." *Bollettino dell'Istituto Storico Italiano per il Medio Evo* (1968), 80:273–317.

—— "Note sul profetismo nel Rinascimento e la letteratura relativa." *Bollettino dell'Istituto Storico Italiano per il Medio Evo* (1970), 82:129–57.

Tondelli, Leone. *Il "Libro delle Figure" dell'Abate Gioachino da Fiore*. 2 vols. rev. ed. Torino: Società Editrice Internazionale, 1953.

—— "Profezia gioachimita del secolo XIII delle regioni venete." In *Studi e Documenti: Romana Deputazione di Storia Patria per L'Emilia e La Romagna, sezione di Modena* (1940), 4:3–9.

Ullmann, Walter. "Avignon Papacy." In *New Catholic Encyclopedia*, 1:1133–36. New York: McGraw-Hill, 1967.

Underhill, Evelyn. *Jacopone da Todi, Poet and Mystic, 1228–1306: A Spiritual Biography*. London: J. M. Dent; New York: Dutton, 1919.

Valois, Noël. *La France et le grand schisme d'Occident*, 2 vols. Paris: Picard, 1869.

Van Cleve, Thomas. *The Emperor Frederick II of Hohenstaufen*. Oxford: Clarendon Press, 1972.

Vasiliev, Alexander Alexandrovich. "Medieval Ideas of the End of the World: West and East." *Byzantion* (1942–43), 16:462–502.

Verhelst, D., ed. *Adso Dervensis: De Ortu et Tempore Antichristi*. CCCM, vol. 45. Turnhout: Brepols, 1976.

—— "De ontwikkeling van Adso's traktaat over de Antichrist: Bijdrage tot de studie van de eschatologische literatuur in die Middeleeuwen." Ph.D. dissertation, Université Catholique de Louvain, 1969.

—— "La préhistoire des conceptions d'Adson concernant l'Antichrist." *Recherches de théologie ancienne et médiévale* (1973), 40:52–103.

—— Review of *De ortu et tempore Antichristi*, by R. Konrad. *Bulletin de théologie ancienne et médiévale* (1970–73) 11:485.

Vielhauer, Philipp. "Apocalypses and Related Subjects: Introduction." In E. Hennecke and W. Schneemelcher, eds., *New Testament Apocrypha*, 2:581–607. Philadelphia: Westminster, 1964.

Vinay, G. "Riflessi culturali sconosciuti del minoritismo subalpino." *Bollettino Storico-Bibliografico Subalpino* (1935), 37:136–49.

Violante, Cinzio. "Eresie urbane e eresie rurali in Italia dall'XI al XIII secolo." In O. Capitani, ed., *L'Eresia medievale*, pp. 157–84. Bologna: Il Mulino, 1974.

Voegelin, Eric. *The New Science of Politics*. Chicago: University of Chicago Press, 1952.

Wakefield, W. L. and A. P. Evans. *Heresies of the High Middle Ages*. New York: Columbia University Press, 1969.

Watt, John A. *The Theory of Papal Monarchy in the Thirteenth Century: The Contribution of the Canonists*. London: Burns and Oates; New York: Fordham University Press, 1965.

Weinel, Heinrich. "Die spätere christliche Apokalyptik." In Hans Schmidt, ed., *EYXAPIΣTHPION: Studien zur Religion und Literatur des Alten und Neuen Testaments. Festschrift Hermann Gunkel*, pp. 141–73. Göttingen: Vandenhoeck and Ruprecht, 1923.

Weinstein, Donald. *Savonarola and Florence*. Princeton, N.J.: Princeton University Press, 1970.

Werblowsky, R. Z. "Messiah and Messianic Movements." In *Encyclopaedia Britannica: Macropaedia*, 11:1017–1022. Chicago: Encyclopaedia Britannica, 1976.

Werner, Ernst. "Popular Ideologies in Late Mediaeval Europe: Taborite Chiliasm and Its Antecedents.'' *Comparative Studies in Society and History* (1959–60), 2:344–63.

Werner, Martin. *The Formation of Christian Dogma.* New York: Harper, 1957.

West, Delno, C., ed. *Joachim of Fiore in Christian Thought: Essays on the Influence of the Calabrian Prophet.* 2 vols. New York: Burt Franklin, 1975.

Westenholz, E. von. *Kardinal Rainer von Viterbo.* Heidelberger Abhandlungen zur mittleren und neueren Geschichte, no. 34. Heidelberg: C. Winter, 1912.

Wheelwright, Philip. *Metaphor and Reality.* Bloomington: Indiana University Press, 1962.

Widmer, Bertha. *Heilsordnung und Zeitgeschehen in der Mystik Hildegards von Bingen.* Basel, Stuttgart: Helbing and Lichtenhahn, 1955.

Wikenhauser, Alfred. *New Testament Introduction.* New York: Herder and Herder, 1958.

Wilder, Amos N. "The Rhetoric of Ancient and Modern Apocalyptic." *Interpretation* (1971), 25:436–53.

Winkelmann, Eduard, ed. *Acta imperii inedita, seculi XIII.* Innsbruck: Wagner, 1880.

—— *Fratris Arnoldi: De correctione Ecclesiae epistola et Anonymi de Innocentio IV. P. M. Antichristo.* Berlin: Mittler, 1865.

Wittkower, Rudolf. "Marvels of the East: A Study in the History of Monsters." *Journal of the Warburg and Courtauld Institutes* (1942), 5:159–97.

Wolohojian, Albert M., trans. *The Romance of Alexander the Great by Pseudo-Callisthenes.* New York: Columbia University Press, 1969.

Worsley, Peter. *The Trumpet Shall Sound.* 2d ed. New York: Schocken, 1968.

Wortley, J. "The Warrior-Emperor of the Andrew Salos Apocalypse." *Analecta Bollandiana* (1970), 88:45–59.

Wright, John. *The Life of Cola di Rienzo.* Toronto: Pontifical Institute of Mediaeval Studies, 1975.

Young, Karl. *The Drama of the Medieval Church.* 2 vols., 2d ed. Oxford: At the University Press, 1962.

Zezschwitz, C. A. Gerhard von. *Vom römischen Kaisertum deutscher Nation: Ein mittelalterliches Drama.* Leipzig: Hinrichs, 1877.

Zimmerman, Benedict. *Monumenta Historica Carmelitana,* no. 1, pp. 296–311. Lerrain: Typis Abbatiae, 1907.

Zoepfl, Friedrich. "Wolfgang Aytinger: Ein deutscher Zeit-und Gesinnungsgenosse Savonarolas." *Zeitschrift für Deutsche Geistesgeschichte* (1935) 1:177–87.

Zumthor, Paul. *Merlin le Prophète.* Lausanne: Payot, 1943.

Name Index

Abbo of Fleury, 89-90, 306nn9-10
Adso of Montier-en-Der, 40, 82-87, 117, 295n10, 304-6 *passim*, 312n14
Aethicus Ister, 156, 302n27, 319n30
Agobard of Lyons, 82, 304n3 (sec. 10)
Akaton, 156-57, 324n34
Alan of Lille, 326n7
Albert the Bear, 113, 311n20
Albumazar (Abu Mashr), 155, 319n28
Alcuin, 40, 292n118, 305nn25, 27
Alexander, bishop of Lincoln, 182
Alexander III, 96, 126, 133, 315n35
Alexander IV, 160, 323n21
Alexander the Great, 44, 56, 73, 299n11 (sec. 3), 320n36
Amaury of Bène, 216, 334n50
Ambrose, 98, 309n31
Ambrosius Autpertus, 40, 292n118
Ammianus Marcellinus, 296n25
Anacletus II, Antipope, 109
Angelo of Clareno, 188, 204, 205-7, 215-16, 246, 330n1, 332n16, 333n47
Angelo of Monte Volcano, 241-42, 338nn17, 19, 20
Anselm of Havelberg, 109-10, 114-16, 128, 310-11 *passim* (sec. 14)
Anselm of Laon, 40, 95
Anselm of Marsico, 328n12
Antiochus Epiphanes, 53, 84, 106, 310n12
Apringius, 292n118
Aquila, 156, 191, 320n33
Arnald of Villanova, 222-25, 334 *passim*
Arnold, brother, O.P., 170
Arthur of Britain, 180-81
Athanasius, 296n25
Augustine of Hippo, 4, 21, 26-27, 39, 51, 62, 88, 127, 146, 291n83, 292nn112, 113, 298nn15, 18, 309n4, 311nn23, 24, 315n30
Augustus, 19

Aytinger, Wolfgang, 271, 274-76, 344-45 *passim* (sec. 33)

Bacon, Roger, 152, 155-57, 187, 190-91, 319-20 *passim*, 329nn20-21
Baronius, cardinal, 306n1
Batu, 151
Bayazit II, 345n20
Beatus of Liébana, 40, 77-79, 292n118, 303 *passim* (sec. 8)
Bede, 40, 77, 83, 292n118, 300n9 (sec. 5), 303n2, 310n11 (sec. 14)
Beliar, 305n25
Benedict XI, 188, 206, 334n48, 337n11
Benedict XII, 337n19, 338nn29, 1
Benedict of Nursia, 134, 199, 228, 229, 316n39, 335n7
Benzo of Alba, 88, 90-91, 297n35, 307 *passim*
Berengaudus, 40, 292n118, 297n10
Bernard Délicieux, 222
Bernard of Clairvaux, 105, 109, 112-13, 186, 263, 310nn4-9 (sec. 14), 311n24, 343n16
Bizas, 90, 307n16
Bonaventure (John of Fidanza), 160, 196-202, 203, 204-5, 206, 321-22n34, 330-31 *passim*, 332nn8, 20, 333n30, 334n7
Boniface VIII, 186, 188, 205, 206, 207, 222, 229, 329n32, 330nn43, 49, 332n23, 333n45, 337n11
Bridget of Sweden, 240, 241, 244-45, 338-39 *passim*
Bruno of Segni, 40, 292n118

Caesarius of Heisterbach, 149, 318n3 (sec. 18)
Catherine of Siena, 241
Celestine III, 321n30
Celestine IV, 169, 172, 323n21
Celestine V, 187-88, 205-6, 210, 213, 318n3 (Intro.), 328-30 *passim* (sec. 22), 333n39, 337nn9, 10, 339n28

365

Celsus, 21
Cerinthus, 23, 303*n*10
Charlemagne, 132, 199, 200, 273, 304-5*n*17, 312*n*5, 319*n*16, 327*n*37
Charles IV, 240, 241, 247, 338*nn*16, 22
Charles V, xiv, 271
Charles VI, 247, 340*nn*9, 22
Charles VIII, 248, 278-79, 345*nn*7, 8, 346*n*13
Charles Martel, 273
Charles of Anjou, 171-72, 210, 247, 323*n*21, 325*nn*49, 54-55, 333*n*37
Charles the Bald, 80
Clement I, 199
Clement III, Antipope (Guibert of Ravenna), 95, 104, 308*n*24, 309*n*33, 310*n*7 (sec. 13)
Clement IV, 319*n*27
Clement V, 205, 207, 222, 239, 337*nn*12-13, 339*n*29
Clement VI, 240, 338*n*29 (sec. 28), 338*n*1 (sec. 29)
Clement VII, 253
Clement of Alexandria, 291*n*92
Clovis, 273
Cola di Rienzo, 182, 240-44, 338-39 *passim* (sec. 29)
Columbus, Christopher, 284-85, 346 *passim* (sec. 35)
Commodian, 22-23, 27, 292*nn*96-97, 294*n*3 (Intro.), 297*n*6, 336*n*10
Commodus, 66
Comnenus, Manuel, 122
Conrad IV, 172, 210, 324-25 *passim*
Conradin, 172, 210
Conrad of Offida, 205
Constans I, 49, 295*n*12, 296*n*31, 312*n*11 (sec. 15)
Constantine, 23, 25, 228, 335*n*7
Constantius, 66
Cyril of Jerusalem, 25
Cyrus, 312*n*11 (sec. 15)

Dante, 15
Decius, 66
Dio Cassius, 290*n*71
Diocletian, 23
Diomedes, 123
Dionysius Halicarnassus, 290*nn*68, 70
Dionysius of Alexandria, 13, 23
Dionysius the Areopagite, 208-9

Dolcino, Fra, 147, 226-29, 261, 335 *passim* (sec. 26)
Dominic, 213, 216, 228, 229, 242, 256, 335*n*7
Domitian, 66, 67, 84, 300*n*6 (sec. 6)

Edmund Crouchback, 325*n*54
Ekkehard of Aura, 89, 92-93, 307*n*24
Elipandus of Toledo, 77
Enzio of Sardinia, 325*n*47, 327*nn*34-35
Ephraem, 39, 60, 299 *passim* (sec. 4)
Ephraem (Pseudo), 60-61, 294*n*3 (Intro.), 299 *passim* (sec. 4), 303*n*36
Ethelbert of Kent, 300*n*9 (sec. 5)
Eugene III, 109
Eugenius of Palermo, 122-25
Euphemius, 301*n*12 (sec. 6)
Eusebius of Caesarea, 17, 23, 25-26, 43, 291*n*83, 292*nn*98-100
Eusebius of Vercelli, 246, 250
Evermord of Magdeburg, 113, 311*n*20

Ferdinand II, 277
Ferdinand of Spain, 284
Ficino, Marsilio, 279, 282-83, 346*nn*21, 22
Florence of Arles, 165, 322*n*40
Francis of Assisi, 160, 197, 200-202, 203, 204, 205, 206, 208-209, 211, 212, 213, 215, 216, 218, 219, 228, 229, 234, 242, 253, 256, 257, 316*n*45, 331 *passim*, 333*nn*29-30, 335*n*7
Frederick I (Barbarossa), 96, 117, 149, 200, 310*nn*14-16, 324*n*24, 327*n*20
Frederick II, 35, 123, 127, 147, 148, 150, 159, 160, 167, 168-79, 181, 209, 210, 211, 219, 222, 247, 251, 319*n*23, 321*n*28, 322-25 *passim* (sec. 20), 326*nn*13-14, 327*nn*22-30, 329*n*16, 333*n*38, 340*n*7
Frederick III, 247, 344*n*7
Frederick of Sicily, 229, 334*n*59, 335*n*8

Gaiseric, 66, 292*n*102
Gaius, 23
Geoffrey of Monmouth, 180, 182-83
Gerald of Wales, 326*n*3
Gerard of Poehlde, 113-14, 311*nn*20, 22
Gerardo of Borgo San Donnino, 160, 196, 320*n*13
Gerberga, 82

Gerhoh of Reichersberg, 96-97, 103-7, 186, 308*n*16, 309-10 *passim* (sec. 13)
Giovanni delle Celle, 235, 337*n*7
Gorritio, Gaspar, 284
Gregory I (the Great), 62-65, 104, 190, 199, 299*n*8 (sec. 4), 299-300 *passim* (sec. 5), 305*n*25, 309*n*6, 311*n*23, 329*n*24, 334*n*4, 342*n*25
Gregory VII, 88-89, 94-96, 99, 104, 168, 308*nn*26, 27, 309*n*31, 310*n*7 (sec. 13), 328*n*2
Gregory IX, 35, 168-69, 173-74, 325*n*43
Gregory X, 150, 187, 191, 329 *passim*
Gregory XI, 253
Gui, Bernard, 218-21, 227-29, 334*nn*57-58, 335*n*3 (sec. 26)
Guibert of Nogent, 89, 91-92, 307*nn*20, 23
Guilloche of Bordeaux, 248, 278

Hadrian, 199
Harold, king of England, 98
Haymo of Auxerre, 40, 83, 292*n*118, 305-6 *passim*, 310*n*11 (sec. 14)
Henricus Aristippus, 312*n*4
Henry IV, 88, 90, 94, 97, 100, 104, 168, 200, 306*n*5, 307*n*16, 308-9 *passim*, 310*n*7 (sec. 13)
Henry VI, 127, 323*n*15, 324*n*24, 327*nn*21, 31
Henry of Harclay, 334*n*2
Henry of Langenstein, 248
Heracleitus, 19
Heraclius, 70, 155, 296*n*15, 299*n*11 (sec. 4), 319*n*25
Herman, Prince of Lorraine, 98
Hermann of Metz, 308*n*27
Hermes Trismegistus, 24
Herod, 163, 317*n*53, 321*n*30
Herodotus, 312*n*1 (sec. 15)
Hildegard of Bingen, 97, 100-102, 308*n*19, 309*nn*39, 43
Hippolytus, 22, 23, 40, 51, 291*n*92, 297*n*8, 303*n*35, 307*n*23
Honorius III, 319*n*22
Hugh of Digne, 159, 223
Hugh of St. Cher, 165, 322*n*38
Hugh of St. Victor, 109, 111-12, 311*n*16, 339*n*35
Hulagu, 151, 155, 319*nn*26, 29
Hunein ben Isaac, 319*n*15

Humbert of Romans, 164, 322*n*35
Hus, John, 259, 263, 343*nn*14, 15
Húska, Martin, 262, 344*n*32

Innocent III, 126, 127, 146, 169, 186, 246, 321*nn*25, 30, 329*n*16
Innocent IV, 35, 152, 169, 170, 175-76, 186, 209, 323*n*21, 324*n*34
Innocent VI, 240, 338*n*29 (sec. 28), 338*n*1 (sec. 29)
Irenaeus, 18, 23, 27, 40, 305*n*25, 307*n*23, 333*n*47
Isabella of Spain, 284
Isidore of Seville, 303*n*7, 305*n*22

Jacob of Serugh, 56-59
Jacopone da Todi, 204, 206-7, 217-18, 234, 332*nn*21-23
Jacques of Vitry, 318*n*4
Jakoubek of Stříbro, 260, 263-64, 343*n*17
James of the Marches, 235
Jenghiz Khan, 150-51
Jerome, 23, 25-26, 27, 39, 91, 157, 285, 292*nn*102, 109, 297*n*7, 305*n*23, 307*n*22, 319*n*30
Joachim of Fiore, 6, 7, 40, 109, 126-41, 145-47, 156, 158-60, 163, 165-67, 170, 180-81, 184, 187, 188, 189, 196-97, 204, 209, 211, 215, 243, 249-50, 253, 254, 274, 280, 284-85, 298*n*14, 311*n*12, 313-18 *passim*, 320-22 *passim* (sec. 17), 323*n*15, 327*n*31, 328*n*12, 331*nn*10, 12, 345*n*2, 346*n*15
John XXII, 205, 206, 207, 208, 234, 237-38, 239, 334*n*60, 335*n*2 (sec. 27), 336*n*1, 337*nn*16, 28, 338*nn*29, 1
John of Brienne, 319*n*20
John of Capestrano, 235
John of Damascus, 294*n*2 (Intro.)
John of Legnano, 254, 341*n*4
John of Parma, 159-60, 164, 167, 196, 206, 321*n*34, 330*n*1, 331*n*15
John of Piano Carpino, 152
John of Příbram, 265-66
John of Rupescissa (Jean de Roquetaillade), 182, 230-33, 239, 247, 253, 327*n*38, 335-36 *passim* (sec. 27), 339*n*36
John of Toledo, 172, 325*n*54
John of Winterthur, 248, 251, 340*n*27

John of Wünschelburg, 248, 251-52
John the Deacon, 299n2 (sec. 5)
Josephus, 285, 298n7
Julian of Hungary, 151, 318n11
Julius Africanus, 291n92, 320n32
Justinian, 66, 67-68, 300nn6-7 (sec. 6)
Justin Martyr, 214

Lactantius, 23-25, 27, 297nn6-7
Ladislaus II, 271, 345n24
Lawrence of Březová, 264-65, 266-68, 343n20
Leo I, 199
Leo VI, 328n8
Lewis of Bavaria, 208
Liberato, Fra, 205
Lichtenberger, John, 271-73, 344-45 *passim*
Louis VII, 117, 118, 156
Louis IX, 156, 171, 318n10 (sec. 18), 328n44
Louis the German, 80
Louis the Pious, 82
Lucius III, 126, 130, 140, 315n35, 318n66
Luke of Cosenza, 314n7

Manfred, 171, 172, 210, 325nn49, 53
Marcus Aurelius, 21
Martianus Capella, 156
Martin V, 254
Martin of Tours, 51, 52
Matthew of Angers, 131
Matthew of Janov, 259
Matthew of Paris, 181, 318n5, 323n11, 326n12
Maximilian, 270-71, 272
Merlin, 156, 180-85, 191, 243, 326-28 *passim*
    (sec. 21)
Methodius (Pseudo), 39, 44, 70-76, 83, 117,
    123, 145, 149, 156, 271, 274-75, 294n7,
    297n34, 301-3 *passim* (sec. 7), 306n30,
    312nn14, 15 (sec. 15), 345n18
Meuccio, Silvestro, 345n2
Michael II, 300n10, 301n12 (sec. 6)
Michael of Cesena, 207, 208, 234
Michael Scot, 326n14
Milič, John, 259
Mohammed, 123, 155-56, 313nn14, 16,
    317n53
Mohammed II, 345n19
Montanus, 21

Nepos of Arsinoe, 292n98
Nero, 17, 23, 52, 54, 66, 84, 97, 137, 171,
    298n13, 317n53, 336n9, 346n22
Nicholas III, 188, 210, 333n36, 335n2 (sec.
    27), 337n8
Nicholas IV, 188
Nicholas Biskupec, 343n13
Nicholas Doxapatres (Doxapater), 122-23
Nicholas of Bari, 172-73
Nicholas of Cusa, 255
Nicholas of Dresden, 260
Norbert of Xanten, 109, 310n6, 311n24
Norseus, 345n18
Notker the Stammerer, 304n17
Nur-ad-Din, 149

Odenathus of Palmyra, 66
Ordericus Vitalis, 326n16
Origen, 23, 25, 291n85, 292n107, 311n18
Orosius, 157, 320n36
Otto IV, 318n3 (sec. 18)
Otto of Freising, 96, 98-99, 109, 117, 118-19,
    308nn14, 15

Papias, 17, 298n20
Paschal II, 307n4
Paulus Alvarus, 303n1 (sec. 8), 305n23
Pedro III (of Aragon), 210, 222, 229
Pelagius, cardinal, 149, 319nn20, 23
Pepin, 199, 273
Peter Abelard, 109
Peter Olivi, 196, 204-9, 215-16, 219, 220,
    331n11, 332-33 *passim*, 334n7, 335n10
Peter Lombard, 127, 159, 314n12, 320n4
Peter Morrone, 188, *see* Celestine V
Petrarch, Francis, 244, 339nn31, 34
Philip I (of France), 98, 309n31
Philip II (Augustus), 319n18, 334n51
Philip of Burgundy, 271, 273, 275, 345n23
Phlegon of Tralles, 291n74
Phocas, 299n11 (sec. 4)
Pico della Mirandola, Giovanni, 277, 281,
    346n21
Piero della Vigna, 169
Pierre d'Ailly, 255
Plato, 19
Pliny, 156, 292n95
Plutarch, 19, 290n67

Poděbrady, George, 262
Porphyry, 292n109
Prester John, 150, 318n8, 319n22
Primasius, 292n118, 310n11 (sec. 14)
Procopius of Caesarea, 66-68, 300n6 (sec. 6)
Prokop the Great, 262
Prosper of Aquitaine, 51

Quintus Julius Hilarianus, 51, 52-53, 299n14
Quodvultdeus, 51, 54-55

Rabanus Maurus, 305n21
Radulphus Ardens, 216, 334n52
Rainer of Florence, 307n4
Rainer of Viterbo, 169, 322-23n7, 323n14, 324nn28, 37
Ralph Glaber, 90, 307nn12, 13
Revolutionary of the Upper Rhine, 147, 271-72, 344n10
Richard I (the Lionhearted), 127, 319n18
Richard of Cornwall, 325n54
Richard of St. Victor, 40
Robert of Uzès, 193-94, 329-30 *passim*
Rudolf, duke of Alemmania, 98
Rupert of Deutz, 40, 95-96, 108-9, 110, 128, 308 *passim*, 310n2
Rutilius Namatianus, 290n73

Saladin, 137, 317nn53, 55, 319n18
Salimbene of Parma, 166-67, 170, 181, 191, 223, 322nn43, 46, 323nn15, 16, 326nn12, 14, 329n27, 335n3 (sec. 26)
Savonarola, Girolamo, 277-83, 345-46 *passim* (sec. 34)
Segarelli, Gerard, 226-29, 335n7
Seleucus, 106
Seston, 156, 320n33
Sigebert of Gembloux, 307n25, 308n28
Sigismund, 254, 261-62, 270
Silvester (pope), 199, 228, 335n1
Simon Magus, 54, 97, 137, 308n25
Stilicho, 20
Sulpicius Severus, 51, 52, 300n8 (sec. 6), 305n26

Tacitus, 290n72
Tancred, 122
Tebaldus Civeri, 254, 341 *passim*
Telesphorus of Cosenza, 182, 246, 247, 249-50, 327n38, 334n6, 340n7
Tertullian, 21, 22, 25, 291n86, 307n26
Theodora, 300n7 (sec. 6)
Theodoret of Cyrus, 294n2 (Intro.)
Theodosius, 43, 98, 309n31
Theophilus of Antioch, 19, 291n92
Thomas Aquinas, 4, 160, 196, 224-25, 334nn7, 8
Tyconius, 27, 77, 184n117, 298n17, 303n5, 305n24, 311n22, 312n20

Ubertino of Casale, 204, 206, 207-8, 212-15, 216-17, 332-33 *passim*, 345n2
Urban II, 89, 307n20
Urban V, 241
Urban VI, 253, 254, 341n14

Valens, 43, 296n25, 299n10
Valentinian, 299n10
Varro, 19
Victor IV (Antipope), 310n15
Victorinus of Pettau, 23, 25
Vincent Ferrer, 254-55, 256-58, 341-42 *passim*
Virgil, 19
Virgil of Salzburg, 319n30

William II (of Sicily), 122
William of Champeaux, 96
William of Ockham, 337n28
William of Rubruck, 318n10, 319n32, 320n34
William of St. Amour, 160
William of Tripoli, 154-55, 319n29
William the Conqueror, 98
Wycliff, John, 259, 343n15

Žižka, John, 261-62
Želivský, John, 260

Subject Index

Abomination of Desolation, 12, 124-25, 224, 237, 264, 278, 343*n*19; *see also* Antichrist

Advent of Christ, *see* Last Judgment and Parousia

Aeons, 8, 288*nn*25, 26, 288-89*n*29; *see also* World ages

Alexander myths, 44, 50, 56-59, 60, 72, 73, 75, 157, 272, 294-95*nn*7, 11, 297*n*36, 298-99 *passim* (sec. 3), 302*nn*23-29, 320*n*36

Anagni, commission, 160, 165-66, 322*nn*38-42

Angelic Oracle of Cyril, 145, 187, 192-93, 215-16, 230, 240, 244, 248, 249, 273, 328*n*4, 329*nn*31-36, 339*nn*25, 30, 340*n*28, 341*n*5

Angelic Pope, *see* Papacy

Antichrist, xiv, 15, 16-17, 22-24, 25, 26, 33, 34, 35, 40, 43, 44-45, 48-49, 49-50, 51-55, 59, 61, 64, 66, 67-68, 71, 76, 80-81, 82-87, 90, 91-92, 95, 96, 97, 99-100, 101, 103, 106-7, 109, 113, 116, 117-18, 119-21, 123, 128-29, 133, 134, 135, 137-38, 147-48, 150 (Mexadeigen), 151, 154, 156-57, 158, 160, 161, 162, 168-72, 173-79, 187, 190, 191, 204-5, 206, 209, 210-11, 212-14, 215, 217-18, 219-21, 223-24, 229, 230, 231-32, 234, 236, 237, 239, 245, 247, 249, 253, 254, 256-58, 259, 260-61, 263, 264, 277, 279, 282-83, 289*n*36, 290*n*62, 292*n*95, 296*nn*27-28, 297*n*40, 297-98 *passim* (sec. 2), 299*n*14, 299*n*11 (sec. 4), 300*n*8 (sec. 6), 303*nn*37, 1, 5, 304*nn*5-6 (sec. 9), 304-5 *passim* (sec. 10), 307*nn*23, 4, 308*nn*20, 22, 309*nn*38-42, 2-3, 310*nn*12, 6, 311*n*19, 312*nn*14, 17-18, 20, 313*n*23, 314*n*18, 316*nn*44, 46, 317*nn*53, 57, 319*n*31, 320*n*14, 321*n*18, 325*n*41, 330*n*56, 333*nn*25, 47, 334*n*7, 336*n*9, 337*nn*24-25, 341*n*9, 342*nn*28, 31, 345*n*25

——imperial Antichrists: Nero, 17, 23, 52, 54, 66, 84, 97, 137, 171, 298*n*3, 317*n*53, 336*n*9, 346*n*22; Antiochus, 53, 84, 106, 310*n*12; Domitian, 66, 67, 84, 300*n*6 (sec. 6); Justinian, 66-68, 300*nn*6-7 (sec. 6); Frederick II, 147, 160, 168-79 *passim*, 211, 226, 324-25 *passim*, 327*n*27

——mystical Antichrist/great Antichrist: 205, 206, 210-11, 212-14, 234, 237-38, 247, 332*n*11, 333*n*37, 334*nn*49, 6, 336*n*9; *see also* Papacy, papal Antichrist

——number of Antichrist (666 of Rev. 13:18), 155, 170, 175-76, 214, 292*n*102; *see also* Abomination of Desolation

——time of Antichrist (three and one-half years), 54, 86, 87, 137, 236, 313*n*23, 337*n*26

Anticlericalism, 118, 119-21, 147, 228, 243, 251, 252, 272, 339*n*27

Apocalypse (literary genre), 2-7, 9, 14-15, 20, 24, 39, 288*nn*10-11, 289*n*35

Apocalypse of Elijah (Coptic Apocalypse), 43, 44, 294*n*3, 295*n*12, 296*nn*13, 30, 298*n*21

Apocalypse of Paul, 14

Apocalypse of Peter, 14, 52

Apocalypse of Sergius-Bahira, 149, 318*n*1 (sec. 18)

Apocalypticism: classical (Jewish and early Christian), xiii-xiv, 1, 2-14, 28, 32; patristic: xiii-xiv, 14-27; later Jewish, 2, 10, 28, 71, 149, 287*n*3 (Intro.); general notion, 1-2, 7-11, 28-36, 287*n*5 (Intro.), 288*n*26, 288-89*n*29, 293*n*127, 294*n*4 (Intro.); Persian (Iranian), 8, 10, 24, 70, 290*n*60, 292*n*103, 301*n*11 (sec. 7), 304*n*2 (sec. 9); Egyptian, 20, 24, 43-44, 291*n*77, 294*n*3 (sec. 1); political aspects, 31-36, 40-41, 66, 70-72, 80, 84, 147-48, 168-79, 181, 226-27, 230-31, 246-48, 270-71, 278-79, 301*n*8, 322*n*3, 339-40 *passim* (sec. 30) (*see also*

Emperor, Last World; France; Germany; Islam; Papacy; Roman empire, etc.); Syriac, 56-59, 60-61, 70-76, 122-23, 296*n*20, 301*nn*2, 11, 302*nn*23, 31; Byzantine, 66-76, 122-24, 145, 188, 300-3 *passim* (secs. 6, 7), 328*nn*8-9

Apostolic Brethren, 226-29, 261, 335 *passim* (sec. 26)

Apostolic Life, *see* Poverty

Ascension of Isaiah, 14

Asclepius, 24, 292*n*104

Astrology, 149-50, 152-53, 155-56, 170, 223, 251-52, 270-71, 283, 296*n*20, 319*n*28, 326*nn*7, 14, 340*n*29

Avignon, *see* Papacy, Babylonian Captivity

Babylon, 32, 52, 90, 118, 131, 132-33, 152, 163, 184, 185, 199, 212, 219, 244, 312*n*11 (sec. 15), 316*nn*36, 44, 321*n*28, 324*n*35, 327*n*32, 328*n*43, 339*n*33

Bar-Kochba revolt, 32, 148

Basel, Council of, 254

Beghards, 343*n*11

Beguines, 205, 208, 218, 334*n*58

Black Death, 31, 338*n*18

Canon, New Testament, 23

Carnal Church, 204-5, 206, 219-20, 227, 332*n*11, 332-33*n*25; *see also* Babylon; Roman Church

Champion of Wales, 184-85, 327*n*37

Charlemagne, Second, *see* Emperor, Last World

Chiliasm (Rev. 20:4-6), 12, 17-18, 22, 23, 26, 32, 53, 78, 88, 265, 267, 290*nn*56, 62, 292*nn*98, 107, 293*n*125, 298*nn*12, 20, 303*nn*10, 34, 308*n*13, 343*nn*28-29; *see also* Millenarianism

Cistercian order, 109, 126, 127, 138, 159, 164, 169, 201, 315*n*27, 316*nn*50, 52, 321*n*33, 323*n*14, 337*n*19

Cognitive dissonance, 321*n*16

Communism (community of goods), 130, 139-40, 221, 261, 265, 272, 317*n*63

Conciliarism, 253-55, 270, 279, 341*nn*2-3

Concordances of Scripture, 103, 127, 131-32, 135, 161-63, 163-64, 164-65, 176-77, 192, 197, 198, 198-99, 206, 209, 266, 272-73, 298*n*14, 309*n*4, 310*n*12, 315*n*33, 316*n*47,

321*nn*20-23, 25, 329*nn*17, 32; *see also* Scripture, interpretation of

Concordat of Worms, 94

Constance, Council of, 254

Conversion, general, 49, 156-57, 205, 209, 220, 284, 333*nn*30-31, 336*n*7; *see also* Jews, conversion of

Cosmic week, *see* World ages

Crusades, 88-89, 90-93, 108, 109, 117, 149-51, 152-55, 168, 235, 247, 262, 272, 297*n*35, 306-7 *passim* (sec. 11), 311*nn*20, 6, 318*n*4, 319*nn*18-22, 327*n*20, 328*nn*42, 44, 329*n*28, 340*n*24; *see also* Islam

Dan, tribe of, 17, 49, 85, 305*n*25

Daniel, Book of, xiii, 1, 3, 6, 7, 12, 13, 22, 23, 26, 39, 54, 70, 71, 73, 85, 87, 89, 91, 98, 132, 135, 145, 158, 224, 233, 257, 264, 269, 297*n*3, 304-5*n*17, 307*nn*22-23, 337*n*26, 340*n*17, 342*n*30; *see also* Four empires

Dominican order, 161-63, 164, 191, 201, 228-29, 230, 277, 321*nn*23-24, 322*n*35; *see also* Mendicants

Dragon with seven heads, *see* Revelation of John

Elijah the prophet, 80-81, 134, 136-37, 161, 208, 232, 304*nn*5-7 (sec. 9); *see also* Revelation of John, two witnesses

Emperor, Last World, 33-35, 41, 43-45, 49-50, 70-71, 72, 75-76, 83-84, 85-86, 88, 90-91, 94, 117-18, 119-21, 123, 124, 128, 147-48, 153, 172, 179, 184-85, 186-87, 200, 222, 227, 228-29, 230, 232-33, 246-52, 256, 270-72, 273, 275-76, 278, 284-85, 294-95*n*7, 295*nn*9-11, 296-97 *passim*, 301*nn*11-12 (sec. 7); 303*n*34, 305*n*29, 306*n*5, 312 *passim* (sec. 15), 313*nn*16, 18, 319*n*14, 325*nn*54-55, 327*nn*37-38, 328*n*43, 331*n*13, 342*n*18; Second Charlemagne, 148, 172, 247-48, 250-51, 278, 326*n*11, 340*nn*7, 21-26, 28, 345*nn*7-8; Third Frederick, 148, 171, 247-49, 251, 252, 270, 277, 333*n*43

End of the World, xv, 1, 2, 4, 6, 13, 16, 22, 25, 27, 28, 30, 32, 33, 36, 39, 41, 51, 57-59, 61, 62, 63, 64, 66, 71, 75, 80-81, 83, 88, 89-90, 92, 95, 96, 102, 103, 106-7, 109, 110, 111,

End of the World (*Continued*)
114, 117, 123, 134, 137, 141, 151, 161, 164, 166, 173, 181, 189, 197, 198, 199, 223-24, 228-29, 247, 249, 251, 253, 255, 256-58, 262, 266, 271, 284, 288-89n29, 291n92, 297n8, 298n14, 299n2 (sec. 3), 300nn9-10 (sec. 5), 301n10, 305n17, 309n32, 310n13, 317n57, 328n39, 332-33n25, 334nn4-5, 342n22, 343n22

Enoch, *see* Revelation of John, two witnesses

Epistle of Barnabas, 17

Eschatology, 3-4, 16, 25-27, 80, 89, 94-95, 287n5 (Intro.); apocalyptic, *see* Apocalypticism

Eternal Gospel, 160, 165-66, 321n34

Evangelical men, *see* Viri spirituales

Evangelical perfection, *see* Poverty, apostolic

Exegesis, *see* Scripture, interpretation of

Figurae, see Joachim's writings, *Book of Figures*

First Enoch, xiii

Flagellent movement, 321n15

Florence, apocalyptic role of, 250, 277-79, 280, 281, 282, 346n19

Florensian order, 127, 158, 159, 167, 215, 314n9, 323n14

Four empires (Dan. 2), 66, 71, 73, 83-84, 86, 94, 98-99, 103, 109, 111, 304-5n17; *see also* Roman Empire; *Translatio imperii;* World ages

Fourth Esdras, xiii

France, apocalyptic role of, 86, 178, 230, 232-33, 246-48, 252, 273, 275, 278-79, 305n29, 340n26, 342n18, 344n14; *see also* Emperor, Last World

Franciscan order, 159-60, 161-63, 164-65, 166-67, 171, 193, 196-97, 200-202, 228-29, 230, 232, 234, 271, 321nn24, 34, 329n18, 331n17, 336nn12, 1 (*see also* Mendicants); Spiritual Franciscans, 147, 188-89, 196, 203-21, 222, 226, 230, 234, 239, 331-34 *passim* (sec. 24), 336n9, 337n14

Fraticelli, 189, 207, 234-38, 240, 241-43, 246, 336-37 *passim* (sec. 28), 338n17, 339n27, 342n27

Generations, computation of, 135, 159, 161, 166, 176, 209-10, 315n21, 316nn39, 42-43, 333n41

Germany, apocalyptic role of, 117-18, 119-21, 246-48, 252, 272, 275, 340n17, 344-45 *passim* (sec. 33)

Glossa ordinaria (Ordinary Gloss), 40, 175, 257, 310n11 (sec. 14), 324n34

Gnosticism, 18, 24, 130, 288n25, 292n104

Gog and Magog (Ezek. 38:2, Rev. 20:7), 50, 53, 54, 56, 57-59, 60, 72, 73, 75-76, 100, 150-51, 156-57, 178, 204, 247, 270, 299nn12, 14 (sec. 3), 317n53, 319n31, 345n25

Gold, Age of, 244, 277, 339n34, 340n17; *see also* World ages

Golgotha, 71, 76, 312n14

Gospel of Nicodemus, 304n5 (sec. 9)

Gospels, 11-12; *see also* Synoptic Apocalypse

Heresy, as apocalyptic sign, 54, 82, 118, 120-21, 173-74, 177, 184-85, 232, 237-38, 280, 298n17, 324nn29, 35, 327-28n38, 334n56

Hermeneutics, *see* Scripture, interpretation of

History, *see* Theology of history

Holy League, 340n7

Holy Spirit, *see* Third *status* of Holy Spirit

Homosexuality, as apocalyptic sign, 74, 124, 232, 302n31

Humanism, 277-79, 345n3, 346n21

Huns, 56, 60, 72, 298n9, 303n36

Hussites, xiv, 259-69, 270, 271, 318n1 (Intro.), 342-44 *passim* (sec. 32); *see also* Taborites

Hypocrisy, as apocalyptic sign, 112-13, 115-16, 118, 120-21, 214, 312n18

Imperial theology, *see* Roman empire

Inquisition, 207, 216, 218-21, 226-27, 234-35, 332n14, 334n57

Intertestamental period, xiii, 3, 11, 97, 108, 148

Ishmaelites, *see* Islam

Islam, 34, 41, 44, 60, 69, 71-72, 74, 75, 77, 88-89, 90-92, 123, 124, 128, 132, 137, 149-57, 169, 173, 177, 179, 183, 185, 190, 191, 209, 220, 226, 232, 242, 247, 250, 301n12 (sec. 6), 302nn19, 30, 303n34, 312n11 (sec. 15), 313nn14, 16, 317nn54-56, 319 *passim,* 324nn35, 39, 336n14, 340n25; *see also* Crusades; Turks

Jacob's Ladder, 14

Jerusalem, 11, 17, 21, 52, 76, 86, 88-89, 90, 91, 92, 106, 107, 115, 117, 119-21, 132, 135, 138, 149, 150, 153, 162, 169, 183, 185, 191, 201, 206, 210, 231, 242, 250, 278, 282, 284, 296n15, 306nn31, 4, 307n26, 311n7, 313n18, 324n23, 325n44, 327n27, 338n21

Jesus (historical), 11-12, 16, 17, 39, 289n42, 296n21

Jews, conversion of, 49, 92, 118, 134, 138, 191, 317n58, 337n23; *see also* Conversion, general

Joachim's writings: *Exposition on the Apocalypse* (*Expositio in Apocalypsim*), 40, 126, 130, 133-34, 136-37, 140-41, 165, 313n2, 315nn19, 28, 317nn56, 64; *Book of Concordance* (*Liber concordiae*), 126, 134-35, 140, 141, 165, 274, 313n2, 314nn13, 19, 315n28, 316nn43-44, 322n41; *Ten-Stringed Psaltery* (*Psalterium decem chordarum*), 126, 140, 165, 313n2, 314n13, 315nn26, 28; *Book of Figures* (*Liber figurarum*), 128, 137-40, 158, 314n15, 315n33, 316n52, 317nn59-63, 321n17; *Commentary on an Unknown Prophecy* (*De prophetia ignota*), 130-33, 314n19; *Treatise on the Four Gospels* (*Tractatus super quatuor Evangelia*), 135-36, 166, 316nn47-49, 322n42; *Against the Enemies of the Catholic Faith* (*De articulis fidei*), 140, 318n67; *Against the Jews* (*Contra Judaeos*), 140; *Life of St. Benedict* (*Vita S. Benedicti*), 317n52, 327n31

Joachite movement, 146-47, 148, 156, 158-67, 170-71, 176-79, 180, 181, 187, 188, 189-90, 192-93, 194-95, 196-98, 203-4, 209, 211, 215, 222, 226, 235-36, 240, 243, 247-48, 250-51, 253, 254, 260, 271, 274, 277, 280, 284-85, 322nn43, 1, 323n14, 332n18, 333n38, 334n55, 335nn7-8, 338n19, 340n26, 343nn24, 29, 345n2, 346nn15, 7; *see also* Third *status;* World ages

Joachite writings: *Letter explaining the Figures* (*Espistola subsequentium figurarum*), 158, 161, 321nn17-18; *Commentary on Jeremiah* (*Interpretatio in Hieremiam*), 159, 161-64, 170, 176-77,

187, 189-90, 320nn8-10, 321nn19, 33, 322n36, 323n14, 324n35, 333n42, 345n18; *Commentary on Isaiah* (*Scriptum super Esaiam prophetam*), 171, 178-79, 320n7, 323n18, 325n53, 333n43; *Commentary on the Angelic Oracle, see* Angelic Oracle *of Cyril; Exposition on the Sibyls and on Merlin* (*Expositio super Sibillis et Merlino*), 171, 184, 326n13, 327nn31-33; *Book of Fiore* (*Liber de Flore*), 181, 189, 328n11; *Book against the Lombard* (*Liber contra Lombardum*), 320n6; *The Burdens of the Prophets* (*De oneribus prophetarum*), 323n16, 326n14; *see also* Papal Prophecies

Kebra Nagast, 301n11 (sec. 7)

Lamb of God, 114, 116, 124, 125, 177, 192, 211, 213, 236, 337n16

Last Judgment, 8, 53, 64, 80, 81, 86, 87, 89, 116, 124, 125, 131, 154, 172, 204, 221, 245, 249, 252; *see also* End of World; Parousia

Lateran Council: First, 94; Fourth, 127, 159, 163-64, 320n4, 321nn25, 28, 32

Leo Oracles, 328nn8-9, 330nn49, 56; *see also* Papal Prophecies

Little Apocalypse (see Synoptic Apocalypse)

Lyons Council: First, 169-70, 209; Second, 196, 204, 329nn26-27

Malachy Prophecies, 118

Mendicants, 320-21n14, 322nn36-37, 330n6; *see also* Dominican order; Franciscan order

Messianism, 2, 8, 17-18, 28, 30, 41, 71, 95, 168-69, 171, 241, 247, 279, 293nn120, 126, 297n33, 298n20, 313n23, 336nn8, 10 (*see also* Millenarianism); abundance of the messianic kingdom, 49, 55, 265, 297n33, 298n20

Mestre Prophecy, 341n5

Michael the Archangel, 50, 87, 297n40

Millenarianism, 17-18, 28, 29-30, 66, 129, 146, 219-21, 261, 267, 268, 272, 279, 287n2 (Intro.), 290nn56, 61, 292n109, 293 *passim*, 298n20, 303n34, 315n25, 335n4 (sec. 26), 343n29, 346n20; *see also* Chiliasm; Messianism

Monasticism, apocalyptic role, 129, 134, 136-37, 138-39, 316*n*51, 316-17*n*52
Mongols, 72, 73, 150-52, 155-57, 190, 232-33, 318-20 *passim* (sec. 18)
Montanism, 21, 291*n*88
Moslems, *see* Islam
Mount of Olives, 50, 86, 87, 91, 250, 251, 296*n*19, 312*n*14
Muspilli, 40, 80-81, 303-4 *passim* (sec. 9)

New orders, *see Viri spirituales*

Oracle of Baalbek, 43-49, 294-97 *passim* (sec. 1); *see also* Sibylline Oracles
Oracle of Hystaspes, 24, 292*n*103

Papacy, general, xiv, 41, 62, 109, 126, 140-41, 152, 159, 160, 163, 168-72, 173-74, 178, 181, 203-7, 216, 218, 222, 226, 228-29, 230, 235, 243, 246, 251, 259, 260, 270, 273, 279, 300*n*8 (sec. 5), 313*n*22, 315*nn*22, 31, 35, 316*nn*48, 49, 51, 317*n*65, 318*n*66, 321*n*30, 323*n*21, 328*n*1, 333*n*28, 335*n*2 (sec. 27), 336*n*1, 340*n*32; papal Antichrist, xiv, 34, 148, 162, 174-76, 187, 188-89, 195, 205, 206, 208, 210-11, 212-14, 220, 234, 236, 237-38, 239, 247, 263, 315*n*19, 318*n*3 (Intro.), 324*nn*32, 34, 328-29*n*13; Great Western Schism, 6, 230, 235, 246-47, 248, 249, 251-52, 253-58, 328-29*n*13, 337*n*5, 340*n*20, 341-42 *passim* (sec. 31); Angelic Pope, 34-35, 103-4, 129, 134-36, 138-40, 145, 147-48, 186-95, 206, 215, 227, 229, 230, 232-33, 242, 247, 249, 250, 274, 279, 314-15*n*19, 316*nn*44-45, 317*n*61, 328-30 *passim* (sec. 22), 335*nn*9-10, 335*n*4 (sec. 27), 336*nn*11-12, 337*nn*21-23, 338*nn*19, 20, 345*n*15; Great Reform, 88-89, 94-102, 104-5, 117, 186, 307-9 *passim* (sec. 12), 309-10 *passim* (sec. 13), 312*n*18; Babylonian Captivity (Avignon papacy), 239-45, 336*nn*7, 15, 337*n*20, 338-39 *passim* (sec. 29), 341-42*n*15
Papal Prophecies (*Vaticinia de summis pontificibus*), 145, 188-89, 194-95, 206, 234, 235-36, 330*nn*44-56, 335*n*4 (sec. 27), 336*n*4, 337*nn*5, 8-26, 346*n*1

Paris, University of, 160, 196-97, 222, 253, 334*nn*50, 52, 334*n*6
Parousia (Second Coming), 12, 14, 15-16, 21, 27, 106-7, 116, 154, 221, 262, 264-65, 267, 294*n*4 (Intro.), 296*n*28, 334*n*2; *see also* Chiliasm; Last Judgment
Peasants' Revolt, xiv, 272
Philosophy, Aristotelian, 196-97, 205, 210, 224-25, 330*n*5, 332*n*10, 334*n*7
Piagnoni, 279
Pikarts, 262, 267-69, 343*nn*12, 25, 344*nn*31, 33; *see also* Taborites
Play of Antichrist, 40, 117-18, 119-21
Poetical apocalypses, 22-23, 40, 57-59, 60, 80-81, 97-98, 119-21, 170, 179, 207, 217-18, 234, 244, 321*n*18, 323*n*16, 325*n*54, 337*n*6
Poor Hermits of Celestine, 205
Poverty, 104, 105, 169, 193, 194, 196, 203, 204-7, 213, 219, 226-28; Apostolic poverty, 203, 208, 209-10, 211, 212, 219, 227, 229, 237-38, 331*nn*2-3, 332-33*n*25, 335*n*5 (sec. 26), 335*n*2 (sec. 27)
Prophecy, 3-4, 5, 7-9, 13, 20, 21, 29, 41, 58, 92, 117, 118-19, 122, 126, 147, 149-50, 156-57, 158, 164, 172, 180-83, 184-85, 188, 190-91, 200-201, 215-16, 228, 230, 241, 243, 244-45, 246-48, 249, 254, 264-65, 270, 271, 277-79, 280-81, 284, 314*n*18, 323*n*15, 325*n*55, 326-28 *passim*, 334*n*56, 339*n*26, 341*n*7, 344*n*2, 345*nn*5, 8, 346*nn*15, 20
Prophecy of Gamaleon, 249, 251-52, 340*nn*16, 29-33
Prophecy of St. Cataldus, 277, 345*n*1
Prophecy of the Son of Agap, 149-50, 153-54, 318*n*4, 319*nn*15-24
Pseudonymity, 5, 6-7, 8, 13, 39, 158, 187-89, 241, 254, 255, 299*n*7, 328*n*8, 341*n*10; *see also Vaticinium ex eventu*

Qumran, 9

Reform (*renovatio*) of the Church, 129, 135, 138-40, 146, 147, 170, 177, 187, 190-91, 200, 222, 226, 230, 232-33, 239, 240-41, 242, 244, 247, 254, 255, 256, 259, 265, 267, 270-71, 273-74, 276, 278-82, 336*n*7,

339*n*33, 340*n*17, 343*n*19, 345*n*11, 346*n*15; *see also* Papacy, Great Reform; Third *status*

Reformation, xiv, 239, 248, 270

Refreshment of the Saints, 26, 87, 102, 124, 258, 306*n*34, 309*n*42, 317*n*57, 342*n*30

Ressurection of the dead, 9, 53, 110, 212, 267, 288-89*n*29

"Restraining force," *see* Thessalonians, Epistles to

Revelation, pseudo-Johannine, 39, 54-55, 66, 292*n*95

Revelation of John, xiii, 1, 12-14, 17, 23, 25-26, 27, 32-33, 39-40, 54, 70, 77-79, 89, 96, 99-100, 113-14, 126, 130, 133-34, 136-37, 140, 145, 158, 163, 165, 173-76, 199-200, 204-5, 206, 208-11, 212, 214, 215, 219, 225, 256-57, 268-69, 274-75, 280, 281, 289*nn*43-47, 294*n*1 (Intro.), 297*n*3, 303*n*5, 311*nn*25, 7, 313*n*15, 315*n*26, 325*n*43, 332*nn*7, 18, 333*n*47, 343*n*13

——angel of the sixth seal (Rev. 7:2), 135, 197, 200, 201-2, 209, 316*n*45, 320*n*12, 331*n*15

——angels of the seven churches (Rev. 1-3), 229

——dragon with seven heads (Rev. 12:3-9), 52, 97, 106, 115, 124, 137-38, 171, 175, 178-79, 184, 217, 268-69, 308*n*22, 317*n*53, 334*n*54

——four horsemen (Rev. 6:1-8), 101, 109, 114-15, 175, 346*n*16

——Gog and Magog (Rev. 20:7), *see* Gog and Magog

——number of the beast (Rev. 13:18), *see* Antichrist, number of Antichrist

——opening of the seven seals (Rev. 5:1-8:1), 54, 110, 114-16, 315*n*33, 325*n*53, 331*n*12

——seven angels with plagues (Rev. 15:1-16:21), 274

——seven trumpets (Rev. 8:2-9:21, 11:15-19), 54, 268, 338*n*14

——ten horns or kings (Rev. 17:12), 52-53, 125, 133, 219, 297*n*10, 337*n*24

——thousand-year kingdom (Rev. 20:4-6), *see* Chiliasm

——two beasts (Rev. 13:1-18, 17:3-11), 113-14, 173-74, 177, 178-79, 210-11, 213-14, 308*nn*23, 25, 317*n*54

——two witnesses, or Enoch and Elijah (Rev. 11:3-14), 48-49, 50, 54, 87, 118, 165, 213, 242, 304*n*5 (sec. 9), 309*n*38, 336*n*12

Revelations and visions, apocalyptic, 5, 7, 10, 13, 14-15, 19-20, 45-46, 54-55, 58-59, 61, 100-102, 123-24, 130, 145-46, 149, 187, 193-94, 220, 227-28, 241, 242-43, 244-45, 249-50, 251-52, 256-57, 272, 280-82, 314*n*6, 315*nn*26, 28, 329*n*38, 330*n*40, 342*n*28; *see also* Prophecy

Revelations of the Pseudo-Methodius, 39, 44, 70-76, 83-84, 117, 123, 145, 149, 156, 271, 274-76, 294-95*n*7, 297*n*34, 301-3 *passim* (sec. 7), 306*n*20, 312*nn*14-15 (sec. 15), 345*n*18

Revolutionism, apocalyptic, xiv, 29-33, 35, 129-30, 141, 146, 148, 226, 230, 231, 252, 259-62, 265-66, 272, 293*n*125, 307*n*1, 335*n*1 (sec. 26), 336*n*8, 343*n*9

Rhetoric, apocalyptic, 6, 30-32, 33-35, 95-6, 109, 168-69, 172, 293*nn*128, 131

Roman Church, xiv, 132, 176, 192, 219, 227, 313*n*22, 332*n*11, 332-33*n*25, 343*n*26; *see also* Carnal Church

Roman empire, 32-34, 41, 52, 61, 71, 83-84, 86, 98-99, 111, 117-21, 172-73, 176-77, 257, 275, 297*nn*39, 10, 301*n*10, 304-5*n*17, 310-11 *passim* (sec. 15), 324*nn*23-27; *see also* Thessalonians, Epistles to

Rome, apocalyptic role of, 104-5, 124, 132-33, 177, 179, 183, 185, 210, 239-41, 242, 252, 259, 270, 273, 279, 281-82, 300*n*4 (sec. 5), 306*n*31, 316*n*44, 321*n*28, 337*n*12, 338*n*21, 339*n*33, 341*n*11

Sabbath, 53, 54, 116, 204, 247; *see also* World ages

Saracens, *see* Islam

Satan, 53, 81, 84, 99-100, 106, 108, 113, 138, 139, 216, 243, 247, 263

Savior, *see* Messianism

Scenario, apocalyptic (apocalyptic drama), 6, 15, 16, 28, 32-35, 40, 94, 104, 146, 172, 186, 247, 297*n*40, 339*n*4

Schism, *see* Papacy, Great Western Schism

Scholasticism, 95-96, 109, 127, 145, 196-97, 206, 209-10, 222, 224-25, 314*n*12; *see also* Paris, University of

Scribalism, apocalyptic, 5, 7, 12, 13, 30, 32, 35, 41, 145-46, 138-39, 171, 293n132

Scripture, interpretation of, 22-23, 25-27, 39-40, 53-54, 62-63, 66, 71, 77-79, 89, 104-5, 111-12, 127, 145, 159, 161-64, 172-73, 176-77, 178-79, 189-90, 197-98, 206, 222-24, 227, 260, 266, 268-69, 281, 298n14, 306n10, 314nn11, 13, 331nn8-10, 335n6 (sec. 26) (*see also* Concordances of Scripture; Tyconian tradition, *and names of individual scriptural books*); Spiritual understanding of Scripture (Joachite), 134, 163, 197, 200, 228, 335n6 (sec. 26)

Second Charlemagne prophecy, *see* Emperor, Last World

Second Coming, *see* Parousia

Seven ages, *see* World ages

Seven persecutions, 131-32, 315n33, 317n53, 345n17

Shortening of the times (Matt. 24:22), 48, 49-50, 86, 137, 269; *see also* Synoptic Apocalypse

Sibylline Oracles, xiii, 7, 18-21, 24, 27, 40, 88, 119, 126, 145, 156, 165, 180, 191, 290-91nn66-87, 296nn19, 22, 299n12 (sec. 4), 307n18, 313nn13, 19, 24-25, 315nn29-30, 325n48; Cumaean Sibyl, 19, 21, 90-91, 306n5, 345n18; Erythraean Sibyl, 19, 122-25, 165, 171, 177-78, 184, 216, 224, 312-13 *passim* (sec. 16), 322n37, 323n16, 325n48, 327n19; Tiburtine Sibyl, 40, 43-50, 83, 122, 172, 294-97 *passim* (sec. 1), 303n2, 307n15, 312nn11, 14 (sec. 15), 340n22; Theodosian Sibyl, 43, 295, 296nn24, 27-28, 297n36; Samian Sibyl, 130-33, 315n31

Sicilian Vespers, 325n55

Spiritual Franciscans, *see* Franciscan order

Spiritual men, *see Viri spirituales*

Status, see Third *status;* World ages

Symbolism, apocalyptic, 5-6, 8, 13, 31, 32, 127-28, 146-47

Synoptic Apocalypse (Little Apocalypse: Matt. 24-25, Luke 21, Mark 13), xiii, 11-12, 57, 61, 85-86, 90, 161, 199, 211, 232, 237, 256, 267, 269, 296n19, 299n12 (sec. 4), 300n4 (sec. 5), 334n53, 343n27

Taborites, 30, 32, 226, 260-62, 263-69, 272, 335n1 (sec. 26), 343nn9, 13, 18-19, 25, 27, 29, 344n31; *see also* Hussites; Pikarts

Tafurs, 89, 306n6

Tartars, *see* Mongols

Testament of the Lord, 15, 22, 291n94, 292n95

Theology of history, 26-27, 96, 127-30, 146, 158, 196-202, 310nn2-3

Thessalonians, Epistles to, xiii, 11, 51, 52-53, 86, 87, 91-92, 106, 137, 175, 177, 187, 211, 266, 289n36; "restraining force" (2 Thess. 2:6-7), 22, 33, 52, 84, 294n134, 297nn39, 10, 301n9, 302n31, 305nn22, 26-28, 306n34; *see also* Roman empire

Third *status* (of the Holy Spirit), 128-29, 133-34, 135-36, 138-40, 147, 160, 166, 171, 187, 197, 209, 242, 315n33, 316 *passim,* 317nn59, 61-62, 323n18, 324n35, 338n19, 342n21; *see also* World ages; Year 1260

Toledo Letter, 149, 152-53, 318nn2, 13, 319n14

Translatio imperii, 84, 86, 96, 109, 111, 305n18, 308n15, 310n3, 340n32; *see also* Four Empires; Roman empire

Trinity, 110, 127, 159, 163, 185, 311nn12-15, 315n26, 321n25

Tripoli Prophecy, 150

Turks, 153-54, 232, 270-71, 274-76, 323n13, 345nn19, 22

Tyconian tradition, 27, 39-40, 54, 77-79, 83, 103, 292nn117-18, 298n17, 303n5, 305n24, 306n10, 311n22, 312n20

Utopianism, 130, 138-40, 317n63

Utraquism, 260, 262, 263, 264, 342n3

Vaticinium ex eventu, 7, 13, 188, 288n20, 294n4 (Intro.), 325n54, 327n34, 340n22, 341-42nn14-15

Venice, apocalyptic role of, 182, 185, 328n41, 340n7

Vienne, Council of, 205, 207

Viri spirituales, 129, 134, 136-37, 138-40, 146-47, 159, 161-63, 164-65, 197, 201-2, 203, 212, 219-21, 227-29, 313n17, 316nn38, 44, 47-48, 321nn20, 34, 330n6, 331nn14, 17-18, 339n34

Vision literature, 14-15, 290n50

Vision of the three lances, 256, 342n24

Visions of the Pseudo-Daniel, 39, 66, 68-69, 296n29, 300nn5, 9 (sec. 6)

World ages, 17, 24, 25, 27, 45-49, 51, 103, 104-5, 128, 147, 204, 244-45, 279, 290n55, 291n92, 297n8, 298n12, 309n1, 309-10n6, 311nn18, 24, 315n33, 316n41, 335n7, 341n9; *see also* Aeons
——ages of the Church, 108-16, 204-5, 208-11, 212, 219-21, 228-29, 325n53, 331n12, 332n20, 333n33, 339n35
——cosmic week (seven millennia of history), 17-18, 22, 27, 51, 57, 52-53, 74, 77-78, 88, 108, 252, 290n60, 303n7, 340n29; *see also* Chiliasm
——double seven ages, 128, 131-33, 137-38, 147, 197, 198-200, 208-11, 212, 331n12, 333n33

——four ages (Pauline), 27, 51, 108, 134
——sixth age or *status*, 197, 199-200, 204-5, 206, 208-10, 210-11, 212, 219-20, 325n53, 331n11
——three *status*, 128, 133-34, 147, 166, 204, 209-10, 314n16, 315n21, 316n39, 332n20, 333nn33, 41; *see also* Third *status*
Worms, Concordat of, 94

Year 1000, 88, 89-90, 306n1
Year 1260, 159, 160-61, 166, 171, 176, 189, 316n43, 320n10, 323n18, 327n27; *see also* Generations, computation of; Third *status*